ROUTES OF PASSAGE

ROUTES OF PASSAGE

RETHINKING THE AFRICAN DIASPORA

VOLUME 1 • PART 2

Edited by

Ruth Simms Hamilton

Michigan State University Press • *East Lansing*

Publication of this book was made possible by The Ruth Simms Hamilton
African Diaspora Series Endowment at Michigan State University. MSU Press is grateful to the donors
who fund that endowment, including Priscilla Hamilton Taylor and Jason Taylor

♾ The paper used in this publication meets the minimum requirements
of ANSI/NISO Z39.48-1992 (R 1997) (Permanence of Paper).

Michigan State University Press
East Lansing, Michigan 48823-5245

Printed and bound in the United States of America.

13 12 11 10 09 08 07   1 2 3 4 5 6 7 8 9 10

LIBRARY OF CONGRESS CATALOGING-IN-PUBLICATION DATA
Available upon request.

Michigan State University Press is a member of the Green Press Initiative and is
committed to developing and encouraging ecologically responsible publishing
practices. For more information about the Green Press Initiative and the use of recycled
paper in book publishing, please visit *www.greenpressinitiative.org.*

Cover and book design by Sharp Des!gns, Inc., Lansing, Michigan

Visit Michigan State University Press on the World Wide Web at **www.msupress.msu.edu**

Acknowledgments

A number of people provided essential support that made the publication of *Routes of Passage: Rethinking the African Diaspora* possible. Among them, Joan Reid, Kimberly Eison Simmons, Michael Hanson, and Raymond Familusi were key to maintaining the spirit as well as the letter of Ruth Hamilton's work.

Contents

The Black Question in Brazil: An Issue Denied

Josildeth Gomes Consorte

IN CONTRAST TO AN INDIAN POPULATION OF ABOUT TWO HUNDRED THOUSAND, people of African descent in Brazil number around 70 million (more than 45 percent of the total). Both groups share a history of slavery, physical annihilation, expropriation, and cultural destruction, yet they have received very different treatment from the church, the state, intellectuals, politicians, the mass media, and public opinion in general. The threatened extinction of indigenous people causes great concern, but the notorious marginalization of blacks and mulattoes generates little interest. They have the lowest income, the poorest school performance, the worst health conditions, and the highest rates of unemployment and crime.[1] What explains the concern for the Indian population and the indifference toward Afro-Brazilians? In other words, what is being defended in the first case, and what is being denied in the second? Finding the answers is not easy, but thinking about them may open new ways of reflecting on the black question in Brazil.

INDIANS AND AFRO-BRAZILIANS

The defense of indigenous peoples is not recent in Brazil. It began during the colonial period, when Jesuit priests, eager to convert the Indians to Christianity, took a stand against their enslavement by Portuguese settlers. Today as yesterday, the context for this issue lies in the development of the capitalist mode of production. The plight of the indigenous population has as background the expansion of capitalism to Brazil's last frontiers, and the dispute arises because they live in areas where enormous national and foreign economic interests are at stake. Today as yesterday, the defense of the Indians stirs deep emotions. In the past the struggle centered on saving their souls or expropriating their land and engaging them as slaves in the economic process. Currently, it involves the radical critique of a mode of production that implies their virtual annihilation and menaces life on earth.

The defense of indigenous groups today revolves around four basic issues. The first is preservation of what remains of the people who were here when Brazil was "discovered," that is, the remnants of five hundred years of destruction inflicted on the legitimate owners of the land. At stake is their right to exist as peoples with their own culture. The second is preservation of their territory, viewed as a necessary condition for ensuring cultural autonomy. The third is preservation of noble values, fundamental to life, insofar as the Indians are viewed as proud, courageous, and lovers of freedom, which gives an emblematic character to their defense. The fourth is the preservation of the environment, in particular the forest of the Amazon Basin, already so devastated by exploitation and so vital to the health of the planet.

The situation is very different for people of African descent in Brazil. As a rule, blacks and mulattoes, whether urban or rural, are totally immersed in the world of capitalist relations.[2] They produce and reproduce their existence within a class society. Mainly low-skilled workers, they seem the same as others in their class, irrespective of origins; their handicaps, failures, and lack of accomplishment are easily explained by factors other than color.

Afro-Brazilians do not constitute ethnic groups with specific territories who speak an ancestral language, and frequently they are unaware of the history of their forebears—when and how they arrived in Brazil, where they originated, and what they brought with them. Their cultural manifestations are totally fragmented (which makes them the object of all kinds of appropriation and manipulation), and their image is very often associated with qualities that may have been formed during slavery. According to official history, patience, humility, and resignation are their most relevant attributes, and suffering and submission (rather than rebellion, resistance, and refusal of slavery) are their most characteristic attitudes. In sum it is taken for granted that Afro-Brazilians do not have territories to defend, that their cultural heritage has been largely lost, and that far from evoking noble virtues, they recall a history that most would rather forget.

Many prefer to see the black question as a thing of the past, a chapter that closed with abolition, a long and painful process punctuated by economic crisis, slave uprisings, and so on. For many, if a debt was ever owed people of African descent, it was paid with the end of slavery. Once they could participate in society with the same rights as others, their future depended entirely on their own efforts. But the debt was not resolved by abolition, as the Golden Law text—the shortest in our history—would have us believe.[3]

When the black question is dismissed or denied in Brazil today, it is because society has never faced what it avoided in 1888, namely, the crucial fact that the restitution of freedom was not accompanied by restoration of the conditions taken away by enslavement, among which access to land was without any doubt the most fundamental. Along with abolition came no means for the former slaves to produce and reproduce their existence as free people, either in the urban areas to which most of them went or in the countryside where many remained.[4] After more than three centuries of backbreaking work to build Brazil, their letter of freedom was more a passport to exclusion from the new social order based on free-market labor and representative government than an invitation to participate.

Changing Views on Afro-Brazilians

Defining the place for people of African descent in Brazil has always been a problem for the state, the elites, and society in general, despite extensive miscegenation and the marks made by African cultures since the beginning. Brought in as slaves, Africans entered the country with the status of chattel. Destined to carry out the extraordinary enterprise of incorporating the newly discovered land into the stream of world capitalism, they were supposed to serve their masters.[5] Their access to land was mediated by slavery, and they were not to own it once liberated. They would then become foreigners, and their return to Africa was a rather common expectation.[6]

The policy of the Brazilian state regarding land ownership by former slaves was made clear in the Land Law of 1850, the absence of agrarian reform in 1888, and the stream of immigrants brought to replace slave labor on farms during the nineteenth century. Access to land would allow blacks to make a place for themselves, to develop more effective roots, and it would give them a stronger basis from which to insert themselves into Brazilian society. Although not always explicitly stated, the message was that they were not welcome. It would be better if they disappeared in some way—by returning to Africa, dying from war or disease, or becoming white and losing their cultural heritage if they remained in Brazil.

At the end of the nineteenth century, when the Republic of Brazil was proclaimed, nevertheless, a major concern was the overwhelming presence of people of African descent. The indigenous population had already been largely destroyed, and whites were outnumbered by blacks in most of the larger cities. Raimundo Nina Rodrigues, a Bahia physician famous for his studies of Africans in Brazil, wrote in the introduction for the French edition of his first book, published in 1900: "We do not dissimulate the little value of these studies. But no matter how incomplete they may be, we are convinced that they will help, even in small measure, in the elucidation of the grave social questions related to our destiny as a people in formation."[7] Unlike the United States, where a rigid color line separated blacks and whites, miscegenation was an undeniable reality in Brazil.[8] More than ever it was necessary to think about blacks' and mulattoes' presence, and in the process anthropology would take its first steps in Brazil.

Rodrigues, informed as he was by evolutionist premises, believed it was essential to investigate the origins of the Africans introduced into Brazil. As can be easily inferred from his writings, an evaluation of their different cultural stages was necessary to appreciate the problem they represented: "The division of the degree of culture of African peoples who have colonized Brazil has thus become a main question for studying our nationality in its basis and living forces."[9] He reached no explicit conclusion regarding the future, but his satisfaction is evident in noting that "negro slaves introduced in Brazil did not exclusively belong to the most degraded, brute or savage among African peoples. . . . More than that, mestizos 'camitas' converted to Islamism proceeded from barbarian African states, yes, but from the most advanced ones."[10]

During the 1930s, when it became theoretically possible to dissociate race from culture and to regard blacks as not being intellectually inferior, two roughly contemporary approaches emerged concerning the future of Afro-Brazilians. One was put forward by another physician, Dr. Arthur Ramos, who was mainly inspired by the works of the French anthropologist Lévy Bruhl.[11] Although intellectually capable, Ramos said, African descendants inherited a culture mediated by another type of rationality, totally inadequate in a country striving to become modern and insert itself into the stream of civilization. In an essay on the religion of Brazil's "backward classes," Ramos commented:

> I do not sponsor in any way the postulates on the negro inferiority and capacity for civilization, as I have so often repeated. These collective representations exist in any culturally backward social group. They are a consequence of prelogical and magical thinking, independently of the racial-anthropological question, because they may arise under other conditions and in any ethnic group. These concepts of "primitive,"

"archaic" are merely psychological and have nothing to do with the question of racial inferiority. Therefore, to accomplish an educational and cultural work, it is necessary to know these modalities of primitive thinking in order to correct it, elevating it to more advanced stages, which can only be done by an educational revolution acting deeply, a "vertical" and "interstitial" revolution that going down the remote steps of the collective unconscious, sets free the prelogical ties to which it is bound.[12]

According to this view African descendants had to overcome their syncretic religious beliefs and superstitions in order to participate in building the nation. In sum, miscegenation would dilute color, and education would eradicate Afro-Brazilian culture.

The other approach, led by Gilberto Freyre and inspired mainly by Franz Boas, far from rejecting the African matrix, credited it as the reason Brazilians had become different from the Portuguese. In the colonial world of the master's house and the slave huts, Africans had made us Brazilians. African culture was already part of ours, and there was no way to reverse the process.[13] In his most famous work, Freyre often pointed out the cultural superiority of certain African groups, both to the indigenous population and to the majority of Portuguese settlers.[14] Yet, by viewing the African cultural contribution as well as miscegenation in an almost idyllic way, Freyre has been made responsible for the myth of the three races, the myth of racial democracy. With time this myth gained increasing academic and official status.

Culturalism was an important advance over the previous perspective derived from evolutionary biology, and it dominated the academic scene for more than two decades. It was responsible for the development of a great number of studies on Afro-Brazilian cultural expressions, mainly in the area of religion. Nevertheless, it brought about a rather radical separation of the cultural dimension from the dynamics of social production and reproduction in the studies of Afro-Brazilians, a bias that can be felt in almost all the work carried out during that period.

The growing interest in race relations in the 1950s led to two lines of research generally treated as mutually exclusive. One continued the interest in Afro-Brazilian cultural manifestations, mainly religious aspects, and the other broke new ground in investigating the integration of blacks into Brazilian class society. Generally speaking, the emphasis on religious forms tended to dominate from Rio de Janeiro northward, whereas the latter prevailed to the south. In other words, where the economy and social setting remained closer to the colonial model, the African cultural heritage was the focus; where industrialization was widespread, race and class relations were the main topic. The first had the merit of pointing out the persistence and importance of an African cultural matrix in Brazilian social formation, while the second revealed the mechanisms through which blacks have been maintained in the lowest social positions. Prejudice and discrimination, always strongly denied but carefully preserved and protected under the cloak of so-called racial democracy, finally were brought under discussion, which shifted the axis of sociological studies toward race and class.

The combination of race, class, and culture in Afro-Brazilian studies appeared only in the 1970s, when the first black consciousness movements began to raise questions about identity. One of these was formed by a group of black undergraduates at the Catholic University of São Paulo who were very active in promoting the debate within and outside the university community from 1978 to 1988. A distinctive mark of that period was the growing number of black investigators and their critical posture toward what had been and what was being written on blacks in Brazil. Not only in the discussion of the black question but also in initiatives to reverse the situation of Afro-Brazilians, and despite a lack of unity, the consciousness movement has been active in many ways ever since: denouncing the lies about slavery in official history; unmasking misrepresentations of blacks' role in Brazilian society; and making more evident every day the reality of prejudice and discrimination.

During the 1980s other actors entered the scene, and new issues were raised. The centennial of abolition in 1988 played an important role in intensifying the debate. The elaboration of a new constitution created other opportunities, although not as many as might have been anticipated.[15] Nevertheless, for the first time racism was characterized as a crime. Among the new actors were Catholic priests and Orisá cult priestesses. In Salvador, Bahia, *yalorixás* (priestesses) of the most renowned and influential *terreiros* (cult territories) began a movement among all Orisá houses to rid the cult of the traditional syncretism. They identified it with slavery and considered it absolutely unnecessary in this new phase of history, when the autonomy and importance of African-based culture was being affirmed not only among blacks but also throughout Brazilian society.

At the same time, in an effort to revise the role of the church in relation to Indians and blacks in Brazil and Latin America in general, progressive Catholic priests developed a specific pastoral message for people of African descent, addressing new forms of participation and action within the church. Efforts included the substitution of 20 November for 13 May as the major date for blacks in Brazil;[16] the celebration of Zumbi, the great Palmares maroon leader and martyr, and other important figures in Afro-Brazilian history during the mass; and the incorporation of drums, dance, food, and even invocations to Orisás into the church ritual. Thus, a segment of the church is seeking to stimulate syncretism, while the Orisá cult is seeking to purge it.

Also during the 1980s, new perspectives and lines of investigation were opened in academic areas. There began a deep revision of black history aimed at searching for concrete ways in which blacks resisted slavery, participated in their own liberation, and developed new social formations in urban and rural settings. This research covers a great range of recurrent and new themes, including capitalism and slavery; rural communities; forms of association and mutual help; master-slave relationships; black consciousness and identity movements; memory and imagery; the slave family and kinship systems; discourse analysis; and the demography of slave populations.

Yet, neither growing interest in the academic world nor the direct involvement of blacks has succeeded in mobilizing Brazilian society as a whole to confront the problems affecting Afro-Brazilians and move them to the forefront of national concern. The lack of consensus on important issues seems to explain a good deal of the difficulty.

THE BLACK QUESTION TODAY

Although some of the current topics are not new and all the relevant issues cannot be covered here, a brief examination of three broad areas illustrates the complexity of the debate.

Prejudice and Discrimination: A Race or Class Problem?

Old as it is, the discussion regarding the role of race and class in the problems faced by Afro-Brazilians has not come close to being resolved, given the difficulty of taking into consideration both perspectives. Combining race and class requires us to face the pervading racism among us, almost a taboo for Brazilians, instead of holding to the narrow but more comfortable perspective that prejudice and discrimination will disappear when class barriers alone are overcome. To include the race dimension requires, necessarily, the recognition of the fact that somatic differences are essential components of the problem (not cultural differences alone), whereas these can be easily dismissed when only class is considered. By viewing the race dimension as irrelevant, the class perspective localizes prejudice and discrimination in the contradictions of the class system alone and perceives their overcoming in the resolution of those contradictions.

There are signs that this situation is changing, however. Since the Constitution of 1988 considered racism as crime, there has been a growing concern about episodes of racism in Brazilian society. Important newspapers and magazines have been devoting considerable space to incidents of this kind,[17] and nongovernmental organizations such as SOS Racismo have taken a firm stand, helping people who have been the object of discrimination to find justice and maintaining vigilance against any kind of racist behavior, no matter what its source. At the same time, victims of racism have become more outspoken on these matters. Although it is not easy to pursue charges of racism in the courts because witnesses are not always willing to testify, the number of reported cases has grown significantly during recent years.[18]

Black Identity: One or Many?

Initiated almost twenty years ago by the black consciousness movement, the difficult debate over black identity seems to have stalled. What separates blacks from the rest of the population? Who are Afro-Brazilians? Where should they look for their identity? In Africa? In Brazil, on this side of the Atlantic? Is there one black identity? Given the diversity of diaspora experiences, can it be manifold? Is black identity inextricably linked to black culture? Under what circumstances is black culture produced and reproduced in Brazil? What are its spaces? What does it look like? All these questions can be summed into just one: Who is black, and what does it mean to be black in Brazil?

Brazil is not a racial democracy. This assertion has been reaffirmed so often that it is almost a truism. But in contrast to what has occurred in the United States, "the perception of phenotype overrides descent as a principle of identity" in Brazil.[19] In this context physical appearance becomes the keystone for evaluating where one fits in the scheme of racial categories, as the above referred research in Rio de Contas, Bahia, shows.[20]

There has been a tendency among analysts of census data to change the three official color categories—white, black, and *pardo*—into a binary system (whites and nonwhites), in order to measure the effects of racial prejudice and discrimination in Brazil.[21] There seems to be in this procedure an implicit assumption that once adopted this binary system would foster consciousness about racial identity among mestizo respondents. Confronted with only those two alternatives, the chance to manipulate the three traditional categories would be minimized, and the number of "nonwhites" would come closer to reality. There is no guarantee, however, that the strategy will have that effect. The absence of the *pardo* category may very well lead to an increase in the number of whites, as the results of the research in Rio de Contas seem to suggest.

The role played by miscegenation in Brazilian society all through its history cannot be ignored if we want to fight racism successfully. We must take into consideration our own experience, that is, the way race relations developed here.

Black Citizenship: What to Strive for?

Citizenship has been a popular topic in recent political campaigns, and for Afro-Brazilians it is necessarily enmeshed with the issue of prejudice, discrimination, and identity. How can they be successful in their fight for citizenship without public recognition of racism? Yet, how can they strive to become equal while remaining different without a clear consciousness of belonging somewhere? How can one defend the right to be different without knowing exactly what that means?

The Catholic University's contribution to the debate has not been entirely academic. In 1978, as mentioned, it made space available to Afro-Brazilian undergraduates who organized under Pontificia Universidade Catolica's Black Group, which remained very active until internal divergences led to its split in 1988. Later, the university created the Institute for Afro-Brazilian Research (IPEAFRO) and appointed as it director an internationally known black intellectual Abdidias Do Nascimento; unfortunately, the results fell very short of expectations. In both cases, however, there was a clear commitment to action.

Nevertheless, the Catholic University of São Paulo does not yet have a special program of studies devoted to blacks in Brazil. Despite the fact that a number of courses concerning Afro-Brazilians has been taught regularly in different postgraduate programs and that a great deal of relevant research has been carried out, both by professors and students at different levels, there is nothing structured in the curriculum. Faculty in the social sciences are in the process of overcoming this lack through the development of a specific nucleus concerned with Afro-Brazilian populations.

Public recognition of the black question in Brazil will certainly take time and will depend greatly on many forces, including the role of intellectuals. Yet, to reach the national level the debate has to assume a more definite political dimension, and tangible objectives must be set. The 1988 Constitution made significant steps in that direction. Besides considering racism a crime, as mentioned, questions considered thus far in relation to Indian populations were raised regarding peoples of African descent. Examples are the official recognition of existing territories connected with black history (maroon settlements) and the right of remnant populations to own them; the recognition of a cultural patrimony—material and immaterial—referred to as the African matrix; and the disposition to protect Afro-Brazilian cultural manifestations.[22] Although small, this is a promising beginning.

Since 1988 there has been evidence that new spaces for African descendants in Brazilian society are steadily growing. Black actors play middle-class roles in television soap operas and commercials, instead of the traditional roles of maid, cook, chauffeur, or porter. Black models are seen in fashion shows. A recent São Paulo magazine dedicated to blacks sold extremely well.[23] But the new visibility of black people has not been restricted to TV and the fashion world.

Since redemocratization in the 1980s, it has become rather frequent for blacks to be elected mayors in a number of state capitals, such as Pôrto Alegre, Vitória, and São Paulo, or governors (Rio Grande do Sul, Sergipe). Benedita da Silva, a black *favelada* (a shantytown resident), was defeated by a very small margin in her race for mayor of Rio de Janeiro in 1992; soon afterward she was elected to the national senate, the first woman to achieve this position in Brazil. These events have given rise to speculations about an ethnic vote. Not long ago Pelé, the famous soccer star who now holds a position in government, ordinarily aloof from such matters, declared himself in favor of blacks voting for black candidates as a strategy for bettering their condition.

Another important sign of change was the official recognition of Zumbi as the most important symbol of the black struggle against slavery during the three hundredth anniversary celebration of his death, held throughout 1995. The nation's president referred to him as "the most important Brazilian black hero." An immediate result of this official concern with African descendants seems to have been the creation at the beginning of 1996 of an interministerial working group to develop concerted action in different spheres to improve conditions for blacks. The demand for quotas for black students in public universities, under discussion since 1995, will certainly be among its priorities.

Conclusion

By blocking access to land ownership by Afro-Brazilians in rural areas and leaving them to fend for themselves in urban areas, the Brazilian state transferred to former slaves and their descendants the entire responsibility for their survival, expressing a total lack of interest in their physical and cultural reproduction. This created enormous obstacles for preserving ethnicity and roots, cultures, and identity. Without an effective basis for physical and cultural reproduction, most Afro-Brazilians were relegated to the lowest positions in society, but the state's project of a modern, white, occidental, and Catholic country did not succeed. Afro-Brazilians did not disappear or become white. Their cultural expressions, such as religion, the samba, and *capoeira* (a mixture of sport and fighting), not only survived but also penetrated most of Brazilian society. The battle against annihilation began the very moment the first African slaves arrived and has continued all through our history. Slavery was not met with resignation, as the official history used to tell. Flights, suicides, rebellions, and maroon settlements punctuated it.

Afro-Brazilians still face prejudice and discrimination. To combat it, they must rescue their history, defend the cultural spaces already conquered, and open others where they can produce and reproduce their culture and above all lead Brazilian society as a whole to become conscious of the racism that pervades it. The new constitutional articles are an important gain in this respect, and the universities and the black consciousness movement still have a fundamental role to play.

Antiracism is a recent phenomenon in the Brazilian scene. As it progresses, we hope the black question will cease to be an issue denied, and racial democracy may finally become a reality.

NOTES

1. This is a generally accepted estimate. According to the national census of 1991, the first one to include the Indian population, Indian peoples amounted to 294,135 individuals, or 0.2% of Brazil's 146,280,918 inhabitants. The same computed 75.7 million white (51.6%); 7.3 million black (5%); 62 million *pardos* (42.4%), and 630,656, yellow (0.4%). There is no information on color for 534,878 respondents (0.4%). Mestizos are commonly termed *pardos* in Brazil.

   According to PNAD data for 1988—Pesquisa National por Amostra de Domicílios (National Household Sample Research)—35% of blacks and 34% of *pardos* earned up to one minimum salary officially established, compared to 12.5% of whites among economically active Brazilians; 33.5% of blacks and 34.9% of *pardos* age 5 and older were illiterate, while only 16.7% of whites were found in this category; 29.1% of blacks and 27.6% of *pardos* age 10 and older went to school less than one year, compared to 12.5% of whites. While 4.7% of whites ran their own businesses as employers only 0.5% of blacks and 1.6% of *pardos* were able to do the same; 18.2% of black and 14.8% of *pardo* families were composed of women with their children while only 11.8% of white families knew the same kind of depravation; 11.1% of blacks and 13.1% of *pardos* lived in "rustic" dwellings throughout Brazil whereas only 2.9% of whites were found in the same condition.

2. Exception is made to some black rural communities, remnants of maroon settlement scattered over the country, that live on a subsistence economy.

3. The Golden Law reads: "Article. 1—Since the date of this law, slavery in Brazil is declared extinct. Art. 2—Contrary dispositions are revoked."

4. "Nothing but freedom," declared Robert V. Richardson, treasurer of the American Cotton Planters Association, referring to what would be given to U.S. emancipated slaves in 1865.

5. This could not be done with the Indians alone, who were insufficient in number, lacked experience in agriculture, and were under the protection of the Jesuits.

6. Soon after the slave revolts of the early nineteenth century, long before abolition, there was a strong official movement to send freedmen back to Africa, although the government could not afford it. Many former slaves succeeded in making their way back to their homeland on their own.

7. R. Nina Rodrigues, *O animiso fetchista dos Negros bahianos* (Rio de Janeiro: Civilização Brasileira S.A., 1935), 9.

8. According to the 1890 census, Brazil had 6,302,198 whites, 4,638,495 *pardos*, and 2,097,426 blacks.

9. Rodrigues, *O animiso*, 9.

10. Rodrigues, *Os africanos no Brasil*, 4th ed. (São Paulo: Cia Editora Nacional, 1976), 268, 269.

11. L. Lévy-Bruhl, *How Natives Think*, trans. Lillian A. Clare (1910, 1926; reprint New York: Arno Press, 1979); L. Lévy-Bruhl, *Primitive Mentality*, trans. Lillian A. Clare (1922; reprint New York: McMillan Company, 1923); and L. Lévy-Bruhl, *The "Soul" of the Primitive*, trans. Lillian A. Clare (1927; reprint New York: McMillan Company, 1928).

12. Arthur Ramos, *O Negro brasileiro* (1934; reprint, Rio de Janeiro: Civilização Brasileira, 1943), 23.

13. Gilberto Freyre, *Casa grande e senzala* (Masters and slaves), vol. 2, 6th ed. (1934; reprint, Rio de Janeiro: Livraria José Olympio Editora, 1950), chap. 4.

14. Ibid., 2:513.

15. The 1988 Constitution dedicates a full chapter to the Indians Capitulo Vuljijulovm-Da Ordoui Serial: articles 68 of the Transitory Dispositions, and articles 215 and 216, section 2, on culture (Capitulo III Titulo VIII-Da Orderu Serial.

16. May 13 is the anniversary of the Golden Law, the abolition of slavery. November 20 is the date of Zumbi's death.

17. *Jornal do Brasil*, *Folha de São Paulo*, and *Veja* are examples of two newspapers and one magazine.

18. According to a survey carried out by *Jornal do Brasil*, fifty incidents of racial discrimination, mostly from Rio de Janeiro, were reported in newspapers between 9 December 1968 and 9 June 1977. See Carlos A. Hasenbalg, *Discriminação e desigualdades raciais no Brasil* (Rio de Janeiro: Edições Graal, 1979), 262, 263. Data from the Center for Afro-Asiatic Studies for 1988 reveal forty-six reports. See Antonio Guimarães, "O recente anti racismo brasileiro: O que dizem os jornais diários (São Paulo)," *Revista USP* 28 (February 1996): 88.

19. M. Harris, J. Consorte, J. Lang, and B. Byrne, "Who Are the Whites? Imposed Census Categories and the Racial Demography of Brazil," *Social Forces* 72, no. 2 (December 1993): p. 452.

20. Respondents were asked to find among a set of thirty-six male and female portraits the drawing that had features most resembling their own. By and large, the drawing chosen showed lighter color, thinner lips and nose, and straighter hair than the person being interviewed. These data have not been submitted to systematic analysis as yet.

21. Carlos A. Hasenbalg, *Discriminação Desigualdades Raciais Nobrasilm Ediçoès Graal LTDD;* Carlos A. Hasenbalg and Nelson do V. Silva, *Estrutura social, mobilidade e raça* (Rio de Janeiro: IUPERJ, 1983); Edward Telles, "Residential Segregation by Skin Color in Brazil," *American Sociological Review* 57 (1992): 186–97; and C. Wood and P. Lovell, "Racial Inequality and Child Mortality in Brazil," *Social Forces* 70 (1992): 703–24.

22. Article 68 of the Transitory Dispositions; Article 216 of section 2, on Culture; Article 215 of section 2, on Culture.

23. *RAÇA BRASIL* (São Paulo) 12 February 1997.

The Evolution of Black Identity
in the Dominican Republic

Edward Paulino

A S A MOSTLY BLACK AND MULATTO CARIBBEAN NATION, THE DOMINICAN Republic is very much part of the African diaspora. From the western border towns of Monte Cristi, Dajabón, and Jimaní to the most eastern provinces of San Pedro de Macorís, La Romana, and Higuey, Dominicans of African descent are ubiquitous. They have been part of the social fabric of Dominican society ever since the establishment of Spain's first colony in the Americas on the island of Hispaniola in the late fifteenth century. From the sixteenth century to the present, Afro-Dominicans and mulattos have been active participants in their nation's history, but until very recently their contributions have been ignored. The reason lies with the Dominican state's effort to create and control its ideal definition of nation.

In the Dominican Republic, the state discourse to create what Benedict Anderson terms an "imagined community" originated in the 1822–44 Haitian unification of the island.[1] That period offered fertile ground for the young and vulnerable Dominican state to define itself in opposition to Haiti by portraying itself as non-black. Subsequent failed Haitian invasions up to the mid-1850s further justified that discourse. This anti-Haitian and by extension antiblack attitude fluctuated through the late nineteenth century, decreasing during the 1861–65 War of Restoration against Spain, and increasing again during the dictatorship of Ulises "Lilís" Heureaux.

By the 1930s, under the dictatorship of Rafael Leonidas Trujillo (1930–61), the state espoused a racist national ideology that anathematized Haiti and rejected black Dominican cultural influences. Capitalizing on the history of conflict with Haiti, the

Dominican intelligentsia created a dogma that portrayed Haitians as racially, culturally, linguistically, and religiously inferior to Dominicans, who were represented as white, Catholic, and descended from Spain. The Trujillo brand of patriotism made Haitians the scapegoat, and the officially sanctioned negrophobia was grounded in a racist historiography that was challenged only after the dictator's assassination in 1961.

This article shows how Dominican national identity was shaped by an authoritarian state intent on creating a new nation. I analyze the racist and xenophobic historiography that excluded consideration of Dominicans of African decent, and contrast it with the post-Trujillo revisionism that attributed an active role to Afro-Dominicans in their country's development. I will also show how returning immigrants have shaped and challenged traditional notions of what it means to be Dominican.

A Tangled History

By the sixteenth century Spain had incorporated Hispaniola into its burgeoning empire, but other European nations soon entered the Caribbean. From 1580 until 1657, Britain and France regularly attacked Spain's New World possessions. In 1586, Sir Francis Drake led an English attack on Hispaniola, raiding the coastal towns and disrupting order in the colony.[2] By the mid seventeenth century, English assaults had given way to marauding by French buccaneers, who gradually established settlements along the northwestern shore, and the Spanish eventually limited their presence to the eastern part of the island. In 1697, contrary to the traditional historiography, Spain and France, which drafted the Treaty of Ryswick, did not cede one-third of the western part of the island to the French (Haiti) and the remainder to the Spanish. Historian Frank Moya Pons writes, "the confusion of some Dominican historians comes from the interpretation that the French gave to the Ryswick Peace Treaty since the belligerent parties in Europe agreed to put an end to the war returning the conquered land and recognizing the possession that each of them had prior to the conflict."[3] But in time, two different sociopolitical cultures emerged, one speaking French and Creole languages in the west, the other speaking Spanish in the east.

The Haitian Revolution in 1791 redefined the French colony on Hispaniola. Black slaves revolted against the whites, and under the leadership of Toussaint L'Ouverture, the Republic of Haiti was created in 1804. This revolution sent shock waves throughout the Americas but most particularly in eastern Hispaniola, which remained a slaveholding Spanish colony until invaded by L'Ouverture in 1801. Haiti, as the first country in the Americas to abolish slavery and the second after the United States to declare political independence, undermined the institution of slavery and the ideological apparatus that sustained the plantation regime. Although colonial Santo Domingo repelled a major Haitian invasion in 1805, Haiti in 1822, under President Jean-Pierre Boyer, ordered an invasion for the unification of Hispaniola. The occupation lasted for twenty-two years. Consequently, Haitian rule provoked an independence movement in Santo Domingo called "la Trinitaria," led by Juan Pablo Duarte, a Creole who would become known as the republic's founding father. On 16 January 1844, twenty-two years after Haitian President Boyer had triumphantly entered the gates of Santo Domingo, the leaders of the Dominican independence movement issued a manifesto that declared, among other things: "Considering, lastly, that because of the difference of customs and the rivalry that exists between us, there will never be perfect union nor harmony, the peoples of the Spanish part of the island of Santo Domingo . . . [are] satisfied that in twenty-two years of attachment to the Haitian Republic they have not been able to draw out any advantage whatsoever but on the contrary have ruined themselves, [and] become impoverished."[4]

Unlike other Latin American colonial independence movements, the Dominican Republic won separation from Haiti, a former French colony, rather than from Spain. Significantly, Dominican patriotism and nationalism grew out of self-differentiation from Haiti, and these sentiments were reinforced by several unsuccessful Haitian invasions from 1844 to 1855. A patriotic article written by General Manuel de Regla Mota in 1855 rallied resistance to the advancing Haitian army and implored his countrymen to recall life under Haitian rule, particularly the "threatening orgies" and "retrograde civilization."[5] Mota was trying to galvanize the populace, which was largely rural and perhaps had stronger ties to its local community than to an emerging and unfamiliar Dominican state. There also may have been some indifference in certain sectors of Dominican society that did not feel threatened politically or economically by another Haitian invasion. In any case, Mota's article represents a period in Dominican history when anti-Haitianism originated and the seeds of a national identity were sown in the alleged racial difference between the two countries. For example, according to some foreign observers, the Haitian invasions provoked many Afro-Dominicans and mulattoes, who equated blackness with Haiti, to say they were "negro, but a white negro" or "although I have black skin, my heart is white."[6]

Although military invasions ceased, Haitians began to cross the porous and unsupervised border in search of jobs in the emerging Dominican sugar industry, which thrived on cheap labor.[7] The Cuban Wars of Independence in the late 1800s reduced the world's sugar supply, and the relatively more politically stable Dominican Republic benefited. Its fertile but unexploited lands, especially along the southern east coast, attracted many sugar investors from the United States and Cuba. The sugar industry developed in Haiti in the 1700s, and in Cuba in the early 1800s, but came much later to the Dominican Republic, where it dramatically transformed the economy. It altered land patterns, dispossessed thousands of farmers, and created over dependency on a single crop. The U.S. economic, political, and military presence in Dominican domestic affairs increased due to the influence of the sugar companies. Furthermore, significant demographic shifts resulted from the demand for cheap labor. One of these was the surge in Haitians seeking jobs.

Haitian labor became essential to the expanding sugar industry, but negrophobic political and cultural elites in Santo Domingo took a dim view of this immigration. Some argued that it endangered Dominican culture. Francisco X. Billini, head of the Colegio San Luis Gonzaga, penned a newspaper editorial suggesting a policy similar to the anti-Asian laws in the United States.[8] As early as 1871 the influx of not only Haitians but also blacks (*cocolos*) from the English-speaking Caribbean concerned officials. In his study on Dominican agriculture Michiel Baud cites a letter from a provincial governor to the Ministry of Interior and Police referring to *cocolos* as those "badly dressed blacks."[9] Other state officials were concerned about the increasing number of black immigrants as the sugar industry in the south and southeast developed.[10]

Color and language were indeed the signs of difference. Haitians, who were black and spoke French and Creole (based on French and African roots), were the most distant from the Dominican white elites, who spoke Spanish. According to Dominican historian Roberto Cassá, "at the heart of the social consciousness [of the Dominican elite] there was determined the idea of identifying the enemy with the Haitian and the Haitian with the black."[11] As the elite struggled to meet international standards of modernity, they sought to marginalize and condemn that which might be considered uncultivated, dirty, or poor. They were sensitive about the presence of both black Dominicans and Haitians, who were invariably considered primitive and uncivilized. Under Trujillo, these historic prejudices would gradually crystallize into official state policy.

Construction of Racialized National Identity, 1930–61

Among the legacies of the 1916–24 U.S. occupation of the Dominican Republic was the Guardia Nacional, which became the vehicle of ascent to power for a young man from the town of San Cristobal. As in Nicaragua and Haiti, the National Guard in the Dominican Republic was a surrogate army comprised of local citizens and represented the economic and political interests of the United States after the withdrawal of the occupation forces. Rafael L. Trujillo quickly rose through the ranks and was a general when he initiated a coup d'état and, after fraudulent elections, became president in 1930. The Trujillo regime became authoritarian and then totalitarian; and in consolidating his power and redefining the nation, he encouraged a state-sponsored intelligentsia to articulate his vision.

The late anthropologist Ernest Gellner suggests that the human condition constructs a "vision of reality" that is antithetical to its present reality and which may be a culture or style of thought constantly in flux. Gellner states that this cultural view must justify itself, "however dogmatic, for selecting that which it does select and for excluding that which it excludes."[12] Trujillo could argue that Dominicans were essentially non-black because they were different from their Haitian neighbors. Haiti was demonized as the "historic enemy" that had once invaded and occupied the eastern part of the island. Moreover, Trujillo sought to capitalize on a shared Dominican history of the black "invaders" during the island's unification. This historiography exhorted its people to remember their courageous struggle for independence from Haiti and the imperative to defend Dominican culture. According to Trujillo, the country "had resisted the hard test of repeated invasions and twenty-two years of [Haitian] domination; she had frustrated the absurd design of the creators of the policy of the neighboring nation of definitively implanting in all the extension of the island of Hispaniola its language, its religion, its customs and its traditions."[13]

A major ideological linchpin for Trujillo's discourse was the notion of *hispanidad:* the centrality of Spain in Dominican culture and identity. Two themes woven into his speeches were Christianity and the Spanish motherland. In Trujillo's nationalism, Dominicans were fanatically Catholic, whereas Haitians practiced pagan rituals in the form of Vodun.[14] Although Haiti was officially a "Catholic nation," the practice of Vodun was widespread and dangerous. According to Trujillo: "Wherever a religion that is not Christian dominates, slavery appears like a law, and there, where this [Christian] religion is weakened, the nation feels, similarly, less susceptible to general liberty."[15]

Trujillo also used the merengue—the national dance—as a political symbol for unity. This music was played everywhere he traveled throughout the country as a way to overcome historic regionalisms and the power of local strongmen (*caudillos*).[16] Much like the Dominican populace, the merengue was a mixture of African and European influences and styles. But its black origins, which ranged from the *tambora* (a two-sided drum played sideways with a wooden stick) to call-and-response vocalization, were denied. Even prominent Dominican musicologists at the time toed Trujillo's ideological line. According to Flérida de Nolasco: "Our songs stem from Spanish rhythms. . . . Even if we admit that our musical folklore is the product of a double culture, the Spanish and the African, the art invariably follows a nobler and purer strain. Dominican folk music is Spanish adjusted to native tastes, and it is only by accident that it is affected by the savage African rhythms."[17]

Trujillo was not the first to espouse this cultural view of Dominican society. Américo Lugo (1870–1952), who rallied Dominicans against the U.S. occupation, was a nationalist who considered whites racially superior to blacks, and he viewed Dominican culture as inextricably linked to Spain, not Africa: "Although open is the mind of the Dominican to all healthy foreign [read European] influence (i.e., the adoption of civil legislation and French trade), at the depths of her culture, by the practical sense and ideal of life, [the Dominican Republic] remains Spanish, based on language, culture, customs, heritage, in its history, traditions, and memory."[18]

According to Dominican historian Frank Moya Pons, however, *hispanidad* collapsed under the weight of racial differences during the attempted Spanish annexation (1861–65), when soldiers and bureaucrats arrived to find that "the people they had come to govern were not as Hispanic as they had been led to believe. The majority of the population were mulattos, and their customs varied enormously from Spanish tradition because of the centuries of isolation during the colonial period, and particularly after 22 years of Haitian domination and 17 years of national independence."[19] The annexationists believed Dominicans should return voluntarily to the colonial fold, but the reinstitution of slavery was a real possibility, since Spain still possessed two slave-owning colonies in the Caribbean, Cuba and Puerto Rico. Again, according to Moya Pons, "What began as a peasant revolt soon became a racial war, since the black and mulatto Dominicans who constituted the majority of the population feared being enslaved again by the Spaniards."[20] Needless to say, the Dominican historiography under Trujijllo failed to make this racial connection.

A leading intellectual during the Trujillo era was Manuel Arturo Peña Batlle (1902–54), who came to symbolize the virulent anti-black historiography of the time. He capitalized on the Haitian invasions and occupation in the previous century to justify his xenophobic disdain for Haitian immigrants, and he wrote about their "natural" inferiority while eradicating all things black from Dominican culture.[21]

Peña Batlle attempted to isolate the black Haitian Other from the mostly mulatto and black Dominicans through cultural distinction. To be Dominican meant being a devout Catholic and fluent in Spanish, and anyone lacking these cultural credentials was categorized as Haitian. Haitian immigrants eroded Dominican Catholic values with their Vodun: "If we consider the growing settlement that is forming in our population's lower classes, the [Haitian] army of that monstrous fetish practice of Voodoo, we will discover that if we do not act with a harsh hand and strong spirit, there will come a moment in which the wrongs will be irremediable between us, such as it is on the other side [of the island]."[22]

The Antiblack Discourse and State Policies

The Dominican intelligentsia's defense of *hispanidad* was echoed in immigration legislation drafted in the early 1930s. The growth of the sugar industry increased the demand for manual labor, drawing thousands of workers from Haiti and the neighboring English-speaking islands of the Caribbean. The Haitian immigration to jobs on the American-owned sugar plantations was in part spurred by the U.S. military occupation of Haiti (1915–34) and the Dominican Republic (1916–24), and its continued dominance in the domestic affairs of both societies.[23] By the early 1930s, Afro-Caribbean and Haitian laborers were prevalent in most of the country's sugar mills (*ingenios*).

In 1932 the government passed a law permitting the selective deportation of Afro-Caribbeans, and the next year an even stricter law targeted all black immigrants. According to the law, at least 70 percent of the sugar industry's workforce had to be Dominican, although economic imperatives of the worldwide Great Depression made enforcement of this law very difficult.[24] The sugar companies opposed this legislation because immigrant labor was far cheaper and they found ways to get around it. For example, at the height of the U.S. occupation in 1920, Haitians in the Dominican Republic numbered 28,258,[25] but by 1935 (two years after the law was passed) the figure was 52,657.[26]

In response to this demographic shift, the Haitian presence in the Dominican Republic was attacked. Historical precedent was used to justify and reinforce Trujillo's new concept of national identity. The intent of these writings was to create the illusion that Haitian immigrants represented an invasion force that would destroy Dominican culture and therefore required a united defense. Emilio Rodríguez Demorizi, perhaps the best-known historian of the Trujillo dictatorship, was among those who portrayed this immigration as a cultural threat. He underscored the connection between the nineteenth-century military campaigns, and a possible modern "invasion." According to Demorizi, unification of the island was impossible because of the stark racial and cultural differences between the two nations, and he warned Dominicans about Haiti's retrograde culture, including "the religious problem of superstitions and of *voudou*, and of the cannibalism that appears in the most bottom layers of that unfortunate Haitian mass."[27]

But the most egregious manifestation of state-sponsored anti-Haitianism occurred in September and October 1937, when the Dominican army and police, along with conscripted civilians and convicts, rounded up and slaughtered between fifteen thousand and twenty-five thousand Haitian men, women, and children.[28] The killings took place primarily but not exclusively along the border. Following the massacre, Joaquín Balaguer (1906–2002), an important intellectual and a relentless apologist for the Trujillo regime who later would be president of the country, denied international charges of mass murder. According to the Dominicanist scholar Ernesto Sagás, the sycophantic Trujillo ideologue (at the time ambassador to Colombia and Venezuela), Balaguer referred to the bloody extermination "as merely incidents between Dominican peasants and Haitian cattle rustlers."[29] Moreover, Balaguer continued to support this official interpretation. He perpetuated Trujillo's anti-Haitian ideology long after the massacre in *La realidad dominicana*, written in 1947. Sagás states that it "makes indistinct use of the terms race and nation, so as to pretend that Haitians and Dominicans not only belong to different nations, but also to completely different races."[30]

OTHER VOICES AND REVISIONIST HISTORY

A few scholars during this period deviated somewhat from the official doctrine and avoided being compromised by the state. Rather than challenge the regime directly, they researched provocative nineteenth-century topics or did not join the chorus of effusive praise for Trujillo. The Spanish cleric Manuel Arjona Cañete, also known as Fray Cipriano de Utrera, falls into this category. Others became political exiles and denounced Trujillo's repressive and authoritarian policies.[31]

Through poetry and fiction, a very small number of writers attempted to examine the long forgotten role and exploited role of black Dominicans. Although Manuel del Cabral, a major figure in twentieth-century Dominican literature published *Doce poemas negros* (Twelve black poems) in 1932, there are those who consider his work detached, "with no real political commitment to revindicating Blacks and Haitians in Dominican society."[32] Nevertheless, Cabral is a precursor of Dominican scholars struggling to resurrect their suppressed blackness, and his poignant poems expose the double bind of race and class exploitation. In "Colá," Cabral writes: "In order to speak with you / with your bone, negro Colá / one need not go inside there, in the twenty cents that you earn daily / nor in the night you have in your amulet / but in the calluses of your fingers that suddenly are turned into silk if you caress your son."[33]

Two prominent writers whose fiction elucidated the marginal and exploitative conditions of black sugar mill workers were Ramón Marrero Aristy and Pedro Mir, the Dominican national poet). Aristy was far from a spokesman for the plight of blacks, but his novel *Over* (1940) describes the corruption, despair, and exploitation endured by the Dominicans, Haitians, and West Indians. In the sugar plantations.[34]

He was killed in 1959 by Trujillo assassins. Pedro Mir wrote his famous poem "Hay un pais en el mundo" (There is a country in the world) in 1949, while in exile. His objective was not to feature the Afro-Dominican per se but to expose his country's impoverishment and brutal subjugation at the hands of a dictator. Nevertheless, the intersections between class and race are very evident in Mir's writings. For example, in one of his poems he writes: "And the sweating profile of the [sugarcane] carriers enveloped in a layer of black muscles."[35]

Others, such as the feminist writer Aida Cartagena Portalatín, began to challenge traditional Dominican literature, which was resoundingly *hispanista* and male-oriented. Although the racial issue in the work of Cartagena Portalatín was not so central during the Trujillo period, this professor, journalist, and poet did begin to question the traditional roles of women, and in the 1950s she gradually came to challenge traditional parameters and Dominican assumptions about race and gender. According to scholar Daisy Cocco de Filippis, Portalatín "discards from the Dominican literary lexicon the terms *sumisa* [submissive], *virginal* [virginlike], and *blanca* [white] as she redefines the boundaries of the female world."[36] Not until Trujillo's assassination in May 1961 and the subsequent popular election of the democratic leftist intellectual Juan Bosch did Dominican scholars begin to reevaluate and revise thirty years of Trujillo historiography.

Much research in the post-Trujillo era falls under the rubric of revisionist history, particularly as a counterweight to historiography during the dictatorship.[37] Revisionist works have challenged and revised the traditional views on race. As early as 1964, Dominican historians questioning such eminent writers as Americo Lugo, for example, Hugo Tolentino and Juan Isidro Jiménes Grullón, initiated a critical debate about Lugo's "historical interpretation and political theory."[38]

Pedro Andres Perez Cabral, in *La comunidad mulata,* addressed the mulatto Dominican majority and the effects of miscegenation. He examined the mulatto propensity for *blanqueamiento* (whitening) and its overall effect on the nation's development. Using Dominican national census data, Perez Cabral found that in the 1935 population of 1,479,417, 13 percent were white, 19.5 percent were black, and 67.5 percent were mulatto. By 1950, the white population had increased to 28.1 percent, and blacks had decreased to 11.5 percent.[39] Part of the explanation for the change may lie in the success of the Trujillo regime's ideological rhetoric of an all-white population, or one at least relatively whiter than Haiti's. Progressive racial mixing (*mulatización progresiva*) to produce lighter offspring and the mulatto's quest for whitening concerned Cabral, who viewed this as a "struggle for aryanization and consequently for de-Africanization."[40]

The new approach to writing and theorizing about Dominican history throughout the early 1960s reflected the nation's reawakening after years of censorship. The movement from "a predominantly 'aristocratic,' heroic interpretation of history to a 'sociologization' of history-writing," states Hermannus Hoetink, is evident in the first part of the 1960s.[41] The freedom to inquire and provocatively ask questions without fear of state reprisal sparked intense intellectual debates on several issues relating to the development of the nation. Intellectuals argued vociferously about the sugar industry and its role in agrarian problems as the U.S. companies absorbed Dominican-owned lands; about the rise of Trujillo; and about the causes of the 1965 U.S. invasion. These debates forced Dominicans to consider civil society and democracy in relation to dictatorships and military juntas, the relationship between foreign capital and exploitation, and national identity issues.[42] In a Caribbean country that, according to Stuart Hall, allows one "to feel closer to Spain and to the Spanish tradition of Latin America," the new approach in the Dominican Republic was indeed unprecedented.[43] But while Dominicans at home were painting a more accurate portrait of the nation, Dominicans abroad also helped shape the evolving conception of race through immigration.

Immigration and Shifting Views of Race and National Identity

The U.S. Immigration Act of 1965 relaxed the quota system and allowed many Dominicans to immigrate, especially to New York City, where a labor shortage in the garment industry offered the possibility of higher pay. Thousands of Dominicans (particularly women) flocked there to work in factories under sweatshop conditions, in restaurants, and in other menial jobs.[44] The large influx of mostly poor and working-class Dominicans arrived at a time of social unrest in the United States, when the civil rights movement and the Vietnam War sparked protest, particularly in large cities.

Many urban immigrants groups became politicized in the 1960s. Black and mulatto Dominicans, coming from a country where racial segregation was not legally institutionalized, encountered the Black Is Beautiful discourse. They also witnessed the spontaneous urban uprisings by African Americans following the assassination of Dr. Martin Luther King in 1968. As historian Clayborne Carson writes, "in a unique display of nationwide racial unity, blacks in numerous cities burned and looted white property and battled the police and military forces sent to suppress them."[45] Although urban rioting and, indeed, revolution were not new to Dominicans,[46] what was different was the social protest and empowerment that revolved around racial politics and ethnic identity.

Dominicans slowly learned that they were black and belonged to a larger African diaspora. Their political and racial education came through daily experiences with white society and from living and working with African Americans. Perhaps for the first time they confronted discrimination based on skin color and segregation in racial neighborhoods. They also interacted with other Latino groups, such as Puerto Ricans in New York City, who forced Dominicans to view themselves in racial terms.[47] This new awareness had a profound effect on Dominican society when these immigrants and their children returned home with a new racial awareness. The coifs, music, spirituality, and clothing associated with the U.S. Black Power movement were as common in Santo Domingo's La Calle el Conde as they were on the Grand Concourse and 149th Street in the Bronx.[48] As historian Frank Moya Pons writes: "The real discovery of the Dominican black roots was a result of the . . . migrants who went back to their [Dominican] communities transformed into new social agents of modernity, capitalism, and racial emancipation."[49]

The Reexamination of African Diaspora Identities, 1970s–90s

According to Carlos Esteban Deive, one of the principal historians of the Afro-Dominican historiographical vanguard, the "interest in Afro-Dominican research originates, fundamentally, from the 1973 celebration of the First Colloquium on the Presence of Africa in the Antilles and the Caribbean in the Universidad Autónoma de Santo Domingo."[50] Since 1964, United Nations Educational, Scientific, and Cultural Organization (UNESCO) had sponsored various conferences throughout the world regarding blacks in the Americas and their respective cultures.[51] Furthermore, the newly independent African states stirred interest in black culture along with an awareness of its world influence. Throughout the 1960s and 1970s, countries such as Brazil, Cuba, and Venezuela hosted conferences that underscored Afro-centric research and traditions. For example, at the First Afro-Venezuelan Cultural Colloquium in 1973, a variety of topics were addressed, ranging from recognition of blacks in the development of the colony to their economic and political history.[52] The colloquium in Santo Domingo immediately followed, in late July and early August.[53]

A variety of influential U.S. publications examining Latin American slavery, *mestizaje* (racial mixing), and the treatment of blacks in literature influenced and accelerated the nascent Dominican discourse on race.[54] Out of all this emerged a number of critical issues central to the reinterpretation of the past as well as to the present and future of racial and national identity on the Dominican Republic. Six themes are particularly significant: slavery, the Haitian invasions, racial prejudice and social inequality, *blanqueamiento* and Eurocentrism, the role of women, and African roots and routes.

Revisiting Slavery

The 1973 conference in Santo Domingo continued the revisionist history that began after Trujillo's death. Part of the growing international interest in African slavery and race relations stemmed from the Tannenbaum thesis, which posited that Latin American (Iberian) slavery was more benign than the North American (Anglo-Saxon) version.[55] According to Tannenbaum, the Latin American race relations that emerged from a legacy of bondage were more fluid and lacked the rigid institutional barriers found in the United States. Efforts to dispel the notion that blacks in the Americas lived in what the Brazilian intellectual Gilberto Freyre called an idyllic "racial democracy," spurred investigation of the long-neglected history of the African contribution to societies in the New World. Yet, some Dominican scholars agreed with Tannenbaum and felt that the absence of an industrialized form of slavery and the predominance of mulattoes in the Dominican Republic indicated "benevolent" race relations, free of what historian Marcio Veloz Maggiolo called a racially stratified society or "ghetto [slavocratic] attitude."[56] To Maggiolo, Haiti symbolized this "ghettoized" reality because it had experienced a very labor intensive form of slavery, a high concentration of blacks, and therefore a heightened racial consciousness. Conversely, the Dominican Republic gradually emerged as a nation without strictly defined racial stratifications because the sugar industry had developed after slavery and independence.[57]

This interpretation was challenged by other historians, who focused on the conditions of black slaves, including their ill treatment and escape rates. *Cimarrones* (runaways) were a poignant example of how Dominican slavery paralleled other exploitative systems throughout the Americas.[58] Blacks and free slaves now appeared as active participants in the unfolding drama of the republic's history, whether in the "militia, clergy, or teaching staff."[59] For the first time, Dominicans were acknowledging that many of their ancestors were black and slaves, and no longer could ignore the legacy of what was once perceived as an exclusively Haitian institution on the island.

Rethinking the Haitian Invasions

Not until the revisionism of the 1970s, notably the seminal empirical colonial study (1822–44) by Pons, did Dominicans realize that many of their ancestors (especially those residing along the border) welcomed and supported Haiti's 1822 invasion.[60]

La dominacion hatiana remains a refreshing example of national history that did not succumb to traditional scapegoating. Indeed, Pons overcame the temptations long associated with a subject that, according to one Dominican scholar, "offers an ideal arena for the traditional, conservative, and anti-Haitian historian to amply exhibit his colors and his beliefs."[61]

A dean of Afro-Dominican studies, Franklin Franco, also helped dismantle the traditional notion that all Dominicans opposed Jean-Pierre Boyer's march on Santo Domingo.[62] Moreover, Franco's research revealed that Dominican independence from Haiti in 1844 was somewhat precarious, and its success relied on the support of many black and mulatto Dominicans, who initially questioned the motives of their own country's resistance leaders. Indeed, a prominent example of black participation in Dominican history occurred shortly after independence; former slaves, terrified that bondage would be reinstituted, mobilized in a section of the capital called Monte Grande and threatened to disrupt the new government.[63] Their fears were not groundless, since there were strong pro-French and pro-Spanish factions in the Dominican revolutionary junta who favored a European protectorate. Furthermore, slavery still thrived in the Spanish colonies of Cuba and Puerto Rico.

When the African-born leader of the black and mulatto insurrection, Santiago Basora, mobilized his followers, he was fully aware of the consequences of political independence without the abolition of slavery. Cause for concern was reflected in the fact that the rallying cry for liberty in 1844 did not call on all Dominicans but was "To arms Spaniards!"[64] These initial words of the tentative national anthem represented an exclusionary attitude toward nonwhites by the mostly Creole (white) independence leaders. Victory for the former slaves came on 1 March 1844, when the new government officially declared abolition, completing the work begun on Hispaniola by Toussaint L'Ouverture almost forty years earlier. The resolution stated that "slavery has disappeared forever from the territory of the Dominican Republic, and whoever propagates the contrary shall be considered a delinquent, pursued and punished."[65] Legal emancipation would not be achieved in Puerto Rico until 1873 and in Cuba until 1886.

Prejudice and Social Inequality

Dominican historians were aware of and influenced by the growing international body of work on blacks in Latin American and their negative portrayals.[66] This literature examined the myriad societal labels in the daily vernacular and folklore: devils, witches, thieves, worthless scoundrels, and docile creatures. In the Dominican Republic, scholars found that the vernacular was also saturated with racial slurs regarding blacks and Haitians. Pejorative maxims about persons of African descent abounded. Deive pointed out that Dominican references to straight hair as "good" and coarse hair as "bad" assigned positive and negative attributes, respectively, to white and black phenotypes.[67] Aphorisms and expressions used daily perpetuated racial prejudice. Blacks were social pariahs: "if you see a white eating with a black, it is because the white owes the black or the food belongs to the latter."[68]

Contrary to the traditional discourse, there was ample evidence of self-affirmation by blacks ever since the colonial period. Scholar and literary critic Silvio Torres-Saillant analyzed nineteenth-century Dominican texts and showed that the elite's notions of the stereotypical black were often challenged by the poor. He found examples of Dominican blacks, especially women, who affirmed their ethnicity while undermining the elite "construction of Dominicans as racially and culturally dichotomous with Haitians."[69] In other words, feelings of solidarity had long existed among the diaspora population on Hispaniola.

Well-respected historians such as Deive continued to challenge the state discourse: "Well, certainly to a less[er] degree, racial prejudice against blacks from the colonial period through today is perpetuated in Santo Domingo."[70] In a pioneering 1975 article, Walter Cordero, scrutinizing the major works of the Dominican literary canon for their racist content, stated that in "Santo Domingo racism against blacks has existed and still exists."[71] This article and a growing number of publications exposed Dominicans to the uncomfortable reality of racial prejudice in their past and contemporary society.

As noted earlier, national poet Pedro Mir challenged the traditional historiography, and he underscored the role of blacks in colonial development. Mir was one of the first intellectuals to describe the linkage of the African slave trade, the sugar mill, and the origins of the Dominican nation. He also was one of the first to challenge an entrenched Euro-centrism reinforced by years of elite rhetoric. In a pioneering work, Mir wrote: "Everyone is more or less in agreement that the black race is not beautiful. Undoubtedly, it is a prejudice, but more difficult to uproot than any other type of prejudice. It cannot be conceived that black could be beautiful with those thick lips, curly hair and black color. However, he could be beautiful in a positive way. What happens is that criteria for beauty applied to blacks are formed with the model established by the whites."[72]

Academics were not the only ones to examine the provocative topic of race. Popular merengue musicians also commented on the racism that affected poor Dominican and Haitian blacks. The cover of Cuco Valoy's album *No me empuje!* (Don't push me!) pictures him being shoved by a white policeman, and Johnny Ventura's classic "El Pique" (The Rage), is a song about the exploitation of Haitians on Dominican sugar estates. Both are significant but rare instances in which black mainstream Dominican musicians have addressed racism and class inequality.[73]

Blanqueamiento and Eurocentrism

Through poetry, music, history, or literature, Dominican intellectuals in the 1970s and 1980s attempted to convince their compatriots that, along with the Spanish and the Taíno, the African was one of their progenitors. Nevertheless, as noted by Carlos Dore Cabral, who has written extensively on the topic of race and nation in the Dominican Republic, Dominicans continued to resist their African heritage: "Many [African] cultural traditions are practiced, [but] few people accept that those customs could be of African origin and, much less, that they might have something do with Africa in ethnic terms."[74]

Introspection about culture and national identity was spurred even more by the five hundredth anniversary in 1992 of the encounter between Europe and the New World. Since Santo Domingo was the first site of European settlement in the western hemisphere, the government organized celebrations and also hosted the visit of Pope John Paul II. Many Dominicans questioned or protested against honoring an event that resulted in the physical extermination of most of the indigenous population.[75] The Centro Dominicano de Estudios de la Educación published a very frank twenty-six-page booklet denouncing the government's manipulation of historical memory. According to this document, "The Spaniards arrived and domesticated and Christianized a handful of people. The rest they sent to Hell. Later, . . . they enslaved Africans and Christianized them. Those they couldn't Christianize they also sent to Hell. That is what we will celebrate. In other words, this is what they [the Spanish] will force us to celebrate. Why don't the Spanish celebrate the years of the Moorish conquest of Spain? In this moment, during these celebrations, while the government denies us as a people the recognition of a strong African cultural influence, we offer this small contribution."[76]

Despite objections, the Dominican government funded lavish events that praised Columbus without addressing the negative repercussions of European contact with native societies. In one pre-government glossy book celebrating Columbus' arrival, President Joaquín Balaguer, a staunch hispanofile and racist who espoused Trujillo's view of Dominicans as Spanish descendants and messengers of Catholicism is stated as saying, "In 1992 the country and the world will celebrate the momentous anniversary of the Discovery of America, an event that changed the course of the history of humanity, and as a result of which the island of Hispaniola played an important role as the catalyst that integrated the American Continent into European Civilization and the Christian Faith."[77] Balaguer, along with the country's right-wing conservative elite, refused to acknowledge the religious and racial diversity among Dominicans, who not only were Christians but also practitioners of a variety of African-based faiths. Despite the state discourse, there were Dominicans who continued to challenge the corrosive and insidious legacy of Trujillista ideology.

Women and Afro-Dominican Identity

The resiliency of hispanidad led several Afro-Dominican women to create the Movimiento por la Identidad de la Mujer Negra (Movement for the Identity of the Black Woman or MIMN).[78] This organization was founded in 1989 to "confront all types of racial discrimination [and] rescue and disseminate contributions of black culture . . . from a gendered perspective."[79] These women represent a radical departure from traditional Dominican attitudes about racial socialization.

For many Dominican women, travel abroad challenged their traditional assumptions of self-identity.[80] Germania Galván, a founding member of MIMN recalls that she was walking along a street in Spain, and "a young child looked at me somewhat startled and said to his mother: 'Mommy, look at the black lady.' From then on, I knew I was a black woman from the Dominican Republic."[81] Asked why a country with no official policies of racial segregation needs an organization that addresses prejudice, Galvan replied that the Dominican society continues to ignore its black cultural heritage, and many Dominicans continue to deny their African roots. She added: "Calling ourselves black women in a country where the population does not consider itself as such is a challenge, a threat. Although the Dominican population is 90 percent black and mulatto, it is not recognized as such. In view of multiple manifestations of racial discrimination that take place in our country, we saw the need to initiate a work of dissemination throughout the population about this subject, given that there are many sectors that insist on entertaining the idea that we are a nation of Hispanic [Spanish/white] ancestry."[82]

The movement also seeks to empower all women and to combat violence while offering support for Dominican women, who face a plethora of political and economic obstacles. Many women who migrate to urban areas are semiliterate and can only find menial jobs. Employment opportunities as domestic or factory workers have dwindled, and some women have been forced to turn to prostitution.[83]

A number of women work in industrial free trade zones: "Though poorly paid and offering few chances of upward mobility, jobs in export manufacturing have provided women workers in the Dominican Republic and Puerto Rico a weapon with which to challenge male dominance in the household."[84] This new economic enfranchisement, however exploitative, has led many workingwomen to organize around economic and social issues that concern them and their children. Women of Haitian descent are in an especially precarious situation because of the systemic and historical discrimination against this nationality. Haitians have for years endured gross violations to their basic human rights in the Dominican Republic, ranging from repatriation, to denial of Dominican citizenship, to deplorable working conditions (particularly in the sugarcane fields).

The Movimiento de Mujeres Domínico-Haitianas (MUDHA) was founded in July 1983 to combat the political and economic disenfranchisement of Haitian women and Dominican women of Haitian descent. Living in a "state of invisibility," these women have to contend with "the pernicious campaign of racism and anti-Haitianism maintained by a government elite that in its extreme [denies] identity and citizenship documents such as birth certificates, national identity cards, passports, and so on, to a million persons, for the sole fact of being descendants of Haitian immigrants, the majority of whom were contracted by the [Dominican] government to cut cane in its period of splendor."[85]

These movements to promote a more inclusive society while combating racial discrimination through educational and social services belie claims that the Dominican Republic is a mulatto nation in which race in general and blackness in particular are irrelevant. Moreover, they offer ordinary Dominicans, who may not be able to travel abroad, an alternative to traditional notions of identity. Furthermore, most of the revisionist history examining Afro-Dominican culture has been written by men and Dominican society retains much of the masculine or machista orientation common to Caribbean and Latin American countries. Not unlike the progressive intelligentsia of the 1970s, these women's groups are fighting racial and economic discrimination, but they also are striving for gender equality.[86]

Rediscovering African Roots and Routes

Negritude in the Dominican Republic, unlike Haiti, cannot be attributed to an intellectual crusade.[87] The U.S. occupation of Haiti (1915–34) forced its intellectuals to reevaluate the traditional elitist historiography, which embraced European cultural superiority. Scholars such as the imminent diplomat and erudite historian Jean Price-Mars challenged this worldview by underscoring Haiti's African roots through a movement that came to be called *negritude* or *indigenist*.[88] The Haitian discourse was mostly sparked from within, whereas it took more than forty years and a flow of migrants to and from the barrios of New York City for Dominicans to undertake a similar process.

By the 1980s and 1990s, the U.S.–born children of Dominicans who had arrived in the United States in the late 1960s were returning to their homeland for temporary and more permanent stays, vacations, or other trans-migratory visits. Immigrants who returned to the Dominican Republic with traumatic stories of racism sensitized or upset their family and friends to the relevance of race. Perhaps more than anything else, immigration was the defining moment for many Dominicans, whose experiences in the United States forced them to see themselves in racial terms. Moreover, these encounters were not limited to encounters with white Americans. Dominican immigrants such as Kathia Fermín were surprised to learn that being a Spanish speaker did not necessarily translate into pan-Hispanic solidarity: Fermín is quoted as saying, "I felt [racism] more in Miami than I have in [New York]. [The Cubans] can get very racial. Cubans, as a rule, think they're the cream of the crop of the Latin community."[89] These immigrants had grown up in the inner cities of the Northeast, where they had been exposed to other marginalized racial and ethnic groups of color. It was in college that many of the second generation of Dominicans confronted the racial segregation in the United States so prevalent between blacks and whites in social settings, and they often chose to socialize and identify with African Americans.[90] Others chose to associate more with whites or exclusively with Latinos. Whatever the case, once outside their insulated urban ethnic communities, they were forced to negotiate the complex terrain of U.S. racial politics and identity.

As historians expanded the interpretation of Dominican history, they ventured into the study of folklore, language, and immigration. They found that Dominican culture was the beneficiary of an important black legacy. The *Almanaque folklórico dominicano* is a collection of readings clearly showing the link with Africa, including an array of photographs depicting religious activities among mostly black Dominicans.[91] In rediscovering their negritude, Dominican writers also used foreign examples of black success to stress a pan-Africanist or universal cultural pride, ranging from North Americans Joe Louis and Dr. Martin Luther King to Cuban musician Bola de

Nieve. Indeed, the Afro-Dominican movement sought to recognize and include other diaspora blacks in its own historiography.[92]

African American immigrants from the United States also were part of Dominican history. During the Haitian unification (1822–44), North American free blacks were invited to settle on the north coast of the Dominican Republic.[93] These English-speaking Protestants survived many hardships and established strong cultural enclaves that persist till this day around Samaná. Clearly, the post-Trujillo historiographical legacy of this revisionist and new history thus reveals that Dominicans are not solely descendants of Catholic Spaniards.[94]

In 1979, Fradique Lizardo, a renowned activist of Dominican folklore, published *Cultura africana en Santo Domingo,* a one-hundred-page book that remains radical nearly thirty years later. For the first time, a vivid connection was shown between Africa and the Dominican Republic, past and present. Maps and illustrations of the Middle Passage, auction blocs, branding tools, and slave whippings and torture reveal that, like Haitians, Dominicans were subjected to the racial prejudice, discrimination, and economic exploitation found throughout the Americas.[95] No less significant was Lizardo's listing of black achievements throughout the country's history and his challenge to Dominicans to view their ancestors as more than an ambiguous agglomeration of Spanish-speaking mulattoes.[96]

Language too provides another way to link Dominican culture with Africa. The early interaction between the numerically small group of Spaniards and the larger African population shaped the linguistic evolution of the Spanish language on the island. "The Dominican Republic should be considered, for reasons derived from its peculiar historical trajectory, as an especially fertile area for the study of linguistic phenomena partially or totally of African origin."[97] Language is constantly being transformed by people who use it. From the original Taino inhabitants, to French-speaking Haitians, to thousands of English-speaking Caribbean workers, to Sephardic Jews, to Syrians and Lebanese, various groups have influenced Dominican Spanish.[98]

In the 1970s, the intensification of the Cold War polarized democratic capitalists and communist socialists. In Latin America the leftist struggles against repressive governments supported by the United States led many artists to express their resistance through Dominican musical and cultural groups. Groups such as Expresión Joven and Convite searched for an authentic voice with which to protest President Balaguer's authoritarian policies and also began to analyze and trace the origins of their music. Convite was a "loosely structured group of musicians, folklorists, and social scientists with a common desire to rediscover and reexamine the country's autochthonous musical traditions, particularly those with clear African roots, which had been most persistently ignored by folklorists and cultural observers since the Trujillo era."[99]

Convite searched the countryside, collecting and transcribing regional musical traditions as examples of a unique Dominican culture. This opened the Pandora's box of racial origins. According to the anthropologist Deborah Pacini Hernández, "the most important question [Convite] raised, Where did meringue [*sic*] come from? symbolically asked the deeper and thornier question, Where did we Dominicans come from?"[100] In its search for Dominican identity, Convite discovered a myriad of regional musical dance genres throughout the nation. Dominican culture, like its music and dance, was no longer considered homogeneous but as fluid and diverse as its people.

Convite explored various regional dances, such as the *tumba, palos* or *atabales, sarambo, zapateo dominicano, carabiné, ga-gá, mangulina, sarandunga,* and *baile de yuca,* which had strong black followings and roots in Africa. The *sarandunga,* for example, was observed specifically in the southern coastal town of Baní and mostly among blacks; it was a "yearly festive dance to celebrate the summer solstice associated with St. John the Baptist."[101] The *baile de yuca* was practiced in the center of the country and according to Luis Brito Ureña, "Rhythmically, it is African with European choreography, probably Spanish. Its name does not originate with the plant of the same name but from the Djukas Bantus of Africa."[102]

In choosing the name Convite, the group's organizers selected a word that means an agricultural cooperative gathering, and the origins can be traced to West Africa. Much like the Amish practice of gathering to build a neighbor's house, a *convite* refers to assisting others with the clearing of fields or planting or harvesting crops.[103] In the 1980s a new musical style, called *bachata,* emerged from the poor neighborhoods of Santo Domingo and grew in popularity. It was associated with the uneducated people who came from the countryside, and its sexually suggestive lyrics and direct references to race disturbed middle-class sensibilities.[104]

This marginal musical genre achieved national recognition and legitimacy through musicians such as Juan Luis Guerra (who is white), and who created arrangements and compositions more palatable to a mainstream audience. Guerra also incorporated into what is arguably the best merengue video, *A pedir su mano* (To ask for her hand), pre-Lenten Afro-Dominican festivities called *ga-gá* (which has origins in Haitian *ra-ra*).[105] Despite Guerra's use of Afro-musical elements, ethnomusicologist and merengue musician Paul Austerlitz believes that these challenges to prevailing views "have not had a substantive impact on Dominican attitudes about race, which on the whole remain Eurocentric."[106]

CONCLUSION: VIEWING DOMINICAN IDENTITIES
THROUGH ALTERNATIVE PRISMS

Since the early 1970s, the Dominican Republic has experienced a cultural metamorphosis concerning national identity. After so many years of an hispanofile dictatorship, it has produced a considerable number of books and articles on Afro-Dominican culture. This shift directly challenged the traditional view of Dominicans as being exclusively of Spanish descent. Intellectuals addressed the long-neglected African contribution to Dominican culture as well as the subtle issues of racism and prejudice. This emerging revisionist history stressed the vitality of pernicious attitudes that originated during the colonial period.

Dominicans, particularly women, have formed organizations that not only seek gender equality but also focus attention on diasporic identities. The Movement for the Identity of the Black Woman and MUDHA realize that gender and race are integral parts of the daily discrimination experienced by Dominican women. According to Sergia Galván, "any study on the subject [of racism] that does not scrutinize the link between gender and ethnicity cannot contribute to a meaningful transformation of the black woman's situation."[107] Today, gender, race, and class are more important than ever in the Dominican Republic, and Galván's caveat should compel researchers to explore how these intersect.

The growing racial consciousness among Dominicans in the United States also coincides with a growing sense of ethnic identity. These *Dominicanos ausentes* (absent Dominicans) often send weekly or monthly remittances home and see themselves as an important diaspora community responsible for the economic well being of their relatives. One scholar writes, "The experience of the [Dominican] diaspora makes us perceive and feel reality in a different way than how we had perceived and felt before the banishment perpetrated against us by the Dominican State more than thirty years ago."[108]

The Dominican Studies Institute in New York City, an activist think tank created by a few dedicated and indefatigable Dominican scholars in 1992, represents a break with the past. It sponsors numerous innovative conferences, seminars, and academic works on Dominican history. Diaspora Dominicans have added a new dimension to the discourse on race, as exemplified by the Institute's 1996–99 research agenda, which indicts Dominican historiography for its continuing skewed, classist, patriarchal, and Eurocentric portrayal of the nation. In a grant proposal to the Rockefeller Foundation, the Institute stated that it wanted to "fill some serious gaps left by the traditional scholarship in representations of ethnicity, culture, class and gender relations in the shaping of Dominican society. Dominican historiography has generally privileged the sagas of a few light-skinned families from the upper classes: the presidents, the generals, the landowners. As a result, most Dominicans, a predominantly black and mulatto population do not normally see their ancestors represented in the standard accounts of the national experience. Overwhelmingly male and Western-oriented, the intellectual elite has generally shown little regard for maroon societies, slave rebellions, folk culture, women's contributions, and spiritual expressions traceable to the African heritage. Our three-year program will undertake to bring into visibility the Afro-Dominican majority of the population, the male and female portions of it, as agent of history and culture from colonial times to the present."[109]

Transnational migration has helped Dominicans see more clearly their society's political, social, and economic deficiencies.[110] In this current era of global communication, Dominicans are linked around the world through such mediums as the Internet, and cyberspace debates have been most contentious and vociferous concerning race. One camp believes racism exists in the Dominican Republic, and the other patriotically defends the nation's image from such unpatriotic rhetoric. An electronic questionnaire by Lester Chase, a student in education at Columbia University, solicited comments on the contemporary state of discrimination and racism in Dominican society. One respondent, Juan T. Libre, noted that "if one reads the society pages of the *Listin Diario* [the oldest Dominican newspaper] . . . you think you are living in Sweden, Germany or Denmark. The blacks of our country do not appear in the society pages. (They appear but too infrequently)."[111]

In a country where the African past and its influence are denied despite more than thirty years of groundbreaking historiography, the Afro-Dominican poet Blas Jiménez uses poetry as an educational and consciousness-raising tool. He believes that "for the Afro-Hispanic writer the decisive field of battle is language" in the affirmation of a black cultural heritage.[112] Dominicans must look at themselves in the mirror and have a dialogue with their blackness: "That black, which I say is a conversant black / left me with many doubts; he left me even without God / but he put me to stare and pay attention to his blackness and transformed his face in the mirror / and as he looked at me directly I knew that the black man was I."[113]

It seems to me that the way to eliminate anti-Haitian and anti-black attitudes is through education. Dominican children are exposed to a Eurocentric curriculum that perpetuates the traditional discourse. A more inclusive curriculum would underscore the role of immigrants as an important first step in constructing a more complex and healthy notion of Dominican identity. Children should learn that the names of their friends represent various groups that have contributed to and transformed Dominican society. The Dominican Republic is not a racial monolith but a multicolored ethnic mosaic. Today, Dominicans of Asian descent are also beginning to question antiquated notions of what it means to be Dominican and not just "chino."[114]

For now, because of overwhelming economic problems, racism seems an unlikely galvanizing force for social protest. In a developing country such as the Dominican Republic, we are not apt to see general strikes or mass marches over racial prejudice by the Dominican majority. People are more concerned about the exorbitant price of flour, cooking oil, milk, and other staples. Nevertheless, such revisionist views of Dominican society will continue to improve our understanding of how poverty, unemployment, infant mortality, and other ills are structurally linked to gender and racial inequality.[115]

NOTES

1. Benedict Anderson, Imagined Communities: Reflections on the Origins and Spread of Nationalism, rev. ed. (New York: Verso, 1991).

2. Ian Bell, *The Dominican Republic* (Boulder, Colo.: Westview Press, 1981), 19. By 1550, the indigenous Hispaniola population, the Taínos (belonging to the Arawak group), had been mostly annihilated by Spanish invasions, forced labor, and disease. For an in-depth study of the pre-Columbian peoples of the Caribbean from an anthropological and archeological perspective, see Irving Rouse, *The Taínos* (New Haven: Yale University Press, 1992).

3. Frank Moya Pons, "The First Border Line" *Rumbo:* 5 (10–16 February 1994).

4. Emilio Rodríguez Demorizi, *Documentos para la historia de la República Dominicana* (Ciudad Trujillo: Editoria Montalvo, 1944), 14. Documents such as these were used by Trujillo's intelligentsia to justify their negrophobic and anti-Haitian discourse. Yet, Mota made no racial references in the citation above.

5. Emilio Rodríguez Demorizi, *Guerra domínico-haitiana: Documentos para su estudio* (Ciudad Trujillo: Impresora Dominicana, 1957), 278. General Mota was also vice-president of the Dominican Republic.

6. See William R. Manning, *Diplomatic Correspondence of the United States: Inter-American Affairs, 1831–1860,* vol. 4 (Washington, D.C.: Carnegie Endowment for International Peace, 1935), 58–59.

7. Catherine C. Legrand, "Informal Resistance on a Dominican Sugar Plantation during the Trujillo Dictatorship," *Hispanic American Historical Review* 75 (November 1995): 559. Two economies developed during the late 1800s: in the north, tobacco and cocoa, and in the south, exclusively sugar.

8. H. Hoetink, *The Dominican People, 1850–1900: Notes for a Historical Sociology* (Baltimore: Johns Hopkins University Press, 1982), 32. Anti-black feeling was evident in a 1912 Dominican immigration law that required non-whites to ask permission to enter the country.

9. Michiel Baud, "The Origins of Capitalist Agriculture in the Dominican Republic," *Latin American Research Review* 22, no. 2 (1987): 144.

10. For an analysis of the role of race and the rise of the sugar industry in the Dominican Republic at the turn of the century, see Stanislao A. German, "The Rebirth of the Dominican Sugar Industry and Its Impact on Dominican Race Relations, 1870–1930" (Master's Thesis, University of Texas at Austin, 1992).

11. Roberto Cassá, "El racismo en la ideologia de la clase dominante dominicana," *Ciencia* 1, no. 63 (1976): 64–65.

12. Ernest Gellner, *Culture, Identity, and Politics* (Cambridge : Cambridge University Press, 1987), 166.

13. Rafael L. Trujillo, *Discursos, mensajes, y proclamas* 5 (Santíago: Editorial El Diario, 1946):178.

14. Vodun is a coherent and comprehensive belief system and worldview in which every person and everything is sacred and must be treated accordingly. "Plants, animals, and minerals share similar chemical, physical, or genetic properties." See Patrick Bellegarde-Smith, *Haiti: The Breached Citadel* (Boulder, Colo.: Westview Press, 1990), 12.

15. Trujillo, *Discursos,* 7:179. For an excellent study on the historic and collaborative inter-border relations see Lauren Derby, "Haitians, Magic, and Money: Raza and Society in the Haitian-Dominican Borderlands, 1900–1937," *Society for Comparative Study of Society and History* (1994): 489–526.

16. Mike Rosenburg, A. Douglas Kincade, and Kathleen Logan, eds., *Americas: An Anthology* (New York: Oxford University Press, 1992), 169.

17. Nícolas Slonímsky, *Music of Latin America* (New York: Thomas Y. Crowell, 1945), 190. Black Dominican musicians such as Esteban Peña Morell and José Dolores Cerón showcased their talents during the Trujillo era. According to Slonímsky, who cites Nolasco, Morell wrote symphonic poems, including Anacaona and Sinfonía Barbara, and viewed negritude as a legitimate force in the Dominican arts. Foreign publications, which were beyond Trujillo's censure, recognized Afro-Dominican contributions. For example, a North American scholar wrote during the 1940s: "Besides European traditions, there is a large, if not at times preponderant, element of African traditions." See J. M. Coopersmith, *Music and Musicians of the Dominican Republic* (Washington, D.C.: Pan American Union, 1949), 2.

18. José Alcántara Almánzar, "Black Images in Dominican Literature," *Nieuwe West-Indische Gids* (*New West Indian Guide*) 61, nos. 3–4 (1987): 164; Américo Lugo, Antología (Ciudad Trujillo: Librería Dominicana, 1949), 71.

19. Frank Moya Pons, *The Dominican Republic: A National History* (New Rochelle, N.Y.: Hispaniola Books, 1995), 206.

20. Ibid., 213. Dominicans were forced to see themselves in racial terms, according to Pons, because the "Spaniards continuously offended the Dominicans, who were reminded that in Cuba or Puerto Rico they would be slaves. This attitude of superiority had its affects on the Dominicans themselves. The lighter-skinned people began to avoid contact with their darker-skinned friends for fear of being associated with them or being considered inferior by the new Spanish ruler" (213).

21. Norberto Pedro James, "Un estudio sociocultural de dos novelas dominicanas de la era de Trujillo: 'Jengibre' y 'Trementina, y Clerèn y Bongó' " (Ph.D. diss., Boston University, 1992), 22–23.

22. Manuel Arturo Peña Batlle, *El sentido de una politica* (Ciudad Trujillo: La Nación, 1943), 15.

23. For the U.S. occupation, see Bruce Calder, *The Impact of Intervention: Some Aspects of the U.S. Occupation of the Dominican Republic, 1916–1924* (Austin: University of Texas Press, 1984).

24. Bernardo Vega, *Trujillo y Haiti, 1930–1937* (Santo Domingo: Fundación Cultural Dominicana, 1988), 1:391; Martin F. Murphy, *Dominican Sugar Plantations: Production and Foreign Labor Integration* (New York: Praeger Publishers, 1991), 46.

25. Ibid., 76.

26. Suzy Castor, *Migraciones y relaciones internacionales: El caso haitiano-dominicano* (Ciudad México: Facultdad Ciencias Politicas y Sociales, UNAM, 1983), 61.

27. Emilio Rodríguez Demorizi, *Invasiones haitianas de 1801, 1805, y 1822* (Ciudad Trujillo: Editora del

Caribe, 1955), 1:10. Demorizi, like most of his contemporaries, denied the African component of Dominican culture by contrasting Dominicans to their darker neighbors to the west: "We are Spanish, and we will always be by blood, by the spirit, by the religion, and the language." Emilio Rodríguez Demorizi, *Lengua y folklore de Santo Domingo* (Santiago: UCMM, 1974), 24.

28. See Robert D. Crassweller, *Trujillo: The Life and Times of a Caribbean Dictator* (New York: MacMillan, 1966), 149–63; Lauren Derby and Richard Turits, "Historias de terror y los terrores de la historia: La masacre haitiana de 1937 en la Republica Dominicana," *Estudios Sociales* 26 (April–June 1993): 65–76; Eric Paul Roorda, "Genocide Next Door: The Good Neighbor Policy, the Trujillo Regime, and the Haitian Massacre of 1937," *Diplomatic History* 20 (Summer 1996): 301–19; José Israel Cuello H., *Documentos del conflicto domínico-haitiano de 1937* (Santo Domingo: Editora Taller, 1985); and Juan Manuel García, *La matanza de los hatianos: Genocidio de Trujillo, 1937* (Santo Domingo: Editora Alfa y Omega, 1983).

29. Ernesto Sagás, "The Development of Antihaitianismo into a Dominant Ideology during the Trujillo Era" (paper presented at the 1995 meeting of the Latin American Studies Association, Washington, D.C., 28–30 September, deposited at the Dominican Studies Institute, City College of New York), 7. Although Balaguer was a prominent anti-Haitian ideologue, Sagás writes that "no other intellectual during the Trujillo Era produced a more coherent and scholarly interpretation of the regime's ideology" than Peña Batlle (7).

30. Ibid., 8. See Joaquín Balaguer, *La realidad dominicana: Semblanza de un pais y de un regimen* (Buenos Aires: Imprenta Ferrari Hermanos, 1947).

31. Historians such as Vetilio Alfau or Rufino Martínez, according to Roberto Cassá, were able to "escape the [historiographical] constraints of the dictatorship." Luis F. Mejía and the Basque Spanish refugee Jesús de Galindez represented "la historiografía del exilio." For an excellent review of Dominican historiography and its theoretical development from the eighteenth century to the 1970s, see Roberto Cassá, "Historiografía de la República Dominicana," *Ecos* 1 (1993): 28–30.

32. Carolina González, "Crossing the Massacre: Haitians in Two Dominican Narratives of the Trujillo Era" (unpublished manuscript, Dominican Studies Institute), 8. González writes: "One of the greatest difficulties in analyzing any aspect of Dominican literature which involves the issue of race is the lack of correspondence that one finds between the literary text's ideology, its expressive qualities, the author's race, social position, and political trajectory." According to González, Tomás Hernández Franco (1904–52) typifies this inconsistency. Franco was a diplomat for the racist Trujillo dictatorship but in 1942 wrote "Apuntes sobre poesía popular y poesía negra" (Notes on popular and black poetry in the Antilles), which González believes is probably the earliest Dominican essay on the topic.

33. Manuel del Cabral, "Colá," in Trópico Negro (Buenos Aires: Editorial Sopena Argentina, 1941), 225. "Para poder hablar contigo / con tu hueso, negro Colá / no hay que meterse allí / en los veinte centavos que ganas diariamente / ni en la noche que tienes metida en tu amuleta / sino en los callos de tus dedos que de súbito se te vuelven de seda si acaricias tu hijo." See also José Luis González and Mónica Mansores, Poesía negra de América (Mexico: Era, 1976), 171–77.

34. Ramón Marrero Aristy, *Over* (1940; reprint, Santo Domingo: Editora Taller, 1988). That such a provocative text could be written within an authoritarian society stems from the "Poesia Sorprendida (Surprised poetry), [which] found that only through an obscurantist surrealist language and support of Spanish Republicans could they obliquely express opposition" (see González, "Crossing the Massacre," 11). For an examination of the batey and the exploitation of Haitian sugarcane cutter, see Roger Plant, *Sugar and Modern Slavery: A Tale of Two Countries* (London: Zed Books, 1987).

35. "Y al perfil sudoroso de los cargadores envueltos en su capa de musculos morenos." Pedro Mir, *"Hay un pais en el mundo" y otros poemas de Pedro Mir* (Santo Domingo: Ediciones de Taller, 1994), 21.

36. Daisy Cocco de Filippis, "Singing to the Beat of Their Own Drum: Dominican Women Poets in

the 80s, an Introduction," in *Gender, Culture, and the Arts: Women, the Arts, and Society*, ed. Ronald Dotterer and Susan Bowers (Cranbury, N.J.: Associated University Presses, 1993), 147. Portalatín, not Manuel del Cabral, is considered by De Filippis "as the first Dominican poet to confront racial issues" while avoiding the romanticization of her racial characters. See Janet Jones Hampton, "The Voice of the Drum: The Poetry of Afro-Hispanic Women," *Afro-Hispanic Review* 14, no. 2 (fall 1995): 18. Portalatín is also compared to the celebrated nineteenth-century writer Salomé Ureña de Henriquez (1850–97) for her influence on the Dominican canon. See Lynn Ellen Rice Cortina's, *Spanish-American Women Writers: A Bibliographic Research Checklist* (New York: Garland, 1983), 115.

37. R. Michael Malek, "Rafael L. Trujillo: A Revisionist Critique of His Rise to Power," *Revista Interamericana* (Puerto Rico) 7, no. 3 (1977): 444–45. Cassá writes that the post-1961 "historiography was marked by the needs to respond to the challenges concerning questions of development. Trujillistas were substituted by younger persons who rejected the current prevalent paradigms as a means to accede contrary conclusions. By a similar measure the post-Trujillo historiographical production has been conditioned by the premises of historical materialism, and this is what confers specificity. The [Dominican] national history has been a privileged terrain for the foundation of political and cultural criticism and the enunciation of alternative projects" (Cassá, "Historiografía de la República Dominicana," 32).

38. Francisco Antonio Avelino, "Elogio y critica del pensamiento de Americo Lugo," *Ecos* 2 (1993): 113. Avelino writes that Lugo's definition of Dominicans as Hispanic in the face of Haitian and Anglo-Saxon aggression was "as a politically defensive measure a success but a sociological error. To be sure, we were neither Haitians nor Anglo-Saxons, but it was also true that we were not Spaniards" (121). Avelino is ambivalent about Lugo, whose "hispanismo did not reach the level of anti-Haitianism," and he considered Haiti "our brother." Yet Lugo believed (as did many Latin American governments) that European immigration would counter the "blackening" of the population. See Francisco Antonio Avelino, *Reflexiones sobre algunas cumbres del pasado ideológico dominicano* (Santo Domingo: Sin Imprenta, 1995), 212–13.

39. Pedro Andres Perez Cabral, *La comunidad mulata: El caso socio-politico de la República Dominicana* (Caracas: Grafíca Americana, 1967), 113. A number of Latin American countries, such as Brazil, Mexico, and Cuba, have adhered to the policy of blanqueamiento, a policy that Richard L. Jackson compares to "ethnic lynching." See Richard L. Jackson, *The Black Image in Latin American Literature* (Albuquerque: University of New Mexico Press, 1976).

40. Perez Cabral, *La comunidad mulata*, 113.

41. Hermannus Hoetink, "Ideology, Intellectuals, Identity: The Dominican Republic, 1880–1980, Some Preliminary Notes," in *Intellectuals in the Twentieth-Century Caribbean*, ed. Alistair Hennessy (London: Macmillan Caribbean, 1992), 2:133.

42. Ibid.

43. Stuart Hall, "Negotiating Caribbean Identities," *New Left Review* 209 (January–February 1995): 6. Hall states that "Haiti, which is in some ways the symbolic island of black culture, [is] where one feels closer to the African inheritance than anywhere else [in the Caribbean]."

44. Dominicans also migrated to the United States for political reasons. Balaguer's 1966 U.S.–supported presidential victory provoked a massive campaign of violence against his old nemesis, Juan Bosch, and his supporters, which forced many to flee into exile. See Catherine A. Sunshine, *The Caribbean: Survival, Struggle, and Sovereignty* (Boston: EPICA, South End Press), 53.

45. See Clayborn Carson, *In Struggle: SNCC and the Black Awakening of the 1960s* (Cambridge, Mass.: Harvard University Press, 1981), 288.

46. Trujillo's assassination ushered in popular democratic elections in 1962 when Juan Bosch was elected president, but he was ousted by a military junta in September 1963. In 1965, pro-Bosch officers initiated a countercoup that escalated into a popular uprising against the illegitimate government

of Donald Reid Cabral. Fearing another Cuba, but under the pretext of protecting American lives, the United States invaded the Dominican Republic on 28 April 1965. See Franklin Franco Pichardo, *Historia de un pueblo,* 2d ed. (Santo Domingo: Sociedad Editorial Dominicana, 1993), 605–54.

47. Dominicans and Puerto Ricans in the late 1970s mobilized at the local level to gain greater control of neighborhood services, such as schools. The Latino Urban Political Association (LUPA) was an example of mutual cooperation and community organizing. See Xavier F. Totti, "The Making of a Latino Ethnic Identity," *Dissent* (fall 1987): 541.

48. Ninna Nyberg Sorenson, "Creole Culture, Dominican Identity," *Folk* 35 (1993): 29.

49. Frank Moya Pons, "Dominican National Identity: A Historical Perspective," *Punto 7 Review: A Journal of Marginal Discourse* (Fall 1996): 24.

50. Carlos Esteban Deive, "Notas sobre la cultura dominicana," *Boletín del Hombre Dominicano* 8 (January 1979): 298.

51. Míguel Acosta Saignes, ed., *Cuadernos afro-americanos* (Caracas: Universidad Central de Venezuela, 1975), 212.

52. Ibid., 205–10. The conference was held on 2, 9, and 16 June 1973.

53. Ibid., 203. According to *Cuadernos afro-americanos,* "the director of this [event] was responsible for the organizational chores and presided over the colloquium. He was Professor Franklin J. Franco."

54. See Robert Brent Toplin, *Slavery and Slave Relations in Latin America* (Westport, Conn.: Greenwood Press, 1974); Thomas E. Skidmore's, *Black into White: Race and Nationality in Brazilian Thought* (New York: Oxford University Press, 1974); and Mauricio Solaun, *Discrimination without Violence: Miscegenation and Racial Conflict in Latin America* (New York: Wiley, 1973).

55. Frank Tannembaum, *Slave and Citizen: The Negro in the Americas* (New York: Vintage Books, 1963). For a good overview of the historiography on race during the 1970s, see Magnus Mörner's, "Slavery and Race in the Evolution of Latin American Societies: Some Recent Contributions to the Debate," *Journal of Latin American Studies* 8 (May 1976): 127–35.

56. Marcio Veloz Maggiolo, "Remanentes culturales indigenas y africanos en Santo Domingo," *Revista Dominicana de Arqueología, Antropología e Historia* 4, nos. 7–8 (1974): 25.

57. Ibid.

58. Carlos Larrazabal Blanco, *Los Negros y la esclavitud en Santo Domingo* (Santo Domingo: Julio D. Postigo e hijos, 1975), 174. By 1980 scholarly works focusing on the colonial slavery period were numerous and included Carlos Esteban Deive's two-tome opus, *La esclavitud del negro en Santo Domingo* (1492–1844) (Santo Domingo: Museo del Hombre Dominicano, 1980). By 1989, Deive had extended his research to runaways in *Los guerrilleros negros: Esclavos fugitivos y cimarrones en Santo Domingo* (Santo Domingo: Fundación Cultural Dominicana, 1989). By the early 1990s there were regional studies, such as Pedro Encarnación Jimenéz's, *Los negros esclavos en la historia de bayona, manoguayabo y otros poblados* (Santo Domingo: Editora Alfa y Omega, 1993), which extended the depth of his twenty-year research into Afro-Dominican history.

59. Larrazabal Blanco, *Los negros,* 175–76.

60. Frank Moya Pons, *La dominación haitiana,* 1822–1844 (Santo Domingo: Editora Taller, 1978), 33. Pons informs us that there was significant support from various Dominican towns, such as Cotuí, La Vega, San Francisco de Macorís, Azua, San Juan de la Maguana, and Neiba, for the Haitian invasion in 1822.

61. Silvio Torres-Saillant, "Historiador conservador o intelectual subversivo? Hacia una relectura de Frank Moya Pons," 7. This speech, to celebrate the publication of Frank Moya Pons, *The Dominican Republic: A National History,* was given at the Hotel Santo Domingo on 29 May 1995. It is a brief but excellent review of Pons's major publications and his invaluable contribution to Dominican history. Copies of the text can be found in the Dominican Studies Institute, City College, The City University of New York.

62. Franklin J. Franco, *Los negros, los mulatos y la nación dominicana*, 5th ed. (Santo Domingo: Editora Nacional, 1977). Indeed, the invasion or unification of the easter island was relatively peaceful, due mostly to the powerful Haitian forces, which only eighteen years before had defeated Napoleon's imperial troops, arguably the world's mightiest at the time (1804). On 9 February 1822, Boyer arrived in Santo Domingo and was greeted by Spanish colonial treasurer Jose Nuñez de Cáceres, who had earlier proclaimed an ephemeral independence from Spain and presented the Haitian leader with keys to the city. Pons, *La dominación haitiana*, 37.

63. Franco, *Los negros*, 160–61.

64. Ibid. The same black and mulatto Dominicans that Trujillo and traditional historiography had proclaimed white and Spanish were responsible for securing not only their freedom but also Duarte's ideal of a democratic and free nation.

65. Demorizi, *Documentos*, vol. 1, *Documentos general de la nacion centenario de la República Dominicana*, 18. The president and vice president of the junta at this time, José María Bobadilla y Briones and Manuel Jiménez, were former slave owners.

66. The Brazilian Paulo de Carvalho-Neto pioneered in this field, including cultural expressions that denigrated blacks. He cited a popular Christmas song: "Dicen que en Belen hay mucho que ver: Un negrito tonto Aprendiendo a leer" (They say that in Bethlehem there is a lot to see: A stupid little black boy learning to read). See Paulo de Carvalho-Neto, "Folklore of the Black Struggle in Latin America," *Latin American Perspectives* 5 (spring 1978): 58.

67. Carlos Esteban Deive, "El prejuicio en el folklore de Santo Domingo," *Boletín Museo del Hombre Dominicano* 8 (January–March 1976): 80.

68. Ibid., 81, 87, 88.

69. Silvio Torres-Saillant, "Dominican Literature and Its Criticism: Anatomy of a Troubled Identity," in *A History of Literature in the Caribbean*, ed. A. James Arnold, vol. 1, Hispanic and Francophone Regions (Philadelphia: Johns Benjamins, 1994), 57.

70. Carlos Esteban Deive, *El indio, el negro y la vida tradicional dominicana* (Santo Domingo: Museo del Hombre Dominicano, 1978), 155. The late philosopher Michel Foucault said once that there are no self-evident truths. Today, walking among the multiracial student body of Dominican universities, it is hard to believe that blacks at the turn of the century were denied admission. This was consistent with other Latin American post-emancipation societies influenced by both domestic elite views of race relations and foreign ideologies about European (white) racial and cultural superiority. So, only in 1906 did Heriberto Pieter Bennet, descendant of former slaves, present his thesis "with very good grades at the Instituto Profesional as the first black to graduate in our university [USAD]. His thesis defense produced stormy protests and the rector, Apolinar Tejera, left the room because he was against the idea of a black graduating in our country." See Fradique Lizardo, *Cultura africana en Santo Domingo* (Santo Domingo: Sociedad Industrial Dominica, 1979), 73–78.

71. Walter Cordero, "El tema negro y la discriminaci_n racial en la Republica Dominicana," *Ciencia* 63, no. 1 (1975): 151. Among Dominican novels critiqued by Cordero for their pejorative references to blacks are *La sangre*, by Tulio Cestero, and *Cosa añejas*, by Cesar Nicolás Penson.

72. Pedro Mir, *Tres leyendas de colores: Ensayos de interpretación de las primeras revoluciones del nuevo mundo* (Santo Domingo: Editora Nacional, 1969), 239–40. Also see Hugo Tolentino's, *Raza e historia en Santo Domingo: Los origenes delo prejuicio racial en America*, vol. 1 (Santo Domingo: USAD, 1974).

73. See Deborah Pacini Hernández, *Bachata: A Social History of Dominican Popular Music* (Philadelphia: Temple University Press, 1995), 146. The chorus of Ventura's song goes: "Vengo con un pique, vengo del batey, de ver tanta gente sin na' que comer" (I'm coming with a rage, I'm coming from the sugar plantations, from seeing so many people with nothing to eat).

74. Carlos Dore Cabral, "Reflexiones sobre la identidad cultural del Caribe: El caso dominicano," *Casa de las Américas* 118 (1980): 77.

75. Pons, *The Dominican Republic*, 37. There were an estimated four hundred thousand aboriginal inhabitants on Hispaniola, reduced to less than three thousand by 1519, according to Pons. For a denunciation of the 1992 celebrations, see Frank Moya Pons stunning rebuke of the 1992 celebrations, "El choque del descubrimento," *Ciencia y Sociedad* 17, no. 3 (1992): 219–42. For an in-depth study of the indigenous role in the development of Dominican society and issues of national identity, see Peter Jordan Ferbel, "The Politics of Taino Indian Heritage in the Post-quincentennial Dominican Republic: When a Canoe Means More Than a Water Trough" (Ph.D. diss., University of Minnesota, 1995).

76. Celsa Albert, *Los africanos y nuestra isla* (Santo Domingo: CEDEE, 1987), 3. Some of the chapter titles are "Who Likes to Be a Slave?" and "Why Are We Dominicans Mulattoes?"

77. Kay Palacios, *Primacías de America en la española* (Englewood Cliffs, N.J.: Hispanic Business and Professional Associations, 1992), 5. Almost forty years before, in a speech to Spanish dictator General Francisco Franco, Trujillo said: "If the old glorious swords that opened the paths in the pagan jungles of the New World passed from Spanish hands to the hands of Spanish sons, then those sons should also be worthy of seizing, with inherited fervor, the luminous symbol of Christ's faith with Spain." Rafael L. Trujillo, *Discursos, mensajes, y proclamas* (Santiago: Editorial el Diario, 1951), 9:166.

78. Kimberly Eison Simmons, Ph.D. candidate in the Department of Anthropology at Michigan State University, first introduced me to the work of the Movimento por la Identidad de la Mujer Negra (Movement for the Identity of Black Women) in 1995. Along with Ginneta Candelario, Kim is one of the leading scholars studying the intersections of gender and race in the Dominican Republic. . Kim's insightful and incisive advice over the years has helped shape the way I see race and gender in the Dominican Republic.

79. Germania Galván, fax interview, 8 December 1995.

80. Helen I. Safa, "Popular Culture, National Identity, and Race in the Caribbean," *Nieuwe West-Indische Gids (The New West Indian Guide)* 61, no. 314 (1987): 123.

81. Galván, fax interview, 8 December 1995. Conversely, dark-skinned Dominican novelist Marrero Aristy, author of *Over*, visited the United States during the 1950s and 1960s and took care not to be mistaken for an African-American by not speaking English. Aristy wrote: "I have been practicing in the hotel with a towel [for a turban] in front of the mirror. I look like Sabu from the movies, a little older, much fatter, but I pass [for a tourist]. From now on every time I come to the United States I put a turban in the suitcase and leave the English-Spanish dictionary. For a little black like myself this is the truth, the great guarantee is not knowing English and money in your wallet. Ah! And suits like these worth $200 and well-known from afar." Hector Inchaustegui, *Escritores y artistas dominicanos* (Santiago: UCMM, 1978), 104.

82. Galván, fax interview, 8 December 1995.

83. Pacini Hernández, *Bachata*, 156.

84. Helen I. Safa, "The New Women Workers: Does Money Equal Power?" *Report on the Americas, NACLA* 27, no. 1 (July–August 1993): 24. Workers in Free Trade Zones are largely at the mercy of profit-driven multinational corporations. According to Safa, these women "are not unionized and receive little support from the government in their struggle for better wages and working conditions, or even to upgrade their skills" (29).

85. See the Mudha website http://www.kiskeya-alternative.org/mudha/

86. Neil MacDonald, *The Caribbean: "Making Our Own Choices"* (Oxford: Oxfam, 1990), 42–43. According to MacDonald, an example of this initiative is the Esclavas del Fogón [Slaves of the stove]. This organization, founded by nine women in 1979, is both a cultural workshop and a social advocacy group: According to one of its members, "Our fundamental aim is to rescue our home grown culture and return it to the communities. For instance, we have many musical forms here which reflect our African heritage—chuines, for example is a traditional form from the countryside. It takes the

form of an improvised lament with a group response. People use it to express their reality—their calamities, their sadness, how hard it is to be a peasant and work so many hours and gain so little. It can be about any theme—love or inflation, or the problem of not having clean drinking water."

87. Frank Moya Pons, "Dominican National Identity and Return Migration," occasional paper no. 1 (Gainesville, Fla.: Center for Latin American Studies, University of Florida, 1981), 23–33. Arhived at the Dominican Studies Institute, The City College of New York.

88. Brian Weinstein and Aaron Segal, *Haiti: The Failure of Politics* (New York: Praeger, 1992), 12–13.

89. Vito Echevarría, "Santo Domingo on the Hudson," *Hispanic* (September 1991): 36.

90. See Sherrie Baver, "Finding African Roots in Latin America," *Hispanic Outlook* (January 1995): 8.

91. Jose Castillo, Ivan Dominguez, and Dagoberto Tejeda, *Almanaque folklóric dominicano* (Santo Domingo: Editora Alfa y Omega, 1978), 157. The authors' interpretation of Dominican culture is distinctly Afro-centric. The last page of the book juxtaposes maps of Africa and the Dominican Republic, and the authors conclude: "This is why if we want to respond to the interrogators in relation to the Dominican culture, Africa is one of the fundamental sources to 'rediscover.'"

92. Carlos Lebron Savñon, *"Este negro a quien debemos querer": Un estudio etnológica acerca del negro en America* (Santo Domingo: Editora Cultural Dominicana, 1978), 123–26 and 136–38. In this work, whose very title (This black whom we should love) suggests frank introspection on race relations, the author concludes on an ironic note: "In the Dominican Republic, racial discrimination does not exist, or [remains a place] where it is least perceived" (227).

93. Jose Agusto Puig Ortiz, *Emigración de libertos Norteamericanos a Puerto Plata en la primera mitad del siglo 19* (Santo Domingo: Editora Alfa y Omega, 1978), 7. Also see Hermannus Hoetink, "Americans in Samana," *Caribbean Studies* 2 (April 1962): 3–22; and two articles by E. Valerie Smith, "Early Afro-American Presence on the Island of Hispaniola: A Case study of the 'Immigrants' of Samaná," *Journal of Negro History* 72 (winter–spring 1987): 33–41, and "A Merging of Two Cultures: The Afro-Hispanic Immigrants of Samaná, Dominican Republic," *Afro-Hispanic Review* 8 (January-May 1989): 9–14.

94. Martha Ellen Davis, *"That Old-Time Religion: Tradición y cambio en el enclave 'américano' de Samaná"* (Santo Domingo: Editora Alfa y Omega, 1984), 97. Into the 1970s, on any Sunday morning one could hear quintessential North American gospel music in Samaná. See also James Cerrulti, "The Dominican Republic: Caribbean Comeback," *National Geographic* 152, no. 4 (October 1977): 538–65. For the contribution of these and other immigrants to the Dominican Republic in the nineteenth century see Hermannus Hoetink, *The Dominican People, 1850–1900: Notes for a Historical Sociology* (Baltimore, Md.: Johns Hopkins University Press, 1982), 19–46.

95. Fradique Lizardo, *Cultura africana*, 14, 30, 38, 44, 84.

96. Ibid., 68. Francisco del Rosario Sánchez was one of the nation's founding fathers and was a person of color. Moreover, according to Lizardo, in 1854 "the New York Saturday Evening Post published a list of the leading families in Santo Domingo showing their black origins, thereby delegitimizing the myth that we were a white European nation."

97. By the early seventeenth century, there were about ten thousand black slaves and around six thousand whites on the island. See Irene Pérez-Guerra, "Africanismos linguisticos en Republica Dominicana: Notas metodologicas," *Boletin del Museo del Hombre Dominicano* 21 (1988): 23–34.

98. Despite their nearly total extermination, the Tainos left a linguistic legacy in such words as casabe or cassava (dried wafer bread), yucca (manioc), and hamaca (hammock). See Bernardo Vega, "La Herencia indigena en la cultura dominicana de hoy," in *Ensayos sobre cultura dominicana*, by Jose del Castillo and others (Santo Domingo: Museo del Hombre, Dominicano, 1981), 14, 140. Many Dominicans would be surprised to learn that a number of words in their culinary vocabulary are appropriated from Haitian Creole, including coconette (a cocoa-powdered bread), cón-cón (charred crust in a rice pot), and mangú (boiled mashed plantains). See Demorizi, *Lengua y folklore de Santo*

Domingo, 65–66.

99. Pciní Hernández, *Bachata*, 121.

100. Ibid., 129. According to one author, "while advocating the preservation of this rural authenticity, Convite also used Afro-Dominican forms as fodder for their own compositions. Groups such as Los Guerreros del Fuego and Asa-Dife, led by José Duluc and Tony Vicioso, continued to work in this idiom during the 1980s and 1990s." Paul Austerlitz, *Merengue: Dominican Music and Dominican Identity* (Philadelphia, Penn.: Temple University Press, 1997), 109.

101. Luis Manuel Brito Ureña, *El merengue y la realidad existencial del hombre dominicano* (Santo Domingo: Editora Universitaria, 1987), 28–32. Anyone studying the intersection of merengue (particularly its regional forms), national identity, and the African diaspora must see the pioneering ethnomusicology studies of Martha Ellen Davis. For a brief but extremely informative article with a thorough bibliography see Martha Ellen Davis, "Music and Black Ethnicity in the Dominican Republic," in *Music and Black Ethnicity: The Caribbean and South America*, ed. Gerard H. Béhague (Miami: North-South Center, University of Miami, 1994).

102. Brito Ureña, *El merengue*, xx. It would be interesting to compare the chenché matriculado dance, which Brito Ureña states has similarities with African acrobatic dances, to the Afro-Brazilian marshal arts dance, capoeira.

103. Carlos Esteban Deive, "La herencia africana en la cultura dominicana," in *Ensayos sobre cultura dominicana* (Santo Domingo: Museo del Hombre Dominicano, 1981), 131. According to Deive, similar types of "juntas campesinas" are prevalent in Trinidad (gayap), Martinique (coup de main), Venezuela (cayapa), Ecuador (minga), and Colombia (cuadros); in West Africa the equivalent is called dokpwe among the Fon of Dahomey. In one convite, writes a field researcher, "more than forty campesinos with their sons and women moved to the [agricultural] grounds. It was a convite [gathering] of hatchets, and the farmers took their hatchets, ploughing and singing while their wives prepared two goats with manioc." Jose Lambourt, *Sana, sana, culito de rana* (Santo Domingo: Ediciones de Taller, 1979), 114. The participants in this convite called the system of "reciprocal favors" a tornapión.

104. Deive, "La herencia." Pciní Hernández writes: "The African descent of bachata practioners and audiences, however, could be clearly discerned in the racially specific language of their song texts. For example, the commonly used terms negro/a, prieto/a, moreno/a—all terms for black or dark men or women—clearly situated the singers, their mates, and, by extension, their audience within an Afro-Dominican social context" (*Bachata*, 135).

105. Austerlitz, *Merengue*, 111.

106. Ibid.

107. Sergia Galván, "Power, Racism, and Identity," in *Connecting across Cultures and Continents: Black Women Speak Out on Identity, Race, and Development*, ed. Achola O. Pala (New York: UNIFEM, 1995), 51.

108. Silvio Torres-Saillant, "Similitudes y un ancho mar de diferencia: Contrapunteo de la tierra natal y la diásporá," *Rumbo* (7–13 May, 1997): 55

109. "Missing Chapters in Dominican History and Culture," Dominican Studies Institute brochure, 1996. Copies can be found at the City College of New York, NAC/107, Convent Ave. at 138th Street, New York, N.Y. 10031.

110. For an excellent monograph on the Dominican community in New York City, see Jorge Duany's, *Quisqueya on the Hudson: The Transnational Identity of Dominicans in Washington Heights* (New York: Dominican Studies Institute, 1994).

111. Juan T. Libre's electronic mail message in dom-rep@darkwing.uoregon.edu list serve, 22 November 1995. The reality is that the Dominican elite is mostly white, and the society pages reflect their control of the economy. In a nation whose majority of inhabitants are non-white, it is absurd and

almost tragicomic that a blond white woman, Sandra Natasha Abreu, was chosen as Ms. Dominican Republic 1996. See *OH!*, a magazine typical of black exclusion, 6 July 1996. In magazines such as *Sucesos* however which detail crime or accidents, blacks are overrepresented in most of the photographs.

112. Blas Jiménez, "El escritor afro-hispano y el proceso creativo," *Afro-Hispanic Review* 14 (spring 1995): 7.

113. Quoted in Rosemary Geisdorfer Feal's, "Reflections on the Obsidian Mirror: The Poetics of Afro-Hispanic Identity and the Gendered Body," *Afro-Hispanic Review* 14 (spring 1995): 28. Afro-Dominican women have been "exalted and dignified" by writers such as Haffe Serulle in his novel *La danza de mingo*, about Florinda Soriano (Mama Tingó), an Afro-Dominican woman who was assassinated in 1974 because of her activism in the shantytowns of Santo Domingo. See Joan T. Eldridge, "The Existential, Socialist and Folkloric Themes in La danza de mingó," *Afro-Hispanic Review* 13 (spring 1994): 10–15; and Haffe Serulle, *La danza de mingó* (Santo Domingo: Ediciones Taller, 1977).

114. Mukien Sang Beng, "Los 'jus' de Enmanuel," *Rumbo* (27 July 1998): 52.

115. Catherine A. Sunshine, *The Caribbean: Survival, Struggle, and Sovereignty* (Washington, D.C.: Ecumenical Program for Inter-American Communication and Action, EPIC, 1985), 145. According to one perspicacious observer, "nothing in their history indicated to the masses of the Dominican people that their precarious material conditions or the overall indignities they suffer constitute a strictly racial form of oppression. As a result, they have not developed a discourse of racial self-defense among their strategies of social resistance. This, no doubt, bewilders observers coming from societies like the United States, where race tends to outweigh many other elements of human identity." See Silvio Torres-Salliant, "The Dominican Republic," in *No Longer Invisible: Afro-Latin Americans Today*, ed. Minority Rights Group (London: Minority Rights Publications, 1995), 132.

The Louvre *Négresse*: Interpretation and Illustration

Anne C. Meyering

W HEN MARIE-GUILLEMINE BENOIST'S *PORTRAIT D'UNE NÉGRESSE* WAS FIRST displayed in 1800, it attracted little attention (figure 1).[1] Today it has become an emblem of the French colonial empire and an all-purpose picture of the universal black female. The sitter's dress is not typical of the *négrillons*, servants dressed in livery in the drawing rooms and gardens of the rich and the well-born, as dark-skinned persons were more often depicted in eighteenth-century French paintings,[2] and her skin color, originally seen as the portrait's major shortcoming, is now regarded by many as its greatest asset.

In its nearly two-hundred-year history the painting has been appropriated for a variety of purposes and presented in a variety of contexts. After its appearance in 1800, it was purchased for the Louvre's collections in 1818, but no further notice was taken of it until the twentieth century. Since 1900 it has appeared in exhibitions or been reproduced in books that deal with one of three major themes: the work of women artists; "exoticism" or "orientalism" in French art; and, most frequently and often simultaneously, the influence of both Élisabeth Vigée-Lebrun and Jacques-Louis David on the art of the period. Since the 1950s, as interest in the painting has grown, myths and misinformation have sprung up around the *Négresse*. Although critics uniformly see it as a remarkable example of David's neoclassical style painted by one of his lesser-known female students, opinions differ on its ideological message. Some view it as supporting abolition, while others regard it as a feminist statement; few have seen it as both. Its use as the cover illustration on ten books in recent years

Figure 1. Marie-Guillemine Benoist, Le portrait d'une négresse, *1800, oil on canvas, 81 × 65 cm. Paris, Musée du Louvre. (Réunion des Musées nationaux/Art Resource, N.Y.)*

confirms its importance as a polyvalent symbol of the contact between blacks and whites. The painting's history reflects the changing nature of perceptions, primarily those of whites concerning blacks, during two centuries.

The portrait was not considered Madame Benoist's best work during her lifetime. Contemporary comment on the Salon of 1800 rarely mentioned it, and when it was discussed, it received muted praise. The most negative comments appeared in a satirical review, *Le nouveau Arlequin et son ami Gilles au musée,* which expressed the racist views of some who visited the exhibition that year. For Arlequin and Gilles it was the subject of the portrait that was contemptible, not the artist's technique or the style in which the subject was presented. Gilles says to his friend that he wants to leave the exhibition because he has seen the devil. "Where?" asks the startled Arlequin. "Look!" Gilles replies, "*Portrait of a Negress* by a woman." Arlequin then sings a ditty: "Who can we trust after such a horror! It was a pretty white hand that made this *noirceur*"

Figure 2. Marie-Guillemine Benoist, **La consultation, ou La diseuse de bonne aventure,** *1812, oil on canvas, 195 × 144 cm. Saintes, Musée des Beaux-Arts. (Musées de la ville de Saintes.)*

(a word that means not only blackness but also an outrageous act).[3] The idea that a white woman had painted a black was repugnant to some salon visitors.[4]

Joseph Esménard, a publicist and poet who reviewed the salon for the *Mercure de France,* only mentioned the picture in passing in discussing the best of the 250 portraits that hung that year in the salon.[5] The Swedish critic Bruun Neergard, in his epistolary review *Sur la situation des beaux-arts en France,* pointed out that the purity of design indicated a student of David.[6] Another critic had a mixed reaction, praising the style and able handling of color but noting that the left clavicle was too pronounced.[7] No one expressed genuine enthusiasm for the canvas.

In 1818 the Comte de Forbin, director of the Louvre under the Restoration, acquired the *Négresse* for the museum along with three other canvases by Benoist: *Une étude, Tête de sorcière, La consultation, ou La diseuse de bonne aventure* (figure 2) and *La lecture de la Bible, ou Les trois âges* (figure 3).[8]

Figure 3. Marie-Guillemine Benoist, La lecture de la Bible, ou Les trois âges, *1810, oil on canvas, 130 × 96 cm. Louviers, Musée de Louviers. (Musée de Louviers.)*

Perhaps Forbin should be credited with anticipating the changing aesthetic tastes of a fickle public. Or perhaps it is the fact that the *Négresse* hangs in one of the world's greatest museums that has preserved or created the artist's renown.

After its acquisition by the Louvre, the portrait attracted little notice until the twentieth century.[9] Walter Shaw Sparrow's *Women Painters,* published in 1905, and an exhibition held in Paris in 1913, *David et ses élèves,* included works by Benoist but not the *Portrait d'une négresse.*[10] Sparrow's book contained a reproduction of Benoist's 1808 portrait of the Princess Borghese, Napoleon's sister, which hangs in Fontainebleau (figure 4). The 1913 exhibition of works of David's students showed the artist's 1786 self-portrait[11] and her 1808 portrait of Doctor Gall.[12] It may be that neither Sparrow's publisher nor the organizers of the exhibition were able to meet the conditions set by the Louvre for reproduction and borrowing, but the inclusion of other works by Benoist in both Sparrow's book and in the exhibition of the

Figure 4. Marie-Guillemine Benoist, **Portrait of Marie Pauline, Princesse Borghese,** *1808, oil on canvas, Fontainebleau: Musée du Château de Fontainebleau. (D. Arnaudet; J. Schormansp; Réunion des Musées nationaux/Art Resource, N.Y.)*

work of David's students indicates that it was not the *Négresse* alone that accounted for Benoist's reputation as a noteworthy artist in the early years of the twentieth century.

Marie-Juliette Ballot's biography of Benoist was published the year following the 1913 exhibition.[13] Viewing the *Négresse* on the eve of the Great War, the author saw coolness and the sharp eye of an academic study. She made no references to the painting's possible association with abolition: "This is a very compact work; the artist is interested only in the model's forms and color, not in composition or emotion; the picture is cold and has the look of an academic study; it is painted with a very masculine discipline and has no feminine graces. The lack of accessories, the simple white ground, chill and distance us, we are close to sharing the opinion of Gilles and Arlequin. . . . It is bizarre to find this negress among the works of Mme. Benoist, who is all grace and freshness."[14]

This "masculine" work, insufficiently decorated and prettied up, showed little influence of the style of Vigée-Le Brun, whose work Ballot preferred and found more prominent in other canvases by Benoist.[15] The biographer explained Benoist's choice of subject by mere convenience. The sitter was the servant of Benoist's brother-in-law and his wife, who brought her with them to France in 1797 when he was on leave from his naval post in Guadeloupe. Ballot also suggested that studies of black people were a common exercise among painters at the time, because working with the color black was particularly challenging, but she provided no evidence to support this assertion.[16]

The *Négresse*'s next appearance was in a 1926 exhibition of eighteenth-century women artists in Paris. This was the first time it was seen outside the Louvre.[17] In addition to the *Négresse* portrait, four other works by Benoist were presented: *Le portrait d'un homme de lettres* (1785); *L'Innocence entre le Vice et la Vertu* (1791); and a pair of portraits of Monsieur and Madame de Briche, dating from the period of the Directory.[18] The catalogue entry paid more attention to the artist's life than to her painting: "At barely 15 years of age (1784), she worked under the direction of Mme Vigée-LeBrun and beginning in 1786, under that of David. She had three paintings in the Young Artists Exposition of 1784 and exhibited there again, in 1785, *le Portrait d'un homme de lettres*, which represents Demoustier, who at that time courted her but without success. It is for her that he wrote *Lettres à Émilie*. In 1792 she married Pierre-Vincent Benoist, whose royalist tendencies threatened considerably the safety of the household during the Revolution."[19]

In the introduction to the exhibition's catalogue, however, Louis Réau contrasted the work of Benoist, in his opinion one of the few female painters marked by the influence of David, with that of a much larger number of women painting at the same time, whose work reflected the influence of Greuze's genre scenes. To buttress his argument, Réau explicitly referred to the *Négresse:* "We recognize sworn followers of David in Mme. Chaudet, wife of the sculptor, and the Comtesse Benoist, née Leroulx-Delaville, the heroine of the famous *Lettres à Émilie* by Demoustier, who redeems some rather dull allegories with a vigorous torso of a turbaned *négresse,* irritatingly displayed against the glare in one of the darkest rooms in the Louvre. Like most of her contemporaries, Mme. Benoist seeks to combine the purity of line typical of David with the supple grace of Mme. Vigée-LeBrun: this feminized David is not without charm."[20] In Réau's opinion, the *Négresse* was noteworthy primarily because it charmingly combined the styles of Benoist's more famous teachers, not because of the choice of subject or any particular originality in composition or technique. After the exhibition the portrait went back to the Louvre.[21]

Three years later, in 1929, a major multivolume work on the paintings in the Louvre appeared. In one of the three volumes covering the nineteenth century, Louis

Hautecoeur, a curator at the museum, shared Réau's opinion of the *Portrait d'une né-gresse:* its main importance lay in combining the styles of Vigée-LeBrun and David.[22] Although Hautecoeur found most of Benoist's work deficient, he provided a striking description of the *Négresse:* "Her works are in general rather poor. She managed, one fortunate day, to produce an excellent painting when, visiting her brother-in-law, the colonial functionary Benoist-Cavay, without concern for mythology or grace, she did a portrait of a *négresse* and, on a yellow-green ground, contrasted the whiteness of the dress and turban, accentuated by the red of a belt and the blue of a scarf, the dark brown of this African torso."[23]

Hautecoeur's 1929 judgment of the painting departed sharply from Ballot's of 1914. Whereas Hautecoeur singled it out as Benoist's most noteworthy accomplishment, fifteen years earlier Ballot had seen it as uncharacteristic of the artist's work and did not like it. Furthermore, Hautecoeur provided one of the most vivid descriptions ever offered of the painting.[24] Not until Andre Trèves described the canvas more than a quarter-century later was it so accurately rendered in prose.

The first time the *Négresse* was shown in the context of exoticism or orientalism was in 1930. In this setting, it has been viewed as an exception that proves the rule.[25] Although students of French painting have argued that the adoption of exoticism or orientalism was associated with the spread of colonization and imperialism, most such exhibitions have featured scenes of figures from the Mediterranean Basin, such as the Levant and North Africa, rather than French North America, the Antilles, or sub-Saharan Africa, parts of the world that also fell under French colonial rule.[26] Nevertheless, Benoist's *Négresse* has been included in these exhibitions, a clear reminder of France's participation in the slave trade and of slavery in its Caribbean island possessions and in its colonies in sub-Saharan Africa as well as in the Indian Ocean.

The event in 1930 that prompted Benoist's portrait of a black woman to be shown in the context of orientalism or exoticism was the celebration of the centenary of the French conquest of Algeria. Jean Alazard, curator of the Musée d'Algers, organized an exhibition and published a companion book.[27] In his book Alazard compared Benoist's *Négresse* to sketches that Géricault made near the end of his life for an ambitious but unexecuted painting of the slave trade, which in Alazard's opinion depicted the most authentic images of black persons ever produced (figure 5): "One does not find much physiognomical truth in the *négresse* of Mme. Benoist; even before a model full of character she remains faithful to the teaching of Mme. Vigée-LeBrun by softening the elements that have some accentuation. In contrast, Géricault is sharp in his analysis of traits; he barely raised the veil on the spectacles of the Orient, but that was sufficient to show what passion for truth moved him to study them."[28]

Figure 5. Théodore Géricault, **Traite des nègres,** *black and red chalk on paper, 30.6 × 43.7 cm. (Paris, École nationale supérieure des Beaux Arts.)*

To Alazard, the image Benoist produced was softened or "sweetened." He reproached her for giving the portrait precisely the characteristics that Ballot had found lacking in 1914. Benoist's representation of a black woman did not have the incisive vision that Alazard found in Géricault's drawing of the slave market. In comparing Géricault's black figures to Benoist's black woman, Alazard implied that Benoist's portrait would have been more realistic if the sitter had been shown working in a cane field or sweating over a laundry tub. But this remark is only speculation. Alazard did not specify which details of the painting have been "sweetened." Was the sitter too "beautiful" for a black woman? Was it because the woman was seated in a fashionable chair over which a shawl of blue silk was draped, as if she were in an elegant Paris drawing room, that makes the portrait lack verisimilitude? Alazard's reading indicated that at least some Frenchmen who viewed this painting in the interwar period found it difficult or impossible to imagine a dark-skinned woman as attractive in 1800.

Since Alazard did not point to specific details in the painting, it is impossible to divine exactly what he meant by "*édulcorant ce qui avait de l'accent*" (softening or sweetening that which had sharpness). Like most published writings on this portrait, Alazard's text did not refer to specific physical features of the sitter.[29] Alazard's description may exemplify a kind of myopia not uncommon in the analysis of portraits of Others, of persons in some obvious way unlike the spectator, in which the viewer finds it impossible to see the image as anything but "unrealistic" or "unobjective." In this case, Alazard viewed a person who was Other not only because of skin color but also because of gender. In addition, the painter was also Other, a female. In contrast to the male author, Alazard, gender difference had not been a factor for Ballot. Yet, she did not regard the *Négresse* any more sympathetically in 1914 than did the (presumably) white male Alazard in 1930 or Gilles and Arlequin in 1800. But whereas Ballot had seen the image as insufficiently decorative, Alazard criticized it for being too "sweetened," "softened," or for lacking the acuity and passion of Géricault's *Slave Trade*.

It is commonplace to find interpretations of images of Others—whether other places, times, or classes—that characterize the image as romanticized or idealized, no matter whether it is physically beautiful or unattractive. Both interpretations distance the subject and the painting from the viewer by saying that the image's resemblance to the sitter is not as compelling or convincing as it might have been, that the painter has reconstructed the sitter other than how she must have been. Both Ballot and Alazard used a standard of verisimilitude in evaluating the *Négresse*. Neither had ever seen the living model; both had a preconceived notion of what she ought to look like, but they arrived at opposite conclusions. Alazard's position distanced the *Négresse* from the viewer by arguing that she was presented more palatably than he presumed she appeared in "real life": black women were never as attractive nor seen in such pleasant settings as Benoist's *Négresse*. Alazard saw Géricault's *The Slave Trade*, a picture of brutality and violence, as a much more realistic image of blacks. In contrast, Ballot suggested the image (or the subject?) had been rendered too austerely, coldly, and "distantly" for the painting to be a realistic portrait. Ballot judged the *Négresse* as a portrait of a woman painted by an eighteenth-century female artist in comparison to portraits of women painted by Vigée-LeBrun; Alazard judged it as an illustration of the "Orient" in French art before Delacroix. The stark contrast in their "readings," fifteen years apart, calls attention to the variety of interpretations this canvas has elicited. Its message has changed, depending on the attitude of the viewer as well as on the historical period in which it has been viewed and the context in which it has been displayed.

The *Négresse* appeared again as an example of exoticism in French art the next year. As part of the International Colonial Exposition of 1931 at Vincennes, on the eastern edge of Paris, two art exhibitions were held concurrently. One was a retrospective of French works, mostly paintings, displayed in the entrance hall of the Musée des

Colonies. The other, in the Pavillon des Beaux Arts, featured works by contemporary artists in France and the colonies.[30] Benoist's *Négresse* hung in the first. The retrospective drew heavily on Alazard's show held the previous year in Algiers.[31] Benoist's painting was not only one of the few works in the exhibition by artists who preceded Delacroix, the French master of "orientalism," but also one of the few showing a person with distinctly dark skin.

If the works shown at the International Colonial Exposition were indicative of public opinion in 1931, then the French associated the colonies with the Orient, which to them meant the Middle East and North Africa. Granted, most of France's vast empire in North America had been lost in 1763, Louisiana in 1803, and Saint-Domingue (Haiti) in 1804, but the retrospective exhibit also included few images of other lands with which France still had connections, such as Senegal, the Antilles, Annam, and Cambodia. The only representations of Asia were Tahitian scenes in works by Gauguin, and aside from Benoist's painting, the only distinctly dark-skinned figures were seen in Géricault's *Tête de nègre* (figure 6) and Chassériau's (1819–65) *Négresse.*[32] The official report on the exposition compared the elegance of Benoist's *Négresse* to the work of Vigée-LeBrun and commented on how pleasing it was, although no more so than the work of an English painter, Bonington (1801–28), who had influenced Delacroix (the report did not specify which of Bonington's works appeared in the show).

In 1951, following the defeat and occupation of France in World War II, Benoist's *Négresse* appeared as number 36 in the show *Delacroix et l'orientalisme de son temps,* which opened on 11 May in his former studio on the rue de Furstenberg.[33] Benoist's painting was one of only five works by four artists who predated Delacroix. These five have now become classic examples of the "oriental" influence on French painting in the nineteenth century.[34] The catalogue pointed out that *Paysage oriental,* by Jean-Baptiste Hilair (1753–after 1822), "announced at the end of the eighteenth century orientalist taste and romantic sensibility."[35] Since Benoist's *Négresse* dated from the same period, and it clearly pictured a person of non-European ancestry, it qualified as an example of "orientalism" in the work of Delacroix's predecessors. The subjects of the paintings in this exhibition were considered exotic, un-French, and un-European, even though the sitter in Benoist's painting was a French citizen when she sat for the portrait sometime in 1798, 1799, or 1800, since slavery was abolished in the French colonies in 1794 and only reimposed in 1802. Again, it is odd to find Benoist's *Négresse* displayed among scenes from the Middle East and the Mediterranean, although the headdress looks like a turban, and her bare breast, dark skin, and full lips may have been considered exotic in France in the 1950s. The catalogue devoted only one sentence to the painting: "This student of Mme. Vigée-LeBrun exhibited at the Salon of 1800 this fine portrait of a *négresse.*"[36] There was no commentary on the canvas—whether it had influenced

Figure 6. Théodore Géricault, **Portrait of a Negro,** *c. 1822–23, 21¹/₂ × 18³/₈," oil on paper mounted on canvas, Albright-Knox Gallery, Buffalo, N.Y., James G Forsyth and Charles W. Goodyear Funds, 1952.*

Delacroix, whether he had ever mentioned seeing it, or whether it was well known among artists of his generation.

Two years later the painting was reproduced in a book on exoticism by Roger Bezombes.[37] The author simply assembled between two covers dozens of excerpts from well-known French writers as well as reproductions of works by noted French artists. The only analysis Bezombes provided occupied a 23-page introduction. The entire discussion of Benoist's *Négresse* Bezombes placed in an endnote. In it he invented a myth about Benoist's work. He noted: "She also painted a number of exotic subjects."[38] Unless the *Tête d'une sorcière* (Head of a Witch), believed destroyed in 1871, or the fortuneteller in *La consultation, ou La diseuse de bonne aventure* (The Consultation, or The Fortuneteller) in the museum at Saintes is considered exotic, Benoist's portrait of the *négresse* was the only remotely unusual subject the artist ever painted.[39]

In 1956 Edith Appleton Standen prepared a book, *Women Artists,* for the Metropolitan Museum of Art series Your Own Museum in Miniatures, distributed by the Book-of-the-Month Club.[40] This small volume was an interesting cultural product in itself; in the mid-1950s, the decade of female domesticity par excellence, here was a book not only devoted exclusively to women artists, but also edited by a woman. In a one-paragraph commentary on Benoist's *Négresse,* Standen merely pointed out that the influence of David was more evident than that of Vigée-LeBrun.[41]

From December 1957 to March 1958, *Portrait d'une négresse* joined other paintings and sculptures at the Orangerie in Paris for a show entitled *Le portrait français de Watteau à David.* Germain Bazin, the chief curator of paintings at the Louvre, singled out Benoist's work in the catalogue's introduction:

> More than one visitor will discover with surprise the *négresse* of Mme. Benoist, which was popular in our galleries before the war; the fact that it was exhibited at the Salon of 1800 allowed us to include in our collection this astonishing masterpiece by a forgotten painter; the removal of some of the yellow varnish that obscured the colors and outlines permits a better appreciation in this picture of one of those virtuoso effects, in an almost monochromatic harmony, at which the French school excelled; the "tour de force" of Mme. Benoist reminds one of d'Oudry's *Canard blanc.*[42]

Note that, according to Bazin, by 1957 Benoist had been forgotten.

For the first time in nearly thirty years, since 1929, when Hautecoeur wrote the entry for the catalogue of the Louvre's paintings, the person in the portrait was identified. The exhibition catalogue stated simply that the sitter was "a domestic servant brought back from Guadeloupe or French Guiana by the brother-in-law of the artist, M. Benoist-Cavay, who was a naval commissary."[43] More important, for the first time the painting was interpreted as a political statement by the artist in support of abolition:

> But Mme. Benoist did not succumb solely to the pleasure of representing an unusual subject, she wanted to allude to the emancipation of the Negroes, a topic then current. Numerous engravings depicting Negro men or women with the caption "I am free . . . , I also am free" had appeared after the decree of the Convention abolishing slavery (4 February 1794). Houdon, who had exhibited in 1781 and 1783 the head of a negress intended for the Parc Monceau, reclaimed the bust to put on the base "given Liberty and Equality by the Convention . . ." and Girodet painted in 1798 Jean-Baptiste Belley (Musée de Versailles), a Negro slave from Saint Domingue who had bought his freedom with his savings and who became a deputy to the Convention, then to the Council of the Five Hundred under the Directory.[44]

It is important to remember that this exhibition of French portraits was held at a point in the nation's history when France's colonial mission was a hotly debated issue. Only three years earlier the French army was defeated at Dien Bien Phu in 1954, and, while the portrait exhibition ran, the war in Algeria was sweeping the Fourth Republic rapidly toward its demise.

Reproductions of the *Négresse* were chosen to illustrate reviews of the 1957–58 show.[45] Maurice Serullaz wrote one for *La Revue des arts,* the journal of the French public art museums.[46] (He also had written the catalogue for the Delacroix exhibition in 1951.) The critic noted that Mme. Benoist, "a sort of Arvers of painting,"[47] had left not a sonnet but a "*Portrait d'une négresse* (Louvre) done in a succulent technique worthy of the brush of Géricault or Édouard Manet!"[48] Serullaz' use of "succulent" and the favorable comparison to Géricault and Manet suggested some viewers in the late 1950s saw eroticism in this portrait by Benoist.[49]

In a short review of the same show in *Le Peintre,* André Trèves singled out Benoist's painting, evidently thinking he was complimenting it by calling it the work of a female artist equal or superior to that of any man. The portrait was also used as the illustration for the article. According to Tréves:

> The visitor stands with emotion before the masterpiece of Marie Benoist, a portrait of a bare-breasted Guadeloupan woman who is very beautiful. She is wearing a white gown that covers her legs. The moderate impasto of the clothing is in a savory white achieved by light bluish contrasts on the planes parallel to the light source or contrarily warmer gray in the folds of the material. The flesh tones and delineation are obtained from a light, rust-colored undercoating which shows through in just the right intensity among little delicate touches thinly overlaid, while the whole is broadly conceived, at once noble, grand. A single regret: the blue of the material resting on the chair is a questionable choice, perhaps it has been chemically altered by the passage of time. This painting of the very first rank belongs in the Louvre. It was shown in 1951 at the exposition in Delacroix's studio and at the Petit-Palais in 1946. Benoist received some training from Vigée le Brun and then was, at the Louvre, one of the first students of David, and also of Gérard. She died in 1826, and her late works are, alas, much inferior to the early ones.[50]

After hanging in the French portraits exhibition at the Orangerie in 1957–58, *Le portrait d'une négresse* was not shown again outside the Louvre until 1972, when it appeared in a major London show, *The Age of Neo-Classicism.* It was also reproduced in the exhibition catalogue.[51] Hélène Toussaint's catalogue entry reiterated previous opinions that Benoist had fallen into oblivion except for this work. Nevertheless the work was important because it showed the powerful influence of David's portrait style. Adding to Bezombes' assertion in 1953 that Benoist painted a number of exotic subjects, Toussaint introduced a new myth about the *Négresse*. She stated that this painting had established Benoist's reputation during her lifetime.[52] We have seen, on the contrary, that criticism of the Salon of 1800 was either tepid or hostile in its assessment of Benoit's only canvas to appear in that show. However, Toussaint redeemed herself as a perceptive observer by calling attention to David's portrait of Madame Trudaine, painted about 1791, as Benoist's inspiration for the composition (figure 7): "Few other works show such complete submission to the master's example: the placing of the model—this black woman who might almost be the negative image of the pale Mme. Trudaine—the restrained draughtsmanship, the cold light, the lustrous finish of the paintwork and the plain background form a combination of elements which corresponds exactly to David's own aesthetic."[53]

In the same year as the London exhibition, Pierre Angrand's book appeared on Forbin, who, as director of the Louvre under the Bourbon Restoration, had purchased four Benoist canvases for the museum's collections in 1818, including the *Négresse*.[54] In noting these acquisitions, Angrand merely listed the titles of three and offered little commentary on "the fourth and most known of these works, an *Étude* [*sic*] *de Négresse* seen down to the knees. A work both *vigoureuse* and *savoureuse*, which moreover was much admired. Taken together, acquisitions of quality."[55] Angrand's choice of "*savoureuse*" (savory [saucy?], tasty, racy) recalls the word "succulent" used by Maurice Serullaz in 1957 and suggests the sensuality and seductive power of the image, a female temptress. Thus, it was only after about the middle of the twentieth century that commentators began to employ words evoking sensuality in writing about the painting. But Angrand also described the image as "*vigoureuse*," a word often used for male figures or artists. By using the two words together, *savoureuse*, implying femininity, and *vigoureuse*, denoting masculinity, Angrand pointed to the ambiguity of the messages the canvas conveyed.

A spate of books on women artists appeared in the late 1970s and the 1980s. Benoist's work, often her *Portrait d'une négresse*, found a place in most of these. Several made only passing references of little value in situating Benoist's work in the corpus of Western painting.[56] Others presented useful insights into her work and its importance in French painting.

Ann Sutherland Harris and Linda Nochlin found room for the *Négresse* in their book, which also served as the catalogue for the exhibition of the same name: *Women Artists, 1550–1950*.[57] The exhibit traveled to Los Angeles, Austin, Pittsburgh, and Brooklyn in 1976 and 1977.[58] Although the portrait did not appear in the show, Benoist was represented by *L'Innocence entre le Vice et la Vertu*, a prosaic if not alto-

Figure 7. Jacques-Louis David, **Portrait of Mme Trudaine,** *1791, oil on canvas, 130 × 98 cm. Paris: Musée du Louvre. (Réunion des Musées nationaux/ Art Resource, N.Y.)*

gether unimaginative allegory.[59] Harris and Nochlin's discussion of Benoist echoed the catalogue copy for the 1972 London show. They reiterated Toussaint's claim that the *Négresse* had made the artist's reputation. They also followed Toussaint in comparing it to David's portrait of Mme. Trudaine. Their main contribution was to quote from a letter written in 1814, in which Benoist agreed to quit exhibiting her canvases in public as a concession to her husband's career. Both he and her mother urged her to do so, arguing that it was inappropriate for a woman married to a *Conseiller d'État* to be a professional painter. After first objecting, Marie-Guillemine relented. Harris and Nochlin's interpretation of this correspondence created yet another myth about Benoist. They argued that the letter showed the oppression of female artists during and after the French Revolution, but that interpretation is questionable.[60]

Benoist's letter to her husband was dated 1 October 1814, a moment of transition between the Empire and the Restoration, just six months after Napoleon's first abdication and five months after Louis XVIII's return to France. The Hundred Days would not begin until the spring of 1815. Under the Empire the painter's husband had risen high in the Ministry of the Interior, where he was given primary responsibility for organizing the administrative system that carried orders from Paris to the eighty-three prefectures and thence to the thirty-six thousand communes of France. The Napoleonic regime had never granted him the recognition that normally accompanied such service, because he was known as a staunch royalist and had made it clear that he would be reluctant to accept them.[61] His steadfastness paid off when Louis XVIII returned, and he was named to the Conseil d'État on 5 July 1814.

Although the artist's husband, Pierre-Vincent had sound royalist credentials, his wife had compromised her reputation as a loyal supporter of the Bourbon dynasty. She had received a gold medal in 1804 from the emperor himself, and she had painted his portrait for the cities of Ghent, Brest, Le Mans, and Angers.[62] In 1805 she also had been commissioned by the new imperial government to execute a portrait of Maréchal Brune.[63] In addition, she had painted several members of the imperial family, including the empress Marie-Louise, Napoleon's sister Pauline, and one of the emperor's nieces.[64] In other words, from the royalist perspective, the artist had been a propagandist for the usurper, and she had accepted from the imperial government an annual stipend of between two thousand and four thousand francs.[65] The restored monarchy was so hostile toward David, her teacher, that he was forced to remain in exile in Brussels.[66] Marie-Guillemine's decision was demanded at least as much by the rapidly shifting winds of French politics as it was by social restrictions on upper-class women, as Harris and Nochlin claim.

This is not to say that Marie-Guillemine was not grief stricken about no longer exhibiting her work at the salons, and she can be considered politically naïve for not realizing earlier that the commissions she accepted from the Napoleonic regime would compromise her and her family if the Bourbons ever returned to the throne. But her decision did not mean that she quit painting, and in 1818 she sold four pieces to the Louvre. In her letters of 1821 she referred to a painting of the Virgin on which she was working for the bishop of Angers, and ultimately it hung in the cathedral there.[67] After 1809, she was increasingly involved in running the chateau of La Motte Baracé, the Maine-et-Loire estate her husband inherited that year from his father. She was particularly interested in planning and supervising its park and gardens.[68] Though she no longer exhibited her work publicly after 1814, she continued to paint and to find other outlets for her artistic talents.

Another survey of women artists was published in 1978, written by Elsa Honig Fine.[69] Fine's discussion of Benoist and her work is a model of succinct and cautious scholarship, although her comments on the colors in the *Portrait d'une négresse* suggest that she was working from a poor reproduction. In a short entry accompanied by a small black-and-white illustration, Fine ably described the *Négresse,* Benoist's life, and her other works.[70] She wrote of the painting: "There exists in the Louvre an extraordinary portrait of a young black woman in a white turban sitting in a green chair on which is draped a cloth of darker green [*sic*]. The uninterrupted background adds to the power and beauty of this painting by Marie Guillemine Benoist, a student of Vigée-LeBrun and David. It is the influence of David, however, that permeates the *Portrait of a Negress . . . .* painted for the Salon of 1800."[71] Like most other commentators, Fine remarked that David's influence in the painting overpowered that of Vigée-LeBrun.

In 1979, at the height of the second wave of the twentieth-century women's movement, the British feminist Germaine Greer included Benoist in her book *The Obstacle Race.*[72] Greer presented Benoist primarily as a student of Vigée-LeBrun and David but also as an accomplished portraitist. The book included a reproduction of the *Négresse,* and Greer referred to it as Benoist's masterpiece, contributing to the belief that this painting established the artist's reputation: "Her masterpiece, *Portrait of a Negress,* relies entirely for effect upon the proud posture of the subject's head and the impenetrable look that she bends on the observer, slightly beneath her. The white cotton draperies emphasize the darkness of her polished skin: every detail works towards the central theme, the still dignity of the alien woman."[73]

Greer was the first critic to call attention to the dignified pose of the sitter. She also observed, as had Hautecoeur in 1929 and Trèves in 1958, how the white dress heightened the impact of the subject's dark skin on the viewer. Whereas in 1930 Alazard had charged Benoist with "softening" or "sweetening" (*édulcorant*) the figure in the frame, in 1957–58 Serullaz had used the word "succulent" to describe Benoist's image of a black woman, in 1972 Angrand had added "*savoureuse*" and "*vigoureuse*" to the lexicon applied to this picture, and Greer applied the word "proud" to the sitter's pose and described her as projecting a presence of "still dignity." Despite all the positive adjectives Greer employed to describe her reaction to Benoist's *Portrait d'une négresse,* Greer acknowledged the sitter's "otherness" when she called her an "alien woman." Thus Greer saw Benoist showing the viewer a figure who was like both the painter and the viewer in gender, yet a stranger, unfamiliar and foreign, in other ways.

Greer's word choices conveyed the ambiguity and ambivalence that this image has evoked in viewers. Along with "alien," Greer's use of "restrained," "cold," "lustrous," and "plain" to describe the image recalled Ballot's 1914 "cold," "masculine," and lacking "feminine graces." Yet, in also describing Benoist's *Négresse* as "proud" and possessing "still dignity," Greer endowed the black woman with self-confidence, self-control, and self-discipline. By endowing the figure in the frame with human qualities of self-restraint and pride, Greer's description was consistent with the entry on the painting in the catalogue for the 1957–58 French portrait show that associated Benoist's portrait with abolition, because abolitionists in 1800 believed that dark-skinned persons had all the human qualities and abilities, as well as weaknesses and frailties, that whites or light-skinned people were believed to possess.

In November 1981 an exhibition entitled *La femme artiste d'Élisabeth Vigée-LeBrun à Rosa Bonheur* opened in southwestern France.[74] Benoist's *La diseuse de bonne aventure* was lent by the Musée de Saintes, and the catalogue only briefly referred to the *Négresse*, calling it the artist's masterpiece.

Although works by Benoist are in the collection of paintings in Versailles,[75] none was chosen by the exhibition curators for *Capolavori da Versailles: Tre secoli di ritratto francese* (Masterpieces from Versailles: Three Centuries of French Portrait), which ran from 16 March to 16 June 1985, in the Pitti Palace in Florence. Nevertheless, the catalogue referred to the *Négresse*, accompanied by a small black-and-white reproduction, as a standard against which to judge portraits done by David's school: "Among the many great works produced by the crystal-clear Davidian syntax (jolting relief of the figure against the simplified sheet of the background, fig. 12 [the *Négresse*]), the exhibition offers the portrait of *Jean-Baptiste Belley, Deputy of Saint-Domingue* (1797, cat. no. 36): where Girodet has exalted, in the emblematic counterpoint of the living and the dead (the black of the skin against the white of the marble), of the integrated ex-slave and the liberal philosophe, the egalitarian principles of the revolution."[76]

Girodet's painting, lent for exhibition in Florence, contained a white marble bust of the Abbé Raynal, author of the anti-colonial *Histoire . . . des deux Indes* and an advocate of abolition of the slave trade, on a pedestal against which Belley leaned. The effect, typical of portraits by David and his students, was to create a sharp contrast between the sitter and his or her surroundings, to make the sitter stand out in sharp relief. Both Girodet and Benoist achieved this effect through the sharp contrast between the black skin color of the sitter and the white objects in the picture. In Girodet's portrait of Belley, the deputy's black skin was juxtaposed to the white marble bust and pedestal depicting the advocate of abolition, Abbé Raynal, as in Benoist's *Portrait d'une négresse*, where the black skin of the seated woman contrasts with the white of her dress and head scarf.

Two books, both on the history of women artists, published in 1987 repeated the assertion that *Le portrait d'une négresse* had made Benoist's reputation.[77] One of them, written by Nancy G. Heller, also repeated Harris and Nochlin's questionable explanation of why Benoist renounced her career. Nevertheless, Heller provided a good one-paragraph summary of Benoist's life and work, identifying her as a student of both Vigée-LeBrun and David.[78] Next to a reproduction of the *Négresse*, Heller's text echoed both Greer and the catalogue for the 1957–58 eighteenth-century French portraits exhibition. Heller described the canvas as the "powerful likeness of a stunning black woman in a white gown and turban . . . [a] dignified portrait . . . , which may have been inspired by a 1794 decree abolishing slavery."[79] Heller could not have known, any more than Alazard, whether the portrait was a "powerful likeness," but this sort of hyperbole was typical of much of the boilerplate writing in historical surveys of female artists. Nevertheless, like earlier viewers, Heller picked up on the way the artist's skillful use of white and black heightened the impact of the image, reiterated Greer's judgment that the sitter was portrayed as "dignified," and explicitly linked the portrait to the abolition of slavery in the French colonies in 1794.[80]

Also published in 1987 was Lawrence Gowing's massive volume *The Paintings in the Louvre,* in which a full-color reproduction of the *Négresse* was accompanied by the following commentary:

> Marie Guillemine Benoist was a distinguished pupil of the studios of both Madame Vigée-LeBrun and David, and the splendid *Portrait of a Negress* that made her reputation at the Salon of 1800, six years after the abolition of slavery in France, had the character of a manifesto both of feminism and of black emancipation. She received commissions from Napoleon and an annual stipend from the government, as well as a gold medal in 1804. But upon the restoration of the monarchy, her royalist husband, the Comte Benoist, was appointed to a high position of state, which required that his wife cease public exhibition. Her heartbroken . . . letter to him ended, "Let's not talk about it again or the wound will open up once more."[81]

Gowing fell into a number of the traps set by historians who preceded him. He repeated Toussaint's 1972 assertion that this portrait had made the artist's reputation. Gowing also made Pierre-Vincent Benoist a count fourteen years before the fact.[82] As was shown above, whether Marie-Guillemine was "required" to cease public exhibition as a result of her husband's new position was debatable. However, Gowing's view was not completely erroneous. He followed the view of others, like the author of the catalogue *Le portrait français de Watteau à David,* in seeing the painting as a statement in support of abolition, but he was the first to assert that it was also a feminist manifesto, although he did not refer explicitly to any of the portrait's details to support this claim.

While the revival of feminism in the 1970s and 1980s accounted for much of the renewed interest in the *Négresse,* generating new myths and misinformation about both the artist and the canvas, the painting's appearance in the fourth volume of *The Image of the Black in Western Art* placed it in a new context for analysis.[83] *The Image of the Black in Western Art* is an ambitious project: to produce an iconography of blacks in Western art from antiquity through the nineteenth century. In 1976 the first part in one volume appeared, covering the period from the pharaohs to the fall of the Roman Empire. In 1979 the second part, covering the period from the early Christian era to the Age of Discovery, appeared in two volumes. In 1989, the fourth part appeared, also in two volumes. Written by Hugh Honour, the fourth part covered the period from the American Revolution to the First World War and contained Benoist's *Portrait d'une négresse.* The third part, covering the sixteenth through the eighteenth centuries, has never been published. Although some of the pictures in *The Image of the Black in Western Art* also appeared in earlier works devoted to orientalism or exoticism in French art, the subject, blacks in art, overlapped rather than coincided with the subject of orientalism or exoticism.

Honour's discussion focused less on the artist than on the work, which he described as "perhaps the most beautiful portrait of a black woman ever painted."[84] He shared the view expressed since the late 1950s that the painting was a statement in support of abolition. In addition, along with Gowing, Honour suggested that Benoist might even have been asserting support for female emancipation in depicting her portrait of a black person as a female. Honour explained how from his perspective the artist's canvas, by the pose and the gaze she gave the sitter, worked to create an image of equality among human beings, whether sitter, painter, or viewer and irrespective of skin color: "There is not the least suggestion of servitude in the painting. The black woman is completely at her ease in this warmly humane and noble image. With perfect poise and self-confidence she looks at us with a gaze of reciprocal equality. The painting is, moreover, a masterpiece of visual sensitivity, the soft black skin being exquisitely set off by the crisp white, freshly laundered cotton headdress and drapery. Few, if any, European images of non-Europeans are as calmly and clear-sightedly objective."[85]

Honour's view had similarities to Greer's. He described the sitter's pose as one of "perfect poise" and "self-confidence," her gaze as one of "reciprocal equality." In Honour's view nothing in the painting suggested servitude, recalling the impression the *Négresse* produced on Greer of "still dignity." Both Honour's and Greer's descriptions of the image included recognition of the sitter's "otherness." Greer used the word "alien," while Honour placed the painter in an ethnocentric position, writing that Benoist's *Portrait d'une négresse* represented a "European" view of a "non-European." But, Honour went on to say, this European artist's rendering of the non-European is "calmly and clear-sightedly objective," that is, it was an exact likeness, not an idealized image, not one that altered the sitter to make her appear more attractive than she was in the flesh. This judgment put Honour's reading in conflict with Alazard's assessment, that Benoist's image was too soft or sweet to be realistic.

Honour did not fail to note the influence of David: "It has, indeed, the sharp focus, the unaffected grace, and the sense of intimate rapport between the artist and the sitter, as well as the firmness and delicacy of line and subtlety of color that distinguish such portraits by Jacques-Louis David."[86] Honour saw the model "as an individual, living, feeling, fellow human being. This memorable image differs from David's portraits only in so far as it represents an anonymous sitter—*une négresse*."[87]

Honour saw the woman in the portrait as beautiful. But, unlike earlier commentators who had seen in the painting a black woman rendered too beautifully to be "real," Honour justified his view of Benoist's *Négresse* by referring to the aesthetic and ethical ideals of the Enlightenment, which prevailed when both the artist and her teacher, David, painted. Honour's text ably situated the painting squarely in its historical context: "In the second half of the eighteenth century intellectual and artistic changes were synchronized as a result of the application of the ideas of the Enlightenment to aesthetics and the call for a new art based on supposedly immutable, eternally valid principles—truthful, rational, and morally elevating. . . . Marie-Guillemine Benoist's *Portrait d'une négresse,* painted in the last year of the century, is an unusual if not unique celebration of the beauty of a black woman rendered in the 'high' neoclassical style originated by David."[88]

These Enlightenment ideals included truth, rationality, and moral elevation, an optimistic belief in progress and human development. Thus, Honour saw in an image of a black woman depicted as "beautiful" a statement by the artist contesting those of her contemporaries, who, like Gilles and Arlequin, could see dark-skinned people only as ugly, dirty, flawed, barbaric, primitive, uncivilized, and unfit for European society, and especially in contrast to those who saw women with dark skin as Jezebels, lascivious and promiscuous. In fact, Honour made no reference in the text to the sitter's bare right breast, except to suggest in a footnote that it may have been a reference to allegories of Liberty produced for the festivals and processions during the republican years of the French Revolution. Honour's evaluation was the opposite of that made the first time the painting was shown in 1800, a reaction still echoed in Ballot's judgment in 1914. Where Honour saw "not the least suggestion of servitude. . . . The black woman . . . completely at her ease in this warmly humane and noble image," Gilles and Arlequin had seen the devil, evil, dirt, and smudges on the body and on the character. Where Honour saw warmth and intimacy between the sitter and the artist, Ballot had seen coolness and distance.

Honour approached the canvas as a scholar examining a painting in light of both the aesthetic ideals and the situation of blacks in France in 1800. Here was a dark-skinned woman painted by a white French female painter, the student of the most prominent painter of her day. The national assembly of a revolutionary government had decreed six years earlier the abolition of slavery in its colonies. In France itself the people had been ravaged and cowed by the Terror a few years before. In 1795 a new constitution had been adopted, creating a new and less violent government, the Directory, but France was still at war. The ongoing struggle between republicans and royalists made everyday life uncertain and insecure, and the ultimate fate of former slaves still hung in the balance in 1800, when Benoist painted the *Négresse*. Honour pleaded for the viewer to see the painting as a portrait, despite the fact that the artist withheld the sitter's name. It is partly her anonymity that contributes to the ambiguity of the painting, making it susceptible to a variety of often conflicting and contradictory interpretations. Her anonymity also suggested to Honour that the canvas may have been, as Ballot argued in 1914, a study in black, an exercise, but, in this case, one that succeeded well enough to be purchased for the national collection of French paintings.

What Honour saw in 1989 contrasted sharply with what James Smalls reported he saw in Benoist's *Portrait d'une négresse* in 1991. Smalls entitled his study of the painting "Black Venus: Marie-Guillemine Benoist's 'Portrait of a Black Woman.'"[89] Smalls argued that in eighteenth- and nineteenth-century French art blacks were "dressed up and displayed," portrayed as ornaments or accessories, mere objects in a white society. He saw in the portrait none of the empathy between sitter and artist that Honour perceived. According to Smalls,

> the contrasting of black skin against crisp white linen gives the work a tactility and sensualness meant specifically for display and decorum . . . [Benoist], like her teacher [Vigée-LeBrun] learned quite well how to neutralize a sitter by cosmetic brushwork, a piquant pose, and a colorful scheme—all used to distract the eye from the truth of slavery and forced servitude and to render seemingly objective reality in an idealized manner. Benoist's portrait reveals nothing of the personality of the black woman portrayed; this "negress" is nothing more than an elegant stylization reflecting the mentality of an ultra-refined society for whom surface polish was of maximum importance.[90]

To support his argument that the sitter was merely an object, "dressed up and displayed," Smalls pointed to the sensuality of the subject, as had Seralluz in 1957 and Angrand in 1972, both of whom had implied that the painting carried an erotic undercurrent.[91] According to Smalls:

> The subject of the painting does, in fact, recall a theme of a modest Venus after her bath. The sitter is a symbol of black beauty presented to us in a manner to arouse

sympathy—she possesses an elegantly long neck on top of which a head reveals an apathetic facial expression whose eyes are puppy-dog large and intended to elicit emotion. . . . After we get past the gaze and the surroundings, we then inquire as to what she is doing. She has been placed there by the artist to encourage us to sympathize with this half-naked, bare-breasted, exotic savage. The black woman's passivity and docility are deemed appropriate qualities for a servant of the artist. Like Girodet's *Portrait of Belley,* Benoist has "civilized" this "primitive negress" by placing her in a morally superior neoclassical context. . . . The sexualization of black flesh forces the viewer not to consider the issue of slavery seriously but instead brings the subconsciously desired slave auction block into the home of the viewer. Images of blacks presented in this manner were designed to make the imagination soar with visions of human possession, bondage, and both physical and psychological violation. Ultimately what we find with Benoist's *Portrait of a Black Woman* is an aesthetically undressed black female who has been shrewdly positioned on the auction block awaiting our decision whether or not to bid. No matter how one sees her, she remains an enslaved "negress."

Either Smalls made contradictory statements about the painting or his argument was a complicated one in which he did not deny that Benoist had rendered the sitter attractive, but in a way that insulted the sitter. Smalls said the sitter was beautiful, but she possessed an "apathetic facial expression," accentuated by "puppy-dog large" eyes "intended to elicit emotion." Puppies are often considered obsequious in their eagerness for attention and affection. The painter has encouraged viewers to sympathize with her, to be drawn to her, even though, according to Smalls, the impression she made was one of a "half-naked, bare-breasted, exotic savage." Although her partial nudity had previously attracted little if any attention, except indirectly, as in the use of words such as "succulent" by Serulllaz in his review of the French portraits show in 1957–58 and "*savoureuse*" by Angrand in his 1972 study of Forbin, the sitter's bare right breast is Smalls' main justification for arguing that the image can be seen in no other way than as one of "an enslaved 'negress.'"

Although much of what Smalls found in the painting is there, in particular the luxury implied by the chair and the blue drapery, his basic reading was flawed. For Smalls, despite Benoist's effort to ennoble or civilize a "savage," the sitter remained "an enslaved 'negress.'"[92] This "black Venus" was designed to appeal to those prurient viewers who found bondage sexually exciting.

Smalls concluded that Benoist's portrait worked to justify slavery. But his text contained contradictions. Benoist had "civilized" this "'primitive negress'" "by placing her in a morally superior neoclassical context." But by placing the sitter in a "morally superior neoclassical context," Benoist could have just as convincingly implied that blacks belonged in Parisian drawing rooms just as much as whites did. The accessories in the painting are less characteristic of a "neoclassical context" than they are of a late rococo interior. The Louis XVI chair and the blue silk shawl might be found in a late-eighteenth-century upper-class, bourgeois or aristocratic, French household, or they might simply be studio props from the same period. Blacks might be found in these households as servants, but that was a dignified status, if they were reliable, hard working, loyal, and competent. Greuze painted his share of white maids and servants, too. Class differences, hierarchy, authority, and deference were an integral part of white society in France in 1800, but that did not make domestic servants slaves, any more than peasants were serfs. Thus, placing a dark-skinned woman in a "morally superior neoclassical context" could demonstrate her humanity, raising the issue of the injustice of slavery, as much as it illustrated the necessity of her enslavement.

For Smalls the sitter's bare right breast plus the color of her skin were the two details of the painting that made impossible any other interpretation than that she was a slave. The bare right breast was an erotic image. Although it is true that around 1800, black women in French literature were often portrayed as lascivious, nevertheless the bare breast is subject to a variety of interpretations.[93] For Smalls it made the sitter a "black Venus." For Honour, the sitter's bare breast linked her to Liberty. But, does the bare breast necessarily take the sitter out of the category of the real and make her into a classical allegory, or make her into an odalisque? The bare breast could just as well have been a symbol of fertility and fecundity as of erotic sexuality.[94] The bared breast, modestly revealed as the woman's plain cotton dress falls from her shoulders, may suggest that the woman was a wet nurse or nanny—common occupations for black women in the Antilles.[95] These women accompanied the children they tended when the families visited France.[96] In addition, it is important to consider the portraits of white women painted in France at about the same time that depicted them with a bared right breast.[97] One in particular makes an interesting comparison—Marie Boulinar's portrait of Aspasie, dated 1794 (figure 8). Aspasie was the friend and counselor of Pericles, noted for her beauty and her wit. Another of these portrait sitters is known to have been governess to the duke of Chartres's children, and another may also have been of a governess.[98] In addition, portraits of respectable white Frenchwomen with one but not both shoulders bared were not uncommon in this period. Perhaps a bared breast or shoulder implied rare physical beauty rather than lasciviousness or promiscuity. Before rushing to the conclusion that the bared breast makes Benoist's *Portrait d'une négresse* an erotic image, the fairly common usage of this pose needs to be considered.

The painting's title also encourages multiple readings of the painting. The anonymity of the sitter makes the portrait available for a wider range of readings than

Figure 8. Marie-Génévière Boulinar, Aspasie, *1794, oil on canvas, 1.63 × 1.27 m. Arras, Musée des Beaux-Arts. (Claude Thériez.)*

if the painter had supplied the sitter's name. A name would have strengthened the sitter's individuality and helped to identify her relationship to the painter. As Honour pointed out, it was only in not naming the sitter that Benoist's portrait is distinctly different from those of David. By not putting the sitter's name in the title of the painting, the artist contributed to the view that her canvas was a study in black. So, while the anonymity maintained in the title by the use of the words *une négresse,* (a black woman), as if the painting could be of any black woman, put distance between painter and sitter, the word *négresse* had more than one meaning in 1800.[99] It did not necessarily mean that the woman was a slave, nor was it necessarily a sexually-charged term. Similarly, the contrast between the simple dress and head scarf and the shimmering blue cloth draped over the chair made the painting susceptible to a variety of interpretations.

Smalls also associated the portrait with French feminism of the 1790s: "By painting a partially nude and sensual black female figure, Benoist was perhaps trying to

La France
et les Français
outre-mer

Robert
et Marianne
Cornevin

Pluriel

Figure 9. Cover of Robert Cornevin and Marianne Cornevin, La France et les français outre-mer *(Paris: Hachette, Éditions Pluriel, 1993). (Reprinted by permission of Hachette Livres.)*

undermine the limitations put on female artists by their male counterparts."[100] Although in this sentence Smalls used the sexuality of the figure depicted by Benoist to argue that the painter challenged the gender stereotypes of her day, in further developing the point, Smalls laid greater emphasis on Benoist's upper-class origins and on the presence of a feminist movement in France during the period when she painted. His logic was that since the artist was an aristocratic white woman, if her canvas was subversive, it was because she harbored feminist rather than abolitionist sentiments. Smalls based this interpretation on a few facts selected from Benoist's biography and on histories of women in the French Revolution without showing any links between. His evidence demonstrates, nevertheless, that some of Benoist's contemporaries saw a direct analogy between the women's and the antislavery movements.

After the Louvre's refurbished Richelieu wing was opened in November 1992, Benoist's *Portrait d'une négresse* attracted renewed attention. In 1993 Sylvain Lavaissière both praised and insulted the artist's talent in the *Guide du visiteur: La peinture française.* Like the entry in the catalogue for the 1957 exhibition *Le portrait français de Watteau à David,* he, too, singled out the unusual nature of the subject. Lavaissière noted the portrait's fidelity to David's style of neoclassicism but went on to say that its high quality made one wonder whether David had a hand in producing it.[101] In other words, it was so good that the artist must have had help. The irony is that Benoist had once put her hand to one of David's most famous works.[102]

Also in 1993, the French publisher Hachette reproduced the *Négresse* on the cover of a paperback edition of a history of French colonization, Robert and Marianne

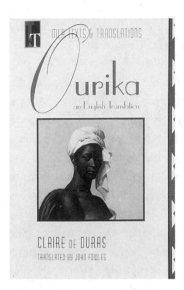

Figure 10. Cover of Claire de Duras, Ourika: An English Translation *(New York: Modern Language Association of America, 1994). (Reprinted by permission of the Modern Language Association of America.)*

Cornevin's *La France et les français d'outre-mer* (figure 9).[103] The painting was cropped to remove the Louis XVI armchair and the blue silk shawl draped over it, as well as the sitter's knees and the right side of her head, taking away the gold hoop earring. With the products of late-eighteenth-century European manufacturing thus removed, the figure was better able to pass for a member of the indigenous population in many of France's colonies. All that remained was the torso of a dark-skinned woman, her right breast exposed, wearing a simple white dress and a turban.

In 1994 the Modern Language Association of America placed another mutilated version of the painting, though cropped differently, on the cover of an English edition of the 1824 novel by Claire de Duras, *Ourika,* translated by John Fowles, the author of the 1970 best-seller *The French Lieutenant's Woman* (figure 10). In less than fifty pages, the Duchesse de Duras told a story based partly on the life of a real Ourika.[104] In the novel, Ourika as a toddler was rescued by the governor of Senegal from being sent into slavery in the Antilles, taken to Paris, given to the governor's aunt, the Maréchale de B., and raised together with the maréchale's two orphaned grandsons. There, in an elegant eighteenth-century townhouse, Ourika was petted and educated just as any white aristocratic girl would have been. Her singing was a pleasure to hear and her dancing a joy to watch. She learned to paint and mastered both English and Italian. Her benefactress made sure she was well read. But when Ourika reached a marriageable age, French society no longer had a place for her. No aristocrat would marry her because of her skin color; the only men in Paris who would consider it were beneath her socially, since she had been raised as an aristocrat, and she could not return to

Africa, because she had become thoroughly French. *Ourika* was certainly not the story of the woman on the cover, a domestic brought back to France from the islands by the brother-in-law of the painter.

As a book cover illustration, the *Négresse* was in some ways less appropriate for the Cornevins' *La France et les français d'outre-mer* than for Duras's *Ourika*. Benoist's sitter and Duras' *Ourika* were contemporaries. Both were young. If the négresse were twenty to twenty-five years old in 1800, she would have been a member of Ourika's generation. The bare breast of the woman in the portrait is firm; her skin has no wrinkles; her body appears vigorous and strong.[105] But small muscles define the shape of her right upper arm, and the veins slightly visible on the tops of both of her hands suggest that she was not a stranger to physical labor. If she had served as a wet nurse, she would have had a child of her own or at least a pregnancy at some point. She reclines slightly, and her long neck and white headdress give her a dignified appearance, as Germaine Greer pointed out, even though the simplicity of the design and the fabric of her clothing disrupt the impression of luxury introduced by the blue shawl. The immaculately white turban and dress have a freshly laundered quality about them, as Hugh Honour suggested. The angle of her right arm frames her bare breast, and the position of her arms is similar to that with which a woman might hold a nursing infant. The tail of the turban falls down from her left temple toward the shoulder, pointing toward her bosom. There is a physicality to the image, but whether it signaled eroticism depended upon the viewer's gaze. She is sensual but perhaps not sexual, exotic but not always erotic.

Although seated, the woman appears tall and straight. Her head is turned to the right, looking toward the viewer or the artist, but in the reproductions her large eyes do not quite focus on the same point; the right one looks off in the distance, while the left is aimed directly at the viewer. Her nose is straight, and, while the nostrils are slightly flared, it cannot be described as flat or broad, as the noses of persons with dark skin were often characterized at the time.[106] Thin, gently arched eyebrows outline her large dark eyes, which the artist has placed in a shadow, so the whites are not brilliant. The shaded eyes lend an air of modesty to her gaze. Her tight curls are visible at her right temple and at the hairline on her forehead, her black hair making a sharp contrast with her white turban.

In the full, uncropped version, the sitter's legs and knees are not clearly defined under the gown, which is not unlike a simple *chemise à la grecque,* in white cotton or linen, a dress fashionable at the time and in which Vigée-LeBrun once painted Marie-Antoinette. The portrait does have some of the characteristics of "dress up and display," and the shawl and the chair would not have been uncommon among the possessions of aristocratic women at the end of the ancien régime, the period

Figure 11. **Portrait d'Ourika** *from L[éonel] de la Tourasse*, **Le Château du Val dans la Forét de Saint-Germain** *(Saint-Germain-en-Luye, 1924), facing page 20. (Paris, Bibliothèque nationale de France.)*

when Ourika grew up.[107] In this regard Benoist's model could pass for Ourika. But the portrait also has some characteristics of the modest class of maids who served these upper-class Frenchwomen. For example, the gold hoop earring is too simple to be typical of the jewelry worn by the wealthy. The painting thus reflects contradictory and conflicting images, which should come as no surprise. The 1790s in France were nothing if not a decade of conflict and contradiction, ambiguity and paradox.

Although aristocratic women of the time were often painted in dresses with low necklines or sometimes with one shoulder or breast bare, they were never represented with both breasts or shoulders bare, as the cropped version on the cover of *Ourika* suggests. A concession is made to French mores in 1800, however, by also cropping the painting below the shoulders, eliminating the bare breast. Nevertheless, despite the similarities between Benoist's *Négresse* and Duras's *Ourika*, other pictures of Ourika

Figure 12. Alfred Johannot, **Ourika,** *steel engraving, 300 × 250 cm. (Paris, Bibliothèque nationale de France.)*

were available which, without cropping, would have made more appropriate cover illustrations for the Modern Language Association edition of *Ourika.*[108]

In 1995, Knopf published a guide to the Louvre that contained a reproduction—cropped—of the *Négresse,* described as an exquisite portrait.[109] On the facing page is a reproduction of David's *Portrait of Mme Trudaine* (figure 7). The juxtaposition provides an opportunity to see why Toussaint and Harris and Nochlin wrote, respectively, that Benoist's painting was "the negative image" and "the black equivalent" of David's portrait.

To conclude this two-hundred-year history of Benoist's painting of a black woman, by making her beautiful, the artist challenged the stereotypes of blacks in the period of the French Revolution, especially those generated by the virulently racist propaganda that followed the slave uprising in Saint-Domingue in 1791. Although the republican National Convention abolished slavery in France's colonies in 1794,

Figure 13. Claire de Duras, Ourika *(Paris: Ladvocat, 1826), facing page 42. (University of Kentucky Libraries.)*

turmoil in France's valuable Antillean colonies kept the debate on slavery alive, if not uppermost in the minds of the French, whose primary concern was to defend the new republic against the combined forces of Austria, Prussia, Russia, and England.[110] By placing the sitter near the plane of the picture frame, Benoist brought her close to the viewer. The artist invited the spectator not to turn quickly away because of the subject's dark skin but to see her as she was: beautiful, modest, and clean, even though she was of foreign origin and low social status. Benoist clothed the model in a simple gown but also surrounded her with luxury and posed her majestically, though modestly. The artist invited the viewer to see a woman with dark skin as something other than a slave. Other portraits from the same period of white French females, of higher social status than the sitter in Benoist's portrait but with a bare right breast, tend to undermine the argument that this portrait carried an erotic message. Rather than a black Venus, the sitter was more likely a nursemaid, a position that, in the wake of Rousseau, carried connotations not only of being a servant but also of natural motherhood, worthy of admiration and emulation.[111]

Over the last two centuries, many people have recorded their impressions of Benoist's *Portrait d'une négresse*. At its first showing the picture was admired by some, but others were disdainful of the subject. Nearly all the critics complimented the work as an outstanding example of the influence of Élisabeth Vigée-LeBrun and Jacques-Louis David, although some regretted that the influence of Vigée-LeBrun was not strong enough, while others regretted that it was too strong. Only in the 1930s did viewers become interested in the painting because it represented a woman with dark skin, an example of "exoticism" or "orientalism" in French art. Not until the late 1950s did anyone mention the possibility that the painting was a statement in support of abolition. No one has ever pointed out that Benoist employed the palette of the tricolor for the textiles—the blue shawl, white dress, and red sash—although Hautecoeur's 1929 description came close.

Only since the revival of the women's liberation movement in the 1970s has the concession Benoist made to the demands of her husband's career been considered of much significance. Although Smalls argued that the portrait is more appropriately placed in the context of the history of feminism than in the context of the history of abolition, little in the painting supports this interpretation, although the tricolor palette may suggest Liberty. Certainly, Benoist did not place a Phrygian cap on the sitter's head or a pike in her hand.[112] Some aspects of Benoist's life, especially her perseverance in pursuing a career as a painter despite the obstacles placed in the path of women, may lend support to an interpretation of her as a feminist, but other things we know about her suggest that she accepted the conventional role of women in French society. She definitely was not a radical. Her father had served Louis XVI, and she married and remained deeply devoted to a man who risked his life to defend the monarchy during the most dangerous days of the Terror.

The recent use of Benoist's *Négresse* on the covers of books about French colonization and French society in 1800 suggests that it has become a symbol of that period in the nation's history, carrying with it all the complexity, ambiguity, and paradox that the word *colonization* and the era of revolution imply. But it is also in danger of becoming an icon of the black woman in the French empire, which would deny the varieties of experience of women of color even under slavery and colonization.

NOTES

The author thanks the late Lucien Abénon, Patience Adibe, Robert DuPlessis, Nancy Fitch, Kenneth Haltman, the late Ruth Simms Hamilton, Earnestine Jenkins, the late Harold Marcus, Jordan Reed, David Robinson, Raymond Silverman, Deirdre Spencer, and Patricia Thompson for comments on and other assistance with earlier drafts of this paper.

1. The entry in the salon catalog reads: "Mme Laville Le Roulx, (M.-G.), femme Benoist, élève de David, 238. Portrait d'une négresse." See *Collection des livrets des anciennes expositions depuis 1673 jusqu'en 1800, Salon de 1800, 42* (Paris: Liépmannsshon éditeur, 1872), 45.

2. See James Smalls, *Esclave, Nègre, Noir: The Representation of Blacks in Late Eighteenth- and Nineteenth-Century French Art,* (Ann Arbor, Mich.: University Microfilms International, 1992), 71. See also Shelby T. McCloy, *The Negro in France* (Lexington: University of Kentucky Press, 1961), 30–32; A. Maurice Besson, "La police des noirs sous Louis XVI en France," *Revue de l'histoire des colonies françaises* 21 (1928): 433–46, esp. 433; Léon-François Hoffman, *Le Nègre romantique* (Paris: Payot, 1973), 63–65. See also William B. Cohen, *The French Encounter with Africans: White Response to Blacks, 1530–1800* (Bloomington: Indiana University Press, 1980).

3. Translated from *Le nouveau Arlequin et son ami Gilles au musée, ou La verité dite en plaisantant. Critique piquante, en vaudevilles, des tableaux, dessins, sculptures et d'autres objets precieux* (Paris: Chez Lacroix, rue des Étuves, no. 393 [1800]), in *Collection de pièces sur les beaux-arts (1673–1808): Dite Collection Deloynes,* vol. 22, no. 624 (Paris: Bibliothèque nationale; New York: Clearwater Publishing Company, 1980), 9; see also Marie-Juliette Ballot, *Une élève de David; La Comtesse Benoist: L'Émilie de Demoustier* (Paris: Plon, 1914), 150.

4. These satirical reviews were meant to amuse and to mock highbrow culture, but they also carried a grain of truth. See Bernadette Fort, "Voice of the Public: The Carnivalization of Salon Art in Prerevolutionary France," *Eighteenth-Century Studies* 22 (spring 1989): 368–95, esp. 390–93.

5. Joseph Esménard, "Exposition de peinture, sculpture, architecture et gravure," *Mercure de France,* in *Collection de pièces sur les beaux-arts (1673–1808),* vol. 22, no. 633, 740, see also Ballot, *Une élève de David,* 150.

6. T. C. Bruun Neergaard, *Sur la situation des beaux arts en France, ou Lettres d'un danois à un ami* (Paris: À l'ancienne librairie de Dupont, rue de la loi, no. 1231, an ix-1801), in *Collection des pièces sur les beaux-arts (1673–1808),* vol. 23, no. 642, 334.

7. *Notice sur les ouvrages de peinture, de sculpture, d'architecture, et de gravures exposés au salon du Musée central des arts, pendant les mois de fructidor, an VIII, de vendemaire et de brumaire, an IX,* par A.D.F. (Paris: se trouve à la porte du Musée central des Arts, et rue du Bacq, no. 467, an VIII [1800]), in *Collection des pièces sur les beaux-arts (1673–1808),* vol. 22, no. 626, 15; see also Ballot, *Une élève de David,* 150–51.

8. See Pierre Angrand, *Le Comte de Forbin et le Louvre en 1819* (Lausanne, Switzerland, and Paris: Bibliothèque des Arts, 1972), and the dossier on the painting in the Centre de la Documentation de la Peinture in the Louvre. Madame Benoist received eleven thousand francs for the four canvases. The price was similar to what Forbin paid for other paintings he acquired for the Louvre in this period. See also Ballot, *Une élève de David,* 229–30 and 274–75.

9. In the English edition of Lafenestre's guide to the Louvre, it is listed in the index, under the artist's name, as "16. Portrait of a Negro Woman," one of the paintings in the Hall of the Seven Chimneys, Gallery 3, but there is no discussion of the painting. See Georges Lafenestre and Eugene Richten-

berger, *The National Museum of the Louvre*, trans. B. H. Gausseron (Paris: Libraires-imprimeries réunies, [1893]), 326.

10. Walter Shaw Sparrow, *Women Painters of the World from the Time of Caterina Virgir, 1413–1463, to Rosa Bonheur and the Present Day* (London: Hodder and Stroughton, 1905); Palais des Beaux Arts de la Ville de Paris, *David et ses élèves*, 7 April–9 June 1913 (Paris: Imprimerie Georges Petit, 1913), 27, Fogg Museum Library, Harvard University.

11. See Ballot, *Une élève de David.*

12. Ibid, reproduction facing p. 192.

13. By referring to "la Comtesse Benoist" in the title of her book, Ballot conferred the rank of count on the artist's husband, Pierre-Vincent Benoist, several years before it was granted to him by Charles X. Madame Benoist died in 1826, but her husband received the title only in 1829. See Celestin Port, *Dictionnaire historique, géographique, et biographique de Maine-et-Loire* (Paris: J.-B. Dumoulin; Angers, France: Lachese, Belleuvre and Dolbeau, 1872), s.v. "Benoist, (Pierre-Vincent)," 1:313–14.

14. Ballot, *Une élève de David*, 149–50.

15. See Jacqueline Lichtenstein, "Making Up Representation: The Risks of Femininity," *Representations* 20 (fall 1987): 77–88, for a discussion of the long tradition that associates ornament and color with femininity.

16. Ballot, *Une élève de David*, 151.

17. *Explication des peintures, gravures, miniatures et autres ouvrages de femmes peintres du XVIIIe siècle exposés au profit de l'appui maternel (Hôpital Tarnier) du 14 Mai au 6 Juin en l'Hôtel des Négociants en objets d'art, tableaux et curiosités* (Paris: De l'Imprimerie de Frazier, 1926), Northwestern University Library Special Collections Department.

18. Ibid., 26. The present locations of the first and the de Briche portraits are unknown. *Innocence* is in a private collection in Paris.

19. Ibid., 25. In addition to identifying the locations of the paintings in the show (*Le portrait d'un homme de lettres* lent by M. Lucien Kraemer, *L'Innocence entre le Vice et la Vertu* lent by the Prince de Croy-Solre, *Une négresse* lent by the Louvre, and the de Briche portraits lent by the Comtesse de Jonquières), the catalog listed several French museums in which Madame Benoist's other canvases could be seen: in Angers, *Napoléon I;* in Louviers, *Lecture de la Bible;* in Saintes, *La consultation, ou La diseuse de bonne aventure;* and at Versailles, *Portrait de la Princesse Borghese.*

20. Ibid. The other woman to whom Réau refers, Jeanne-Elisabeth Gabiou, Madame Chaudet, had one work in the show, no. 23, *Amour à la rose.* She exhibited in the salons from 1798 to 1817.

21. Both André Linzeler and J.G. Goulinat reviewed the 1930 show, but neither had a word on Benoist or her paintings. See André Linzeler, "L'exposition des femmes peintres du XVIIIe siècle," *Beaux-Arts* (1926): 161–62; and J.-G. Goulinat, "Les femmes peintres au XVIIIe siècle," *L'Art et les Artistes*, n.s., 13, no. 65 (March–July 1926): 289–94.

22. Louis Hautecoeur, *La peinture du Musée du Louvre, école française, XIXe siècle*, first part (Paris: L'Illustration, [1929]), plate 31, 23.

23. Ibid., 30–31.

24. Hautecoeur was less eloquent in a later work on female portraitists of the First Empire: "Mme Benoit [*sic*] . . . attempts to borrow from her teachers, Mme Vigée-LeBrun and David, the grace of the first and the solidity of the second, and she succeeded in one work, the picture of a negress in the Louvre." Louis Hautecoeur, *L'art sous la Révolution et l'Empire en France, 1789–1815: Architecture, sculpture, peinture, arts appliqués* (Paris: Guy Le Prat, 1953), 74.

25. Following Mary Sheriff's study of Vigée-LeBrun, one might argue that Benoist tried to make the sitter in her *Portrait d'une négresse* an individual and especially a member of the human race, endowed with all the same strengths and weaknesses that humans, both male and female, possess. The painter tried to raise the sitter above the servility of the group in which she has been placed by the

prevailing racist stereotypes, but to do this the sitter must simultaneously partake of and transcend the qualities stereotypically assigned to the black female, servant but not servile, exotic but not erotic, sensual but not sexual. In much the same way Vigée-LeBrun had to prove she was a woman because her ambition to be a painter, a male profession, created fears and suspicions about her, threatening to undermine her credibility as an artist. See Mary D. Sheriff, *The Exceptional Woman: Élisabeth Vigée-LeBrun and the Cultural Politics of Art* (Chicago: University of Chicago Press, 1996).

See also Hoffman, *Le Nègre romantique*, in note 2 above. Hoffman argues that it was only with the Enlightenment that French literature began to treat blacks as individuals.

26. This disjuncture between orientalism and European imperialism and colonization is confirmed by Michael Rogers in his review of John M. Mackenzie's *Orientalism: History, Theory, and the Arts:*

> While British and French Orientalists were different in many respects, their allegedly imperialist works generally pre-date the imposition of direct imperial rule. Nor were long-standing imperial territories—the Antilles, the Cape, the Antipodes or North America—given such attention. The Orientalists' interest was in the biblical and classical legacy of the Near East, which travel had made increasingly accessible. Admittedly, they often make the local inhabitants mere actors in a scene not of their own making—insulting, if one is looking for offence, but not a conspiracy. Their works, moreover, were often tinged by fantasy and did not always avoid vulgarity; but misrepresentation was more than balanced by Romantic idealization. And in so far as they pretended social criticism, they were critics of their own societies, seeking in the East the values they felt were lost in their own cultures.

Michael Rogers, "The Foggy Orient," *(London) Times Literary Supplement*, no. 4859, 17 May 1996, 28.

27. Jean Alazard, *L'Orient et la peinture française au dix-neuvième siècle, d'Eugène Delacroix à Auguste Renoir* (Paris: Plon, 1930).

28. Ibid., 10

29. Aside from the mention by the anonymous reviewer in 1800 of the left clavicle (see note 7 above), Hugh Honour's comment in 1989 on her bare breast; see *The Image of the Black in Western Art*, vol. 4, *From the American Revolution to World War I*, pt. 2, *Black Images and White Myths* (Cambridge, Mass.: Harvard University Press, 1989), 8 n. 5. In 1991 Smalls made several references to the sitter's sensuality; see Smalls, *Esclave, Nègre, Noir*, 67–103.

30. Ministère des colonies, Exposition coloniale internationale de 1931, *Rapport général présenté par le Gouverneur Général Olivier*, vol. 5, part 1, *Les sections coloniales* (Paris: Imprimerie nationale, 1933), 387–445, "L'art et les colonies et les beaux-arts à l'exposition coloniale internationale." The official guide does not specifically mention Benoist's painting, nor does Edna Nicoll's *À travers l'exposition coloniale* (Paris: E. L. Nicoll, 1931). Nicoll only gives the name of each building and a general description of the displays, extolling what the visitor would have seen. On the Pavillon des Beaux-Arts exhibition, she mentions that the works of French artists were by far the best on display. The show in the museum vestibule was reviewed in "Le palais permanent des colonies," *Beaux-Arts* 7 (1931): 3, but the article did not mention *Portrait d'une négresse*. For an analysis of the importance of the Colonial Exposition as a representation of the French Empire in the interwar period, see Catherine Coquerel-Vidrovitch, "Apogée et crise coloniales," in *Images et colonies: Nature, discours et influence de l'iconographie coloniale liée à la propagande coloniale et à la représentation des Africains et de l'Afrique en France, de 1920 aux indépendances* (Paris: Syros, ACHAC, 1994). See also Herman Lebovics, *True France: The Struggle over French Identity, 1900–1945* (Ithaca, N.Y.: Cornell University Press, 1994), chap. 2; "The Seduction of the Picturesque and the Irresistible Magic of Art," 51–97, on the International Colonial Exposition of 1931.

31. The official report of the 1931 exhibition drew on an article by Raymond Isay, "Art et colonies" (see

Ministère des colonies, Exposition coloniale internationale de 1931, *Rapport général*, 399). Isay discussed the significance of France's colonies in the evolution of French art:

> Now the Islands, while suggesting to our artists a thousand exquisite frivolities, gave birth only rarely to great works. The taste for the Island is manifested in the decorative rather than the "major" arts. It is like the taste for bibelots, that is, for an artistic reality which, ever since the time when the West remained secret, continually became less important, thinner, smaller. And that partly explains the ruin of the colonial empire: the Colony—whether a "warm land" or "acres of snow"—was never truly taken seriously by the Ancien Régime. By regarding it as a luxury good, an objet d'art, a jewel or a bauble, one unwittingly prepared to accept its loss. . . . At Aboukir, at Trafalgar, it is the old France of beyond the seas, an entire world, that collapses. In the nineteenth century, in contrast, the Colony, reconstituted in new forms, will bring us a very different message. It will cease to incarnate an "artificial Paradise" for the use of the sophisticated and will become, definitively this time, an empire. Thereupon, its aesthetic role will alter completely: rather than a pleasant pastime, it will bring to France and to Europe a new and forceful art lesson.

See *Revue de Paris* 38 (15 October 1931): 818–48; the quotation is from 831–32.

Isay did not see any significant disruption in the French aesthetic due to colonial influence on the art produced in France before Delacroix and Gauguin. France's colonial enterprise contributed only decorative elements to artistic forms and styles that remained essentially "French" until Delacroix.

Isay did not mention *Portrait d'une négresse*. The lack of response to Benoist's painting, both at the time of its first showing in 1800 and by Isay, lends support to Isay's 1931 view. "Major" French arts—painting, sculpture, and architecture—did not adopt the theme of, or reflect, the slave trade, contact with Africa, or life in the Antilles, the North American possessions, or the territories in the Indian Ocean. Thus, Isay helps perpetuate the view that France's colonies before 1830 contributed little, if anything, to "French" culture, a view that includes collective amnesia about France's role in slavery.

32. Ministère des colonies, Exposition coloniale internationale de 1931, *Rapport général*, 409. The report did not make clear which of Chassériau's drawings or paintings of dark-skinned women were displayed in the retrospective. See Marc Sandoz, *Théodore Chassériau, 1819–1856: Catalogue raisonné des peintures et estampes* (Paris: Arts et métiers graphiques, 1974).

Catherine Coquery-Vidrovitch ("Apogée et crise coloniales," 27–33) has recently shown how the 1931 colonial exposition reflected and contributed to the construction of the myth of the colonies in the minds of the French in the interwar period. See also Charles-Robert Ageron, "L'exposition coloniale de 1931, mythe républicain ou mythe impériale?" in *Lieux de mémoire*, ed. Pierre Nora (Paris: Gallimard, 1985), 1:561–91; and Catherine Hodeir and Michel Pierre, *L'exposition coloniale* (Paris: Complexe, 1991).

33. In 1946 the *Négresse* was hung in the Petit-Palais in the show *Chef d'oeuvres de la peinture française du Louvre*. See the dossier on the *Portrait d'une négresse* in the Louvre's Centre de la Documentation de la Peinture. I have been unable to find out anything about this exhibition, but it may be linked with remodeling or refurbishing of the Louvre galleries at the time.

For the Delacroix show, see Société des Amis d'Eugène Delacroix, *Delacroix et l'orientalisme de son temps* (Paris: À l'atelier du Maître, 1951), in the George Washington University Gelman Library, Washington, D.C. It appears that the author of the catalogue, Maurice Serullaz, borrowed heavily either from the report on the 1931 exposition or from Alazard's book.

34. Sociéte des Amis d'Eugène Delacroix, *Delacroix et l'orientalisme*, 16 and 22–23.

35. Ibid., 23.

36. Ibid., 16.

37. Roger Bezombes, *L'exoticisme dans l'art et la pensée* (Paris: Elsevier, 1953), 68 n. 194.

38. Ibid., 177.

39. See Ballot, *Une élève de David*, 245–54, for the closest thing to a complete list of Benoist's works and for the largest number of reproductions in black and white.

40. Edith Appleton Standen, ed., *The Metropolitan Museum of Art Miniatures: Women Artists*, Your Own Museum in Miniatures series (New York: Book-of-the-Month Club, 1956).

41. Ibid., no. 18. This publication has no page numbers.

42. Germain Bazin, *Le portrait français de Watteau à David*, 2d ed. (n.p.: Éditions des Musées nationaux, Decembre 1957–Mars 1958), xi.

43. The naval personnel dossier for Benoist-Cavay at the Services des Archives d'Outre-mer (EE 156–57) in Aix-en-Provence contains a summary of his service in the French navy from 1789 to 1809. It indicates that he served in Guadeloupe from 1789 to 1791 and from 1792 to 1797. He served at Cayenne, in French Guiana, from 1800 to 1809.

44. Bazin, *Portrait français*, 40.

45. *La Revue des arts* (26 December 1957): 283; and *Les nouvelles littéraires*, 26 December 1957. Although the painting was used on the cover of the latter, the review inside did not mention *Le portrait d'une négresse*.

46. M[aurice] Serullaz, "Salles de l'orangerie, le portrait français de Watteau à David," *Revue des Arts* (26 December 1957): 283–90.

47. Félix Arvers (1806–56) was a poet and playwright best known for one book of poetry, *Mes heures perdues* (1833), and especially a sonnet he wrote for Marie, the daughter of Charles Nodier (1780–1844), the noted and early proponent of romanticism.

48. Ibid., 288.

49. See the discussions below of Angrand, *Le Comte de Forbin* and of Smalls, *Esclave, Nègre, Noir*. See also the discussion of the reproduction of *Le portrait d'une négresse* on the cover of the 1994 MLA edition of *Ourika*, later in this essay.

50. André Trèves, "Le portrait français de Watteau à David," *Le Peintre* (1 January 1958): 7–8. See also the dossier on the painting in the Centre de la Documentation de la Peinture in the Musée du Louvre.

   In the introduction to the exhibition catalogue, Germain Bazin suggested that the painting had recently been cleaned.

   The comment that Benoist's last works were much inferior is puzzling. She began exhibiting in 1784 and stopped twenty-eight years later, with the salon of 1812. She won a gold medal at the Salon of 1804, two-thirds of the way through her public career and four years after the *Négresse* was first shown. She was awarded the medal in the same year she completed a commissioned portrait of Napoleon as first consul for the city hall of Ghent. See Ballot, *Une élève de David*, 154–56, 211–14, 252–55; see also Edward D. Lilley, "Consular Portraits of Napoleon Bonaparte," *Gazette des Beaux Arts* 106 (November 1985): 143–56, and Nicole Hubert, "À propos des portraits consulaires de Napoléon Bonaparte: Remarques complémentaires," *Gazette des Beaux Arts* 108 (July-August 1986): 23–30.

51. The Royal Academy and the Victoria and Albert Museum, Fourteenth Exhibition of the Council of Europe, *The Age of Neo-classicism*, 9 September–19 November 1972 (London: Arts Council of Great Britain, 1972), 18–19 and plate 10.

52. "When it appeared at the Salon of 1800, the painter's reputation was made" (ibid., 18–19). Toussaint was a curator at the Louvre.

   As was pointed out earlier in this essay, the picture received little critical attention when it appeared in the Salon of 1800, and the notice it did receive was lukewarm at best. Benoist did not receive a gold medal until 1804.

53. Ibid., 19.

54. Pierre Angrand, *Le Comte de Forbin et le Louvre en 1819* (Paris: Bibliothèque des art, 1972). The négresse's portrait was reproduced facing page 142.

55. Ibid., 142.

56. These include Hugo Munsterberg, *A History of Women Artists* (New York: Clarkson N. Potter, 1975), 48–49; and Karen Petersen and J. J. Wilson, *Women Artists: Recognition and Reappraisal from the Early Middle Ages to the Twentieth Century* (New York: New York University Press, 1976), 60–62.

57. Ann S. Harris and Linda Nochlin, *Women Artists, 1550–1950* (New York: Alfred A. Knopf, 1976), 49.

58. In 1976 another major exhibition, *French Painting, 1774–1830: The Age of Revolution,* also toured the United States. None of Benoist's works were included.

59. Ballot, *Une élève de David,* reproduction facing p. 64.

60. Harris and Nochlin, *Women Artists,* 49.

61. Anne Meyering, "Constructing an Aristocratic Identity in Nineteenth-Century France: Denys Benoist d'Azy and His Father" (paper presented at the annual meeting of the Society for French Historical Studies, Boston, 21–23 March 1996). See also Adolphe Robert, *Dictionnaire des parlementaires francais* (Paris: Bouloton, 1889–91) 1:253.

62. See Lilley, "Consular Portraits"; Hubert, "À propos des portraits consulaires"; and Ballot, *Une élève de David,* 156–214, esp. 164, 187–88, 250–51, and 262–65.

63. Ballot, *Une élève de David,* 166–67.

64. Jean-Pierre Samoyault, *Guide to the Museum of the Chateau of Fontainebleau* (Paris: Éditions de la Réunion des musées nationaux), figures 213, 237, and 240 (pp. 163, 187, and 189); Jean Pierre Samoyault, "Tableaux, sculptures et meubles provenant d'Elisa Bonaparte," *Bulletin de la Société de l'Histoire de l'art français* (1983): 85–90; and Ballot, *Une élève de David,* 183–84, 196–97, 199–200, and 252.

65. R. B. Holtman, *Napoleonic Propaganda* (Baton Rouge, La.: Louisiana State University Press, 1950), 164.

66. Angrand, *Le Comte de Forbin,* 110–38.

67. Ballot, *Une élève de David,* 215–33, esp. 232, 253.

68. Archives nationales, 161 AQ 9.

69. Elsa Honig Fine, *Women and Art: A History of Women Painters and Sculptors from the Renaissance to the Twentieth Century* (Montclair, N.J.: Allanheld and Schram, Prior, 1978).

70. Ibid., 54–55.

71. Ibid., 54.

72. Germaine Greer, *The Obstacle Race: The Fortunes of Women Painters and Their Work* (New York: Farrar, Straus, and Giroux, 1979), 270–71, 298–300.

73. Ibid., 298–300.

74. At Donjon Lacataye in Mont-de-Marsan, from November 1981–February 1982.

75. See Claire Constans, *Musée national de Château de Versailles: Les peintures* (Paris: Éditions de la Réunion des musées nationaux, 1995), 1:81, no. 441, *Portrait of Pauline Bonaparte,* and no. 442, *Portrait of Napoléone-Élisa Bacciochi.*

76. *Capolavori da Versailles: Tre secoli di ritratto francese* (Florence: La Casa Usher, 1985), 31.

77. Nancy G. Heller, *Women Artists: An Illustrated History* (New York: Abbeville Press, 1987); and Lawrence Gowing, *The Paintings in the Louvre* (New York: Stewart, Tabori and Chang, 1987).

78. Heller, *Women Artists,* 63 and plate 37. See also Nancy G. Heller, *Women Artists: An Illustrated History,* revised and expanded ed. (New York: Abbeville Press, 1991), 63–64 and plate 37.

79. Heller, *Women Artists,* revised and expanded ed., 63–64.

80. Benoist's work was not mentioned in Wendy Slatkin, *Women Artists in History from Antiquity to the Twentieth Century* (Englewood Cliffs, N.J.: Prentice-Hall, 1985).

81. Gowing, *Paintings,* 562.

82. Benoist's husband, Pierre-Vincent, was not made a count until 1829, while the painter ceased showing her work in public when he was named to the *Conseil d'État* (Council of State) in 1814.

83. Hugh Honour, *The Image of the Black in Western Art,* vol. 4, *From the American Revolution to World War I.*

Although similar to the 1930s and 1950s publications and exhibitions on the theme of exoticism or orientalism, *The Image of the Black in Western Art* contained more pictures of dark-skinned persons, in whatever part of the world or whatever setting, than did the earlier works. Yet all three themes—exoticism, orientalism, and "blacks in art"—suggest distance and difference from the viewer-commentator.

84. Ibid, 4:7.

85. Ibid.

86. Ibid.

87. Ibid., 4:8. Compare the views of Hoffmann, *Nègre romantique*, on the French literature of this period, which he argues looked for the first time at blacks as individuals rather than as stereotyped members of a group.

88. Honour, *The Image of the Black*, 4:12.

89. Smalls, *Esclave, Nègre, Noir*, chap. 3, "Black Venus: Marie-Guillemine Benoist's *Portrait of a Black Woman*," 67–103. Since this article was submitted in 1997 for publication in *Routes of Passage*, Smalls has published a much more sophisticated, nuanced, and detailed reading of the painting. See James Smalls, "Slavery is a Woman: 'Race,' Gender, and Visuality in Maire Benoist's *Portrait d'une négresse*," *Nineteenth-Century Art Worldwide* 3, no. 1 (Spring 2004). Nevertheless, he comes to substantially the same conclusions: "In the end, both Benoist and her 'negress' were slaves to a male-dominated culture" (24). I regret that it is not possible for me to substitute an analysis of the more recent article for my discussion of the chapter from his 1991 doctoral dissertation.

90. Ibid., 82–83.

91. It was a common belief in the eighteenth century that blacks, both males and females, were more concupiscent than whites. See Hoffmann, *Nègre romantique*, 99–146, esp. 121–23. This belief persisted for a long time. See also Sander L. Gilman, "Black Bodies, White Bodies: Toward an Iconography of Female Sexuality in Late Nineteenth-Century Art, Medicine, and Literature," in *"Race," Writing, and Difference*, ed. Henry Louis Gates Jr. (Chicago: University of Chicago Press, 1985–6), 223–61.

92. It is true that the freedom of many former slaves in metropolitan France and the colonies was short-lived; abolished in 1794, slavery was reimposed in the French colonies in 1802. See Susan Peabody, *There Are No Slaves in France* (New York: Oxford University Press, 1996).

93. See Hoffmann, *Nègre romantique*, 122–23; see also Ignacy Sachs, "L'image du noir dans l'art européen," *Annales: Économies, Sociétés, Civilisations* 24 (July–August 1969): 883–93. Sachs concludes: "As colonization and the slave trade expanded, the image of the Negro grew worse and became loaded with racial prejudice. The tradition that had never died—the Negro as symbol of the darker side—took on renewed life and certain stereotypes about the emotionality and sexuality of blacks, in opposition to European cerebralism, began a long and tenacious career, of which, alas, we have not yet seen the end" (891).

94. See Marilyn Yalom, *A History of the Breast* (New York: Alfred A. Knopf, 1997).

95. Hoffmann, *Nègre Romantique*, 63–65; see also Arlette Gautier, *Les soeurs de Solitude: La condition féminine dans l'esclavage aux Antilles du XVIIe au XIXe siècle* (Paris: Éditions Caribéennes, 1985), 205–7; Nicole Vanony-Frisch, "Les esclaves de la Guadeloupe à la fin de l'ancien régime d'après les sources notariales (1770–1789)," *Bulletin de la Société d'Histoire de la Guadeloupe*, nos. 63–64 (first and second quarters 1985): 89–98; and Guy Lasserre, *La Guadeloupe: Étude géographique* (Bordeaux: Union française d'impression, 1961), 1:291–303.

96. McCloy, *Negro in France*, 48, cited in note 2 above.

97. See Joseph Baillio, "Vie et oeuvre de Marie Victoire Lemoine (1754–1820)," *Gazette des Beaux Arts* 127 (April 1996): 125–64.

98. See *Portrait présumé de Madame de Genlis*, 1781, by Marie Victoire Lemoine, in ibid., 128, and figure 24, 147. When the portrait was painted, she was the governess of the children of the duke of Chartres.

See also *Jeune femme avec un chien*, c. 1796, by the same artist, ibid., 137, figure 15, 138, and 155–56. The latter is one of three paintings, none of which is signed or dated, that Baillio places around 1795 and states that they seem to form a family group. See also *Aspasie* (1794) by Marie Boulinar, in Mont-de-Marsan, Donjon Lacataye, *La femme artiste d'Élisabeth Vigée-LeBrun à Rosa Bonheur*, plate no. 8, 26.

99. See Simone Delesalle and Lucette Valensi, "Le mot 'nègre' dans les dictionnaires français d'ancien régime: Histoire et lexicographie," *Langue française* 15 (September 1972): 79–104; and Serge Daget, "Les mots esclave, nègre, noir et les jugements de valeur sur la traite négrière dans la littérature abolitioniste française de 1770 à 1845," *Revue française d'histoire d'outre-mer* 60, no. 221 (fourth quarter 1973): 511–48.

Although some evidence supports the view that the word *nègre*, and by extension *négresse*, always carried a pejorative connotation, the matter is quite complex. Whether both have the same history remains to be investigated.

100. Smalls, *Esclave, Nègre, Noir*, 94.

101. Sylvain Lavaissière, *Guide du visitéur: La peinture française* (Paris: Réunion des Musées nationaux, 1993), 121.

102. In his memoirs, Alexandre Lenoir recounts that David had taken a break from sketching the figures for his *Supplice des enfants de Brutus*, leaving in his studio the unfinished drawing of the head of a Roman girl. Marie-Guillemine came by, picked up a pencil, and completed it. Just as she was putting the final touches on the drawing, David walked in. He complimented her work but took a pencil and altered it slightly. Then he pointed out to her that she had made it a Greek when it was supposed to be a Roman. See Alexandre Lenoir, "Souvenirs historiques," *Journal de l'Institut historique* (9 December 1835), quoted in Ballot, *Une élève de David*, 49–53.

103. Robert Cornevin and Marianne Cornevin, *La France et les français outre-mer: De la première croisade à la fin du second empire* (Paris: Hachette, Éditions Pluriel, 1993).

Copies of the book were for sale at the annual meeting of the French Colonial Historical Society held in the Hôtel Fumé of the Université de Poitiers in June 1996, where one of the authors, Marianne Cornevin, was in attendance. When asked what had led to the selection of Benoist's painting for the cover, Cornevin expressed surprise and said she did not know why it had been chosen.

The edition published by Éditions Tallandier in 1990 had used on the cover a portrait of Colbert, the map of an island, and a detail of a painting that appears to represent the arrival of French explorers in the tropics.

104. Roger Little, ed., "Mme de Duras et *Ourika*," in *Ourika*, by Claire de Duras (Exeter, England: University of Exeter Press, 1993), 37–42.

105. Ibid., 34–42, 48–49.

106. Hoffmann, *Nègre romantique*, 125, quotes from J.-J. Virey, *Histoire naturelle du genre humain* (Paris: Crochard, 1824), 2:3–4: "[The shape of the Negroid nose] somewhat resembles that of the orang-utang. Everyone knows the kind of muzzle Negroes have, the wooly hair, the big lips so swollen, the large flattened nose, the receding chin, the round and bulging eyes, which distinguish them and which would be recognizable at first glance, even if they were as white as Europeans. Their forehead is low and rounded, their head narrow around the temples; their teeth slant outward."

107. On the dress see Baillio, "Vie et oeuvre"; see also Margaret A. Oppenheimer, "Nisa Villers, née Lemoine (1774–1821)," *Gazette des Beaux Arts* 127 (April 1996): 165–79. Especially on the ambiguity of the dress, see Sheriff, *Exceptional Woman*, 143–47.

108. See Little, *Ourika*, "Table des illustrations" and "Cahier iconographique," nos. 3 (reproduced here as figure 11), 7 (very similar to the one reproduced here as figure 12; both were engravings by Charles-Henri-Alfred Johannot after a painting by François Gérard done in 1823), and 8 (reproduced here as figure 13).

Figures 12 and 13 would have been better choices because both were produced as illustrations of the novel at the time it was published and therefore reflect the sensibilities of artists of the period. It is not clear when figure 11, owned by la Maréchale-Princesse de Beauvau, who reared Ourika, was produced. All could have been used unmutilated and still satisfied modesty. By the early 1820s, when *Ourika* was first published, the austerity of Davidian neoclassical portraits such as Benoist's *Négresse* was no longer in vogue in France. See, for example, Walter Friedlaender, *David to Delacroix*, trans. Robert Goldwater (Cambridge, Mass.: Harvard University Press, 1952). I spoke with the MLA editor in charge of the project, who said that the suggestion to use Benoist's *Portrait d'une négresse* on the cover of *Ourika* came from the author of one of the two introductions. The editor added that other illustrations had been considered, but that Benoist's painting was preferred. She also said that sometimes the most authentic illustrations do not make the best cover art. When I asked why the painting had been cropped, she responded that perhaps a bare-breasted black woman would not be considered appropriate.

Since Benoist painted a woman with one breast bare, the cover of the MLA edition of *Ourika* is to me a bowdlerized version of the original "text." It is surprising that the MLA and the scholars involved would have treated a picture with less concern for how it was produced or what it "said," how it mirrored the era in which it was produced, than they did the prose text. The intent may have been to raise the model from the servant class to the aristocracy, but the two bare shoulders defeat that purpose, as I explained earlier. The sanitized cover illustration may make it easier to avoid a discussion of Ourika's sexuality with students, one audience for the book although sexuality is one of the issues at the heart of the novel.

Hoffmann, *Nègre romantique*, 123, suggests that Puritanism made Anglo-Saxons more uncomfortable about sexuality, especially black-white sexual relations, than some other groups (by implication, the French). This cultural difference may in part explain why the version of Benoist's *Portrait d'une négresse* on the cover of the Cornevins' book, presumably intended for a Francophone audience, reveals the bare breast, while the version on the MLA edition of *Ourika*, presumably intended for readers in the United States, does not.

109. Knopf Guides, *The Louvre* (New York: Borzoi Books, Alfred A. Knopf, 1995), 230–31.

110. See Hoffman, *Nègre romantique*, 117–46.

111. See George Sussman, *Selling Mothers' Milk: The Wetnursing Business in France, 1715–1914* (Urbana: University of Illinois Press, 1982).

112. See Lesueur's gouache pictures of women in the French Revolution at the Musée du Carnavalet, the Musée de l'Histoire de la Ville de Paris.

The Politics of Space, the Poetics of Place: Africville, Africadia, and the African Diaspora in Canada

Raymond Familusi

Listen here, son. Did you think this were gonna work? Were you fool enough to think this were gonna work? They ain't gonna let us put nothing up like that and leave it. They don't intend to let us git it back. You ain't a place. Africville is us. When we go to git a job, what they ask us? Where we from . . . and if we say we from Africville, *we are Africville!* And we don't git no job. It ain't no place, son. . . . They took away the place. But it come'd round, though. Now that culture come'd round. They don't just go out there and find anybody to talk about Africville, they run find us, show us off—them that'll still talk, cause we Africville.

—*Fredrick Ward, "Dialogue #3: Old Man (to the Squatter)"*

W HEN FREDERICK WARD'S FICTIONAL OLD MAN DECLARES "WE ARE *Africville!*" he reveals a history of associations among place, people, and culture that plays a constitutive role in the social construction of "race," and blackness in Canada. Viewed a product of nature rather than culture, these associations provide signposts in the negotiation of social and cultural terrains.[1] Like the old man said, you "don't git no job" if you are from Africville; you "don't git no job" if you *are* Africville. There is more to settlement than residency: there is also identity. The historical association of black bodies with marginal places and social deprivation in Canada generally looms large in the contemporary struggle of black Nova Scotians for equity in a racialized social order.[2]

In 1930, Ida Cecil Greaves argued that being neither a public responsibility nor an economic menace, blacks in Canada have "remained an ignored minority."[3] In his 1971 comprehensive history *The Blacks in Canada*, Robin Winks concluded that despite three hundred years of settlement, blacks remain an alien presence on Canada's ethnic landscape[4]—like the Simmelian stranger "who comes today and stays tomorrow."[5] Anthropologist Frances Henry's 1973 published study of two black Nova Scotian communities is entitled "Forgotten Canadians."[6] Her 1994 study of the Caribbean diaspora in Toronto is subtitled "Learning to Live with Racism."[7] Mainstream ethnic studies in Canada, the discipline devoted to "difference," is largely silent on the place of race and the race of place in Canada's "ethnic landscape," at least before the post-1960 "arrival of visible minorities."[8] After "their" arrival it remains largely "preoccupied with 'absorptive capacity,' the ability of the country to adjust to the presence of 'the Other.'"[9]

"We are Africville and Preston. . . . / We are here and not here, / We are gone but never leave," laments Maxine Tynes in her 1990 poem "Black Song Nova Scotia," which ends with the repeated lines: "We are here, We are here, We are here."[10] In the context of African Nova Scotian history, remarked George Elliott Clarke, "that line is important because we constantly have the feeling that 'We aren't here. We aren't here. We aren't here.' in terms of the larger society."[11] "We have been erased," argued Esmeralda Thornhill, "and with erasure goes any consciousness of our daily experience of racism."[12] Any study of the black experience in Canada that seeks to explore the struggles engaged and the resistances enacted is confronted by erasures, absences, and silences, which like the margins of this page provide the structure of a narrative already in place.[13]

In a 1969 House of Commons debate, former Prime Minister Pierre Elliot Trudeau argued that "There have been some aspects of Canadian life which we have felt more than seen. Of these, the most evident and undoubtably the most important, is the spirit of tolerance and goodwill that is an invaluable Canadian characteristic. Canadians take for granted what so many persons elsewhere seek and envy: human relationships that, by the large, accept without question difference in colour or origin or language." These sentiments were codified in 1971 with the introduction of an official multicultural policy identifying ethnic diversity as a public good to be supported and encouraged institutionally. Black and other "visible minorities" (in the language of the state) were to be acknowledged as full fledged (cultural) members of Canadian society. Beyond debates over the underlying political motivations of the federal Liberal Party's embrace of ethnic pluralism at this time, state-sponsored multiculturalism has certainly had for many the salutary effect of enhancing Canada's image at home and abroad as a place of tolerance.

Whatever may be argued in theory regarding the virtues of multiculturalism as a national ideal, in practice the identification of tolerance as a characteristic of some deeply felt core Canadian identity infects it with considerable ambivalence for those who are today "tolerated." Certainly the 1971 introduction of a national multicultural policy, following as it did the lifting of racially restrictive immigration policies in the 1960s, marked a definitive or at least significant break with a history of efforts to construct a national identity rooted in white settler notions of superior northern (European) culture purportedly uniquely suited to Canada's northern geography. However, continuity with these efforts remains evident in the projection of tolerance as an ineffable 'Canadian' characteristic. While "multiculturalism" embraces a plurality of racially and ethnically defined cultural groupings, "tolerance" rather ironically reinscribes a White/Other, subject/object dichotomy in its celebration of the agents of tolerance.

Thus, on the one hand, multiculturalism as national discourse serves ideologically to mask a history of violence and repression dating back to the founding of the Dominion of Canada and beyond to the colonization of First Nation lands and the institutions of slavery. Multiculturalism as the official regulatory domain of "difference," deflects attention from this history of struggle and resistance, repression and accommodation which paved the path by which yesterday's unwanted have become today's tolerated. On the other hand, as a "political discourse relying on a language of culture and ideological constructions of ethnicized and racialized communities," multiculturalism "had or has the merit of deflecting critical attention from a constantly racializing Canadian political economy." Therefore, while African Canadians are no longer the "ignored minority" written of by Ida Greeves in 1930, they remain subject to a well-documented array of structural roots in Canadian society have been at best obscured, at worse "erased." Thus, the old man's reference to "culture come'd round" with the razing, the erasure of Africville as a physical community offers a metaphor for the construction of Canada's "house of difference."

Focusing on black settlement as an artifact of the Canadian nation imagines as a white community, the first part of this chapter provides a schematic overview of the history of black settlement in Nova Scotia, the founding and then razing of Africville, and the social and political climate in Canada surrounding the nineteenth century settlement of blacks. I then look more closely at the relationship between settlement space, race, and (national)identity in a review of two articles published in nationally distributed Anglophone publications. Each was published at a time of heightened national tension over the prospect of black immigration to Canada. In the period of approximately 1910 to 1913, African American homesteaders again looked to the North Star to escape Jim Crow and settle in western Canada. Except for a small number, their efforts were largely thwarted by a concerted if somewhat covert campaign by Canadian officials to restrict the entry of black Americans. In the late 1960's, on the other hand, the opening of Canadian immigration to non-Europeans generated a different set of public fears as government agencies acted to forestall the movement of "radical" and "subversive" blacks into Canada due to the concern they would cause 'trouble' in Canada's black "urban slums." Each article, with important differences, cites black settlements in Nova Scotia as exemplary examples of the type of settlement and people deemed undesirable to "Canadians."

The remainder of the chapter returns to the theme of culture "come'd round" but in a second sense employed by Ward's old man; that is, culture as the product of a "people" in defiance of efforts to erase their history of struggle and survival from the annals of the land. This is the story of and Africville 'reborn' as it is reimagined by black Nova Scotians which occurred in parallel with the emergence in the 1960s of a more secular oriented oppositional politics of place and identity.[14] The chapter concludes with a critical look at the "myth" of Africville in relation to what might be described as the quest for an 'authentic' blackness both rooted and rootless in Nova Scotia.

AFRICVILLE AND BLACK SETTLEMENT IN NOVA SCOTIA

Referred to intermittently by white settlers as "African Village" in the late nineteenth century, the contraction "Africville" was in general use by the twentieth century. The widely accepted but contested view is that Africville was established sometime before 1840 on the northern boundaries of the British naval garrison of Halifax, on the east coast of Canada, by former black refugees who were escaping poverty and starvation in surrounding communities.[15] They called their settlement Campbell Road, after the dirt street that ran through it, and sometimes Seaview, which referred to its idyllic location on the edge of Bedford Basin.[16]

However, from about the 1850s Africville was increasingly less than idyllic. Industries and institutions not wanted in white communities were placed there: Rockhead Prison, "night soil" disposal pits, an infectious diseases hospital, a bone-mill plant, a tar factory, a foundry, two slaughterhouses, a cotton factory, and so on. By the end of World War II, the settlement was more urban than rural and more industrial than residential. Still, it had its own neighborhood stores, a segregated school almost sixty years old, midwives and war veterans, the Seaview African United Baptist Church (established in 1916), a distinctive sense of itself as a community, and a post office with an address: Africville, Nova Scotia, Canada.[17]

By 1959, after decades of targeted neglect, a survey found that Africville had no access to recreational facilities and inadequate fire and police protection.[18] Its sole source of drinking water ran dry in the summer and was polluted by sewage, although three Halifax sewer lines ran beneath the community.[19] Numerous petitions to the city from the middle of the nineteenth century onward to extend sewer, water, and electrical services were refused or ignored, and the consistent disregard of residents' rights to welfare and social services "was obviously punitive."[20] No residents had attended university, and less than 1 percent had attended high school. One-third of the employed residents earned less than $1,000 a year, and less than 1 percent earned more than $4,000 a year. Income was directly related to the types of jobs available to residents, who provided a pool of semi- and unskilled labor for surrounding urban communities. These jobs were primarily service oriented or seasonal or both and generally involved work as porters, kitchen help, maids, maintenance workers, and general laborers.[21]

In the early 1960s, poised on the brink of demolition in a citywide redevelopment scheme, Africville "had not only a common geographical reference, but a widely shared connotation as a deviant slum community."[22] The church remained, attended by families who could trace their lineage to Africville's founding and who continued to struggle for the community's survival. But many who could leave did so, while others with nowhere else to go began occupying the community's margins. Africville's reputation as a site of deviance had grown slowly since the end of World War II. It now had a reputation amongst both blacks and whites: "Blacks elsewhere in Halifax advised their children not to go near the community; middle-class whites advised their friends that Africville was an interesting but dangerous place to visit."[23] The reality was far more complex, but this was dwarfed by Africville's reputation and image.

By 1968, all that remained of the "slum by the dump" placed there by the city of Halifax in the 1950s were a few bulldozers leveling the ground upon which once stood Africville's social and symbolic center, the Seaview African United Baptist Church. Africville comprised only about 10 percent of those relocated in Halifax during this period (at the height of redevelopment, about two hundred families per month were moved to outlying areas of the city or into public housing),[24] but it emerged as the most notorious of urban redevelopment schemes that targeted working-class neighborhoods in the city and across the country in the 1960s and 1970s.

The approximately four hundred predominantly black indigent or working-class residents of Africville were dispersed, with a few exceptions, to other areas of the city.[25] Many, whose possessions were transported by municipal dump trucks, were settled in public housing in the North End, an adjacent "black district" in Halifax.[26] Almost one-quarter of former residents were assigned to city-owned temporary housing and forced to relocate, in some cases as many as three more times before being allowed to settle permanently.[27] Today, the former site of Africville is occupied by Seaview Park, little used and windswept, crowded by a container port to the west and a bridge access road to the east.

Africville was one of a number of what are sometimes called "old line" or "old growth" black settlements in Nova Scotia established in the eighteenth and nineteenth centuries. These settlements were primarily the product of two group migrations enticed north from the United States by the British promise of land and emancipation. Black loyalists during the American Revolution were the first significant influx of free blacks to British North America, most of whom went to Nova Scotia. Despite British promises, when the first group arrived in 1782–83, "they found that neither land nor provisions were ready for them."[28] This experience would prove paradigmatic, and the majority of the black loyalists departed for West Africa in 1792, where they joined other African "returnees" in founding Freetown. The lands they had occupied in Nova Scotia were permanently resettled by a second wave of migration, the "black refugees" from the War of 1812.[29]

The War of 1812 between the United States and Great Britain brought prosperity to Nova Scotia and high demand for the labor of blacks in the colony, but by 1816 the economy was very weak following the end of the war and the colony was beset by widespread crop failures. Restricted to parcels of marginal land with poor soil at the best of times, black settlers in many cases suffered near-starvation as well as the hostility of whites who no longer needed their labor. These settlers were marginalized people occupying marginal spaces,[30] and in 1830 H. C. Hart succinctly and starkly describes a black settlement in Guysborough County: "They had their quarters on the hill . . . called 'Niggertown Hill.' They suffered severely from famine and many died from want."[31] In the words of Beckles Willson, refugee blacks who joined the British cause were privileged "to enjoy the comforts of political freedom and physical starvation under the British flag in Nova Scotia."[32]

Several factors shaped the course of black settlement in Nova Scotia: (1) the poor quality and inadequate amount of land granted to blacks;[33] (2) racism and segregation, which isolated black communities and cut them off from governmental and local assistance provided whites;[34] (3) black dependency for economic survival on hostile white settlements, which simultaneously sought to maintain and criticized their dependency; and (4) receipt of only licenses of occupation from 1815 to 1842, rather than the outright land grants provided white settlers.[35] For twenty-five years blacks were therefore unable to move "without abandoning their investment."[36] They also refused to be moved under the terms offered by the British. They refused to be relocated to Trinidad, for fear of reenslavement, and they refused to be redistributed in small groups around the province, for fear of greater exploitation by whites.

With the Emancipation Proclamation of 1863 by the U.S. government, the welcome for fugitive blacks in British North America "vanished with the cause in which it originated"—abolition.[37] The northward flow associated with the Underground Railway, primarily into central Canada, reversed course, and thousands of free and fugitive blacks returned to the U.S. Nova Scotia again became the main area of black settlement in British North America.

In 1867, the British North America Act established the Dominion of Canada with the political unification of Lower and Upper Canada (present-day Ontario and Quebec), New Brunswick, and Nova Scotia. Canada was intended to be not "just similar to but actually a British society"—socially, politically, and demographically.[38] Those of non-British descent would be restricted from entering, in part subject to the demands of the labor market. Non-Europeans already in the country "would not be accorded a 'proprietary' interest in the new Dominion" and would remain, through the judicious management of social policy, sufficiently small in number as to draw little attention to their status as permanent aliens.[39] The informal and effective "White Canada" policy served this purpose, defining a hierarchy of preferred racial groups for immigration, until the late 1950s, "a strict hierarchy of preferred racial groups for immigration."[40] The place of "Africans" in this hierarchy is made clear in a 1909 correspondence between members of the Federal Immigration Branch: "There are certain countries . . . and certain races of people considered as suited to this country and its conditions, but Africans, no matter where they come from are not among the races sought, and hence, Africans no matter what country they come from are in common with other uninvited races, not admitted to Canada."[41]

Confronted in the early 1900s by the prospect of group migration by African American homesteaders threatened by the introduction of Jim Crow legislation in Oklahoma, the Canadian government moved to block their entry. Conducting research on American immigration in the National Archives of Canada, David Harvey observes: "Hundreds of American blacks wrote Ottawa between 1910 and 1913, inquiring about opportunities in the West and attitudes toward their immigration and settlement. Most letters were from Oklahomans, semi-literate, on lined paper, pathetically optimistic and referring to those of their race who had 'followed the North Star' to find freedom 'between the lion's paws.' The response they received was a chilling form letter referring to climate."[42]

Climatic suitability, the idea of an inherent relationship between race and environment, provided a "scientific" explanation for barring non-European immigrants by the Canadian state. It was the foundational ideology of a northern white settler nationalism that found its earliest expression in the writings of the Canada First movement in the late 1800s.[43] Eva Mackey writes of Canadian nationalists from the colonial period up to the 1950s: "One of the most persistent benefits articulated about Canada was that, unlike the United States, its northern climate would keep the country 'uncontaminated' by weaker southern races." Canada's climate provided "'a fundamental political and social advantage . . . over the United States,' because it resulted in a 'persistent process of natural selection.'" It would ensure that Canada "would avoid the 'Negro problem,' a problem 'which weighs like a troublesome nightmare upon the civilization of the United States' (in Berger 1970: 131). Canada . . . would [instead] be a nation of the 'sturdy races' of the North (in Berger 1966: 8–9)."[44]

By the 1860s the dual emplacement of African Nova Scotians—geographically on the margins of white settlements and metaphorically on the margins of Canadian society—was established and remained essentially unchanged for the next one hundred years. From the beginning this constituted the landscape within which blacks in Canada were imagined by whites.

BLACKS IN THE WHITE IMAGINATION

Maclean's Magazine, 1911: *Blacks and the Border Within*

In a 1911 edition of *Maclean's,* when Canadian fears about African American migration to western Canada were at their height,[45] columnist Britton Cooke offered two reasons "the colored man . . . should be checked" at the border: "first that the colored man is nine times out of ten unsuited to the development of the highest sort of citizenship in Canada, that his sense of humor and predisposition to a life of ease render his presence undesirable in Canadian cities . . . and is liable to cause race troubles; and secondly, that he cannot be assimilated as can the white races, and if he is assimilated, he must leave a tinge of the colored blood in the *Ultimate* Canadian Race—a race which should be bred from the best "stock" that can be found in the world."[46]

In support of this argument, twelve photographs, purportedly taken in the southern United States, accompanied Cooke's article. They offer typology of "Negro" characteristics and the environments within which "Negroes" reside to provide the reader with an unambiguous assessment of the worth or lack thereof of potential black immigrants to Canada. The image of a "characteristic" family group, for example, directs the reader to observe not only the "stalwart" individuals but the large size ("numbers") of the family and the poor condition of "the array." The threat implied in the attention drawn to the family's size would be readily grasped by the magazine's readership.[47] On the other hand, the 105-year-old man referred to as "Old Uncle Jo" is described as the "good type of negro": industrious, hardworking, and still on duty despite his advanced years. The age of Uncle Jo is not insignificant. Taken in the context of the other images offered and the discussion of immorality and degeneration in "typical" black communities, it suggests "good negroes" born before the Emancipation Proclamation are of an era that is coming to an end. It is the younger generations of blacks seeking to settle on the Canadian prairies that constitute a concern for maintaining Canada's racial "stock."[48]

The two photographs of purportedly southern U.S. black dwellings that are presented in the conclusion of Cooke's article offer two sets of contrasting images linking race with place and Nova Scotia with the southern United States. The first contrast is between a "sunny" southern environment with its "happy-go-lucky" way of life as the "natural" environment of blacks, and the northern climate of a "cold country" as the "natural" environment of northern Europeans. Embedded in this contrast is the central premise of the idea of climatic suitability: environmental determinism. The moral character of people is determined by their "genetic" or "racial" inheritance, which is determined by their environmental origins.

The second contrast distinguishes the image of "The Nigger Quarter!" with the "Negro Quarter" Cooke describes in Nova Scotia, and both with the image of "A Home in Sunny Land." While the "*Negro* Quarter" in Nova Scotia is "the abode of little more than innocent shiftlessness," the "*Nigger* Quarter" provides a concrete example of how such places are susceptible "to the breeding of vice and crime."[49] The image of "A Home in Sunny Land" points to the American south as the natural environment of blacks ("happy-go-lucky") and suggests the dangers of blacks settling in a more "demanding" and thus unsuitable climate. Cooke, with particular reference to Booker T. Washington, notes: "Persons of fair mind cannot fail to admit that there are good citizens [in the United States] whose skin is dark."[50] However, this observation merely strengthens his argument to exclude blacks from Canada, as evidently some can progress if left in their "natural" environment.

The distinction between "good" and "bad" Negroes is important to Cooke's argument, which is threefold. First, 1911 is not 1850, when blacks were threatened by slavery; because they are now able to "progress" in the United States, Canadians are not morally obligated to accept them. Second, Canadians should be proud of their history of tolerance, as shown by the story of the Underground Railway, and an effort to exclude blacks should not be read as contradicting this fact. Third, Canada's climate is incompatible with the progress of blacks, whether "good" or "bad." Thus, not only should Canadians restrict blacks to a southern environment for their own good, but also, given the "breeding of vice and crime" to which a black settlement inevitably will succumb, black immigration must be restricted for the protection of white Canadians and the national goal of an "ultimate race."

Cooke seeks to avoid any implications of racial prejudice by emphasizing the Underground Railway as evidence of Canadian tolerance. Canada was "a place of refuge for these people in the days of slavery, and . . . many a poor beaten black man, or heart-broken negress found safety on Canadian soil."[51] Such an approach, which both highlights the acceptance of fugitive slaves before 1860 and rationalizes the exclusion of blacks thereafter, selectively appropriates the history of black Canadian settlement in the service of a white Canadian nationalism. As Afua Cooper notes, "Canada . . . styled itself as a haven for the oppressed, those Blacks who had fled the United States because of slavery and virulent racism."[52] This is illustrated by the near mythic place of the Underground Railway in Canadian history—an event that Walker reports is more familiar to Canadian high school students than the name of the first prime minister of Canada.[53] This affirmative acknowledgment, however, rests on an "erasure" of black Canadian experiences.[54] What is erased is that "on coming to Canada, many Blacks found that the only difference between the new country and the old was that in the new country the law protected ex-fugitives from re-enslavement."[55] The hopes of the first generation of black settlers proved illusory, wrote Greaves in 1930: "The most to which the Negroes of to-day can look forward is to re-cross the border over which their ancestors came so hopefully, the path to Canadian freedom has proved a cul-de-sac."[56]

Whereas the saga of the Underground Railway resonates with the "dramatic force" of black liberation in the historical narratives of the United States,[57] in Canada it appears as its fulfillment, that is, the end of history for black Canadians. The story of the mid-nineteenth-century escape toward the North Star by African Americans fleeing "northern racism and southern slavery"[58] is the path by which blacks simultaneously enter and exit Canadian history. The figure of the fugitive slave representative of the Underground Railway (for example, in the celebrated Canadian Heritage Minute series)[59] straddles the line drawn between the "tolerant" nation of the north and its "violent" alter ego to the south.[60] Black Canadians are written into the conflicted narratives of Canadian identity, but as the artifacts of competing white nationalisms. Cooke's "Negro Quarter" in Nova Scotia is the border within, imagined by white Canadians as that which the nation is not: the place where Negroes reside.

The Globe and Mail, 1969: *Blacks Are in but Not of the Nation*

With the emergence of "black" as a cultural and political category in the early 1960s, "subversive" and "extremist" blacks became the object of scrutiny in Canada. Journalists warned of impending violence and directed their readers to look south of the border for a portent of things to come. The Security Service arm of the Royal Canadian Mounted Police (RCMP), which has federal law enforcement responsibilities, mobilized in response. "Having become more conscious of their black identity, the danger is that Canadian blacks of nationalist persuasion will become more tuned in on themselves and become more willing to protest," reported an internal RCMP Security Service document.[61] Informants were hired, and "countering activities" were pursued.[62] In a campaign targeting "black nationalists,"[63] in cooperation with Canadian immigration officials as well as intelligence and law enforcement communities in the United States,[64] the RCMP monitored and sought to restrict the movement into Canada of "suspicious" blacks from the United States and elsewhere. In some cases, they collaborated with immigration officials to deport individuals without regard to due process.[65] At the same time, faced by pressing labor needs, in an international political climate sensitive to the issue of racism and a national confederation threatened by a revitalized French ethno-nationalism, Canadian immigration policies were revised in 1965 to allow the entry of substantial numbers of non-Europeans.

It was in this context that the *Toronto Globe and Mail* published a special issue in 1969 entitled "The Blacks of Canada." Substantial space was devoted to Nova Scotia, the radicalization of the indigenous black population, and what were now described as "black slums" rather than "Negro quarters."[66]

Accompanying the issue was an editorial entitled "Not Necessarily Inevitable":

Is the Canadian mosaic, in a small but somehow dramatic way, taking on a faint black hue? . . . There are about 60,000 Negroes in Canada—double the number of 10 years ago. . . . And from the remnants of Africville in Halifax to the relatively calm and contented descendants of immigrant slaves in Southwestern Ontario, the question almost inevitably arises. When? As if the currents from the South were simply too powerful to resist—swirling floodwaters against a frail border-dike—many anticipate a Canadian Watts or a Toronto Harlem with each nervous glance at the deliberately meager immigration statistics.[67]

If the introductory paragraphs are alarmist, the closing paragraphs offer reassurance:

Candid . . . would be the admission that most of the blacks in Canada, from the West Indies, Africa, Britain and the United States, are better-educated and more self-sufficient than, say, a cross section of U.S. Negroes.

This alone presupposes a different racial situation than in the United States. Our children will not meet the heritage of oppression that goes back to the days of slavery. And because immigrants to Canada are selected for certain skills and educational standards, they will be more articulate and ready to react to injustices.

Unlike 1911, "good" blacks are now acceptable immigrants to Canada, that is, properly screened and not representative of that cross-section of U.S. Negroes whose characteristic environment is evident in the "black slums" of Nova Scotia. With Africville recently demolished, and with attention drawn to the condition of Beechville, among other black Nova Scotian settlements, the *Globe and Mail* readership is assured that Canada's "Negro problem" is being addressed effectively.[68] The reference to "the relatively calm and contented descendants of immigrant slaves in Southwestern Ontario" simultaneously identifies Canada, and specifically Ontario, as the tolerant terminus of the Underground Railway, while emphasizing the alien quality of this black population.[69] They are alien even though their communities predate Canada's founding as a nation-state. As the "descendants of immigrant slaves," they continue to be imagined as an "American" body occupying a "Canadian" space. They may reside within the nation, but they are not of it.

The Case of Africville and Its Re-imagination

Stuart Hall writes about the emergence of "black" as a political category in Great Britain in the 1970s, of "the search for roots [in which] one began to speak the language of that which is home in the genuine sense."[70] He draws attention to the significance of the interrelationship of place and identity in the struggle of subaltern groups to construct an identity and a politics that speaks from the "margins." This was an "enormous act of . . . imaginary political re-identification, re-territorialization and re-identification, without which a counter-politics could not have been constructed."[71] Just such a process occurred in Nova Scotia, where by 1969, "Africville was more than a designation on the city's old maps, . . . it was a word to which militant black Nova Scotians now rallied."[72]

Despite calls from across the country going back more than a decade to remove this "blight" and "blot" upon Canada's international image, the congratulatory atmosphere following Africville's demolition soon began to dissipate. The demolition metamorphosed from a triumph of social welfare liberalism into a symbol of a racist social order that black activists and their allies publicly decried. Liberal social reformers depicted the razing as an act of compassion for a downtrodden community, but critics pointed to the Machiavellian maneuvers by city officials in their efforts to force people to relocate, the raft of promises that were not kept, and the desire by the city of Halifax to obtain valuable land on an increasingly crowded peninsula.[73]

In a striking example of a counterdiscourse, Africville was resurrected from its status as a "neighborhood of exile"[74]—"a 'dumping ground' for poor people, downwardly mobile working-class households and marginal groups and individuals"—to a community of deep moral worth (*gemeinschaft*) deemed lost to the machinations of city politics, institutional dominance, and racism.[75] The historical articulation of place and identity in the racialized construction of blacks in Nova Scotia (and Canada generally) was challenged with the symbolic recuperation of a black urban settlement stigmatized by both blacks and whites as a "shack town," "ghetto," "slum," and "deviance service center." Against the representation of black settlements as static islands of economic dependency and moral decline, their inherent value was asserted by black Nova Scotians, which provided a symbolic call to arms to similarly threatened communities that remains relevant to this day.[76]

Black organizations that either failed to intercede on behalf of Africville or collaborated in its removal were criticized for being too moderate or accommodationist.[77] The arrival of members of the Black Panther Party in 1968 at the invitation of black activists not only crystallized the distance between Nova Scotia's "traditional" church and urban-based black leadership and its younger, secular challengers but also provoked "indignation and even fury" among white Nova Scotians. By 1970, the inauguration of a provincewide organization by and for black Nova Scotians occurred when the Black United Front (BUF) was founded.[78]

George Elliott Clarke points to the razing of Africville and the creation of BUF as the emergence of "Nova Scotia's own Black Consciousness Movement." He argues that at this moment an African–Nova Scotian nationalism rooted in religion and culture became an "Africadian" neonationalism rooted in socioeconomic analysis of "the people."[79] *Africadia* is the term Clarke uses to reimagine black settlement in Nova Scotia and, by extension, Canada along the lateral axes of the African diaspora through the "re-membering of a dismembered" Africville.[80] According to Clarke, "Africadians remember Africville because this lost place represented our innocence," the innocence of "local cultures . . . rooted in rural and conservative religious traditions," as against "the incursions of technological, liberal capitalism, the most dynamic and vulgarly progressive ideology of our common era."[81] Using Africville as an allegory of black community, Africadia reclaims black settlement from the wastelands of Canada's racial geography and is the means by which black Nova Scotians are rerepresented within the complex intertwining of the local and the global.[82]

Clarke describes black settlement in Canada as "an *archipelago* of blackness."[83] He thinks through the heterogeneity of black passages to posit an overarching national identification (*African Canadianité*) that embraces supranational tensions, distinctions, and experiences.[84] He also opens space for the indigenization of particular black experiences, laying claim to the nation by emphasizing *spora* through *dia,* the seeding of dispersed peoples within Canada, giving rise to new-old identifications. Thus Africadia offers "not a model, but a *modal* 'blackness.'"[85] That is, Africadia is one of a number of different articulations of blackness in Canada: interrelated and overlapping but distinct.

As an avowedly cultural nationalist project, Clarke's Africadia asserts a distinctive place for black Nova Scotians in Canada. First, it offers a response to the unprecedented streams of black immigration since 1965 that shifted the demographic balance (and cultural and political influence) of the black population from the east coast to central Canada (specifically Toronto). Second, to use Paul Gilroy's critique, Africadia is a response continentally to an African *Americanism* viewed by some as an ethnic absolutism that seeks hegemonic play in the location of an authentic "blackness" within the domain of U.S. black culture.[86] Finally, globally Africadia offers a response to transnational, diasporic constructions of black social, cultural, and political praxes, which appear to recenter rather than decenter claims to national authenticity, as in Gilroy's much-celebrated notion of a "Black Atlantic."[87]

More than thirty years after its demolition, Africville is celebrated nationally in songs, poetry, plays, movies, jazz albums, CD-ROMs, museum exhibits, web pages, and even by the federal government for its "community heritage."[88] The city of Halifax has erected a memorial on the former site, Seaview Park, on which the names of the founding families are engraved. But the iconic rise of Africville has occurred in tandem with the dramatic demise of the post-1968 black organizations. The militant Afro-Canadian Liberation Movement (ACLM) vanished almost as quickly as it appeared. The doors of the Black United Front were closed in 1995. Even the progressive potential of what some have called Nova Scotia's "black renaissance" appears largely blunted. There is no black independent political organization with a provincial scope in Nova Scotia today.

Meanwhile, former residents of Africville continue to struggle for various forms of compensation, restitution, and (more controversially) reparation for their dislocation.[89] The historic lands and community integrity of once isolated black settlements are threatened by white suburbs and private capital.[90] The largely illusory fear of organized violence by blacks in the 1970s was replaced by the reality of spontaneous eruptions in 1989, 1991, 1996, and 1997.[91] The violence—ranging from school yard fights between hundreds of black and white students to an attack on a convoy of police vehicles occupying a black community—has drawn national attention to so-called race relations problems in Nova Scotia.[92]

To add to the complexity, a new black Nova Scotian professional class and fledgling middle class have made breakthroughs in terms of political representation and institutional change. In some cases the change is unprecedented continentally—such as the legislation of designated seats on public school boards for African Canadians.

CONCLUSION

Clarke's notion of Africadia can be a discursive strategy to subvert the dominant discourse by unmasking practices of white exclusivity embedded within the ideology of multiculturalism as it is practiced today.[93] Clarke's effort recharts the nation's racial geography, through an appropriation of Africville's history in the linking of culture, people, and land broadly consistent with Canada's historical concern with ethnic congruity, albeit in an atmosphere sensitive to nonwhite demographics.[94] This appropriation, however, raises troubling questions regarding the political efficacy of an Africadia erected upon the rubble of Africville. On the one hand, Africville as an "imagined community" represents a counterhegemonic narrative of a unitary black experience in Nova Scotia. It reveals and critiques the structures of racism that shaped the social domains of black life. On the other hand, such a strategy conceals and erases the heterogeneity and particularity of lived experiences.

In her incisive analysis of the construction of Africville as an imagined community in black Nova Scotian literature, Maureen Moynagh points to how social differences are ignored to reveal "the power relations and technologies of violence at play in the [Canadian] nationalist imaginings" while simultaneously resisting "the conventional homogeneity of imagined communities through a foreground of the competition over the way a community is imagined."[95] In other words, difference is reinserted into the imagining of Africville with the revelation that there are contested views of it as a community. Moynagh argues that this alternative homogeneity papers over class divides and urban-rural splits, but to the extent that "this unity is scripted as a political strategy in response to disenfranchisement, exclusion, and dispossession, it simultaneously refuses to become fixed as an identity."[96]

At issue is whether a political strategy of cultural representation is equivalent to a cultural strategy of political intervention. Clearly, it is not. A politics of representation that not only identifies but also resists "the structural racism that produces and destroys Africvilles" can speak but not act without a politics of collective action.[97] The slogan Remember Africville, a rallying cry in the resistance of black Nova Scotians to the specific incursions of (white) political and economic elites over the last three decades, highlights the strategic potential of linking the cultural and the political. However, it is in the conflicted and contradictory daily experiences of black Nova Scotians as they seek to create and maintain a politics of collective action (that also defines a collective culture) that such a strategy is defined. This is important to acknowledge in order to resist not only a slide into a kind of romantic or nostalgic reconstruction of Africville as the expression of a universal black Nova Scotian experience but also the appropriation of Africville as an imagined community by the very hegemonic nationalist and racialist discourses an Africville reimagined by African Nova Scotians seeks to resist.

A 1998 federal government "Backgrounder" on Africville, published by Parks Canada, is an example:

> It was only after [Africville's residents were] settled elsewhere that they realized they had lost the heart of their community life. . . . Inspired by the American Black Power movement, community leaders called for action. Community members spoke out against the injustice that had been committed against them, and they took pride in themselves, in Black communities and their traditions. . . .
>
> The site where Africville was located is now a deserted park, but the spirit of Africville lives on. It has become the rallying point for Nova Scotia's Black community, and an impetus for Black people all over North America to fight racism—a symbol of the link between social well being and community heritage.[98]

Neither the tenuous place of Nova Scotia's fledgling black middle class nor the generations living in impoverished urban and rural neighborhoods are captured by the state's multicultural embrace of Africville's "spirit." The material divide between "community heritage" and "social well being" is evident in the persistent high levels of unemployment in black communities, the ongoing struggle to protect community lands from dump sites and urban expansion, the continued struggle to obtain equitable access to education facilities, and the pervasive role of federal and provincial government institutions in shaping the scope and expression of black community aspirations.[99]

With its postdemolition status as "mythico-history,"[100] "allegory,"[101] and "metaphor,"[102] the Africville erased is the Africville embraced. It is the absence of black community, rather than the presence of the lived experience of contemporary black Nova Scotians, whose "spirit" is celebrated. While black Nova Scotians continue to struggle for social justice, in the political void left by BUF's demise the myth of Africville is vulnerable to co-optation by "the 'real' and 'true' Canadians," the dominant political community, as long as it is isolated from the political praxis.

Michael Echeruo writes that the first liability of a counterdiscourse is that it "must begin with a premise from the primary discourse."[103] What is required for an African Canadianism, an Africadianism, is an identity that is as authentic as the terms of the dominant political community in Canada demand. In this respect, Clarke's representation of historically rooted rural and antimodern black settlements as the authentic core of an Africadian (black Nova Scotian) identity meets the demands for an essentialist, bounded, historical object consistent with the project of Canadian nation-building. But to what end? Clarke's quest for a "primordial ethnic specificity" in the form of Africadia contests the content but not the terms by which ontological authenticity is overdetermined within the Canadian national formation.[104] As Mackey cogently argues, "the Project of Canadian nation-building has not been based on the erasure of difference but on controlling and managing it. Difference is allowed—in defined and carefully limited ways—as long as the project of Canadian nation-building comes first. In this structure of difference and Canadianness, those defined as the 'real' and 'true' Canadians are the ones who define the appropriate limits of difference."[105]

Masked by the construction Africadia are the conflicting and contradictory tendencies inherent in the idea of an overarching black identity as a lived experience in Nova Scotia. If the demolition of Africville was required for the reimagination of black Nova Scotians, as Clarke implies, then arguably the demolition erased the contradictory and conflicted relations within and between black communities that is the domain of contemporary cultural and political struggle. Again, it is the absence of Africville rather than the presence of the lived experience of contemporary black Nova Scotians that sutures internal difference. It is important to ask why Africville and not "Little Preston" in Dartmouth, or the racialized housing projects of Mulgrave Park or Uniacke Square in the North End of Halifax, or the black communities of North and East Preston, or the southwestern black communities of Nova Scotia provides the representational grounds upon which a distinctive black Nova Scotianness is expressed.

The danger is that a mythical Africville has no place for those who no longer have claims to historically black lands, who reside in housing projects, impoverished urban neighborhoods, and racialized inner cities in Halifax and beyond. Ironically, this includes the former residents and descendants of the community of Africville. Like the old man said: "It ain't no place, son . . . cause we Africville."

NOTES

1. James Ferguson and Akhil Gupta, "Culture, Power, Place: Ethnography at the End of an Era," in *Culture, Power, Place: Explorations in Critical Anthropology*, ed. James Ferguson and Akhil Gupta (Durham: Duke University Press, 1997), 4.

2. The disputed boundary between the black community of East Preston and the new, predominantly white suburb of Lake Major is a particularly poignant example. Brian Hayes, "Communities at Odds over Boundary," *Halifax Mail-Star*, 6 February 1997, A1; Chris Lambie, "Residents Disagree over Role of Racism in Boundary Dispute," *Halifax Daily News*, 7 February 1997.

3. Ida Cecil Greaves, *The Negro in Canada*, vol. 16, *Mcgill University Economic Studies: National Problems of Canada* (Orillia, Ontario: Packet-Times Press for the Department of Economics and Political Science, McGill University, 1930), 75.

4. Robin W. Winks, *The Blacks in Canada: A History*, 2d ed. (Montreal: McGill-Queen's University Press, 1997), 476—83.

5. Aleksandra Llund, "The Stranger: Ethnicity, Identity and Belonging," in *The Future of the Nation State: Essays on Cultural Pluralism and Political Integration*, ed. Sverker Gustavsson and Leif Lewin (New York: Routledge, Nerenius and Santérus, 1996), 84.

6. Henry Frances, *Forgotten Canadian: The Blacks of Nova Scotia*. Don Mills, Ontario: Longman Canada Limited, 1973.

7. Frances Henry, *The Caribbean Diaspora in Toronto: Learning to Live with Racism* (Toronto: University of Toronto Press, 1994).

8. Alan B. Anderson and James S. Frideres, "Explaining Canada's Ethnic Landscape: A Theoretical Model," in *Perspectives on Ethnicity in Canada: A Reader*, ed. Warren E. Kalbach and Madeline A. Kalbach (Montreal: Harcourt Canada, 2000), 7.

9. Elliot L. Tepper, "Immigration Policy and Multiculturalism," in *Ethnicity and Culture in Canada: The Research Landscape*, ed. John W. Berry and J. A. Laponce (Toronto: University of Toronto Press, 1994), 103.

10. Maxine Tynes, "Black Song Nova Scotia," in *Fire on the Water: An Anthology of Black Nova Scotian Writing*, ed. George Elliot Clarke (Lawrencetown Beach, Nova Scotia: Pottersfield Press, 1991), 74.

11. Maureen Moynagh, "Mapping Africadia's Imaginary Geography: An Interview with George Elliott Clarke," *Ariel: A Review of International English Literature* 27, no. 4 (1996): 80–81.

12. Esmeralda Thornhill, Royal Commission on the Donald Marshall Jr. Prosecution, Consultative Conference on Discrimination against Natives and Blacks in the Criminal Justice System and the Role of the Attorney General (Halifax, Nova Scotia, 24–26 November 1988), 66.

13. Barnor Hesse, "Black to Front and Black Again: Racialization through Contested Times and Spaces," in *Place and the Politics of Identity*, ed. Michael Keith and Steve Pile (New York: Routledge, 1993), 162–82.

14. Donald H. J. Clairmont and Dennis William Magill, *Africville: The Life and Death of a Canadian Black Community*, 3rd ed. (Toronto: Canadian Scholars' Press, 1999). George Elliot Clarke, "A Community that Refuses to Die," *The Toronto Star*, 26 September 1992, K13; George Elliot Clarke, "The Death and Rebirth of Africandian Nationalism," *New Maritimes: A Regional Magazine of Culture and Politics* 11, 5 (1993): 20–28.

15. This version is based on the work of Clairmont and Magill, whose account is consistent with the events of the time, but former community members have differing accounts, some of which contradict or dispute Clairmont and Magill. See Donald H. J. Clairmont and Dennis William Magill, *Africville: The Life and Death of a Canadian Black Community*, 3d ed. (Toronto: Canadian Scholars' Press, 1999).

16. Ibid., 55.
17. Africville Genealogy Society, ed., *The Spirit of Africville* (Halifax: A Maritext Book–Formac Publishing Company, 1992); and Clairmont and Magill, Africville, 46—48.
18. Clairmont and Magill, *Africville*, 62.
19. Bernard MacDougall, "Urban Relocation of Africville Residents: A Study of the Influence of Urban Relocation on Displaced Residents, with Particular Respect to the Africville Relocation" (master's thesis, Maritime School of Social Work and Saint Mary's University, 1969), 35.
20. Clairmont and Magill, *Africville*, 62.
21. MacDougall, "Urban Relocation," 10—13.
22. "37 Africville Residents Approve of Rose Report," *Halifax Mail-Star*, 10 January 1964; "City to Make Africville Move as Painless as Possible, Mayor Says," *Halifax Mail-Star*, 17 January 1964; "Africville May Disappear by Year's End," *Halifax Mail-Star*, 5 January 1966, 4; Clairmont and Magill, *Africville*, 38; Dulcie Conrad, "The Colour Bar on Our Doorstep," *Observer*, 1 May 1966, 10–13, 20; Susan Dexter, "The Ghetto That Fears Integration," *Maclean's Magazine*, 24 July 1965, 16; and Sylvia Fraser, "The Slow and Welcome Death of Africville," *Star Weekly*, 1 January 1966, 2–7.
23. Clairmont and Magill, *Africville*, 124.
24. Carleton University History Collaborative, *Urban and Community Development in Atlantic Canada, 1867—1991*, vol. 44, *Mercury Series Paper* (Hull, Quebec: Canadian Museum of Civilization, 1993), 79—80.
25. Some former residents arguably gained from the relocation program because they negotiated sufficient compensation for their property to purchase a home elsewhere in Halifax, but they lost their home within a few years to foreclosure.
26. Africville Genealogy Society, *The Spirit of Africville*; Clairmont and Magill, *Africville*; and Stephen Kimber, "Taking Back the Neighbourhood: Halifax's North End Resists a Legacy of Racism and Poverty," *Canadian Geographic* 112, no. 4 (1992): 32—41.
27. Clairmont and Magill, *Africville*, 212—21.
28. Winks, *Blacks in Canada*, 35.
29. This account does not address the smaller streams of black migration into Nova Scotia, including, most significantly, Caribbean migrants who settled in the Whitney Pier area of Sydney Cape Breton in the early 1900s and the Jamaican Maroons exiled by the British to Nova Scotia in 1796. The approximately five hundred Trelawny Town Maroons proceeded to Freetown in 1800. Mavis Christine Campbell, *The Maroons of Jamaica, 1655—1796: A History of Resistance, Collaboration and Betrayal* (Trenton, N.J.: Africa World Press, 1990); Mavis Christine Campbell and George Ross, *Back to Africa: George Ross and the Maroons: From Nova Scotia to Sierra Leone* (Trenton, N.J.: Africa World Press, 1993); and Vinson H. Sutlive, *Nova Scotia and the Fighting Maroons: A Documentary History*, vol. 41, *Studies in Third World Societies* (Williamsburg, Va.: Department of Anthropology, College of William and Mary, 1990).
30. See J. Yolande Daniels, "Black Bodies, Black Space: a-Waiting Spectacle," in *White Papers, Black Marks: Architecture, Race, Culture*, ed. Lesley N. N. Lokko (Minneapolis: University of Minnesota Press, 2000), 195–217.
31. G. A. Rawlyk, "The Guysborough Negroes: A Study in Isolation," *Dalhousie Review* 48 (spring 1968): 24–36.
32. As quoted in Clairmont and Magill, *Africville*, 28.
33. Rawlyk, "The Guysborough Negroes," 25.
34. Winks, *Blacks in Canada*, 36.
35. Clairmont and Magill, *Africville*, 28.
36. Ibid.
37. Greaves, *The Negro in Canada*, 43.

38. James W. St. G. Walker, "'Race' Policy in Canada: A Retrospective," in *Canada 2000: Race Relations and Public Policy*, ed. O. Dwivedi et al. (Guelph, Ontario: Department of Political Studies, University of Guelph, 1989), 2.

39. Ibid.

40. Jock Collins and Frances Henry, "Racism, Ethnicity and Immigration," in *Immigration and Refugee Policy: Australia and Canada Compared*, ed. Howard Adelman et al., vol. 1 (Toronto: University of Toronto Press, 1994), 528–31; Freda Hawkins, *Critical Years in Immigration: Canada and Australia Compared* (Kingston, Canada: McGill–Queen's University Press, 1989), 17; Christine Inglis, Anthony Birch, and Geoffrey Sherington, "An Overview of Australian and Canadian Migration Patterns and Policies," in *Immigration and Refugee Policy*, 1: 8–16; and John Schultz, "White Man's Country: Canada and the West Indian Immigrant, 1900–1965," *American Review of Canadian Studies* 12, no. 1 (1982): 53–64.

41. As quoted in Schultz, "White Man's Country," 54.

42. David D. Harvey, *Americans in Canada: Migration and Settlement since 1840* (Lewiston, N.Y.: E. Mellen Press, 1991), 10.

43. Joan Anderson et al., "Constructing Canada: An Introduction," in *Painting the Maple: Essays on Race, Gender, and the Construction of Canada*, ed. Joan Anderson et al. (Vancouver: University of British Columbia Press, 1998), 8—11; and Eva Mackey, *The House of Difference: Cultural Politics and National Identity in Canada* (New York: Routledge, 1999), 30—32.

44. Mackey, *House of Difference*, 30—31. Mackey cites Carl Berger, *The Sense of Power: Studies in the Ideas of Canadian Imperialism, 1867—1914* (Toronto: University of Toronto Press, 1970); and Carl Berger, "The True North Strong and Free," in *Nationalism in Canada*, ed. Peter Russell (Toronto: McGraw-Hill, 1966), 3—26.

45. Trevor Sessing, "How They Kept Canada Almost Lily White: The Previously Untold Story of the Canadian Immigration Officials Who Stopped American Blacks from Coming to Canada," *Saturday Night* 85, no. 9 (September 1970): 30—32; Bruce R. Shepard, "Plain Racism: The Reaction against Oklahoma Black Immigration to the Canadian Plains," *Prairie Forum* 10, no. 2 (1985); and Jason Howard Silverman, *Unwelcome Guests: Canada West's Response to American Fugitive Slaves, 1800—1865* (New York: Associated Faculty Press, 1985).

46. Britton Cooke, "The Black Canadian," *Maclean's Magazine*, November 1911, 11, emphasis in original.

47. Ibid., 4.

48. Ibid., 6.

49. "The Nigger Quarter!" Britton Cooke, *Maclean's Magazine*, November 1911.

50. Esmerelda Thornhill Nova Scotia, The Royal Commission on the Donald Marshall, Jr., Prosecution. 1988. "Consultative Conference on Discrimination against Natives and Blacks in the Criminal Justice System and the Role of the Attorney General." Halifax: McCurdy's Printing and Typesetting Limited.

51. Ibid., 6.

52. Quoted in George Elliott Clarke, "Contesting a Model Blackness: A Meditation on African-Canadian African Americanism, or the Structures of African Canadianité," *Essays on Canadian Writing* 63 (1998): 45 n. 8.

53. James W. St. G. Walker, *"Race," Rights and the Law in the Supreme Court of Canada: Historical Case Studies* (Toronto: Osgoode Society for Canadian Legal Studies, 1997), 1.

54. Nova Scotia, 1988, 66; Adrienne L. Shadd, "'Where Are You *Really* from?': Notes of an 'Immigrant' from North Buxton, Ontario," in *Talking about Difference: Encounters in Culture, Language and Identity*, ed. Carl James and Adrienne Shadd (Toronto: Between the Lines, 1994), 9.

55. Quoted in George Elliott Clarke, "Contesting a Model Blackness," 45 n. 8.

56. Greaves, *The Negro in Canada*, 60.

57. Keith S. Henry, "Black Politics in Toronto since World War I," in *Occasional Papers in Ethnic and Immigration Studies* (Toronto: Multicultural History Society of Ontario, 1981), 8.

58. Howard Law, "'Self-Reliance Is the True Road to Independence': Ideology and the Ex-slaves in Buxton and Chatham," in *A Nation of Immigrants: Women, Workers, and Communities in Canadian History, 1840s—1960s*, ed. Franca Iacovetta, Paula Draper, and Robert Ventresca (Toronto: University of Toronto Press, 1998), 83.

59. Sponsored by the C. R. Bronfman Foundation, the Underground Railway was one of the original Heritage Minutes broadcast to Canadian viewers as an illustration of an important moment in the nation's history. The one-minute historical drama showed nineteenth-century white Canadians welcoming a black fugitive to freedom:

    > *Between 1840 and 1860, more than 30,000 American slaves came secretly to Canada and freedom.* "When my feet first touched the Canadian shore, I threw myself on the ground, rolled in the sand, seized handfuls of it and kissed them." These were the words of Josiah Henson recalling his first moments as a free man. Henson had escaped to Canada along the "underground railroad," a network of secret paths, hiding places and safe houses that stretched from southern states to the borders of Canada. Like countless other immigrants, Henson came to Canada as a refugee escaping brutality and oppression. (http://www.histori.ca/minutes/minute.do?ID=10166&sl=e).accessed 4 April 2003.

60. Donald H. Clairmont and Fred C. Wien, "Race Relations in Canada," in *Ethnicity and Ethnic Relations in Canada: A Book of Readings*, ed. Jay E. Goldstein and Rita M. Bienvenue (Toronto: Butterworths, 1980), 309–24; and David R. Hughes and Evelyn Kallen, *The Anatomy of Racism: Canadian Dimensions* (Montreal: Harvest House, 1974).

61. A 1972 RCMP Security Service document, *Black Nationalism and Black Extremism in Canada*, quoted in "Commission of Inquiry Concerning Certain Activities of the Royal Canadian Mounted Police, Freedom and Security under the Law" (Ottawa: Minister of Supply and Services, Canadian Government Publishing Centre, 1981), 503.

62. In a particularly notorious example of an illegal but ultimately successful "countering" activity, designed to thwart a meeting between members of the Black Panther Party and the militant Front de libération du Québec (FLQ), Security Service operatives burned to the ground a barn on a farm at Sainte-Anne-de-la-Rochelle in Quebec. Paul Palango, *The Last Guardians: The Crisis in the RCMP—and in Canada* (Toronto: McClelland and Stewart, 1998), 74–75.

63. Caroline Brown and Lorne Brown, *An Unauthorized History of the RCMP* (Toronto: James Lorimer and Company, 1974); Commission of Inquiry Concerning Certain Activities of the Royal Canadian Mounted Police, "Freedom and Security under the Law" (Ottawa: Minister of Supply and Services, Canadian Government Publishing Centre, 1981); and Palango, *The Last Guardians*.

64. Brown and Brown, *An Unauthorized History of the RCMP*.

65. Clive Cocking, "How Did the Canadian Mounties Develop Their Unfortunate Habit of Deporting People They Don't Happen to Like?" *Saturday Night* 85, no. 6 (June 1970): 28–30; and Farrell Crook, "Man Deported to U.S. Despite Appeal Rights," *Toronto Globe and Mail*, 24 October 1972.

66. Martin O'Malley, "In the Panther's Wake," *Toronto Globe and Mail*, 15 February 1969, 21, 23, 25; "Rocky the Revolutionary," *Toronto Globe and Mail*, 15 February 1969, 24.

67. "Not Necessarily Inevitable," *Toronto Globe and Mail*, 15 February 1969.

68. As long as "white attitudes" do not again prevail, which is a sly dig from the "metropolitan" core of central Canada at "provincial" cousins in Nova Scotia. The enlightened thinking of Canada's metropolitan elite is further highlighted in reference to blacks in Ontario as "the relatively calm and contented descendants of immigrant slaves," as opposed to the decidedly less "calm" activities of indigenous black activists.

69. When asked "in a 1989 survey which word best described the 'ideal Canadian,' Canadians put 'tolerant' in first place." In contrast, "Americans in the same survey picked 'independent minded' for themselves." Walker, *"Race," Rights and the Law,* 3.

70. "Black is not a question of pigmentation. The Black I'm talking about is a historical category, a political category, a cultural category. In our language, at certain historical moments, we have to use the signifier. We have to create an equivalence between how people look and what their histories are. Their histories are in the past, inscribed in their skins. But it is not because of their skins that they are Black in their heads." Stuart Hall, "Old and New Identities, Old and New Ethnicities," in *Culture, Globalization and the World System,* ed. Anthony D. King (New York: State University of New York at Binghamton, 1991), 53.

71. Ibid., 52—53.

72. Winks, *Blacks in Canada,* 456.

73. Clairmont and Magill, *Africville;* and Donald H. J. Clairmont et al., *Africville Relocation Report,* vol. 102, *Institute of Public Affairs, Dalhousie University* (Halifax: Institute of Public Affairs, Dalhousie University, 1971).

74. Loïc J. D. Wacquant, "Urban Outcasts: Stigma and Division in the Black American Ghetto and the French Urban Periphery," *International Journal of Urban and Regional Research* 17, no. 3 (1993): 366–83.

75. Africville Exhibition Steering Committee, *Africville: A Spirit That Lives On* (Halifax: Art Gallery, Mount Saint Vincent University; Black Cultural Centre for Nova Scotia; Africville Genealogy Society; National Film Board, Atlantic Centre, 1989); Africville Genealogy Society, *The Spirit of Africville;* Donald H. Clairmont and Dennis William Magill, "Africville Relocation Report: Supplement" (Halifax: Institute of Public Affairs, Dalhousie University, 1973); Clairmont and Magill, *Africville;* George Elliott Clarke, "The Death and Rebirth of Africadian Nationalism," *New Maritimes: A Regional Magazine of Culture and Politics* 11, no. 5 (1993): 20–28; and Maureen Moynagh, "Africville: An Imagined Community," *Canadian Literature: A Quarterly of Criticism and Review* 157 (summer 1998): 13–34.

76. Online publication Accessed 20 October 2002. http://imprint.uwaterloo.ca/issues/021601/ 4Human/features02.shtml. Anonymous, "The Other Africville," *Cities,* October 1989, 19–23; Golda Arthur, "Fight for Africville Church Continues," *NOVANEWSNET,* accessed 5 December 1998, http://novanewsnet.ukings.ns.ca/stories/97–98/980305/africville.htm; Marla Cranston, "East Lake Site Picked for Landfill," *Halifax Daily News,* 1 March 1992, 3; Elaine Flaherty, "Demolished Africville Threatened Again; Blacks Fear Memory of N.S. Community Will Be Desecrated," *Montreal Gazette,* 27 July 1991, B4; Greg Hare and Dan Leger, "Violence in the Streets Looms as Blacks Face Loss of Lands," *Dartmouth Free Press,* 22 June 1977; Susanne Hiller, "Dump Choice 'Insensitive,'" *Halifax Daily News,* 25 July 1997, 3; Cathy Nicoll, "Preston-Area Dump Foes Say Heritage Threatened," *Halifax Daily News,* 19 December 1991, and "Effect of Dump Choice Is Racist, Group Charges," *Halifax Daily News,* 16 March 1993, 5; Charles Saunders, "Landfill Fight: Preston Exercises Its New Clout," *Sunday Daily News,* 15 September 1991, 17; Estelle Small, "Tears Falling Still at Loss of Africville," *Halifax Daily News,* 19 June 1985, 1; and Melanie Stuparyk, "Africville: The Devastating Story of a Black Settlement in Halifax," *Imprint Online* 23, no. 27, (16 February 2001).

77. In particular, the African United Baptist Association (AUBA) and its secular arm, the Nova Scotia Association for the Advancement of Coloured People (NSAACP).

78. Frank Stanley Boyd, "The Politics of the Minority Game: The Decline and Fall of the Black United Front," in *Fire on the Water: An Anthology of Black Nova Scotian Writing,* ed. George Elliot Clarke (Lawrencetown Beach, N.S.: Pottersfield Press, 1992), 43–52; Nancy Lubka, "Ferment in Nova Scotia," *Queen's Quarterly* 16, no. 2 (1969): 222; and Jennifer Bradford Smith, *An International History of the Black Panther Party: Studies in African American History and Culture* (New York: Garland, 1999), 87–111.

79. Clarke, "Africadian Nationalism," 27. Clarke provides two related explanations of the origins of the neologism. In his editorial contribution to a special issue of the *Dalhousie Review* focusing on the literature, culture, and history of black Nova Scotians, he explains that "the term *Africadia* [is] a neologism combining both Africa and Acadia (the historic name of Nova Scotia and New Brunswick)" (151). The explanation emphasizes the overlapping history of two diaspora waves in the Maritime provinces, both of which suffered exploitation and repression under British colonialism: the African diaspora and the French diaspora; the Acadians were brutally uprooted and exiled from the Maritimes by the British upon their victory over the French. The second explanation is found in a journal article, "*Must All Blackness Be American?*" Clarke writes that Africadia is derived from "a fusion of *Africa* and *cadie*, the Mi'kmaq term for 'abounding in' (and the probable cognate of the French toponym *Acadie* [Acadia])" (67 n. 1). In both cases, the terms *Africadia* and *Africadian* "serve to stress the long history of Africans . . . in Maritime Canada" (ibid.). The latter emphasis holds a certain different political connotation, however, in a colonial history in which black Nova Scotians settled on lands taken from the aboriginal peoples (the Mi'kmaq). George Elliott Clarke, "Must All Blackness Be American?: Locating Canada in Borden's "Tightrope Time," or Nationalizing Gilroy's the Black Atlantic," *Canadian Ethnic Studies* 28, no. 3 (1996): 56–71, and editorial, *Dalhousie Review* 77, no. 2, special issue (1997): 149–53.

80. Ruth Simms Hamilton, "Toward a Conceptualization of Modern Diasporas: Exploring Contours of African Diaspora Social Identity Formation," in *Contemporary Diasporas: A Focus on Asian Pacifics*, ed. H. Eric Schockman, Kay Song, and Eui-Young Yu, Occasional Papers Series (Los Angeles: Center for Multiethnic and Transnational Studies, University of Southern California, 1995); James Clifford, *Routes: Travel and Translation in the Late Twentieth Century* (Cambridge, Mass.: Harvard University Press, 1997).

81. Clarke, "Africadian Nationalism," 24.

82. George Elliott Clarke, "Contesting a Model Blackness: A Meditation on African-Canadian African Americanism, or The Structures of African Canadianité," *Essays on Canadian Writing* 63 (spring 1998): 42.

83. Ibid., 27, 43. Clarke's use of this phrase is reminiscent of Derek Welcott's discussion of race, history, and identity in the Caribbean which he refers to as "this archipelago of the Americas." Derek Walcott, "The Muse of History: An Essay" in *Is Massa Dead? Black Moods in the Caribbean*, ed. Orde Coombs (New York: Anchor, 1974), 27.

84. Ibid., 27.

85. Ibid., 43.

86. Paul Gilroy, "Cultural Studies and Ethnic Absolutism," in *Cultural Studies*, ed. Lawrence Grossberg, Cary Nelson, and Paula A. Treichler (New York: Routledge, 1992).

87. Paul Gilroy, *The Black Atlantic: Modernity and Double Consciousness* (Cambridge, Mass.: Harvard University Press, 1993). See the following by Clarke: "Africadian Nationalism"; "The Birth and Rebirth of Africadian Literature," in *Down East: Critical Essays on Contemporary Maritime Canadian Literature*, ed. Wolfgang Hochbruck and James O. Taylor (Trier, Germany: WVT Wissenschaftlicher Verlag Trier, 1996), 55–79; "Must All Blackness Be American?"; and "Contesting a Model Blackness."

88. The cultural and political significance of Africville particularly for black Canadians is demonstrated by its salience as a theme in cultural and intellectual production over the last three decades. The following are some select examples of works in print, film, and music exploring various dimensions of the history of Africville and the experience of its former residences produced since the community's destruction in the late 1960s.

Examples of a focus on Africville in print include Frederick Ward's 1974 novel in Black English, *Riverlisp: Black Memories* (inspired by conversations with former Africville residents); a 1992 edited volume by the Africville Genealogy Society, *The Spirit of Africville*, with five essays on various dimensions of Africville, ranging from a fictional walk through the community to social analysis to comments from former residents. A number of poems of Africville have also been published in, for example, Frederick Ward's 1983 collection *The Curing Berry* (Toronto: Williams-Wallace Publishers), George Elliot Clarke's 1983 collection *Saltwater Spirituals and Deeper Blues* (Porters Lake, Nova Scotia : Pottersfield Press), Maxine Tynes' 1990 publication *Woman Talking Woman* (Lawrencetown Beach, Nova Scotia: Pottersfield Press,), George Borden's 2000 collection *A Mighty Long Way!: From Africa to Africadia* (Dartmouth, Nova Scotia: G.A.B. Consulting) and David Woods' 1990 collection "Africville: Requiem" in a special edition of the *Dalhousie Review*, edited by George Elliot Clarke (77:263–265) which includes, amongst other pieces historian James Walker's essay on Africville as an allegory for the black experience in Canada.

Films and television broadcasts exploring various dimensions of Africville range from Shelagh Mackenzie's poignant 1991 documentary *Remember Africville* (National Film Board of Canada) to George Elliot Clarke's 1999 made-for-television romantic tragedy *One Heart Broken into Song*, to the critically acclaimed 1999 short film *Welcome to Africville* by Dana Inkster, awarded the Best Canadian Female Film Director at the 1999 Toronto Images Film Festival. In 1997 the Canadian Broadcasting Corporation show *Adrienne Clarkson Presents* broadcasted "Africville—A Celebration of Canada's Oldest Black Community." Produced and directed by Peggy Shkuda, it was a multimedia production (music, songs, archival footage, film, and interviews) which sought "to celebrate the people of Africville by bringing to a wider audience an important piece of Black Canadian history. (See, for example http://www.tv.cbc.ca/acp/97–98/index.html.)

Finally, a number of songs inspired by Africville have been produced and performed over the years including *Africville* written by George Elliot Clarke and performed by the African Nova Scotian a cappella group Four the Moment on their 1995 CD *In My Soul* (Just A Minute Productions). Two full length albums that stand out are Faith Nolan's 1986 debut album *Africville* (http://www.nexicom.net/~faith/music .html) and Joe Sealy's 1996 Canadian Juno Award winning CD *Africville Suite* (Sea Jam Recordings)—described by one commentator as "a profound spiritual and cultural tribute to an important Canadian historical community" (James Hale, "Jazzman Captures Spirit of Africville," *The Ottawa Citizen*, 5 July 1997, H2).

Parks Canada, "Backgrounder: Africville," accessed 8 September 2001 (http://parkscanada.pch.gc.ca/library/background/44e.htm).

89. "Former Africville Residents to Sue Halifax," *Halifax Daily News*, 26 October 1998, 5; Arthur, "Fight for Africville Church Continues"; Jeremy Copeland, "'We're Not Going to Fold Up Shop': It's Victor and Eddy Carvery's Second Winter Protesting What They See as the Mistreatment of Africville Residents," *North End News*, 6 October 1995, 4–5; Jennifer Ferguson, "Africville Delays Frustrate, Anger Descendants," *North End News*, 6 October 1995, 4; Dalton Higgins, "Slaves in Canada: Blacks Demand Reparations for Racist Past but Confused about How to Do It—Cash to Individuals or Education?" *NOW Magazine Online Edition* 29, no. 45 (2001), accessed 14 July 2001, http://www.nowtoronto.com/issues/2001–07–12/news_spread.html; Michael Lightstone, "Africville Claim Getting Assist from City Hall," *Halifax Daily News*, 4 February 1994, 3; and Heather Speirs and Mark Evans, "Why Move Squatters? Carverys Need Support," *North End News*, 3 March 1995, 5.

90. Christine Doucet, "Core Dwindles: Household Size Drop, Lack of Land Key Factors in Decline," *Halifax Herald*, accessed 5 December 1997, http://www.herald.ns.ca/cgi-bin/home/displaypackstory?1997/12/05+155.raw+Poppartnine; David Jackson, "'Exurbia' Booms Beyond Suburbs," *Halifax Herald*, accessed 5 December 1997, http://www.herald.ns.ca/cgi-bin/home/displaypackstory?1997/12/05+132.raw+Poppartnine; Chris Lambie, "Residents Disagree over Role of Racism in Boundary Dispute," *Halifax Daily News*, 7 February 1997; Jeffrey Simpson, "Not in Our Backyard, Beechville Says," *Halifax Chronicle Herald*, 25 July 1997, A7.

91. Greg Hare and Dan Leger, "Preston Residents Want Non-violent Solution," *Dartmouth Free Press*, 26

July 1977; "Violence in the Streets Looms as Blacks Face Loss of Lands," *Dartmouth Free Press*, 22 June 1977.

92. Glen Allen, "A Smouldering Race Issue; Nova Scotia Blacks Seek School Reform," *Maclean's Magazine*, 27 February 1989, 14; "N.S. Symphony Embraces Black Musicians," *Halifax Daily News*, 2 October 1991, 22; "Parents Call for the Removal of 'Unfair' Teachers at School Complain That Black Students Being Harassed and Intimidated," *Toronto Star*, 8 October 1997, A6; Elaine Flaherty, "Blacks Hopeful after Report on N.S. Racism," *Montreal Gazette*, 16 October 1991, B6; "Catalyst for Racial Change?" *Ottawa Citizen*, 26 July 1991, A10; Graeme Hamilton, "School Tries to Soothe Scars of Racism: Graeme Hamilton Finds a Halifax School Trying to Overcome Its Past," *Ottawa Citizen*, 29 September 1997, A3; Susanne Hiller, "Police Discuss Preston Rift: Halifax Cops Miffed at RCMP-Union," *Halifax Daily News*, 16 May 1996, 4; Randy Jones and Lisa Clifford, "Police Pelted after Standoff: Officers Hurt. Cars Damaged in Aftermath," *Halifax Chronicle Herald*, 14 May 1996, A1; Chris Lambie, "ATV Fights RCMP: Mounties Seek Preston Answers in Tape," *Halifax Daily News*, 17 May 1996, 5; Michael Lightstone, "Cop Car Stoned in North Preston," *Halifax Daily News*, 29 December 1996; Maureen Murray, "Blacks Call for Action after Riot in Halifax," *Toronto Star*, 20 July 1991, A1; Charles Saunders, "A Comeback from a Setback," *Sunday Daily News*, 2 June 1996, 16; Charles Saunders, "A Setback for Preston: Vandalizing Police Cars No Way to Break Down Negative Stereotypes," *Halifax Daily News*, 19 May 1996; Paul Schneidereit, "A Tale of Extremes," *Halifax Herald*, accessed 17 November 1997, http://www.herald.ns.ca/cgi-bin/home/displaypackstory?1997/11/17+125.raw+Poppartone; and John Spears, "Blacks, Whites Unite to March in Halifax," *Toronto Star*, 2 August 1991, A11; John Spears, "Violence Highlights Fight for Equality after Centuries of Conflict," *Toronto Star*, 27 July 1991, D4; and John Spears, "Year after Halifax Race Riot Blacks Work to Ease Tensions," *Toronto Star*, 22 August 1992, D5.

93. Mackey, *House of Difference*, 70.

94. Clairmont and Wien, "Race Relations in Canada."

95. Moynagh, "Africville," 18—19.

96. Ibid., 19.

97. Ibid., 18.

98. Parks Canada, "Backgrounder: Africville."

99. Of the seventy-five recommendations made in 1997 by a consultant for Cole Harbour High School in the wake of nearly a decade of race-related conflicts that culminated in several large and violent confrontations, five have been implemented.

100. Clairmont and Magill, *Africville*, 285.

101. James W. "Allegories and Orientations in African-Canadian Historiography: The Spirit of Africville," *The Dalhousie Review* 77 (1997): 155.

102. Moynagh, "Africville," 19.

103. Michael J. C. Echeruo, "An African Diaspora: The Ontological Project," in *The African Diaspora: African Origins and New World Identities*, ed. Carole Boyce Davies, Ali A. Mazrui, and Isidore Okpewho (Bloomington: Indiana University Press, 1999), 7.

104. Maureen Warner-Lewis, "Cultural Reconfigurations in the African Caribbean," in ibid., 22.

105. Mackey, *House of Difference*, 148.

Reflections on the African Diaspora in Israel, 1997

Mark Shapley

IN SUMMER 1997, I WENT TO ISRAEL WITH A PARTICULAR INTEREST IN ITS THREE largest black communities: the Beta Israel or Ethiopian Jews, the Ethiopian Orthodox Christian communities, and the Hebrew Israelites, an African American Judaic Community. I wanted to understand why these African diaspora communities had come to Israel and the nature of their experiences there. This study is based on qualitative data gathered from interviews with community leaders, students, business- and professional people, soldiers, and others. I attended religious services in both synagogues and churches, went to cultural performances, and visited homes. I also examined primary and secondary sources.

Between 1 June and 17 July, I traveled to a number of places and interacted with many different people. In Jerusalem I met pilgrims from around the world as well as local residents. At the Mount of Olives I made contact with a number of Palestinians around my same age who took me into their neighborhoods on the West Bank. In the Galilee area I encountered many Israelis and Palestinians who provided me with a better understanding of Tiberias and the Galilee region. I spent time in Beersheba with many Beta Israel and others in Tel Aviv who informed me about their life on the coast. In Dimona I was well received by the Hebrew Israelites, who shared many important aspects of their lives with me.

In the discussion that follows, the Beta Israel are examined first. The focus is on the complexities of their incorporation into Israeli society, highlighting such aspects as language, education, military service, and economic well being. I also discuss their struggle with rabbinical Jewry and the transitions in their Ethiopian identity as well as their political and organizational activism.

Attention then shifts to the Hebrew Israelites, who have been in the country for three decades. In particular, I examine how and why they came to Israel and their struggle to establish themselves despite often hostile resistance from the state.

I conclude with reflections on the Ethiopian Orthodox Christians and their historical presence and residency in Israel. Central to their story is the struggle over property rights in Jerusalem and other holy places that are important to their faith.

Beta Israel (Ethiopian Jews): Unfolding Identities and Realities in Everyday Life

The massive resettlement of Ethiopian Jews in Israel around fifteen years ago is a fascinating episode in the displacement of African people to a new land. This group represents two diasporas. Before 1982, they were part of the ancient Jewish dispersion, and now they are part of the "neo-African diaspora" (as distinguished from the New World dispersal due to the slave trade). The complexities of their experiences in Israel are reflected in the following comments:

> It is written in our scriptures that we were to return to our forefathers' land that was promised. By our faith we knew we had come home. What is here we could not have in Ethiopia; for our children there is work and education. Ethiopia is our land from where we come, but our spiritual home is here. Some things we had to change to live here, but our love for Ethiopia is the same because we are Ethiopians.
>
> —*(an elderly male)*

> I was born in Ethiopia, but was raised here—so I do not remember anything about Ethiopia. I love Ethiopia because that is my place of birth, and I love Israel because it is where I live now, so I am of two worlds made in one within me.
>
> —*(a teenage female)*

> I will return to Ethiopia because I have never been to my "motherland," although I do not know whether I will stay.
>
> —*(a young adult male)*

My family desires to return to Ethiopia. It may not be a permanent move, but there is freedom to go between two countries. For my parents life was better in Ethiopia, as we still have family there.

—(a female college student)

There are benefits and opportunities found in Israel that are not available in Ethiopia. I do get homesick, but Israel is my new home now, and with no relatives remaining in Ethiopia, how can I return home?

—(a middle-aged man)

For the Beta Israel, emigration changed their material conditions, perceptions of self, and communal identity. Furthermore, the nation of Israel is grappling with the search for identity, that is, the basic issue of who is a Jew. The minority Ashkenazi (Jews of Central and Eastern Europe) exercise cultural and political dominance over the Mizrahim, the Jews from Africa and Asia who constitute more than 65 percent of the population, and over the Palestinian Israelis, who constitute 20 percent. How does the African Other, the Ethiopian fit into this mosaic?

Incorporation and Its Complexities

Insights about how Ethiopian Jews have carved a niche for themselves in Israeli society and how they view that society can be gained from their experiences with education and language proficiency, military service, and employment. For example, there is a marked intergenerational difference in terms of exposure to the Israeli education system.

EDUCATION AND LANGUAGE

For those born after resettlement, enrollment in Israeli schools has played a central role in their socialization, whereas the older generation was educated in Ethiopia. Language proficiency is closely related to age and education, and it is a significant factor in incorporation and in the degree to which cultural ties are maintained.

Upon arrival, most of the Beta Israel spoke either Amharic or Tigrinya. Many young Ethiopians adopted Hebrew quickly, but there are still a large number of people who communicate in their mother tongue, especially in the older generation, which tended to have less contact with Hebrew-speaking Israelis upon arrival. In some cases older Ethiopians can speak and understand Hebrew but not read or write it with equal proficiency. The younger generation may use Amharic or Tigrinya at home or within the community, but at school or work they communicate in Hebrew. Three young men interviewed (ages fifteen to twenty) were born in Ethiopia and arrived as Tigrinya speakers but within three or four months had learned Hebrew. They were also fluent in English. They preferred to speak among themselves in Tigrinya but otherwise used Hebrew. One young woman said she was brought up speaking Hebrew. Her mother spoke Amharic but did not teach it to her; she learned it from two roommates in boarding school.

For those who began their education in Ethiopia, it was often a challenge to start over in Israel. In addition to learning Hebrew, they had to adjust to different teaching methods and in some cases different subject matter. Three high school students expressed a desire for more Ethiopian teachers, as there are many issues and concerns not clearly understood or recognized by less sensitive non-Ethiopian teachers. One recent high school graduate articulated the need for Ethiopian history and culture to be taught, arguing that it was important for all Israelis to know about his former country.

Interviews with Ethiopian students at Ben Gurion University revealed the importance of a college education for job prospects. They planned to enter diverse fields, including social work, philosophy, medicine, and political science. As the first generation to attend Israeli universities, they foreshadow an Israeli-generated Ethiopian professional class. One woman, who was just finishing her degree in social work, explained that she chose this field in order to help improve the living conditions of Ethiopians throughout the country. As we spoke, she drew my attention to a man walking across the plaza and said he would be the first Ethiopian to graduate from the medical program. He had almost finished his studies at Addis Ababa University when he emigrated, but much of his work had to be re-credited requiring almost another five years.

MILITARY SERVICE

Mandatory military service brings younger Ethiopians into another important aspect of Israeli life. Many Ethiopians Jews began serving in the army upon their arrival. I spoke with two young men in their second year of service who said that military life is extremely demanding. There is time off for family and friends, but they are always on call. One said he would prefer to be working or in school, but he understood the need to protect his family and the nation. They also saw benefits to service, such as gaining good skills and training for the future, and said that it gave them the opportunity for

contact with other Israelis, which they feel is lacking in their closely knit communities: "You can meet good friends while in the service, and it gives us a chance to learn
more about each other."

The military has had its problems with racism, which some attribute to high
suicide rates, as there has been some twenty suicides between 1994 and 1996 among
Ethiopian Jewish recruits.[1] In March 1997 an Israeli Defense Forces (IDF) major was
dismissed because, when an Ethiopian under his command requested medical aid,
he said the doctor should post a sign saying "No blacks allowed." The incident raises
questions about the extent of racist sentiments in the IDF, which my research was
unable to answer.

For Ethiopians, securing a job in Israel is a central concern and in some instances a
major problem. The immigrants and the government have been greatly challenged to
find work opportunities, and unemployment is high among Ethiopians. Most high-
paying careers demand university training or special skills, so many Beta Israel have
jobs in small stores, restaurants, hotels, delivery services, and gas stations. A very
small percentage work in public transportation, as bus or taxi drivers, and an even
smaller number in banks or post offices.

Avi, a young man from Tel Aviv, said very few Ethiopians own businesses because
these require start-up capital. He knows of only one Ethiopian restaurant in the whole
country, in Tel Aviv, and he showed me a small shop that sells Ethiopian music exclusively, but the owner was not a Beta Israel and did not appear to know much about
his wares.

A student at Ben Gurion University commented that very few Ethiopians hold
government posts, administrative positions in education, or operate private businesses as entrepreneurs and producers. He surmised that the Beta Israel community
is still establishing itself.

Are You Really Jewish?

One of the first sites I visited upon my arrival in Jerusalem was the Western Wall,
one of the holiest places for Western Jewry, and my visit coincided with the thirtieth
anniversary of Israeli control over the city. This was a very important occasion for
most Israelis, but the few Ethiopians I saw there were young. The older generation of
Ethiopians retained Ethiopian traditions, thus the celebrations of Western Jewry at

the wall were largely irrelevant to their theology. On several other occasions I rarely saw any Ethiopian Jews praying at the wall. This may be because their population in Jerusalem is quite small, but it also points to a challenge they have faced since their arrival, the significant differences of traditions that distinguish Ethiopian Judaism from Western Jewish observances.

From the beginning, pressure was put on the Ethiopians to alter their traditional religious customs. The debate over "Ethiopian Jewishness" was based mainly on the comparisons between the ancient Beta Israel traditions and the rabbinical forms adopted in the West. The refusal of many Israelis to accept the fact that the Ethiopians were indeed Jews led to the special conditions and terms by which the Israeli religious authorities were going to accept them. These terms included ritual "recircumcision" by the Western rabbis, which meant that they were still not recognized as legitimate Jews. This caused a great uproar among the Ethiopians and especially angered the *quesotch* (Ethiopian priests), many of whom refused on the ground that their Jewish faith and observances were beyond question. Another condition was that the Ethiopians take Hebrew names. One young man from Beersheba explained that he has two names: Makonnen (Ethiopian) and Moshe (Hebrew for Moses).

The rabbis went so far as to discredit existing marriages, demanding that the state recognize only marriage contracts presided over by certain rabbis. This caused a major protest by the Ethiopians, who refused to have their identity as Jews questioned. It was like saying everything sacred they believed about their religious heritage did not exist and was valueless. Furthermore, in Christianized Ethiopia, Beta Israel had a long history of struggle including discrimination because they were Jews, which made the attitude of the rabbinical authorities in Israel even more insulting.

A soldier I met in Jerusalem felt the Beta Israel brought greater diversity to Israel by showing that Judaism has a history in Africa. He said Ethiopians had the oldest Torah in the world and brought this symbol of ancient Judaism back to Israel with their immigration. He acknowledged that the Ethiopian presence made Israelis think more about race. His friend felt Israeli society was "set in its ways" and difficult to change because of Ashkenazi domination.

A student at Ben Gurion University felt strongly that traditions held by the Ethiopians were forms of the "original faith unchanged" and gave them even more claim to Israel than many of the Russian or Ashkenazi Jews. He also said that as Africans they challenged Western Jewry to look beyond race in defining Judaism. He believes Ethiopian contributions to Israel will grow as the community becomes more politically and economically active and therefore more visible and influential. He pointed out that there has been only one Ethiopian representative in the Knesset, and more are needed in order for their community to be heard and to have an effect on Israeli society.

The task of determining who is or is not a Jew and who has the authority to make such decisions remains a critical issue in Israel. The questioning of Ethiopian Jewishness persists as a major problem and is a barrier to full acceptance in Israeli society.

Cultural Production and Agency: Transitions in Ethiopian Identity

When I asked two young men in the military where I could find an Ethiopian synagogue in Jerusalem, they said there was none, that most Ethiopians just went to the nearest synagogue for prayers. As we spoke more about their faith, they emphasized the uniqueness of Ethiopian Judaism, describing the prerabbinical rituals of the *orit* (Ethiopian Torah), still observed by many of the older generation. Both of the soldiers were from Beersheba and advised me that I should go there if I wanted to observe a traditional service, as that is where the largest Ethiopian synagogue in Israel is located.

Beersheba, where the greatest proportion of Ethiopian immigrants settled, is an Ethiopian cultural center. Connected to the synagogue complex is the Ethiopian House of Jewry, where services ranging from health and prenatal care to such immigration concerns as housing and employment are offered. New institutions have been developed, including restaurants and a nightclub as well as recreation facilities. The small nightclub is one of the few local hangouts for young Ethiopian Jews to enjoy themselves and their popular music.

Like many other diaspora communities, the Beta Israel reestablished their social and religious spaces after resettlement, but even some of the most fundamental traditions that have sustained the community have changed in the process of incorporation. In particular the Ethiopian synagogue, although Ethiopian synagogue life remains at the heart of the community, it is undergoing incremental change. Traditional rituals continue but are slowly assuming new forms. Perhaps the most dramatic change is the increasing significance of Western rabbinical worship.

Beersheba is one of the few places where the traditional services in the ancient language of Geez are still performed. The service begins at sundown on Friday, as in rabbinical practice, and then resumes for Sabbath services early Saturday morning, at 5:00 A.M. sunrise. When I arrived about 5:30 A.M., the synagogue was completely empty except for an elderly priest reciting the Geez prayers from memory. For more than an hour we were the only people there. Later two elderly men came and joined the priest in the Geez prayers. By 6:45 A.M. there were five more elderly men. All these men were wearing the traditional Ethiopian *shemmas* (white shawls) and recited all the prayers from memory.

Later, others entered the sanctuary wearing rabbinical *kippurs* and shawls and carrying Hebrew prayer books. They did not join the Geez prayer but instead quietly sat and recited in Hebrew. About 7:30 A.M., the Geez prayers subsided, and the Ethiopian *quesotch* were replaced by an Ethiopian rabbi, and the Hebrew service commenced. The rabbi was dressed in a black suit and hat very much like the garb of the Hasidic sect, which has roots in Europe and did not emerge in the Middle Eastern until the late 1800s. By 8:00 A.M. the synagogue was full, mostly of middle-aged men, some women about thirty-five years of age or older, and a number of boys probably ranging in age from six to fourteen. There were virtually no young adults (age fifteen to twenty). My two acquaintances in Jerusalem had told me they rarely attend services.

The men who had participated in the Geez service sat to the left of the pulpit, facing the congregation, but did not take part in the rabbinical service and did not have Hebrew prayer books. During rabbinical service, after certain passages of the Torah were read, the reader would leave the pulpit to allow the edge of his shawl to be kissed by the greater congregation; significantly, he always went first to the elders near the pulpit. While I was present, only one European Israeli came in, and he left before the service ended. One middle-aged man informed me that the elders are the only ones who know the Geez prayers. Other men who have been taking on communal leadership roles have opted to become rabbis rather than continue the Geez legacy. An acquaintance at Ben Gurion University also made the same comment, explaining that the desire or interest to go through the rigorous training and study of Geez under the priests is not as strong as it may once have been. This lack of interest by the younger generation in learning Geez and the ancient tradition may be lost if the language is not passed on. He said that the university plans to hire a local Ethiopian priest to teach Geez, and he intends to take the class, although he is not immediately considering the priesthood.

In reflecting on this, I think the form and content of worship may be one of the most significant changes faced by Ethiopians. Is it inevitable that the Ethiopian Jewish community will forgo their rich cultural traditions, the last remnants of a prerabbinical Judaism? Will the Judaism of the ancient past, which always housed different sects within its branches, pass on along with the traditions of the Beta Israel?

The generation gap between the elder Ethiopian Jews born and raised in Ethiopia and the youth born in Israel is quite pronounced. Yet the older generation, who witnessed some of the greatest changes, remain the "cultural stewards" who retain the Ethiopian traditions and heritage from whence they came; they are the memory keepers. Perhaps it will only be through young Ethiopian Jews like my university friend, who for example have an interest in learning Geez, that the Ethiopian Jews may lay claim to their own ancient Judaic past and retain the practices of their forefathers.

Like most African diaspora communities, the Beta Israel struggle with sociopolitical problems of rejection and discrimination. They have dealt with many of these challenges through a new political activism. Several organizations have represented political interests within the Ethiopian Jewish community since immigration. In the late 1980s the Ethiopian Student Organization was founded, and the National Committee for Ethiopian Jewry was revived after being inactive for a number of years. By 1990 there was mounting factionalism within the community, and the varying political currents attempted to unify under the Umbrella Organization of Ethiopian Jewish Organizations, but factions continued to emerge, some of which developed out of a resistance to domination of the Umbrella Organization. Finally, the United Ethiopian Jewish Organization became a prominent political presence under the founding leadership of Addisu Messeleh, who eventually became the first Ethiopian a representative in the Knesset.

The thread linking these organizations is the focus on socioeconomic and political issues in order to foster communal development and incorporation into Israeli life. A new Ethiopian political consciousness is demanding fundamental rights and privileges. Problems of racism and discrimination have become prevalent and have sparked political activism. Two recent examples illustrate racial conflict.

The first case was the Israeli blood scandal, which led to massive riots in Jerusalem in February 1996. About ten thousand Ethiopian Jews converged on the prime minister's office to protest the secret policy of Israeli medical authorities to destroy blood donated by Ethiopians. The fear was that it was more likely to be tainted with HIV, which in turn led to rumors about AIDS in the Ethiopian community. The blood dumping had been going on for five or six years before it became public knowledge.

One college student said the Ethiopians were infuriated by this lack of acceptance and betrayal, which shook their trust in the government. Another added that the incident allowed him to see how Israeli officials really felt about the Ethiopians.

The second case occurred in July 1997, when a young Ethiopian man was killed by Israeli soldiers. The twenty-three-year-old was shot nine times by soldiers at a home in Beersheba, which investigators later declared may have been a matter of mistaken identity. The enraged Ethiopian Jewish community immediately protested outside the police consulate in Beersheba, and there were charges of police brutality. A student pointed out to me that there has been a rise in police violence toward Ethiopians in such areas as Ashkeland, Natalia, and other areas heavily populated by Beta Israel. A political science student at Ben Gurion commented that one of Israel's most wanted Hamas leaders, allegedly responsible for a series of suicide bombings, was arrested and held without so much as a scratch on him, yet the police shot an Ethiopian Jew nine times by "mistake."

In May 1997 a program produced by Ethiopians was aired on Israeli television, *Through Our Eyes*, which was their first attempt to become involved with the mainstream TV media. The concept stemmed from an earlier documentary on Beta Israel life since emigration. With the assistance of an Ethiopian-born film producer, Daniel Waldeman, the idea of a weekly program became a reality. Waldeman spoke to me regarding the importance of educating Israelis about Ethiopian community issues, concerns, and cultural heritage. Given questions about their Jewishness and racial stereotyping, the program provides a much-needed forum for addressing misconceptions.

I was introduced to at least two radio programs that were broadcast weekly. The one from Tel Aviv is in Amharic and Tigrinya and provides news about Ethiopia and the world, accompanied by Ethiopian music. The program from Jerusalem features new Ethiopian music as well as reggae, rap, and R and B.

African Diaspora Popular Culture and Implications for Identity

The demand for black music by Israeli youth in general and the Ethiopians in particular has opened new windows in the Israeli market and media for African diaspora popular culture. Radio stations have slowly diversified their formats to meet the demands of a growing young audience. Many radio programs targeting younger listeners are still dominated by popular music from Europe and the United States, but have come to include such black artists as Whitney Houston, Boys II Men, and Bob Marley. In turn music retailers also have expanded their selections of black music.

The 1980s marked a new period in music history as satellite and cassette technology made the world a much smaller place, while economic recession forced the industry to look to international markets for further growth.[2] By early 1993, MTV's global audience was nearly one-quarter of a billion households (60 million in the United States), or more than half a billion viewers in seventy-one countries.[3] Yet MTV has only recently begun playing rap or certain other forms of African American music on a regular basis.[4] MTV is a major source of African diaspora music in Israel, and along with exposure to the music of urban black America comes styles in clothing and hair, some of which are appropriated by Ethiopian youth. From short braids to dreadlocks, Young Ethiopians have picked up the cultural rhythms of their Western cousins.

The younger Ethiopian Jews are captivated by the music produced in the United States, especially rap and R and B, as well as reggae from Jamaica. Artists such as Snoop Doggy Dog, Tupac, Mary J. Blige, and many others are favorites. Reggae artists Buju Banton, Bob Marley, and Israel Vibration are also popular. Young Israelis of other backgrounds are taking an increasing interest in this music as well, which is heard more often in discos and nightclubs.

In Tel Aviv, the Soweto Club features a prime-time reggae format coupled with hip-hop and R and B. It has become the hot spot for young Israelis, including Ethiopians. They come from as far away as Haifa and Ashqelon on the weekends. As noted earlier, Tel Aviv has the country's only Ethiopian restaurant, and it also is a hangout for young Ethiopians. Across the street is a small shop selling mainly music, books, posters, and other products from Ethiopia, but it is not owned by an Ethiopian. As in other diaspora situations, black consumers are not necessarily the providers of their own cultural products.

The annual reggae festival concert is a major event. The 1997 headliners were international reggae superstar Buju Banton, the famous dance hall artist from Jamaica, and Misty and the Roots, a very popular band from London. Nationwide promotions pictured an inset photo Bob Marley's in the Star of David. The concert was held on a beach in Ahkziv, only a mile from the Lebanese border, and Ethiopian reggae lovers flocked to it from all over the country, wearing their motherland's colors of red, gold, and green, Bob Marley T-shirts, and dreadlocks. The festival started about five years ago and continues to grow. Reggae has played an important role in the spread of black popular culture in Israel.

The strong identification with reggae is also connected to the Rastafarian spiritual movement, which is linked to the Solomonic tradition in Ethiopia. For many Ethiopians born in Israel, these associations with a "motherland" most have never seen are very powerful. One manifestation of this "community of consciousness" is hairstyles. Many young Ethiopians I met said they wanted dreadlocks like mine, and a soldier in Beersheba proclaimed that after he left the army he not only planned to grow his *rasta* (the Beta Israel term for dreadlocks) but also intended to visit Jamaica. This is but one example of the strong symbolic identification the Beta Israel youth have with Rastafarianism through the music experience.

What is so fascinating is in Jamaica I found that the Rastafarians look to their cousins in the East with equal enthusiasm and reverence. What I call the African diaspora mirror of identity reflects and refracts the African heritage (and cultural identity is refracted) throughout the diaspora as people (re)connect with one another. Rastafarians refer to this as the "I and I concept," a recognition of the spiritual self or equal in others, which expresses the oneness or commonalties of the global African family being made up of "communities of consciousness."

Jamaican Rastafarians in their search for cultural heritage looked to Africa for redemption, with Ethiopia as the promised land, and to Haile Selassie, emperor of Ethiopia, a black Messiah. This is part of the belief system of the Rastafarian messianic movement out of which came dreadlocks, reggae music, and the colors of Garveyism: Red, Black, and Green. Ethiopianism, Garveyism, and the Rastafarians of the West did not take root in Ethiopia until more recently, as they were cultural manifestations of an African diaspora experience—looking toward Africa and Ethiopia, as the promised land.

The Ethiopian Jews of the African diaspora join Jamaicans and others in the search for ways to deal with alienation, racism, displacement, and identity issues. Black movements such as Garveyism crystallized in the 1920s- and 1930s–period of world depression and economic dislocation. Thus Ethiopian youth identification with Rastafarians is akin to the "closing of the circle." It is a way for them to identify with "blackness," their Africanness, through cultural productions and practices of the New World African diaspora. Even in Jamaica, Rastafari appealed to young politically conscious, many poor but not exclusively, as some were students and professionals. They saw Jamaica as a land of oppression—one venue of escape was to create their own identity space.[5]

As immigrants, the Ethiopian Jews share the diaspora experience of being marginalized others in a land founded and shaped in the modern age largely by Western European Jewry. As recent African emigrants, Ethiopians are subordinated, as are the majority Sephardic and the fifth of the population who are Palestinian. Ethiopian Jews' political, economic, and cultural conditions result in their looking at themselves in some of the same ways as other peoples of the diaspora in similar situations: a subordinated and indeed racialized Other as one aspect of their identity. In Ethiopia, they were a religious minority in a Christian country; in Israel their minority status is based in large part on an externally defined and racialized African heritage.

The new experiences have led them, like other diaspora communities, to affirm and express their African identity through creative culture, especially music. It is important to note that the younger Beta Israel have begun to see themselves as a part of the global African diaspora. Furthermore, their cultural expressions are having an effect on Israeli mainstream culture.

As Barnet and Cavanagh point out: "The products of the global pop-music industry are American [and by extension New World African diaspora] in beat and feel, and the market is dominated by American artists. . . . The black experience in America—the yearnings, pathos, intensity, and energy inspired by a mix of African rhythms, slave songs sung in a strange land, and the speed and din of life in America—produced a cultural mix that has excited people everywhere in the twentieth century. This authentically American art form touches people across divisions of race, nation, and class in ways no other musical experience can equal."[6] For Beta

Israel youth, hip-hop, reggae music, dreadlocks, and other cultural manifestations are a way to rebel against a social system that does not recognize or value their blackness or African heritage; but even more importantly, they are a way to affirm their cultural self and place in Israel. But as African immigrants in a turbulent land of religious, racial, political conflicts and violence—they too can define Israel as a type of oppressive "Babylon," in much the same way their diaspora cousins in the West view their oppressors.

THE BLACK HEBREWS

The African Hebrew Israelites, also called Black Hebrews or Hebrew Israelites, often refer to themselves as The Nation. They have settled in the Negev not far from Beer-sheba, in a smaller city called Dimona, and are people of African descent primarily from the United States. One of their beliefs is that their ancestors, the Israelites of biblical times, were Africans:

> Now these are the generations of the Sons of Noah, Shem, Ham, and Japhet: and unto them were sons born after the flood.
>   And the sons of Ham; Cush, and Mizraim, and Phut, and Canaan. (Gen. 10:1)

The group was formed on the south side of Chicago in the early 1960s, one of the many black Jewish groups that emerged in the U.S. as part of a black cultural tradition, dating as far back as the 1920s and 1930s, if not earlier.[7] These particular Black Hebrews left America for Liberia in 1967, when about 134 members of what was then called the Abeta Israel Cultural Center made their "exodus." They never intended to settle permanently in Liberia, and 39 members of the group left for Israel in 1969 seeking citizenship under the Israeli Law of Return, to prepare the way for the rest of the community.

The group forced many obstacles from the state bureaucracy initially, especially questions regarding "Jewishness," and the advance party was finally allowed provisional status as immigrants, but not as Jews. Under the leadership of Ben Ammi Israel, they moved into an abandoned Russian compound and proclaimed their right to the land through their claimed descent from the original Hebrews. After 30 years this highly self-reliant community, scattered in various towns, has finally begun to receive some recognition from a very reluctant government.

Encounters in Jerusalem, Tel Aviv, Tiberias, and Sfat

My first contact with a Hebrew Israelite was during my first week in Jerusalem. I met a man selling incense and oils who suggested that I go visit the larger community in Dimona. He spoke for quite some time about the political and spiritual situation of blacks in the United States and the need for radical change and their evacuation. He emphasized the Hebrew Israelite doctrinal beliefs that blacks, especially from the United States, are the true Israelites and chosen people of Yah, destined to inherit the Holy Land. At this man's suggestion, I went to Tel Aviv and sought out the Hebrew Israelite restaurant, one of the few vegetarian restaurants in Israel. There I met Abshalom, one of the Hebrew elders, who explained he had come to Israel in the mid-1970s and settled in Dimona. That is the main settlement, although there are also smaller communities of Hebrew Israelites in Tel Aviv and Tiberias, where one of his daughters lives. A professional musician originally from New York, Abshalom emphasized how blacks in the West, especially America, need to return to the land and the law of their ancestors, which is promised as their inheritance. He spoke of how the Hebrew lifestyle of prayer, exercise, and diet are the sacred remedies for the physical and psycho-spiritual ailments that afflict blacks in the West.

In Tiberias I spent an afternoon talking with Abshalom's daughter, who was born in Israel, fluent in Hebrew, and loved her home. She was not interested in visiting the United States and had heard a lot of negative things about the black experience there. She has not had many problems with racism in Israel, to which she attributed to her fluency in Hebrew, but is aware of racial incidents. She had been educated in part in Israeli schools but had not planned to go onto college yet. At the time she lived with a number of other Black Hebrew community members in Tiberias. As for contact with Ethiopian Jews, she said some lived in her building complex but they rarely spoke. She had tried to make conversation, but the response was not very cordial. She believed the Ethiopians were told by European Israelis not to interact with the Hebrew Israelites.

In Sfat, known for its historical legacy as the home of Jewish mysticism and for its art colony, I met Kim Weston, originally from Detroit, Michigan, whose 1965 hit, "Take Me in Your Arms (Rock Me a Little While)," was number four on the R and B charts in the United States. I talked with her over dinner in a place called the Memphis Restaurant with some of her greatest hits playing in the background, as she explained her life as a Hebrew Israelite and years as a singer returning to the stage in Israel. She had joined the Hebrew Israelites in the 1970s, decided to settle in Israel, and now performed there and throughout the Middle East. She feels at home in Israel, where she has created an artistic niche as a performer of historic R and B. She lives in Sfat but visits Dimona often to see friends and for special celebrations.

Dimona: Cultural Center of the Hebrew Israelites

I was warmly received by the small black neighborhood in Dimona, where one of the elders described the hard conditions experienced in the first five or six years, including no electricity or running water and serious food rationing. I observed drill teams of boys, ranging in age from four or five to thirteen, and was told they are responsible for the daily cleaning of the neighborhood streets as well as the drill exercises. My guide explained that several community members had received military training in America, and that was useful in establishing and maintaining the community's security forces. He added that it was important for the youth to develop a sense of environmental awareness and readiness at an early age.

The compound at Dimona included about thirty-five mobile homes; the community dining hall; stores that sold foodstuffs, hardware, and household items; a tailor shop where most community clothes were made; and a shop with African-style fashions, jewelry, and sculpture. There was a vegetarian restaurant, and a new recreation and visitors' center was under construction, which will have a swimming pool and sauna. Across the street was a newly built school provided by the Israeli government, which apparently believed the Hebrew Israelite community was permanent. One woman said it was an attempt to "control the education of the Hebrew Israelite children, signaling the first steps toward attempts at brainwashing."

Much of the community's income is provided by a factory, about fifteen minutes away on the outskirts of town, that produces tofu, soy ice cream, and other soy products. The equipment was imported from Japan, where three community members were trained in making tofu. The ice cream really began to flourish upon the arrival of a man who had owned that kind of business in Atlanta, Georgia. The factory also had a bakery. All products were marketed to Israeli supermarkets, used at the restaurant, or sold for local consumption. The plan was to promote health foods to the Israeli population and eventually enter the international market.

Health consciousness and daily exercise are the required routine for all adults and children as the basis for a divine lifestyle. Each adult is expected to run at least thirty minutes every day. Other activities including martial arts, such as Tai Chi and karate, along with yoga and mediation are also encouraged. An elder who is the group's fitness expert and trainer said the physical regimen is essential to sustain and purify the bodily "temple." He also said that men are considered priests, and their responsibilities range from judicial and ceremonial activities to overseeing work, construction, and transportation. Earlier that morning he had performed the blessing of a newborn child.

He talked about the Hebrew Israelites "call to Black people in America" to awaken to their true identity as descendants of the original Israelites and the need to free themselves from the bondage and oppression that shackled their minds and souls to the Western path leading to destruction. He also noted that the Hebrew Israelites had contributed to the African American Heritage version of the bible, serving as advisors about terms and geographic locations and as models for the illustrations, wearing the traditional Israelite clothing.

One of the older community leaders, who had lived in Israel for twenty-three years as a "keeper of memories," gave a very detailed account of the harassment in the past. At first, the Israeli police would continually arrest members and often deported them to America. There were stories of people who left for work and were never heard from again. He said that many of the confrontations came to blows. Once the police were holding four or five male Hebrew Israelites and questioned them about their Jewishness. The men proclaimed themselves to be Israelites with divine rights to the land. The police refused to believe them and demanded that they drop their pants, to see whether they had been circumcised. The prisoners adamantly refused and told the police: "You can try to take these pants off yourself, but we are gonna fight you down!" The frustrated police finally let them go for fear of creating a riot or worse. The harassment eventually lessened as the authorities realized the group "was not going to be moved," regardless of the tactics.

Events climaxed in the mid 1980s, when the compound was surrounded by soldiers and tanks to prevent a march on Jerusalem the Hebrew Israelites had organized to protest conditions and treatment. "Armed with the spirit of *Yah*," as one woman said proudly, and dressed in white, the community came out in tight drill formation and started toward Jerusalem. The soldiers could not open fire on the weaponless group, and eventually negotiators were sent to reason with the leaders about their demands.

These kinds of incidents reveal the unified strength of the Hebrew Israelites, their political resolve, and their struggle for respect as a legitimate community. Ironically what was once a thorn in the side recently was called "the miracle in the desert" in the Israeli press. Through resilience and determination, these blacks from the United States have forged their own destiny in one of the most barren places in Israel. The status of the group has grown nationally, and the widely known Hebrew Israelite choir was asked to perform at the opening of the 1997 Maccabee Games, to which Jewish athletes from around the world come to compete.

A BET television special on the Hebrew Israelites and other communities of African heritage in Israel aired on 4 January 1998. Among those interviewed were Ben Ammi Israel, leader of the Hebrew Israelites; Baht Ammi Baht-Israel, a pioneer settler; Prince Gavriel Ben-Israel, founding member of the Dimona settlement; Karaliah Ben-Israel, a founding female member; Prince Asiel Ben-Israel, Dimona's ambassador at large; and

Yesherchar Ben-Israel, who recounted that he was working at the Wrigley Gum Factory in Chicago when he decided to emigrate. He did not feel accepted in the United States and took his five children with him, but his wife refused to go. Prince Asiel Ben-Israel made it clear that it is important to understand how the Hebrew Israelites perceive and define themselves. When they left for Israel, the Law of Return said that those who believed they were Jewish would be awarded full citizenship. In 1971 the law was changed, and only those with a Jewish mother would receive citizenship. After more than thirty years, the Hebrew Israelites have still not been granted citizenship.

Despite challenges and resistance, the Hebrew Israelites have demonstrated a capacity to endure and use creative energies to shape their identity. According to one elder, the "advent of the Messianic Kingdom is manifest as we speak." He added: "This is Zion, in the way we are living—it is not in outer space or heavenly never-never land, it is here on earth, right here in Dimona, and Ben Ammi is our Messiah Leader. We are living the divine life in all its ways, every day—we just hope our brothers and sisters in America can see this before it is too late for them."

ETHIOPIAN ORTHODOX CHRISTIANS

Yet another black religious community in Israel is the Ethiopian Orthodox Christians, one of the oldest Christian communities in the world. The Ethiopians have been settled in Jerusalem as well as Bethany, Bethlehem, and Jericho for centuries. Saint Jerome, who lived in Bethlehem between 386 and 412 A.D., describes in a letter "the arrival and presence of Ethiopian monks in the Holy Land." These pilgrim groups eventually took up residency near several holy sites, establishing chapels and monasteries.

I met Zion and Solomon, two Ethiopian Christians in their late twenties, on one of my first visits to the Old City. They were on their way to the Ethiopian church and monastery known as the Dier Sultan, located on the upper levels and roof of the Church of the Holy Sepulchre complex.

The tradition is that this place was first given to the Ethiopians by King Solomon during the visit of Makeda, queen of Sheba, and was used as shelter by Ethiopian officials who visited Palestine from time to time. One of these was the eunuch and finance minister of Candace, queen of Ethiopia, who would eventually be baptized by the apostle Philip.[8] Father Doubdan wrote in 1661: "Continuing our way we went to the parvis of the Holy Sepulchre to see the dwelling of the Abbysinians who are the subjects of Preston John, Primate. (Preston John or Emperor Lebna Dengal of Ethiopia.) This dwelling is on the Mount Calvary where we went upstairs to a little courtyard on the terrace at the entrance of which there is a little wild olive tree in the form of a bush . . . where Abraham found a ram attached by its horns, which he sacrificed instead of his son Isaac. They to whom it belongs preserve it."[9]

Zion was a nephew of one of the monks and had been living in Jerusalem about four months. Solomon had been there much longer. Both spoke Amharic and a little English, and Solomon was fluent in Hebrew, which Zion was still learning. Most Ethiopians living in the Old City are relatives of people connected with the church and have jobs in greater Jerusalem.

Solomon lived near the church and monastery of Debre Gennet and Kidane Mihret, located on Ethiopian Street, which is near the largest Ethiopian population in Israel. The church of Debre Gennet (Mount of Paradise) and the monastery of Kidane Mihret (Covenant of Mercy) are dedicated to the Virgin Mary and were built by emperors Yohannes IV and Menelik II between 1882 and 1901. During that era several other properties were acquired as well, including Holy Trinity Monastery, situated on the River Jordan, where Christ was baptized by John the Baptist; the convent and church at Jericho; and the Monastery of Saint Tekla Haimonet at Bethany.

At the church and convent in Jericho, which served as a monastery compound, I met an elderly Ethiopian woman, who was one of the attending nuns along with an Ethiopian man who was a groundskeeper, who shared stories about Ethiopian traditions that extend back into Old Testament times. One of these stories was based on Ebed Melech, the Abyssinian who saved Jeremiah from the pit of death,[10] the Ethiopians claim rights to Jerusalem and Israel through the promise of Yahweh, who commended Ebed Melech to Jeremiah for his faith in the chosen prophet. New Testament passages (such as Acts 8:26–39) refer to the Ethiopian eunuch, the first African to be converted to the new faith centered around Jesus the Messiah. Eusebias speaks of him as the first fruit of the faithful in the whole world, indicating that Ethiopia was one of the earliest nations to accept Christianity.

The Ethiopians maintain they were the first to establish the central monastery at the Church of the Holy Sepulchre in Jerusalem and controlled much of the Old City church site, long before the Armenian, Coptic, or Greek churches settled in began to force their way into the area. Over time, Ethiopian properties have been lost, now two Ethiopian chapels are the only passage between the ninth and tenth stations of the cross on the Via Del Larosa, the route Christ walked to Calvary, and possession of the keys to these sanctuaries has been the subject of controversy between the Copts and the Ethiopians.

The debate over property rights goes back centuries and also involves other properties around the Holy Sepulchre. Ethiopian claims were recognized as far back as 636 A.D. in a decree by Khalif Omar, the Muslim power ruling Jerusalem at the time:

That tranquility reign among them [Christians] in all other places of adoration which are under their authority in Jerusalem and outside, which are: the Quamma or the temple of resurrection and the big Church of Bethlehem where the birth of Christ took place. That the Iberian and Abyssinian Communities, residing from the Greek nation be there; that all the other nations go there for their pilgrimage, the Latins, Copts, Syrians, Armenians, Nestorians, Jacobites and Maronites must submit to the said Patriarch [Sophoonios of Jerusalem].[11]

Emperor Haile Selassie, whose ascendance to the Ethiopian monarchal throne was based upon his lineage descending from the Solomonic line, was conferred with the title of Lion of Judah at his coronation in 1930, further representing the integral Ethiopian connections to Jerusalem and Israel. During the Italian invasion in 1935, Emperor Selassie went into exile, arriving in Israel in the month of May 1936, and reestablished his seat of government in Jerusalem.[12] His entourage doubled the size of the Ethiopian community. After Italy's initial occupation of Ethiopia there followed an intense and drawn out court litigation in the Jerusalem courts between Italy and the Ethiopian Orthodox Church and Government concerning Ethiopian religious properties. These legal disputes suggest Italy's interests in invading Ethiopia were also greatly focused on controlling historical Ethiopian sacred sites in Jerusalem as well as throughout Israel.

Conflicts between the Ethiopian Christians and the Egyptian Copts concerning Deir Sultan have also surfaced in recent years in the Israeli supreme courts, in spite of these land disputes the Ethiopian Christian community continues to thrive and receives hundreds of devoted pilgrims each year. As Israel's oldest diaspora community, the Ethiopian Orthodox Church represent an important historical legacy of Africans in the holy land.

CONCLUSION

The presence of African people in Israel demonstrates how the diaspora has moved through time along geographic, political, cultural, and religious dimensions. The Ethiopian Orthodox Christians arrived in biblical times, the Black Hebrews in the late 1960s, and the Beta Israel in the 1980s. Each group had to deal with issues of incorporation and identity. For all three groups, Israel and especially Jerusalem are at the heart of religious life. For the Beta Israel, the idea of return has long been part of their theology. In 1862, for example, during the reign of Negus Tewodros (1855–68), six Beta Israel priests led thousands of Jews from their villages northward to the Red Sea, believing Yahweh would perform a miracle and divide the waters as he had done in the Exodus. For the Hebrew Israelites, migration to Israel is essential for establishing the messianic kingdom. For Ethiopian Orthodox Christians, visiting the holy sites demonstrates commitment to their faith, and their right to a presence there rests on biblical grounds.

These contemporary communities are heirs to a rich legacy of African presence traced throughout ancient Israelite and biblical history. For example, Ethiopian presence has been evident as early as the time of Moses, who took an Ethiopian wife Zipporah. In the book of Jeremiah, the Ethiopian Ebed Melech saved Jeremiah from the pit of death. Moreover, Chronicles chapter 9 describes the visit of the Ethiopian queen of Sheba to Israel and her gifts of gold and frankincense given to King Solomon, the basis for the canonical book *The Kebre Negast* (Glory of the kings), a pillar of the Ethiopian Israelite traditions and Solomonic dynasties found in both the Beta Israel and Ethiopian Orthodox Christian faith. Moreover, Ethiopians are referred to in the New Testament, in Acts 8:26; where Philip meets and converts the Ethiopian eunuch, a devout Jew heading toward Jerusalem to worship. His baptism symbolized the Ethiopian presence among the earliest Christians, as Eusebius spoke of him as the first fruit of the faithful in the whole world.

This black presence in Israel highlights the significance of Ethiopia and Ethiopianism in diaspora identity and the circularity of influence among New World African peoples. Since the 1700s, especially within the early black theological traditions, references to Ethiopia in the bible served as symbolic links for the forcibly displaced Africans. Ethiopianism became even more prevalent during the mid to late 1800s and early twentieth century in America and the West Indies, making up the golden era of black nationalism and pan-Africanist movements, including Garveyism and later the Rastafarians. Most notable today is the appropriation of the Rastafarian ideology concerning Ethiopia, cultural expressions in hairstyles, and the interest in reggae music favored by young Ethiopian Jews. Their "African diaspora mirror of identity" is important in understanding the meaning and significance of the African diaspora experience as a global phenomenon. The struggle of diaspora people to define themselves within societies that refuse to accept them fully for who they are is central to an understanding of their persistence and survival. The common threads among these black "communities of consciousness" in Israel are their determination to establish themselves, gain respect, and uphold their religious beliefs. In doing so they have created new pathways and framed a new sense of themselves that combines both continuity and change.

The presence of these groups remains significant, as they reveal the important historical connections between the land of Israel, the people of African descent, and the destiny of the Judaic faiths.

NOTES

Financial support for summer research in Israel was provided by the African Diaspora Research Project (ADRP), under the direction of Dr. Ruth Hamilton. Dr. Lee June, vice president of student affairs, also contributed financial support through his office. I was a participant in the study abroad program in Israel under the direction of Dr. John Greene of the Religious Studies Department at Michigan State University.

Due to the fact that original research for this article was conducted in 1997, many issues and names of places have naturally changed over time. Among some of the major issues that changed, the Black Hebrew-Israelites have since become Israeli citizens, a culmination of the struggle discussed in this article.

1. See Serge Schmemann, "Ethiopian Jews in Israel: Melee over AIDS Fear," *New York Times*, 29 July 1996, A3.
2. Reebee Garofalo, "Culture versus Commerce: The Marketing of Black Popular Music," *Public Culture* 7 (fall 1994).
3. Benjamin R. Barber, *Jihad vs. McWorld: How Globalism and Tribalism Are Reshaping the World* (New York: Ballantine Books, 1996).
4. Todd Boyd, "Check Yo Self, before You Wreck Yo Self: Variations on a Political Theme in Rap Music and Popular Culture," *Public Culture* 7 (fall 1994).
5. Leonard Barrett, *The Rastafarians: Sounds of Cultural Dissonance* (Boston: Beacon Press, 1977).
6. Richard J. Barnet and John Cavanagh, *Global Dreams: Imperial Corporations and the New World Order* (New York: Simon and Schuster, 1994), 112.
7. Morris Lounds Jr., *Israel's Black Hebrews: Black Americans in Search of Identity* (Washington, D.C.: University Press of America, 1981).
8. Acts 8:26–39; Archbishop Yesehaq, *The Ethiopian Tewahedo Church: An Integrally African Church* (New York: Vantage Press, 1989), 177. (ISBN number: 5–533–0760–2)
9. Ibid., 178
10. Jeremiah 38:7–12.
11. Correspondence *Respecting Abyssinians at Jerusalem*, 1850–1867, Presented to the House of Commons, in pursuance of their address dated 5 December 1867, with further papers presented by command of Her Majesty, 1868 (London: Printed by Harrison and Sons; Asmara: Kokebe Tzebah Press), 38.
12. Kirsten Pederson, *The History of the Ethiopian Community in the Holy Land from the Time of Emperor Tewodros II till 1974* (Jerusalem: Habesch, Commercial Press, 1983), 102.

Redefining a Collective Identity in the Struggle for State and National Identity in Ethiopia and Israel: The Case of Ethiopian Jews (Beta Israel)

Ruth Simms Hamilton with Getahun Benti

THE MAKING OF THE BETA ISRAEL IN ETHIOPIA

Ethiopian Jews lived for over two thousand years in small communities in Abyssinia (Ethiopia). They resided in the northwestern region, living in small villages of around two hundred residents scattered throughout the Semien Mountain region, near Lake Tana, Tselemt, Walqait, Wagara (all in Gondar province), and in southern Tigray and Wollo.[1] They were domiciled in small numbers in towns of Shoa province but a larger majority has lived in the region of Gondar. Those in the Gondar area are primarily Amharic speakers while those in Tigray speak Tigrinya. Both languages are spoken in their locations in Tselemt, Semien, and Walqait, locations between Tigray and Gondar. Internally differentiated linguistically and socially, the largest group, the Amharic-speaking Jews, especially those who lived in and around the town of Gondar (like the Amharic-speaking Christians in Ethiopia), have traditionally been more urban and of higher socioeconomic status.[2]

With their fellow nationals, Ethiopian Jews share the same languages and employ the same ecclesiastical and liturgical language in holy texts written in Geez, also known as Ethiopic.[3] Linguistically, the people of Ethiopia fall into four major groupings: Cushitic, Nilo-Saharan, Omotic, and Semitic, each with its own subdivisions. The Cushitic is the largest in terms of population and further divided into four main branches—northern, southern, eastern, and central. The majority of Jews are associated with the central

Cushitic division and one of its subpopulations.[4] Both Christians and Jews use Amharic given names or names taken from the Bible.[5]

The introduction of Christianity to Abyssinia in the fourth century A.D. and the conversion of the royal family to it no doubt limited the spread of Judaism but did not prevent its dissemination or stop the adoption by the Christians of "certain Jewish practices."[6] For example, the Ethiopians "clung to those remnants of the Mosaic law [even] after their conversion to Christianity."[7] Orthodox Christianity, drawing significantly from the Old Testament and as practiced by the Ethiopians, has many Judaic elements in it:

> features of the Ethiopian Orthodox Church seem to reflect significant Judaic influence
> . . . the placing in every Ethiopian Church of a tabot, or a symbolic representation of
> the Ark of the Covenant supposedly granted by God to Moses, before which Ethio-
> pian priests would on occasion dance, thus recalling the practice of King David and
> "all the house of Israel" as described in the Second Book of Samuel. The tabot (which
> did not exist in any other Christian country) resembled the Jewish Scrolls of Law in
> that it alone gave the church its sanctity.[8]

The long isolation of Ethiopian Christians from the larger outside Christian world resulted in less external influence and in the maintenance of earlier practices and forms of Christianity that bear much similarity with Judaism. The reverse is also characteristic of Judaism in Ethiopia.[9] The religious practice of Ethiopian Jews "is based on the Pentateuch, the first five books of the Old Testament" without knowledge of modern Hebraic law and its interpretations regarding Judaism.[10] Thus the religious practices of the Jews, some of which were borrowed from the neighboring Christians, have over many centuries maintained a strong Mosaic character.[11]

In Ethiopia, among the common elements that both religions have is the symbolic representation of the Ark of the Covenant, called *tabot,* which was supposedly given to them by Moses. They use Geez, a language only for church liturgy and religious services; they also have similar "division of places of worship into separate concentric compartments."[12] In both religions women are segregated and use a separate section during worship. Use of similar prayer sticks, beating of drums, use of umbrellas during religious processions, prohibition of smoking, and wearing white turbans by the priests are all common to followers of both religions. Both groups do not eat meat and dairy products on two days of the week, but on different days—the Christians on Wednesdays and Fridays and the Jews on Mondays and Thursdays. In general, both "religious groups shared similar organizational structures and identical designations."[13] Both have similar religious authorities with the same names, *debtaras* (lay clerics), deacons, monks, and nuns.[14] Thus, many similarities between Christianity and Judaism (as practiced in Ethiopia) are observable even today. As pointed out by Pankhurst, "in Ethiopia the two religions, Christianity and Judaism, blended in a manner virtually unknown elsewhere in Christendom."[15] Clerics from both ranks have defected to each other's religion, and Christian scribes were solicited to make copies of the Torah for the Jews. In essence, the interpenetration has been long and complex, with the two religious communities sharing a common Ethiopian way of life, some philosophical and religious ideas, and many national social institutions and customs.[16] Yet as Hagar Salamon states, Ethiopian Jews "regarded themselves as a distinct religious group. . . . Their faith clustered around the *Orit,* the Old Testament written in Ge'ez, the language of both Jewish and Christian sacred writings. As a group, the Beta Israel . . . constructed their identity in reference to their Christian neighbors, rather than to a Jewish 'other.'"[17]

State Subjugation and the Imposition of Falasha Identity

Until the first decade of the fifteenth century, Jews were an integral part of the social fabric of Abyssinian society. Thereafter came a turning point in history—their major confrontation with the Christian kingdom under King Yishaq and their subsequent defeat and reduction to subjects. The name *Falasha* was given to them in the early fifteenth century during the reign of Yishaq, 1413–30, following their resistance to Christian Amhara encroachment and attempts to evangelize them. Having failed to achieve this, Yishaq issued an edict that he hoped would force them to accept Christianity: "He who is baptized in the Christian religion, may inherit the land of his father; otherwise let him be a *Falasi.*"[18] Consequently the Jews were labeled *Falashoch,* meaning exiles. Moreover, King Yishaq absconded with their land and built many churches in places such as Dambya and Wagara. They were not completely forced to leave their lands nor did they become completely landless. They were, however, transformed into subjects and reduced to tributaries of the Amhara kings and lords. Even then, those who "remained loyal to king Yishaq and fought on his side" against their own kin were allowed to keep pieces of land for themselves under Amhara overlordship.[19]

The ownership of land must be understood within the context of Ethiopia's feudal system, whereby land tenure was primarily linked to service to the state and military. Hence, the Jews were engaged in major wars with Christians for centuries, but they also served as soldiers of the Christian state. This was not only the case for King Yishaq but also for almost all of his successors too. For instance, under King Susneyos (1607–32), there was a special Jewish regiment, Kayla, renown for scaling the highest peaks in the Semien Mountains for the emperor.[20] Some Jews were raised to positions of political importance, especially in the military, to serve the interests of the Amhara. But following the political chaos (known in Ethiopian history as the *zemene massafint*, or era of the princes) of the late eighteenth and the nineteenth centuries, they even lost that role and therefore their degree of marginalization was escalated. Thus, "the [Ethiopian Jewish] elite no longer played any significant political role in the general society after the *zemene massafint*."[21]

Over time, usufruct rights to land by Jews remained subject to frequent takeovers and tribute payments. With ensuing political and social transformations, the Amhara encroached even more on the small pieces of land they used as tenant farmers. In a Christian monarchial feudal state, especially among the northern Christian Amhara and Tigre, land ownership had been and still is communal. Everyone is entitled to a piece of land, although very small, as it is divided among offspring, generation after generation. However, Jews were denied even this traditional right of communal land-ownership in the northern setting.

In an agrarian society where access to land for farming is essential, Jewish material existence became more problematic. Consequently, like their disenfranchised co-religionists of the *Judenstadts* (ghettos) of fifteenth-century (some as early as 906 A.D.) Central Europe,[22] Ethiopian Jews became artisans, masons, carpenters, potters, weavers, blacksmiths, and tanners. Women pursued pottery crafts. As a result of their skills and artisanship, the Jews were associated with term *tebib*, referring to those who possess "secret knowledge."[23] Eventually their skills and products were in demand, resulting in an economic niche whereby they provided the Amhara with iron, clothes, leather, and pottery products. Over centuries they supplied their Christian neighbors with "ploughshares and the metal parts of other tools, as well as spearheads, woven cloth, and pottery of many shapes and sizes."[24] They were skilled and efficient builders and masons and were central to the construction of the historic castles, Ethiopian Christian churches, palaces, and residential houses in Gondar[25] and other reigning towns and were instrumental in the building of the current capital city of Addis Ababa and Gondar; the latter was the capital of Christian Ethiopia from the seventeenth century up to the 1860s.

The practices of social distancing and labeling those who engage in handicraft activities as inferior is prevalent among many Ethiopians, but especially the dominant Amhara and Tigre Christians in the north of the country.[26] They viewed Jews with a mixture of fear and repugnance,[27] defining them as evil-eyed people who became hyenas in the night and human beings in the daytime, and further stereotyping them as sorcerers, cannibals (*budas*), and evil people who used superhuman forces that resulted in persecution and bodily harm.[28] Jewish men "specialized in weaving and smithery and the women in pottery. The latter two occupations employed fire. . . . To the Christians, the power to transform otherwise useless things into useful objects by means of fire was surely supernatural. If they could change the form and function of things, what might they also do to people—including themselves?"[29]

Ideologies, myths, stereotypes, and labels are invoked by the powerful as a means of justification and legitimation of their actions, but also as a powerful mechanism of psychological and cultural control. The subjugated are therefore confronted with an externally imposed, unflattering stigmatization and negative identity. The condemnation, labeling, and stigmatization of the Jews were part of a culture of control to maintain their political impotence. Moreover, the practice of ideology through discrimination had the added effect of further neutralizing their possibilities of effectively contesting the economic and political power of the dominant groups. Socially, they were marginalized and became victims of blatant oppression, an outcast group in Ethiopia.

Re-defining the Collective Self: The Emergence of the Beta Israel

Though the Amhara and the Tigre despised the manual arts and stigmatized the practitioners as inferiors, Ethiopian Jews placed great value on their skills as craftsmen. In their communities, "blacksmiths were considered to be respected and wise men," which could be expressed in the very fact that members who were lazy or "unskilled" in craftsmanship were considered useless.[30] Moreover, the Jews used their high level of artistry and craftsmanship to empower themselves and to denigrate Christians through the metaphorical use of the Amharic term *dohone*, a clay vessel made of mud and straw which could only be sun-dried and used to hold dry foodstuffs:

> The *dohone* was the only clay vessel made by Christians, and the Beta Israel stressed the fact that no skill was required in making it. In those regions where both religious groups dwelled together, fired vessels were made exclusively by Beta Israel. Thus calling a Christian a *dohone* suggested that he was made of inferior, less sophisticated stuff. . . .
>
> While the *dohone* was of no use as a drinking vessel, fired vessels were useful not only for drinking but also for cooling water and improving its taste. Since Beta Israel provided all the drinking vessels in regions where they lived, this praxis formed the basis for the idea by which all religions benefited from Judaism as from a draught of cold water. But Christianity, as a *dohone*, could not fulfill any such task and hence could not be "imbibed."[31]

For Jews, this high valuation of their talents and skills was confirmed in practice as well as by observant international travelers. Early European travelers from Portugal, Germany, France, and Scotland variously characterized them as "the best craftsmen in the country."[32] For example, "early in the 17th century, the Falashas were described by the Portuguese Jesuit Manoel de Almeida as 'great smiths'; and Hiob Ludolf, a German scholar, later observed that they were much involved in the weaving of cotton and made the Heads of Spears and several other pieces of workmanship in Iron."[33]

Because they were committed to their religion and maintained a strong identity as Jews,[34] they called themselves the *Beta Israel* or *Ayhud*, literally meaning people of the House of Israel, Israelites, and Jews respectively.[35] This counterchallenged the name *Falasha* imposed upon them by the Amhara and, therefore, revealed their defined self or group image. To change or adopt a name is a rite of passage, a significant social transition.[36] In other words, *Falasha* was unacceptable to them, and accordingly, the group took on the signifier, *Beta Israel*, that represented the kind of people they wanted to be, a passage to a new group image and identity. This was a reflection of their "community of consciousness" and agency, creative and direct cultural action for themselves.[37]

There has also been much speculation about the origins of the Beta Israel or when and how they arrived in Ethiopia.[38] Over time, the Beta Israel have passed along their own story of origins directly linked to the "national" Ethiopian Kebra Nagast legend. The latter is based on the biblical story of the Cushite queen of Sheba who has an illegitimate son, Menelik I, by the Palestinian King Solomon. With the Beta Israel as escorts, Menelik I, accompanied by his mother, the queen of Sheba, returned to Cush on a spiritual mission to bring Judaism, the religion of his father. Moreover, the Ark of the Covenant, containing the Ten Commandments and carried from Jerusalem, is said to rest in the town of Aksum, where it is believed the queen of Sheba ruled. For the Beta Israel, their community of origin was indeed ancient Israel, also the putative homeland of Menelik I, whom they escorted to Ethiopia. Thus, the Beta Israel, claiming the same origins, demonstrated that they were not inferior to the Amharas, and that they too have equal legitimacy and are empowered to define and control their destiny. The dominant group can control some of the identity of the subordinated group, but it is seldom complete. One can be labeled, but the stigmatized can negotiate their identity, creating their own myths, stereotypes, and worldviews. Very important, they can name and rename, define and redefine themselves, advancing their own symbols and language of opposition. Hence, subjugated social space can become the loci for the valorization and empowerment of the collective self.

The multiple faces of oppression—economic and political, ideological and cultural—contributed to the definition of Beta Israel peoplehood. Being identified by the dominant group as inferior is certainly incorporated into the historical memory as a locus of consciousness, which at the same time creates a relational dialectic, giving rise to new acts of collective self-definition and creative actions. Consequently, for the Beta Israel, historical forces created a conditioning situation for the continuation of their peopleness in process.

The Beta Israel underwent various religious affirmations in defense of their own ideologies and religious practices.[39] One dimension of this was the development of a strong religious revival in the nineteenth century. This revivalism was of such a magnitude that it assumed the form of a millennial movement that called for returning to the promised land, Israel.[40] Some Ethiopian Jews pursued passage to what they perceived to be a zone of safety, not unlike enslaved Africans in the Americas who sought freedom by fleeing their captivity and forming *quilombos,* or maroon communities, far beyond the reach of their oppressors. Accordingly in 1862, under the leadership of a respected and charismatic *kes (priest),* Abba Mahari, large numbers set out on a pilgrimage to Jerusalem. Thousands of Beta Israel from the Gondar region attempted to reach the Holy Land via northern Ethiopia to the Red Sea. Many died along the way. Because of the difficult terrain and the winter season, and with many suffering from hunger and the cold, the journey became overly hazardous, forcing them to return to their villages in Ethiopia.[41]

They continued to practice *attenkugn* (in Amharic, law of purity, or "don't touch me") to isolate themselves from their neighbors. Ritual barriers separated them from non-Jews to avoid contamination; thus contact with outsiders required ritual absolutions before rejoining the community.[42] Moreover, their village " . . . was surrounded by stones or fences with hedges to show visibly and symbolically the demarcation line between purity and pollution. The villagers never bought or accepted any food from outsiders who did not follow their religion, not even those items which are permitted by the Bible, because they considered them to have become contaminated by contact with the outsiders."[43] Great attention was paid to distinctions between pure and impure, "whether in everyday life or on important occasions such as birth or a death."[44] Jewish religious rules of purity were strictly observed and set Beta Israel apart from others for centuries. Thus their sense of who they were, their values, and their ideal behavior were located within their built environment and social spaces.

The practice of *attenkugn* should not be interpreted to mean that the Jews were totally isolated without any meaningful relationships with their Christian and Muslim neighbors. It was not unusual to find mutual friendships and support of each other in times of joy and sadness, illness and death, weddings, and other sacred and secular celebrations. While the extent of participation varied regionally and over time, the key was knowledge of and adherence to the norms of participation for each other's rituals and observances.[45]

Abbink describes in detail another historical ritual affirmation of Beta Israel identity, the *Seged* celebration or *Mehlala*. *Seged*, an Amharic word, means to bow down or venerate oneself before God. *Mehlala* is the Geez term meaning to go down on one's knees to appeal, pray, or supplicate.[46] For centuries the Seged observance was a day of prayer, pilgrimage, fasting, and religious rituals conducted in hallowed, uncontaminated locations in Ethiopia. Held annually in November, it was located mainly in areas with a high priest such as Ambover (near Gondar), Gedebge (Wagara), Mudrago (Saqalt), and Bet Maryam (Tigray). Moreover, it has been a celebration with meaning only for the "true Israelites." "It is . . . a ritual enacting the drama of Falasha history and destiny, encompassing all relevant moments of their existence: defeat, supplication, revival through the example of the monks resisting and defending the Falasha tradition, loyalty to and dialogue with their God (through pilgrimage, fast, prayer, reading central religious texts, commemorating the dead, partaking of a communal meal)."[47]

Members of all religions are associated with rituals of commemoration of their origins, values, meanings, and significant aspects of their history such as the Passion and Last Supper for Christianity, fasting and Ramadan for Islam, and Passover for Judaism. Yet ceremonies of particular communities "bear the impress of the local conditions to which the Jewish [Islamic, Christian] community in the country in question was subjected."[48] In this context, it can be argued that aside from the sacred and spiritual sustenance provided by the *Seged*, the annual event is a way of remembering and recalling, in the present life of the Beta Israel, major formative experiences and events in the history of their community in Ethiopia. This commemoration, performed at a pure and sacred sites, gives meaning and identity to those who shape and practice it: here the story is told not only in the past but in a "metaphysical present." At their sacred site, "temporal difference [is] denied and the existence of the same, the 'true' and 'authentic' reality [is] annually disclosed."[49] Rituals, religious or secular, if understood within the ideological sphere of underlying meaning and significance for those who adhere or practice them, reinforce boundaries of group consciousness of themselves, their culture, and solidarity.

Connecting with World Jewry

For two thousand years the Beta Israel consistently and tenaciously adhered to their religion without connection to the larger-world Jewish diaspora. There is evidence that awareness of their presence has been known since the ninth century. Apparently a Jewish traveler, Eldad HaDani, reached eastern Africa and described the practices of Jews living beyond the rivers of Cush (the biblical term for Ethiopia).[50] More definitively, however, the issue of the religious identity of Ethiopian Jews was raised and answered in the sixteenth century. Details of the legal issues and cases related to this are discussed in greater detail in the writings of Bleich (1977) and summarized in a more recent study by Schindler and Ribner.[51] In the sixteenth century, the scholar and chief rabbi of Egypt, David ibn Zimra (Radbaz), ruled that Ethiopian Jews were descended from the tribe of Dan, one of the ten lost tribes, and that they were captured and exiled by the Assyrians in the eighth century B.C.E. (before the Christian Era, or B.C.):[52]

> Radbaz . . . was presented with an halachic question which not only called for a clarification of the religious status of the Falashas but also describes the adversities which they suffered. A Falasha town or settlement was attacked, the males slaughtered and the women and children taken captive. One woman, whose husband was presumably among the slaughtered, was purchased as a slave by a Jew who subsequently entered into a sexual liaison with her which resulted in the birth of a son. Later, the son sought to marry a young lady of Jewish parentage and Radbaz was asked for a ruling with regard to the permissibility of the forthcoming marriage.[53]

Based on this and another case, Radbaz was specific that Ethiopian Jews were indeed "of the seed of Israel, of the tribe of Dan."[54]

It was not until the eighteenth and nineteenth centuries, however, that Ethiopian Jews became more closely connected to the world Jewish diaspora. The news of the Beta Israel was first brought to Europe by James Bruce, who visited Ethiopia during his mission to discover the source of the Blue Nile between 1769 and 1772. Then around the middle of the nineteenth century, Protestant missionaries began to arrive and clearly defined the Beta Israel as Jews, as evidenced by the London Society for Promotion of Christianity, which attempted to convert them. To some extent proselytization was successful, as it has been estimated that missionaries, in their fifty-year presence in Ethiopia, converted about 1 percent of the total Jewish population, or approximately two thousand. Jews who converted to Christianity during this period took on the appellations *Feresmura/Feresmukra*, *Felesmura*, or *Falash Mura/Falashmura*.[55] Not unexpectedly, some converted because they desired to be part of another religion or group, but many may have converted because they anticipated that by becoming Christians their socioeconomic status would improve, especially in regard to land acquisition.[56] Common wisdom among many Ethiopian Jews is that "the conversion of individuals or whole families *failed to 'really change' them*. The dominant Christian society continued to view them as a separate minority, even though they were no longer part of Beta

Israel." Relatedly, "The Christian says come, I'll give you my daughter and I'll give you land. So then, after he converts to Christianity, he doesn't give him what he promised. Even when the converts' children play with other children, the children know that the father is a Jew. *One could pass through generations and never forget that he was a Jew*" (emphasis added).[57]

Becoming a convert and existing in another social space obviously creates their own problems of identity formation and "in-betweeness." In this context, many New World African people, past and present, have lived in "passing" spaces, hoping to make a transition from blackness to whiteness and therefore to assimilate into the dominant white culture and society.[58] But there are also the parallels between Felesmura and the *conversos*, or Marranos, Spaniards of Jewish origin who were largely forced to convert to Christianity in the fourteenth century. The latter were very successful in public life, attaining high positions and honors, but during the fifteenth-century Spanish Inquisition they were denounced as Jews and expelled from Spain. Although they were legitimate converts, Marranos were still viewed as Jews by non-Jewish "old" Christians. Of great import, however, is that the Marranos looked on themselves as a distinctive ethnic group with an identity separate from Jews and "old" Christians.[59] Significantly, Felashamura conversion was largely voluntary through the appeal of proselytizing Christian missionaries; moreover, upward mobility was not a factor characterizing their reality. It appears that similar to the *conversos*, Felashamura "maintained their identification with Beta Israel—and particularly with their family and the people in their villages—as their emotional center of gravity."[60] These examples are once again a reminder that who people are and what they become is always a process depending on the intersections of their own definitions of who they are and would like to become, and the actors, internal and external, to their historical "ethnic" spaces; thus, who is a Jew?

During the last half of the nineteenth century, Ethiopian Jews came to the attention of Jewish organizations such as the Alliance Israelite Universalle in France and the Jewish Chronicle of London, and to prominent Jewish leaders and rabbis in Europe.

Missionary activities in the mid-nineteenth century brought strong reaction from Agudat Israel, the Orthodox stream of Judaism. Rabbi Azriel Hildesheimer of Germany encouraged others to travel to Ethiopia and assist the Beta Israel in their education and religious activities. In 1867, three years after Hildesheimer's efforts, the frontiers of the Ethiopian Jewish community were further opened when a French Semiticist, Joseph Halevy, accumulated information about how the Beta Israel were faring in light of the challenges they were facing. Through his encouragement, Jacques Faitlovich, who was to become a central figure in advocating the cause of

Ethiopian Jews, was recruited and settled in Ethiopia. . . . Financial assistance by Baron de Rothchild enabled him to extend his stay and create social and educational services.[61]

The most prominent person involved in the campaign to include the Beta Israel in the World Zionist movement was Jaques Faitlovich, who went to Ethiopia in 1905. He made an all-out campaign in Europe and the United States by establishing "Falasha support communities" as well as by taking some young Ethiopian Jews to Europe and Palestine for education.[62] During the early and mid twentieth century, Jewish support groups were established in England—collectively known as the English Falasha Welfare Association. Among its members were British, Canadian, and United States Jewish organizations such as the Jewish Colonization Association, the Jewish Agency, the American Joint Distribution Committee, and the Central British Fund. They raised money for the Beta Israel and "lobbied for the tribe's immigration to Israel."[63]

In the 1950s twenty-five Beta Israel went to Israel, partly sponsored by organizations of the Jewish diaspora and the Jewish Agency of Israel. Having received religious and vocational training, nearly all of them returned to Ethiopia to work for the state or in Jewish villages as teachers.[64] They implemented a number of educational, religious, and health care projects for their community, some with the assistance of international Jewish organizations. This pattern continued into the early 1980s as work expanded in the Gondar region, benefiting not only the Jews, but Ethiopians of other religions.[65] These young Jews became important cultural workers for their communities in Ethiopia, and some who stayed in Israel later played significant roles in the campaign to secure the immigration of their co-religionists to Israel.

With the establishment of the State of Israel in 1948, there was little or no support for Beta Israel immigration to the promised land. Top Israeli government and religious authorities doubted their Jewishness. An Israeli diplomat reportedly argued that "the Jewishness of the Falashas is exaggerated," because their religious traditions are too similar to other Ethiopians:[66] "They [Ethiopian Jews] are certainly not Jews by race. They are one of the indigenous Agaw stock of Abyssinia and speak a Hamitic language. They know no Hebrew, and their scriptures are the Ge'ez version of the Old Testament. Their Judaism is of a curiously archaic type. They do not possess the Mishna or the Talmud, and they do not observe the feast of Purim, nor do they celebrate the dedication or the destruction of the second temple."[67] Although Jews have been historically treated as aliens and strangers in diaspora, late-nineteenth-century European racist ideology, rooted in the "new" Darwinism and directed toward "nonwhites," also racialized Jews by *socially* defining them as having inferior racial characteristics in comparison to the superior Germans of Aryan origins. This should not be interpreted to mean that Jews are a "biological" race. Race and the process of racialization are always *historically specific* and *socially defined.* The above quotation is a reflection of what might be called *dual essentialism.* That is, the definition of Jews is based on a European or Ashkenazi background and on Western rabbinical Judaism. This is consistent with the reality that for some Israeli authorities, "The Falashas were considered too primitive to become Israelis."[68] Their religion was perceived to be "old and odd," and "too orthodox," to create problems of accommodation. Hence, the Falashas were perceived as strangers, alien to Judaism and at the bottom of Israel's list of immigration priorities.[69]

Prior to 1980, there were small numbers of Ethiopian Jews immigrating to Israel. The published research of Abbink and Soroff provides details about this group, characterized as "veteran Ethiopians," most of whom arrived between 1965 and 1979.[70] Approximately 50 arrived during an eight-year period between 1965 and 1972, and over 350 from 1973 to 1979.[71] Hence over this fifteen-year period, roughly 400 Jews arrived in Israel from Ethiopia, and of this number, the largest single group of 121 arrived in 1977. Menachem Begin, Israel's prime minister at the time, made secret arrangements in 1977 with then Ethiopian leader Mengistu Haile Mariam "to exchange Israeli arms for Ethiopian Jews."[72] In general, the "veterans" came as individuals or as a family, were not organized as an *edot*, or ethnic community, and were relatively well educated, with 56 percent having attended secondary school and 27 percent having attended university. They came to Israel primarily for religious reasons, yet, upon arrival in the Jewish homeland, their acceptance as "religious Jews was more problematic, since they were not always viewed by the rabbinate as Jews."[73] They were not yet officially received as Jews, a de jure condition under the state's Law of Return, which at the time automatically granted citizenship to those officially recognized as Jews in diaspora. It was not until 1973 that the Sephardic chief rabbi of Israel ruled that the Beta Israel were "descended from the Tribe of Dan," an affirmation of the decision reached by sixteenth-century rabbi David ibn Zimra (Radbaz). In 1975 an interministerial committee of the Israeli government agreed that their immigration status was legal, paving the way for acquisition of citizenship in Israel under the Law of Return.

Revolution in Ethiopia and Beta Israel Passages to Israel

The situation created in Ethiopia following the overthrow of Emperor Haile Selassie in 1974 was attended by endemic drought, famine, and war. Ethiopians of all faiths suffered under the new government, and thousands fled the country as their very survival was threatened. This was particularly the case for residents of Tigray, a stronghold of rebel activities since the late seventies, and Wollo, the most drought- and famine-stricken province. On this account, inhabitants of these areas sought security and survival by fleeing the country; most headed for the Sudan.

Of the close to 500,000 refugees in Sudanese camps in 1980, approximately 3,000 were Judaic Ethiopians; by 1984, their numbers had more than doubled. They were reported to have strongly supported the socialist government of Ethiopia with the hope of getting land, which for centuries was denied them by Amhara rulers. Their expectations were not met. Moreover, they were defined as Zionists and CIA agents, thus becoming victims of gross brutalities of the regime. Their existence in these camps was quite fragile, and many died from dangerous and tenuous life conditions compounded by disease, starvation, and malnutrition.[74]

For a decade, 1980–90, significant numbers of Beta Israel refugees and displaced persons were airlifted to Israel, shifting their population concentrations from Ethiopia to their new homeland. Many arrived in Israel by circuitous routes, and their number totaled around 1,400 by 1981.[75] By November of 1984 it is estimated that there were over 7,500 in Israel, most of whom were from the Tigray province and adjoining districts of Ethiopia.[76]

The geo-social movement of the Beta Israel was caught in the web of trans-statist politics, including the ongoing Middle Eastern conflict between Israel and Islamic and Arab countries; Cold War relations and interests of the United States and the former Soviet Union; internal warfare in Ethiopia; and the civil war in the Sudan between Arab Muslims of the North and black African Muslims (especially those in the Nuba region), Christians, and other religious groups in the South. Teshome Wagaw provides details of how the "return" of Ethiopian Jews to Israel was impacted by a minefield of conflict in the international political arena, with each state and stateless people driven by their respective interests and locations within the hierarchy of world political and economic power.[77] An aspect of this population transfer to Israel involved "arms-and-money-for–Beta Israel" exchanges, a pathetic reminder of the trucks-for-blood episode to help save Jews during the Nazi holocaust.[78]

It should be noted, nonetheless, that the campaign to "rescue" the Beta Israel was heightened not by the Israeli state, but by the social activism of North American Jews. One such organization was the American Association for the Ethiopian Jews, which procured funds for the purpose of quickly evacuating the group to Israel or other countries that would receive them.[79] In November 1981, thirteen activists from the Association for Ethiopian Jews in the United States and Canada visited Ethiopia. They reported that the Beta Israel "were being arrested and tortured and their villages deprived of educational and other government services."[80] On their way back

Table 1. Immigration Cycles of Beta Israel from Ethiopia to Israel, 1954–99

TIME FRAME	APPROX. NUMBERS	ORIGIN & CHARACTERISTICS
1954–57	25	Students to Israel for religious and vocational training; most returned to Ethiopia to serve their communities and country.
1965–79	400 (+)	Selected individuals and families immigrated under bilateral agreement between the governments of Ethiopia and Israel; others came during this time for education and training, a significant number of whom where young men.
February 1980–November 1984	7,500 (+ or –)	Early immigrants, more urban and mainly from Tigray province; others from Walqait, Tseggede, Tselemt (Gondar province), and Lasta (Wollo province).
21 November 1984–6 January 1985	8,000 (+ or –)	Refugee Beta Israelis airlifted to Israel from the Sudan in Operation Moses, mainly from Gondar, Tigre, and Eritrea regions.
March 1985	800–900	Additional refugees from the Sudan—Operation Joshua.
1985–91	500 (+ or –)	Small groups immigrating to Israel, many well-educated urbanites from Addis Ababa, young and well-trained other professionals in the areas of education, health, and administration.

the visitors returned through Israel to report their findings to Israeli authorities. It was this American-Canadian group that lobbied Israel, the United States, and Canada to take Beta Israel evacuation seriously, thus giving new impetus to the immigration question. They had some success in convincing Israeli authorities to give more serious consideration to the evacuation issue.[81]

One outcome of the various state–Jewish diaspora collaborative activities was the secret and massive 1984–85 repatriation from the Sudan known as Operation Moses. Between 21 November 1984 and 6 January 1985, about 8,000 Beta Israel were evacuated from the Sudan to Israel in Operation Moses.[82] In March 1985, with the help of the U.S. military and the CIA, another airlift under the code name Operation Joshua brought some 800 to 900 Beta Israel to Israel.[83] As noted in table 1, from the 1980s to early 1990s between 32,000 and 48,000 Ethiopian Jews immigrated to Israel,

May 1991	15,000–20,000	A more rural group (from different regions) as part of the massive airlift out of Addis Ababa— Operation Solomon.
1993–96	4,000–5,000 (+ or –)	Many rural Jews from Gondar and other regions granted visas under family reunification priority.
1997–98	4,000 (+ or –)	Falashmura occupants of refugee compound in Addis Ababa.
1999	3,800	Predominately rural from remote, mountainous Quara region along the Sudanese border; many under age 18.
TOTAL	44,646–50,146*	

*Approximate range. As of 2000, it is estimated there are approximately 70,000 Ethiopian Jews in Israel.

SOURCES: Table constructed from the following sources: Jan Gerrit Abbink, *The Falashas in Ethiopia and in Israel: The Problem of Ethnic Assimilation* (Nijmegen: ISCA, 1984); Ian Fisher, "Tangling of Jewish Roots Bars Ethiopians from Israel," *New York Times*, 19 April 2000, A3; Bernard Gwertzman, "Sudan Lets U.S. Fly 800 Ethiopian Jews to Israeli Refuge, *New York Times*, 24 March 1985, A1 and A15; Simcha Jacobovici, "Ethiopian Jews Die, Israel Fiddles," *New York Times*, 15 September 1984, A23; Sam Jaffe, "Struggles of Israel's Ethiopian Jews," *Christian Science Monitor*, 17 March 1997, 9–11; George A. Lipsky, *Ethiopia: Its People, Its Society, Its Culture* (New Haven, Conn.: Harf Press, 1962), 45; Ruth Mason, "The Ethiopian Exodus Continues; Solomonic Sequels," *Hadassah Magazine* (November 1998): 13–15; Clifford D. May, "Ethiopia Attacks Jews' Departure," *New York Times*, 5 January 1985, A3; Richard Pankhurst, "The Falashas, or Judaic Ethiopians, in Their Christian Ethiopian Setting," *African Affairs* 91 (1992): 567–82; Lila Perl, *Ethiopia: Land of the Lion* (New York: William Morrow and Company, 1972), 108; David K. Shipler, "Torture Reported of Ethiopian Jews," *New York Times*, 15 November 1981, A9; Teshome Wagaw, "The International Political Ramifications of Falasha Emigration," *Journal of Modern African Studies* 29, no. 4 (1991): 557–81; and *For Our Soul: Ethiopian Jews in Israel* (Detroit: Wayne State University Press, 1993).

their origins and backgrounds diverse. In the last massive evacuation, the ousted head of state of Ethiopia, Mengistu, is reported to have taken $35 million in exchange for about 15,000 Beta Israel in what came to be known as Operation Solomon. The post-1980 massive removal of Jews from Ethiopia reached a high point in 1984–85 and peaked in 1991.

Continuing Passages

For eight years (1991–98), during the last decade of the twentieth century, the immigration of Jews remaining in Ethiopia has been subject to wide debate, investigated by a number of commissions and committees in Israel and in Ethiopia and lobbied for by

Ethiopian Jews in Israel. Jews remained in the Semien Mountains, the Tigray region, the city of Gondar, and in refugee camps in Addis Ababa, the capital city of Ethiopia. The actual number remaining in Ethiopia varies considerably, from an estimated low of 10,000 to a common wisdom number of around 26,000.[84] Many were family members of those who were part of the earlier operations. Small numbers immigrated to Israel, and in 1996, it was estimated that between 120 and 140 left monthly on commercial flights,[85] resulting in some Beta Israel reunited with their families. Priority was given to Jews in the rural areas because they did not convert to Christianity and not given to those in the urban refugee camp. Falashmura, Jews who converted to Christianity in the nineteenth century were not allowed to board planes during Operation Solomon in 1991. They refused to leave Addis Ababa and remained encamped in a refugee compound near a community center and synagogue with support from the New York–based American Joint Distribution Committee (AJDC) and the North American Conference on Ethiopian Jewry (NACOEJ).[86]

Many in Israel believed the country should not have moral responsibility toward those who leave the faith. For others the position of the Falashmura was compared to the Marranos of Europe—Jews who were forced to convert to Christianity during the Roman Catholic Inquisition of the thirteenth century. Some Falashmura contended they were forced to convert under persecution but retained their Jewish customs and identity.[87] Then there were significant reservations in Ethiopia about allowing another major airlift. Government officials in Ethiopia have been very sensitive to criticism levied against the Mengistu regime and the country by other Africans who viewed the earlier airlifts as unconscionable and akin to complicity of Africans during the slave trade—an African government failing to rescue its citizens and selling them for money and arms.

In June of 1997 the Israeli cabinet decided to give permission for the Falashamura to immigrate to Israel under the Law of Entry and not the Law of Return. After many years of waiting in a refugee camp in their country of birth, the small band of Falashmura reached the promised land, beginning a new chapter of their lives. The most recent emigration of Jews from Ethiopia consists of about 3,800 men, women, and children from the remote and mountainous Quara region of Ethiopia along the Sudanese border. After seven years of investigation, Israeli state officials concluded that the Jews from Quara are indeed Jews, left behind during the earlier operations of the 1980s. Beginning 22 June 1999 over forty flights, scheduled throughout the year, brought what might be perceived as the last major "organized twentieth century exodus" of Ethiopian Jews to Israel.[88]

In summary, Jews have lived in Ethiopia for centuries, contributing significantly to the ancient history and legacies of the country. The fifteenth century, however, was a major turning point when Jews were reduced to subjects by the feudal Christian mo-narchial state, alienated from the land, and stigmatized as Falasha. Nonetheless, the Beta Israel acted in their collective self-interest by creating new road maps for living, affirming their Jewishness through worship, ritual, and organized celebrations and collective myths, attempting pilgrimage to the promised land, and living in purified and unpolluted physical and social spaces as they developed relationships with their Muslims and Christian neighbors. They further negotiated their identity by renaming themselves and becoming the Beta Israel.

In the late nineteenth and early twentieth centuries they became more connected to world Jewry, primarily in Europe and North America. In the last quarter of the twentieth century their very existence became imperiled as Ethiopia plunged into civil war following the overthrow of Emperor Haile Selassie in 1974 and the emergence of a military state. Forced to flee their places of domicile, significant numbers sought refuge in the Sudan. They were in an untenable position, with their survival caught in the web of transnational state relations extending from continental Africa to North America, Europe, and the Middle East. The monetary and lobbying support of Jews, primarily from the United States and Canada, is an important reminder that the "con-sciousness and agency" of mobilized diasporas can be effective actors in the broader interests of their "imagined communities."[89] With its wealth, politically effective organizations, and post-Holocaust and -Israel self-consciousness, it is possible that North American Jews carried the mantra on behalf of their Ethiopian coreligionists by default. Another more engaging possibility, however, is that North American Jews, who are as secular as they are sacred and are well integrated in their national spaces (Canada and the United States), may also affirm their own identities by reaching out to support Ethiopian Jews. Regardless of motives, the action of the Jewish diaspora is indicative of the increasing visibility and significance of trans-diasporic action, for example, Armenian, Palestinian, and African. The ongoing global consciousness of diaspora peoples, organized to act locally and globally, can be a major force in impact-ing the social situation and conditions of their "imagined communities."

Ethiopian Jews in Israel: Identity Re-formations and Contestations

Most of the writings about the Beta Israel in Israel document their experiences in absorption centers where all new immigrants are taught to "cope with a modern western society."[90] The emphasis is upon official mechanisms of absorption, success, and failure and, in general, how emigrating Ethiopians are assisted in making transitions to their new homeland.[91] One scholar contends, for instance, that absorption centers are operating paradoxically, slowing down the pace of absorption rather than accelerating the process. "although necessary, the absorption centers tend to isolate the immigrants from the larger society and circumscribe, distort, or under certain conditions even work against the ultimate goals of successful absorption. The sooner the immigrants move out and learn to function in the real and larger world, the better."[92] Not unexpectedly, there are explanations of differences in "adjustment" varying with age,[93] gender, marital status, and previous cultural norms and expectations.[94] Some contend that education of the relatively youthful population has been a priority and has met with some degree of success.[95] Apparently over one hundred Ethiopians with the initial group in the 1980s entered the Israeli army.[96] According to another analyst, the state has been successful in relocating the Ethiopians in twenty different towns and cities,[97] some with significant concentrations, such as Afula,[98] Ashqelon,[99] Beersheba,[100] Hebron (Kiryat Arba), Ramot Gan,[101] Rehovot, Rishon, Le Zion, Netanya, and Hadera.

Importantly, the literature also tends to take a social problems approach to the Beta Israel, emphasizing such factors as their adjustment problems in a Western, high-tech Israeli social order; their lack of skills, education, and ability to speak Hebrew; and their strange Judaic practices.[102] In this sense their refugeeness and uprootedness from Ethiopia tends to follow the discourse of refugee studies historically, the "pathologization of uprootedness," or the "problematization of refugees." "They are not ordinary people, but represent, rather, an anomaly requiring specialized correctives and therapeutic interventions." Thus "their problemness" is located "within [their] bodies and minds (and even souls)."[103]

In the discussion that follows, the approach is structural, with an emphasis on how the nature and extent of the incorporation of Jewish strangers from "far away places" are impacted by the social organization of a society, socioculturally, economically, and politically. Of particular concern are the state and its apparatuses, the institutionalization of religion in relationship to the state, ideologies and cultural beliefs about the nation and the state, and very importantly, the social fabric of the society in relationship to the intersections of class and social positioning, ethnicity, and nationality, race, and religion. The assumption is that how the Beta Israel are incorporated into Israel will depend upon social relations, ideological practices, and power relationships that define and condition their material realities, their everyday lives. What is the significance of these social forces on how Ethiopian Jews redefine themselves or become a "new people" in a changing and evolving body politic such as Israel? Just as important, nonetheless, is how changing perceptions of their collective self takes on new meaning in relationship to the way they create and institute new road maps for themselves. Will Israel become a meaningful and socially acceptable home for Ethiopian Jews, or will Israel become the exilic African diaspora home for Ethiopian Jews?

Contesting the State, Religion, and Citizenship

Since Jewishness and citizenship are legally intertwined in Israel, the Beta Israel were "given Israeli citizenship and issued identity cards" within twenty-four hours of their arrival.[104] Yet according to Orthodox rabbinical circles their Jewishness was not a given. Whereas in Ethiopia they were marginalized and subordinated largely because of their refusal to convert to Christianity, in Israel their fundamental identity for thousands of years became a major question for Orthodox rabbis in particular.

As previously noted, in the sixteenth century Rabbi David ibn Zimra (Radbaz) of Egypt declared the Beta Israel Jewish, although his position was that they were subject to all biblical and Talmudic laws regarding marriage and divorce and that ignorance of the law could cause major "genealogical damage."[105] In the early 1970s, the late Ashkenazic Rabbi Moshe Feinstein, among others, did not consider the Beta Israel as legally Jewish, but conceded that since they believed themselves to be Jewish the only solution was for them to undergo full conversion according to Jewish law—the only avenue to full acceptance. In contrast and during the same period, the Sephardic Chief Rabbi Ovadiah Yosef considered the Ethiopians to be Jewish and recommended a case-by-case approach at the time when the issue is relevant to the individual, for example during marriage or divorce. Yet, even among those who shared Rabbi Yosef's position the belief was that "to remove all doubt, new Ethiopian immigrants should undergo one aspect of the conversion process, ritual immersion, not as conversion per se, but as a 'renewal of covenant.'"[106] With the arrival of the first group of Jews via Operation Moses in 1985, the issue of conversion became a hotly contested issue for the Beta Israel, becoming an active site of contestation and identity transformation for them.

In 1985, then Ashkenazic Chief Rabbi Avraham Shapira and Sephardic Chief Rabbi Mordechai Eliyahu both considered the Ethiopian immigrants as fully Jewish but "maintained that because of widespread intermarriage and divorce practices that violated Jewish law, Ethiopians would have to undergo a symbolic conversion ritual for full admission [entry into Judaism]."[107] Initially the conversion ritual required symbolic circumcision for males; immersion in a ritual bath, the *mikveh*, or traditional bath of purification; and affirmation of the Torah. The chief rabbis ruled that since

Ethiopians had been separated so long from other Jews, they had to undergo a symbolic act of return to the covenant.[108] Extreme Orthodox Jews especially insisted on their conversion, some of whom threatened to deny the Ethiopians services such as admission to schools or to take the more extreme action of closing schools rather than accepting the "unconverted" Ethiopians.[109]

CONTESTING THE STATE

The situation of the Beta Israel raises a fundamental question about whether Israel can be a homeland for all Jews and at the same time be a Jewish state. This was an issue at the inception of the state over fifty years ago and it remains a center of contestation today. From a diaspora perspective a homeland is where all exilic people can aspire to return and feel welcomed. Thus if Israel is a homeland for *all* Jews, all should feel at home, notwithstanding their diversity of cultural backgrounds and ways of practicing their faith. Apparently this was what the Zionist founders had in mind: to create a homeland where all Jews could feel "normal." However, from the inception concessions were made to Orthodox Jews as a matter of "temporary expediency." In essence, the civilian leadership promised to "the Orthodox that in the imminent Jewish state, matters of personal status would be regulated by religious law; that the Sabbath would be the official day of rest; that Jewish dietary laws would be observed in government facilities; and that religious education would be provided if parents desired it for their children . . . [these] concessions that seemed a temporary expedient in 1947 have, fifty years later, come to haunt the Jewish state."[110]

While more than half of the 5 million Jews in Israel are secular, religious Jews range from the fundamentalist ultra-Orthodox Haredim groups to liberal Orthodox, Reform, and Conservative. Estimates vary considerably, but the common wisdom is that the ultra-Orthodox Haredim constitute 14–20 percent of Jewish Israelis, and another 20–30 percent are Orthodox. Importantly, through various political alignments, the Orthodox are effective political players and power brokers in the coalition governments of the country. The extended quotation below puts the situation in context:

> In Israel . . . the politics of proportional representation have meant that Orthodox parties have been key participants in every coalition government since independence. For nearly thirty years, as if they were themselves uncertain of their staying power, they were relatively circumspect in the price they demanded in return for their support. But that was when the decisively secular Labor Party was Israel's virtually unchallenged establishment. With the displacement of Labor by Likud in 1977, a new day dawned.

Likud was more sympathetic to the Jewish religious tradition, and, more important, its core constituency included the mass of Sephardic [Jews from Asia-Africa (*yotzei*, Asia-Africa)] voters, whose loyalty to religious tradition was rock solid. In the meantime, the center of Orthodox gravity had moved from the moderation of the early years to a militant ultra-Orthodoxy. An invigorated Orthodox began to press its own expanded agenda, and the Orthodox political parties—especially Shas, the party of the Sepharadic traditional—expanded as well. With that new strength have come the perquisites of power, in the form of government subsidies; these have fueled the schools, daycare and community centers and other services that have led the Orthodox parties to thrive rather than merely survive.

The 1996 elections . . . brought the Orthodox parties to unprecedented representation in the Knesset (23 out of 120 members), hence also to unprecedented demands. . . . And, recognizing . . . their own strength, they are now ratcheting up the price of [their] support.[111]

Under these circumstances, the religious sectors are able to empower themselves and press their ultimate agenda for a Jewish state. For the Orthodox, the Jewish law, *halacha,* is absolute; the 613 commandments of the Torah cover all aspects of life, so civil law is not necessary. The battle is for power to control the state, whether to create a theocracy following God's law, observing the Jewish calendar, and legislating the Sabbath, or whether to maintain a secular, civilian controlled, democratic government. Closely linked to the contestation of the state is the question of who is and who is not a Jew in Israel and the resulting implications for the diaspora.

CONTESTING RELIGION AND CITIZENSHIP: WHO IS A JEW?

From a religious perspective, the question of who is a Jew in Israel has gone through several revisions since the 1950 Law of Return. Shortly after the formation of the State of Israel, the governing body known as the Knesset passed the Law of Return on 5 July 1950, granting every Jew the right to immigrate to the country. The original law did not specify or define who is a Jew for purposes of Israeli citizenship. Subsequent changes further narrowed the boundaries of Jewishness such that by 1960 the legal definition of a Jew was based on matrilineal descent, one born of a Jewish mother. Later legal refinement in 1970 circumscribes a Jew as a person born of a Jewish mother or a convert to Judaism, but the law was further amended to specify that a "candidate for Jewishness must not be a member of another religion—must, especially, not flaunt the fact that he or she has adopted the beliefs, rituals, obligations, or life style of a religion other than Judaism. Active conversion to another religion now became grounds for excluding someone born of a perfectly acceptable Jewish mother from membership in the Jewish people."[112]

At the time of the Ethiopian immigrations to Israel the boundaries of Jewishness were again tested, with rabbinical gatekeepers clearly demonstrating the power of Orthodox Jews. In more recent years the authority of the Orthodox community of Jewish Israelis has opened up the possibility for a more exclusionary definition of who is not a Jew. Thus the contested nature of Ethiopian Jewishness presaged a deepening crisis, with major implications for the larger world Jewish diaspora. Since late 1997 and into 1998, legislation has been pending in the Israeli parliament, the Knesset, which would legalize a de facto policy by which *only* Orthodox rabbis can conduct conversions to Judaism in Israel. Currently Orthodox Jews have a monopoly on religious functions such as marriages, burials, and other religious rites. For example, only religious weddings are permitted in the country and only Orthodox rabbis can perform them for Jews. The pending legislation would also legally bar non-Orthodox representatives from serving on local religious councils that allocate money to community groups.

Perhaps most significant is that by having *legal* control over conversions, only Orthodox rabbis will decide who is a Jew, thus deciding who is eligible for automatic Israeli citizenship.[113] Leaders of the Reform and Conservative movement in Israel have sought support from Israeli courts in seeking recognition for the conversions they performed. These leaders say "that . . . the government ministries responsible for registering converts as Jews have refused to [recognize non-Orthodox conversions that were previously recognized as valid]."[114]

> In the meantime, the non-Orthodox movements have taken their appeals to Israel's highest court to force the state to recognize the conversions. Among the cases are Israeli couples who have adopted babies abroad, had their infants converted abroad by non-Orthodox rabbis, and were unable to register their children as Jews. . . .
>
> To preempt a court decision that would have ruled in favor of the Reform and Conservative movements, the Orthodox want to turn the unwritten "status quo" into law.[115]

Although the question of who is a Jew is not new to Judaism, how the question is answered at this time directly relates to deeper questions of power to control inclusiveness and exclusiveness with respect to citizenship and religious identity.[116] Hence the conflicts and contradictions surrounding the Ethiopians expose fundamental fault lines in the social fabric of Israel. These include the struggle for religious control of the state and religious culture, with a deepening disrespect and intolerance for cultural variation and diversity. Fundamentally, it is a battleground over religious freedom, which not only applies to Jews in Israel but also to other Israeli citizens who are Muslims, Christians, and Druze. The current situation begs the question of freedom of religion and freedom to be Jewish. Although the issue is raised within the context of Ethiopian Jews, the concern goes to the heart of identity for other Jews of the diaspora.

With the current pending legislation, 80 to 90 percent of North American Jews, similar to the Ethiopians, would not be recognized by the Orthodox chief rabbinate in Israel. The Judaic practices of Conservative, Reform, and Reconstructionist Jews in the United States would be repudiated, and should they seek Israeli citizenship, conversion by Orthodox rabbis would be required. Just as the religious practices, views, and interpretations of Ethiopian Jews have been historically conditioned within the larger Ethiopian social milieus over thousands of years, so too has been the history of North American Jews. Over generations, the latter have adjusted their practices within the time span of their largely European and New World rootedness, as symbolized by the emergence of Reform Judaism in nineteenth-century Germany. Among the more "modernized" North American groups women can become rabbis and cantors; there are liturgical changes, for example, the recognition of patrilineal descent in contrast to matrilineal descent only, as recognized by Orthodox law. As noted by a conservative rabbi of New York University, there are few American Jewish families where there has not been an intermarriage, or where there is not a convert by a Reform or Conservative rabbi. Hence, "When Israel starts carrying on and saying these are not Jews, we are being informed that many of our nieces and nephews and, alas, some of our children and grandchildren are not Jews."[117]

This point is reinforced by the recent debate surrounding the legitimacy of the Jews of Venta Prieta in Mexico, a community founded in the mid nineteenth century by descendants of families escaping the Spanish Inquisition. Conservative Rabbi Samuel Lenen in commenting on the debate asked the question: "How many Jews can prove they are Jewish beyond three generations?"[118]

Becoming Visible: Resisting and Redefining

(Re)conversion elicited a great deal of hostility among the Ethiopians, many of whom were unwilling to accept the demands to undergo conversion in order to be called Jews and to become integrated into the religious community of Israel.[119] In his study, Wagaw provides rich details of the conversion controversy.[120] What is most interesting, however, is that a significant number of the group of immigrants arriving before 1984, while unhappy with the requirement, went through conversion with little resistance. This was a group consisting of more men than women, large numbers of younger children, and people mainly from Tigray province; they also tended to be poorer rural dwellers.

The immigrants arriving after 1984 as part of Operation Moses rebelled against the demand and refused what they saw as an indignity: "They were almost all from the Gondar region and had a different psychological makeup and political persuasion." They had also "languished for up to three years in the refugee camps in the Sudan."[121] Within a short time of their arrival the Ethiopian Jews were struggling for their identity as Jews. It is reported that "Some Ethiopians, who had already been living in Israel for several years, began to encourage their newly arrived brethren to refuse any kind of conversion process, specifically citing ritual immersion as kin to the forced baptism that had periodically been the fate of Beta Israel in their native country."[122] The group engaged in an extended period of protest, including camping outside the chief rabbinate headquarters in Jerusalem:

> During the spring and early summer of 1985, the Ethiopian community staged protest marches through the streets of Jerusalem. They attempted a march to Ben-Gurion airport, meant to symbolize their preference for a return to Ethiopia rather than the humiliation of conversion in Israel. The leaders also threatened mass suicide and possible attacks on both Ethiopians and Israelis who actively supported the Rabbinate's demands. A mass demonstration, held in Jerusalem across from the Chief Rabbinate headquarters, escalated into a general strike. Ethiopians left their absorption centers throughout the country and made their way to Jerusalem to camp out in a small park in front of the Plaza Hotel. 500 to 1,000 Ethiopians remained there for more than a month.[123]

In staging public demonstrations the Ethiopians used what power they had to fight for their identity as Jews. Seemingly, the rabbis relented a little by taking the position that only Ethiopian Jews wishing to marry would either appear before the rabbinical court to determine their Jewishness or undergo the *mikveh.*

Blue ribbon committees looked into the matter; Prime Minister Shimon Peres, Labor leader Abba Eban, and other government leaders were drawn into the controversy as they looked at the broader issues of the state and religion in Israel. The recommended outcomes were essentially the same, and the Ethiopians felt they were discriminated against for reasons other than religion. The conversion requirements had not been imposed upon immigrating European Jews from the former Soviet Union, the Russian Jews. It has been estimated that over a third of the eight hundred thousand immigrating Russians are not legitimate Jews as defined by the strict Orthodox laws of rabbinical authorities.[124] Yet the former Soviet Jews were not subjected to the rebukes and humiliating negation of their religious identity as were the Ethiopian Jews. Thus many Ethiopians considered conversion "to be racist and an insult to their piety and loyalty to Judaism through two thousand years. Some educated Ethiopians have refused to participate in it."[125] This point is further amplified when one considers that "No previous migrant group suffered the demeaning challenge to its authenticity as did the Ethiopians, nor were any other immigrants required to undergo procedures such as ritual immersion before being granted full Jewish status. Further undermining their ethnic integrity was the decision of the Israeli religious establishment to delegitimize the office of the *kes* [traditional Ethiopian rabbis] prohibiting these men from exercising many of their traditional functions and in practice, rendering the community leaderless."[126] Yet, many Ethiopians have turned to the *kes* who still perform marriages although they are not recognized by law as legitimate. For those near the city of Netanya or who can travel there to be married, the Chief Rabbi of the city, David Shloush, will perform Ethiopian marriages that are legal and which do not require ritual conversion.

ASSERTING A "UNIQUE" SPIRITUALITY: "WE ARE CLOSER TO THE SOURCE"

Resistance and struggle against attacks on the authenticity of their Jewishness required the Beta Israel to look at their individual and collective past and present and to look at these lived experiences in a new light. The one aspect of their cumulative history they never expected to be an issue in their new pathways was their Jewishness, their religious identity. A study of Ethiopian heads of household reveals some representative insights regarding their bitterness.

- A male, age forty-four, "How can a small group (the Orthodox religious establishment) dictate to us how to be Jews? . . . There is no end to my suffering."
- A female, age sixty, "If they do not want us, then why did we struggle so to come here?"
- A male, age thirty-seven, "So I live with pain and bitterness because my Jewishness has been called into question."[127]

Additionally, most felt that Israeli rabbis, with the exception of Rabbi Shloush of Netanya, were obstructionists in clarifying their religious identity of two thousand years. Another respected elder of the early group of Beta Israel immigrants also expressed frustration and disappointment: "We suffered so much on our way here [Israel] and they question our Jewish identity? . . . people think that we had come because of hunger, which infuriates me! After all we have suffered because of our Jewishness on the journey."[128]

For Ethiopian Jews, conversion requirements struck a blow to their sense of meaning and existence. It also brought into sharp relief views of their own authenticity and observant practices as Jews in contrast to the more secular Jews in Israel, where the latter constitutes the vast majority of Israeli Jews. That is, most are not ritually observant and tend to treat holidays as national and not religious. Not surprisingly, when the early Ethiopian immigrants arrived, what they saw was quite different from their expectations:

> They had expected, nearly without exception, that the Israeli Jews would be religiously observant, at least respecting the Shabbat and the dietary laws. But they found that this was true only for a minority of Israeli Jews. Furthermore, it was paradoxical to them that the religious (rabbinic) establishment often ignored or rejected traditional notions and usages of Falasha Judaism, almost completely neglecting Falasha priests in Israel. They were also surprised to find that the general public only paid token respect to the rabbinic establishment in its role as part of the legal order of the State. These realizations also led to a revaluation of the elements of their own ethno-religious tradition."[129]

For Ethiopians, then, the extent to which religious practices were maintained, particularly observance of the Sabbath, was related to being Jewish—it was what distinguished them from other people and religions. From the perspective of their own traditional values, the Beta Israel felt more religious than other Jews, especially in terms of adherence to rituals of purity and impurity: "they maintain an underlying sense of group pride. . . . The reasons given are a) their age-long adherence to Judaism in most difficult conditions and b) the originality of their traditional form of Judaism in Ethiopia. From the fact that they have not been influenced by Talmudic tradition, many . . . conclude that their Judaism as practiced in Ethiopia was 'more close to the source' to the Judaism practiced in the golden days of the Temple (up to 70, C.E.)."[130]

From the perspective of their own traditional values, they defined themselves as more religious than other Jews, yet their authenticity was questioned. For them, their move to Israel was one of moving from "purity to impurity" in terms of rituals of pollution and purification; not unexpectedly, this was important in the process of reformulating their identity. It was a way of resisting onslaughts on their identity as Jews and on ways of life that have been so critical to their survival as Jews in diaspora. In amplifying their religious behavior as "good Jews" they also saw a certain amount of hypocrisy in Sabbath practices of the ritually observant. Beta Israel defined practices by some Israelis to circumvent the prohibition on lighting a fire on the Sabbath as "impossible hypocrisies": "With one exception, they were unanimous in stating that they never made use of the hot plate, which for them was a symbol of a hypocritical compromise. They continued to eat only cold meals on the Sabbath."[131]

Individual and group identities are always constructed in relationship to others. And in mediating their identity as Jews, under very different conditions, the Beta Israel counterchallenged an imposed Otherness as they have done centuries earlier during the *zemene massafint* in Ethiopia. Now in Israel, they marched, staged public demonstrations, and appealed to the Israeli supreme court. Very importantly, however, in their private lives and in their spiritual and moral definitions of themselves, they saw purity and sacrifice, but they also defined their observant practices as closer to the "source" or "roots" of Judaism than those who dared to question and deny them their religious identity and authenticity. Indeed, they maintain that "we Ethiopians are purer and closer to the source."

In their struggle for inclusion in Israel, the experiences of Ethiopian Jews provide a window on how the state and its legal apparatus compete with the religious apparatus for power to control the boundaries of the nation-state, the content and limitations of "nationness," the relationship between religion and citizenship, and very importantly, the parameters of Jewishness. Such processes and contestations directly contribute to the construction of difference and Otherness, creating insiders and outsiders and imposing negative identities on the designated Others. As characterized by Dominguez, the contestation about control over the objectification of Jewish peopleness is about determining the outermost limits of the in-group and the innermost limits of the out-group and about exclusivity and inclusivity. Importantly, "It is about Otherness as much as it is about the collective self."[132] The conversion controversy is a dynamic site of contestations over the construction of an Israeli nation-state, its social formations and relations; it is about a complex and diverse society in search of identities and definitions. Will Israel become a secular-democratic state under civil law or a state governed by religious law and Orthodox religious authorities? Even more fundamental is that the case of the Ethiopians reveals the ongoing and ever present contestation over the very meaning of Jewishness—who is or who is not a Jew in Israel—and the implications for the identity of Jews in diaspora worldwide.

NOTES

This paper is dedicated to Dr. Ruth Hill Useem and to the memory of the late Dr. John Useem, wonderful friends, colleagues, and mentors. The senior author is grateful to those who read earlier drafts and provided useful comments, contributed valuable references, or both: the Useems, Elliott Skinner, Ruth

Harris, Steve Gold, Rabbi Matthew Kaufman, Beatrice Rabin, and Gabriele Kende. They are not responsible for the content and interpretations of this chapter; these are the responsibility of the senior author.

1. Spellings in Ethiopia vary considerably (e.g., *Semien* may also be spelled *Semyen*). Thus we shall maintain consistency in our spellings throughout the chapter.
2. Brian Weinstein, "Ethiopian Jews in Israel: Socialization and Re-education," *Journal of Negro Education* 54, no. 2 (spring 1985): 213–24, 221. According to a census taken in 1984, the total population of the Agaw was 489,834. Office of Population and Housing Census Commission, *Population and Housing Census of Ethiopia*, 1984 (Addis Ababa, 1990), 44. The same document states that the population of the Beta Israel was 34,056 (page 45) by the time of the census. But as quite a good number of them lived in Tigray province, which was then beyond the reach of the government due to intensive civil war, and as most of them had already taken refuge in the Sudan because of famine, the reliability of the data regarding northern Ethiopia in general and the Beta Israel in particular is doubtful.
3. Richard Pankhurst, "The Falashas, or Judaic Ethiopians, in Their Christian Ethiopian Setting," *African Affairs* 91 (1992): 567–82.
4. For detailed information see M. Lionel Bender, *The Non-Semitic Languages of Ethiopia* (East Lansing: African Studies Center, Michigan State University, 1976), 8, 66–297; Donald N. Levine, *Greater Ethiopia: The Evolution of a Multiethnic Society* (Chicago: University of Chicago Press, 1974), 34–35.
5. Pankjurst, "The Falashas," 575.
6. A. H. M. Jones and Elizabeth Monroe, *A History of Ethiopia* (Oxford: At the Clarendon Press, 1955), 42–43.
7. Ibid., 39 and 43; James Arthur Quirin, "The Beta Israel (Falasha) in Ethiopian History: Caste Formation and Culture Change, 1270–1868" (Ph.D. diss., University of Minnesota, 1977), 226; Wolf Leslau, *Falasha Anthology* (New Haven: Yale University Press, 1954), xxv.
8. Pankhurst, "The Falashas," 574.
9. Menachem Waldman, *The Jews of Ethiopia: The Beta Israel Community* (Jerusalem, 1985), 11. Ami-Shau, Center for Aid to Ethiopian Immigrants
10. Lila Perl, *Ethiopia: Land of the Lion* (New York: William Morrow and Co., 1972).
11. Jones and Monroe, *A History of Ethiopia*, 39 and 43; see also Quirin, "The Beta Israel (Falasha) in Ethiopian History," 226; and Leslau, *Falasha Anthology*, xxv.
12. Richard Pankhurst, "The Falashas in Their Ethiopian Setting," *Ethiopian Review* 6 (June 1992): 23–25.
13. Ibid.
14. Ibid.
15. Pankhurst, "The Falashas," 567.
16. Ibid., 567–82.
17. Hagar Salamon, *The Hyena People: Ethiopian Jews in Christian Ethiopia* (Berkeley: University of California Press, 1999), 4.
18. Taddesse Tamrat, *Church and State in Ethiopia, 1270–1527* (Oxford: Clarendon Press, 1972), 201. For good but brief information on the history of the Beta Israel, especially for the period between the fourteenth and the nineteenth centuries, see an article by Robert L. Hess, "An Outline of Falasha History," in *Proceedings of the Third International Conference of Ethiopian Studies, Addis Ababa, 1966*, 1:99–112. For more information on how the name *Falasha* was invented, see Steven Kaplan, *The Beta Israel (Falasha) in Ethiopia: From the Earliest Times to the Twentieth Century*, (New York: New York University Press, 1992), 53–69.
19. Kaplan, *The Beta Israel (Falasha) in Ethiopia*, 56.
20. Pankhurst, "The Falashas," 571–72. Based on extensive interviews with Ethiopian Jews, Salamon said most informants found the term *Kayla* derogatory, "as Christians used it for minority groups to

whom they attributed super natural powers." For more extensive meaning attributed to the term see Salamon, *The Hyena People*, 11–12.

21. Quirin, "The Beta Israel (Falasha) in Ethiopian History," 207–11. For good information on this period of Ethiopian history, see Mordechai Abir, *Ethiopia: Era of the Princes, 1769–1855* (New York: Frederick A. Praeger, Publishers, 1968), 27–43. That some Beta Israel were involved in the politics of the power structure dates back to the very days of their conquest by Yishaq (Kaplan, *The Beta Israel (Falasha) in Ethiopia*, 56).

22. For an overview of the *Judenstadts* see Leo Spitzer, *Lives in between: Assimilation and Marginality in Austria, Brazil, West Africa, 1780–1945,* (London: Cambridge University Press, 1989), 73–100.

23. Salamon, *The Hyena People*, 30.

24. Pankhurst, "The Falashas," 571.

25. Quirin, "The Beta Israel (Falasha) in Ethiopian History," 202.

26. Perl, *Ethiopia*, 107–8; Louis Rapoport, *The Lost Jews: Last of the Ethiopian Falashas* (New York: Stein and Day Publishers, 1980), 100.

27. Quirin, "The Beta Israel (Falasha) in Ethiopian History," 212–13. For good information on cast formation among the Beta Israel and their systematic marginalization by the Amhara, see Quirin's Ph.D. diss. in general and his chap. 5 in particular, where he discusses the issue in detail.

28. Teshome G. Wagaw, "The International Political Ramifications of Falasha Emigration," *The Journal of Modern African Studies* 29, no. 4 (1991): 559–61; see his notes 4 and 11. It should be noted that the persecution of Muslims and Roman Catholics has been historically evident in Ethiopia.

29. Salamon, *The Hyena People*, 30.

30. Quirin, "The Beta Israel (Falasha) in Ethiopian History," 201.

31. Salamon, *The Hyena People*, 107 and 109.

32. Pankhurst, "The Falashas," 571–72.

33. Ibid., 571.

34. Perl, *Ethiopia*, 76. Back in 1986, the research assistant was personally told by his Beta Israeli friend who was working for his master's program in the English language in Addis Ababa University that his people strongly feel offended when they are addressed as *Falashas.*

35. See Quirin, "The Beta Israel (Falasha) in Ethiopian History," whose very thesis consistently refers to them as the *Beta Israel.* For an extensive discussion on the invention of the name *Falasha* by the Amhara and its enforcement on the Beta Israel, or the *Ayhud,* see Kaplan, *The Beta Israel (Falasha) in Ethiopia,* 53–78.

36. Anselm L. Strauss, *Mirrors and Masks* (New York: The Free Press, 1959).

37. See Ruth Simms Hamilton, *Creating a Paradigm and Research Agenda for Comparative Studies of the Worldwide Dispersion of African Peoples,* monograph no. 1 (East Lansing: African Diaspora Research Project, Michigan State University, , 1990), 23–24.

38. For a summary of these views see Kay Kaufman Shelemay, *Music, Ritual, and Falasha History* (East Lansing: Michigan State University Press, 1989). See chap. 1, *Perspectives of Falasha History.*

39. Quirin, "The Beta Israel (Falasha) in Ethiopian History," 212–13.

40. Ibid., 222 and 225.

41. Shoshan Ben-Dor, "The Journey to Eretz Israel: The Story of Abba Mahari," *Pe'amim: Studies in the Cultural Heritage of Oriental Jewry* 33 (1987): 5–31. (Hebrew) as reported in Gadi Ben-Ezer, "Ethiopian Jews Encounter Israel: Narratives of Migration and the Problem of Identity," in *Migration and Identity,* vol. 3, International Yearbook of Oral History and Life Stories, special eds. Rina Benmayor and Andor Skotnes (Oxford: New York: University Press, 1994): 101–17, 104.

42. See Ruben Schindler and David Ribner, *The Trauma of Transition: The Psycho-social Cost of Ethiopian Immigration to Israel* (Brookfield, Vt.: Ashgate, 1997), 17; and Louis Rapoport, *Redemption Song: The Story of Operation Moses* (San Diego, Calif.: Harcourt Brace Jovanovich, 1986).

43. Emanuela Trevisan Semi, "The Beta Israel (Falashas): From Purity to Impurity," *The Jewish Journal of Sociology* 27, no. 1 (June 1985): 103–14, 106.

44. Ibid., 107.

45. Salamon, *The Hyena People*, provides rich ethnographic details regarding sociability, cooperation, and exchange relations among religious groups in chaps. 4–6.

46. J. Abbink, "Seged Celebration in Ethiopia and Israel: Continuity and Change of a Falasha Religious Holiday," *Anthropos* 78, nos. 5–6 (1983): 789–810.

47. Ibid., 795–98.

48. Paul Connerton, *How Societies Remember* (New York: Cambridge University Press, 1989), 46.

49. Ibid., 43.

50. Schindler and Ribner, *The Trauma of Transition*, 11.

51. J. D. Bleich, *Contemporary Halakhic Problems* (New York: Ktav, 1977); Schindler and Ribner, *The Trauma of Transition*, 11.

52. Weinstein, "Ethiopian Jews in Israel," 214; and Schindler and Ribner, *The Trauma of Transition*, 34–35.

53. Bleich, as reported in Shindler and Ribner, *The Trauma of Transition*, 34.

54. Ibid.

55. Ruth Mason, "The Ethiopian Exodus Continues: Solomonic Sequels," *Hadassah Magazine* (November 1998): 13–15, 13.

56. Salamon, *The Hyena People*, 65–71.

57. Ibid., 66 and 67.

58. See Spitzer, *Lives in between*, chap. 4; Gregory Howard Williams, *Life on the Color Line: The True Story of a White Boy Who Discovered He Was Black* (New York: Dutton, 1995); Richard Graham, ed., *The Idea of Race in Latin America, 1870–1940* (Austin: University of Texas Press, 1990).

59. For discussion of these issues see Henry Kamen, "The Secret of the Inquisition," *New York Review of Books*, 1 February 1996, 4–6; Willard F. King and Selma Margaretten, *The Spaniards: An Introduction to Their History* (1971; reprint, Berkeley: University of California Press, 1985); Norman Roth, *Conversos, Inquisition, and the Expulsion of the Jews from Spain* (Madison: University of Wisconsin Press, 1995); and Benzion Netanyahu, *The Origin of the Inquisition in Fifteenth Century Spain* (New York: Random House, 1995).

60. Salamon, *The Hyena People*, 69.

61. Schindler and Ribner, *The Trauma of Transition*, 16.

62. Rapoport, *Redemption Song*, 175–76; Tudor Parfitt, *Operation Moses: The Story of the Exodus of the Falasha Jews of Ethiopia* (London: Weidfield and Nicolson, 1985), 23.

63. Rapoport, *Redemption Song*, 178.

64. Teshome G. Wagaw, *For Our Soul: Ethiopian Jews in Israel* (Detroit: Wayne State University Press, 1993), 564.

65. Wagaw, "The International Political Ramifications," 563.

66. Rapoport, *Redemption Song*, 197.

67. Jones and Monroe, *A History of Ethiopia*, 40–41.

68. Ibid., 195.

69. Ibid., 186–87.

70. Jan Gerrit Abbink, *The Falashas in Ethiopia and in Israel: The Problem of Ethnic Assimilation* (Nijmegen, The Netherlands: ISCA, 1984); and Linda Begley Soroff, *The Maintenance and Transmission of Ethnic Identity: A Study of Four Ethnic Groups of Religious Jews in Israel* (Lanham, Md.: University Press of America, 1995).

71. Abbink, *The Falashas in Ethiopia*, 112; and Soroff, *The Maintenance and Transmission of Ethnic Identity*, 46.

72. David K. Shipler, "Torture Reported of Ethiopian Jews," *New York Times*, 15 November 1981, A9.

73. Soroff, *The Maintenance and Transmission of Ethnic Identity*, 150.

74. For greater detail see Wagaw, *For Our Soul*, chap. 3.

75. Ibid.

76. Ibid., 73.

77. See ibid., chap. 3.

78. For analysis see Tom Segev, *The Seventh Million: The Israelis and the Holocaust* (1991; reprint, New York: Henry Holt and Company, 2000), chap. 4.

79. Harley, "West Ponders How to Help," B4.

80. Shipler, "Torture Reported," 9. This could be an overexaggeration meant to win the support of the world public. In general all Ethiopians suffered in the hands of the military government.

81. Ibid.

82. Ahmad Karadawi, "The Smuggling of the Ethiopian Falashas to Israel through the Sudan," *African Affairs* 90 (1991):45.

83. Wagaw, *For Our Soul*, 66, 73.

84. Ian Fisher, "Tangling of Jewish Roots Bars Ethiopians from Israel," *New York Times*, 19 April 2000, A3.

85. Judith Matloff, "Black Jews Seek Promised Land," *Christian Science Monitor*, 18 April 1996, 6.

86. Ibid.

87. Fisher, "Tangling of Jewish Roots"; and Ruth Mason, "The Ethiopian Exodus Continues: Solomonic Sequels," *Hadassah Magazine* (November 1888): 13–15.

88. Hilary Anderson, "Final Exodus for Ethiopian Jews," *BBC Online Network*, 22 June 1999, http://news.bbc.co.uk/2/hi/africa/375112.stm.

89. Benedict Anderson, *Imagined Communities* (New York: Verso, 1983).

90. Thomas L. Freedman, "For Ethiopian Jews, Israel Is Another World," *New York Times*, 4 January 1985, 1; Wagaw, *For Our Soul*; and Weinstein, "Ethiopian Jews in Israel."

91. Esther Hertzog, *Immigrants and Bureaucrats: Ethiopians in an Israeli Absorption Center* (New York: Berghahn Books, 1999).

92. Wagaw, *For Our Soul*, 215.

93. Freedman, "Israel Is Another World," 1.

94. Sabra Chartand, "For Ethiopians of '84, Some Unsettled Matters," *New York Times*, 3 June 1991, A4; Donna Rosenthal, "Israel: The New Exodus," *The Atlantic* 269, no. 5 (May 1992): 38. See also Joel Greenberg, "Exodus to Isolation: Ethiopians Endure Hardships," *New York Times*, 11 July 1992, 2Y; Wagaw, *For Our Soul*, provides a detailed analysis of many of these problems.

95. Henry Kamm, "Ethiopian Jews Have Trouble Fitting In," *New York Times*, 30 March 1986, 3. Wagaw, *For Our Soul*, has devoted considerable attention to the educational experiences and programs.

96. Weinstein, "Ethiopian Jews in Israel," 218.

97. Ibid.

98. Wagaw, *For Our Soul*, 82. It is reported that those in Afula are not well educated.

99. There are around one thousand Ethiopians out of sixty thousand residents, most of whom are Moroccan or North Africans. It is also reported that those in Ashqelon are mainly from Tigre province in Ethiopia. See Semi, "The Beta Israel (Falasha)," 103; Wagaw, *For Our Soul*, 138.

100. To receive the 1984 group of immigrants an absorption center was opened exclusively for Ethiopians in Beersheba. Ninety-five apartments were made available for five hundred residents. Sixty-five families took up residence, sixteen of which lived together in large apartment complexes. Weinstein, "Ethiopian Jews in Israel," 216–17. Also see Wagaw, *For Our Soul*, 222.

101. Wagaw, *For Our Soul*, 124, 127, 147, 256.

102. Hertzog, *Immigrants and Bureaucrats*.

103. Liisa Malkki, "National Geographic: The Rooting of Peoples and the Territorialization of National Identity among Scholars and Refugees," *Cultural Anthropology* 7, no. 1 (1992): 24–44, 32.

104. Leon Wieseltier, "Black Jews and the Meaning of Zionism: Brothers and Keepers," *The New Republic*, 11 February 1985, 21–23, 21.

105. Shindler and Ribner, *The Trauma of Transition*, 33–35.

106. Ibid., 35.

107. *The Christian Century*, 2 October 1985, 857–58.

108. Weinstein, "Ethiopian Jews in Israel," 219.

109. Chartand, "For Ethiopians of '84," A4.

110. Leonard Fein, "Israel's Un-orthodox Battle," *The Nation*, 7 July 1997, 21–24, 22.

111. Ibid., 22.

112. Virginia R. Dominguez, *People as Subject, People as Object: Selfhood and Peoplehood in Contemporary Israel* (Madison: University of Wisconsin Press, 1989), 173.

113. See the following for various perspectives on the "conversion controversy from which much of this summary has been culled": Laurie Goodstein, "American Jews Grow Fearful of Being Cast Aside by Israel," *New York Times*, 16 November 1997, 1 and 6; Ilene R. Prusher, "Israel's Orthodox Want Only One Way to Pray," *The Christian Science Monitor*, 14 November 1997, 6; William Safire, "A Passover Sermon," *New York Times*, 23 April 1997, A21; Serge Schmemann, "'Who's a Jew' Puzzle Gets More Tangled," *New York Times*, 27 January 1998, A5; Serge Schmemann, "In Israel's Bitter Culture War, Civility Is a Casualty," *New York Times*, 21 July 1998, A1 and A6; editorial, "A Schism among Jews?," *New York Times*, 20 April 1997, section 4, 14; and Joel Greenberg, "In Dispute over Who Is a Jew, a Grace Period," *New York Times*, 29 October 1997, A3. For more information on how Jewishness is determined in modern Israel, see Simon N. Herman, *Jewish Identity: A Social Psychological Perspective* (New Brunswick, N.J.: Transaction, 1989), 75–83.

114. Prusher, "Israel's Orthodox," 6; also Schmemann, "'Who's a Jew,'" A3.

115. Prusher, "Israel's Orthodox."

116. Consult the following references for detailed discussions on who is a Jew: Lawrence H. Schiffman, *Who Was a Jew: Rabbinic and Halakhic Perspectives on the Jewish-Christian Schism* (Hoboken, N.J.: KTAV Publishing House, 1985); Simon N. Herman, *Jewish Identity: A Social Psychological Perspective*, 2d ed. (New Brunswick, N.J.: Transaction Publishers, 1989), chap. 5, "Who Is a Jew," 75–83; and Charles E. Shulman, *What It Means to Be a Jew* (New York: Crown 1960), chap. 1, "What Is a Jew?"

117. Goodstein, "American Jews Grow Fearful," 6.

118. Alison Gandy, "Emerging from the Shadows: A Visit to an Old Jewish Community," *NACLA Report on the Americas* 27, no. 2 (September–October 1993): 11.

119. "Ethiopian Jews Claim Israel Denies Equality," *Chicago Tribune*, 14 September 1992, section 1, 4; *The Christian Century*, 2 October 1985, 857–58.

120. Wagaw, *For Our Soul*, 108–19.

121. Ibid., 113.

122. Shindler and Ribner, *The Trauma of Transition*, 39.

123. C. Rosen, "Ethiopian Jews in Israel," in *The Jews of Ethiopia: A People in Transition* (Tel Aviv: Beth Hatefutsoth, Nahum Goldman Museum of the Jewish Diaspora; New York: Jewish Museum, 1986), 80, as cited in Shindler and Ribner, *The Trauma of Transition*, 39.

124. Laurie Goodstein, "American Jews Grow Fearful," 1 and 6.

125. Weinstein, "Ethiopian Jews in Israel," 219–20.

126. Schindler and Ribner, *The Trauma of Transition*, 80.

127. Ibid., 41–42.

128. Gadi Ben-Ezer, "Ethiopian Jews Encounter Israel: Narratives of Migration and the Problem of Identity," in *Migration and Identity*, 101–17, 114–15.

129. J. Abbink, "The Changing Identity of Ethiopian Immigrants (Falashas) in Israel," *Anthropological Quarterly* 57, no. 4 (October 1984): 139–53, 146.

130. Ibid., 144.

131. Semi, "The Beta Israel (Falashas)," 110.

132. Dominguez, *People as Subject*, 169.

Asphalt Stages: Pickup Basketball and the Performance of Blackness

Michael Hanson

Jazz is an art of individual assertion within and against the group. Each true jazz movement . . . springs from a contest in which each artist challenges all the rest, each solo flight, or improvisation, represents (like the successive canvases of a painter) a definition of his identity: as individual, as member of the collectivity and as link in the chain of tradition.

—Ralph Ellison

And there was basketball, a game that worked better on asphalt than grass. . . . City ball was faster, louder, more stop-and-go, and like bebop defiant of established standards of performance.

—Nelson George

S INCE THE MID 1980S, BASKETBALL HAS REGISTERED EXPLOSIVE GROWTH IN popularity as mass popular sport, expressive cultural form, and global revenue-generating enterprise. Central to this growth has been an amplification of the racial dynamics of the sport; increasingly, basketball has been invested with a particular African American aesthetic, cultural, and participatory identification. The racial particularity of this association is conditioned by structural, cultural, and historical forces and in turn shapes dominant styles of play, the general visibility and reception of the game, and the specific desires and expectations that are mobilized for its consumers.

The current popular status of basketball emerges in part from the stylistic reconfiguration and economic vitalization of the National Basketball Association (NBA) in the eighties. During this period the NBA institutional apparatus, led by new league president David Stern, successfully navigated the emergent racial anxieties of marketing an increasingly black game to white audiences. Ironically, this achievement was realized by reinscribing the league's ascendant black style and dominance as its desirable offering to white consumers.

David Leviatin notes that the percentage of black players in the NBA went from only 12 percent in 1955, to just under 50 percent in 1965, to 1978 and through the present when the percentage of black players lies between 70 and 75 percent. Meanwhile, the number of black starters, a much stronger indicator of black predominance and racial consumption, has been 80 to 85 percent since the mid-1980s, while virtually all of the stars are black.[1]

In 1980 the NBA was facing an imminent collapse. Having recently absorbed some of the teams, players, and style from the American Basketball Association (ABA), which was largely acknowledged to be a looser, flashier, and more improvisational league, the NBA's image and white fan-base was increasingly diminished by concerns of widespread drug abuse among players and competitive disparities due to monopolization. As league commissioner, Stern introduced salary caps and antidrug policies while effectively resignifying white desires for and identification with the black basketball aesthetic.

The NBA's rehabilitation marked a stylistic paradigm shift that foregrounded a perceived black racial authenticity, flamboyance, and theatrical presence in post–Julius Erving newcomers such as Michael Jordan, Magic Johnson, Charles Barkley, and Dominique Wilkins, not to mention the widely perceived yet rarely articulated racial rivalry between the white and equally talented Larry Bird and some of the league's black stars. Enabled by an enlarged share of national television exposure, the complex racial politics of college basketball were often rehearsed far beyond the actual game for high visibility teams such as the Georgetown Hoyas and the UNLV Runnin' Rebels. Today, United States basketball is positioned at the center of a far-reaching international basketball market that exchanges bodies, products, icons, and identifications, while in the realm of popular mass media, the latest turn in racial representation at once celebrates and demonizes the black body and urban life as objects of both public consumption and civic threat. Finally, the strong black identification with basketball, as leisure pursuit, indigenous craft, and cultural site, amplifies the already racialized signifiers of the game.

The sport is now situated in a sort of transcendent black aesthetic that unites and articulates with a variety of black cultural practices, from music to fashion to urban youth culture and style. In this way basketball functions as a primary representational nexus through which the complexities of racial subjectivities are rehearsed, produced, and contested. Without reducing it to an index of Afro-diasporic culture or values, this study departs from the premise that basketball occupies what Michael Eric Dyson refers to as a "metaphoric center of black juvenile culture, a major means by which even temporary forms of cultural and personal transcendence of personal limits are experienced."[2] In this sense, the game provides an analytic space in which to interrogate the way structural, cultural, and political forces implicate the informal daily practices, or what Michel de Certeau calls "tactics," of the disempowered.[3]

This analysis inquires into the multiple approaches and meanings available to and articulated by participants within the pickup basketball universe. The focus is pickup or informal basketball, which has widespread participation at all competition levels and is distanced, at least institutionally, from the disciplining and commodified elements of professional and competitive collegiate play. In this informal arena we can observe, in a less mediated way, some of the routine features of black expressive style. As an embodied cultural practice, basketball is formalized by both the game's internal structures and rules and the unique social and physical traits that actors bring to the game. Bodily expression is the physical source for varied gestural and meaning-giving practices that articulate in basketball's cultural space. Erving Goffman defines performance as "all the activity of an individual which occurs during a period marked by his continuous presence before a particular set of observers and which has some influence on the observers."[4] This notion of public, intersubjective presence informs my treatment of black performativity—the catalog of styles, gestures, self-productions, and general ways of being in the social world that have historically developed as Afro-diasporic cultural practices. Here, in the performative register, features of social identity are expressed, negotiated, and made intelligible. Three dimensions of black performativity will be explored: the aesthetics of play, black vernacular styles, and the pursuit and maintenance of a positively managed self. The analyses presented here derive from ethnographic and observation data collected while participating in a localized, highly competitive pickup basketball scene.[5]

Talent, Performative Difference, and the Racial *Habitus*

By foregrounding racial differences in playing style and orientation to the game, this study risks reproducing a racial biology of sport that bases athletic difference on genetic expression, physiology, and constitutional variation.[6] For my purposes, race is defined provisionally as a discursively produced, historically contingent social designation that is largely enabled through arbitrary references to and conflations of phenotypical difference and sociohistorical location. It is a nominal term, but one that is nonetheless a fundamental organizing marker of social privilege, institutional access, and historical outcome.[7]

My aim is to explore the dimensions of white-black differences in playing *style,* particularly a unique black performative approach to the game. Style in this sense is a culturally conditioned constellation of practice, orientation, and sensibility that coheres in body-based expression. Distinctions of style are nonstatic, shifting delineators of difference that appear as intensities rather than indexes of discrete practices. The "black style" referred to here is typified by a self-conscious, expressive, improvisatory, deceptive, spontaneous, and individualistic athletic self-production, such that the aesthetic dimension of performance often structures or accompanies primary processes of play. Conversely, "white style" is often premised on absorbing the individual within the team structure (strategic ball movement in creating open shots, egalitarian opportunity among players, and so on) and privileges a deliberate, fundamentally sound offensive pace and an instrumental rather than aesthetic-oriented technique.[8]

Tendencies in playing style are largely the product of social histories and collective group practices. Donal Carlston notes the role that sociomaterial environment plays in the formation of particular approaches to the game. Certain features of social and physical space—population density, availability and crowding of recreational areas, the presence and participation of spectators, and situationally determined levels of appropriate playing intensity, physical contact, and rule compliance—shape the development of distinct playing styles.[9] Here, racially segregated living spaces and the local cultural forms that are produced therein contribute to what kinesiologist Gary Sailes calls the "sport socialization process."[10] These variable features of space and cultural norms significantly dictate performance orientations.

As racial style and sociostructural location are intimately linked, athletic performance might be viewed as a type of structured practice, where "schemata" for acting are generated. This places a specific racial stress on Bourdieu's notion of *habitus,* a "subjective but not individual system of internalized structures, schemes of perception, conception, and action common to all members of the same group or class and constituting the precondition for all objectification and apperception."[11] To the degree that it expresses and embodies collectively held and structurally shaped values and sensibilities, race becomes the articulation point of cultural style and embodied expression. As these practices become routinized through the ritual enactments of practice and play, they complicate, as Loïc Wacquant has shown in his work on boxing, fundamental distinctions between mind and body, the physical and the cultural.[12] In this way performative practices are not essentially biological but are products of historically conditioned yet shifting structural and cultural forces: the life-world of the city, the symbolic sphere of collective black identity, the political investments in racial self-representation, and so on.

Yet, the historical constitution and effect of minoritized social space on processes of play do not solely account for the sharp aesthetic distinctions, orientations, and productions of this play. The cultural and representational dimensions of differentiated yet coherent Afro-diasporic identities are significant formative influences beyond the immediacy of place or environment. Playing style and to some degree skill derive from the successful appropriation, imitation, and incorporation of extant dominant approaches, sensibilities, and ways of playing—literal rehearsals of "being like Mike." Style develops through a process of identification, a cogitized yet always embodied practice. The reproduction and appropriation of "black" style and orientation among black players may be less a function of *physical* location—the valorized inner-city game that prioritizes crafty inside moves and the capacity to self-create shots in defensive traffic for instance—than of *cultural* location, the abstracted historical processes of black in-group identification and subject formation.[13] In the face of persistently truncated access to mainstream institutions and resources, black expressive practices often replace or accompany social and political processes within what political theorist Nancy Fraser terms the "informal counterpublic sphere"—a localized, informal site to play at, dramatize, contest, and envision alternative realities and liberated futures.[14] These practices may rely on masked insubordination, disruptive counterstrategies ("hidden transcripts"), and the body as a symbolic site of resistance and celebration. The expressive economy of basketball, the temporary joy and transcendence through the everyday poetics of physical work and pleasure, and the game's black vernacular structure confirm the social significance of immediately available forms of cultural, corporeal, and gestural expression. This oppositional and organizing efficacy of cultural practices is a defining feature of the early subcultural models of cultural resistance.[15] Here, style is perceived as a fundamental organizing feature of cultural identity: "Symbolic objects—dress, appearance, language, ritual occasions, styles of interaction, music"—are appropriated, cultivated, and deployed by particular social groups to "form a *unity* with the group's relations, situation, experiences: the crystallisation in an expressive form, which then defines the group's public identity."[16] Black style amplifies the reflexive, self-conscious, and stylized expressions of the performed self. The emotive, rhetorical, and gestural are privileged aesthetic modes, and the form and process of cultural practice are often foregrounded in contexts where instrumentally derived ends are limited or denied.[17] Repetition, a will toward perpetual newness and innovation, an emphasis on the pleasure and power of the spoken word (*nommo*), and a foregrounding of public performance are primary delineators of black cultural forms.

Basketball is a dynamic cultural field that functions through the exchange of physical and symbolic capital—the reflexive, kinetic, and somatic dimensions of bodily expression and the social features of cultural practice are embodied in and deployed by players to varying degrees. Criteria for judging the value of "good" or "bad" play generate from this field, and to the extent that stylistic elements are privileged by racial *habitus*, black style becomes the archetype of good play. Consumption and judgment of the game is shaped by racialized perceptions, and in this way good players are disproportionately reproduced by race, as black or urban style is the aesthetic index against which stylistic valuations are made.

Black style in basketball—individual expression, intragame contests, self-conscious and often ironic presentations of an overdetermined cool and stylized self, the projection of confidence and competence—is articulated in a metaperformative modality. The metaperformance, or "playing at playing," occurs simultaneously with the actual dynamics and flow of play that comprise Goffman's elementary performance. As actors objectify their own performance in a manner that comments or signifies on the process of play as it occurs, the metaperformance transcends the expressive and functional conventions that frame traditional structures of the game. The following analyses should be viewed as brief ideal-typical descriptions of some formal, gestural, and processual elements that structure pickup basketball and black performance.

RACIALIZED SPACE AND THE CULTURAL DIMENSIONS OF THE PUBLIC SELF

Pickup basketball is a highly routinized, context-specific, often nonverbal and embodied discursive system. Direct verbal engagement or attempts to explicitly elicit information from participants risk transgressing the widely accepted norms and expectations that structure fluid processes of this cultural space. The flow of primary events and action, the selection of teams, or the jurisdiction of rules, for instance, occurs in a sophisticated intersubjective yet tacit manner. Nonverbal enactments, even where audible expression is constant, are the primary codes of conduct and function as the semantic foundation for unfolding interactions.

The "rules of the game"—the codes of communication and understanding that are the main foci of ethnographic inquiry—are ritualized, implied, and presupposed. Explicit verbal interventions are in fact discouraged in this communicative system, as they can be perceived as disruptive or, worse, reveal the naïveté, inexperience, or incompetence of the transgressor. As will be elaborated below, the efficacious self-production of competence, talent, and desirability translates into social authority and inclusion in this cultural space. To be "out of the know" significantly diminishes status on the symbolic level and access to playing time on a practical one. Thus, the significant portion of this data consists of observational and interpretive accounts of the action and focuses on the visual, emotive, expressive, and physical registers of basketball culture.

In this account, play occurred in a large gymnasium that housed two courts. From the outset, I observed a distinct pattern in the self-regulation, selection, and negotiation of public space that articulated along racial lines. The court nearest the main entrance was predominated by black players, the farther court by whites, although this arrangement was not generally perceived as impermeable. Indeed, games integrated by one or two players on each court in the minority were common, and the racial arrangement was frequently determined by factors that superficially appeared unrelated to race or social grouping—the need for enough players to fill two sides or players entering games on either court to avoid waiting.[18] However, the racial delineation sharpened as the gym became fuller, more active, and competitive.

The gym was mainly accessed through doors located near one corner of the baseline of the so-called black court. Whites often entered and, with little discernible hesitation or acknowledgment of activities on the black court, proceeded directly along the baseline toward the court on the other side of the gym. Blacks would enter and congregate around the baseline of the black court or linger in the doorway to observe while waiting for an opportunity to play. Any number of factors may contribute to this pattern of racialization: the inertia of precedence, grouping based on previous acquaintance, affinities of style, self-assessed court placement by skill level, and so on. Comments by white players usually referred to some combined notion of skill and style: "It's too run and gun over there" or "the pace [on the black court] is definitely faster. You have to warm up here [on the white court] first before trying to get in games over there." Remarks about tempo can be read either as white players wanting a more "controlled" or moderate pace versus one characterized as "run and gun" or as an assessment of black play—the need for a warm-up suggests a certain elevation of this style, one that requires preparation before engaging. Observations from black players also reveal a tacit recognition of a style and skill difference; for example: "Let's wait for a game here. It's too slowed down over there." Black and white players often referred to the exact style dynamic, yet for each, the perceived game tempo or level of individualistic play was inflected with different value and desirability. Participating on the court that was most compatible with one's style took priority over simply playing, even if it meant waiting.

The production, experience, and negotiation of social space were also invested with racial meaning. On the predominantly black court, space seemed more "public," that is, participants—players, spectators, bystanders—appeared self-conscious of their presence and performance before others. Participants were "onstage," in constant engagement with the action via informal comments, critical or humorous observations, and gestural and bodily expression that conveyed a reflexive communicative intentionality. A strong sense of intersubjective observation, acknowledgment, and criticism often structured the social processes of black play. The environment of "publicness" had a communal, antiphonal quality that blurred boundaries of playing-observing, game-event, functional talk–informal conversation. This degree of sustained performativity was rarely demonstrated on the white court, where action and expression was significantly more instrumental and where the social space of the game rarely flowed across the sidelines. Black counterpublic sphere practices, including quotidian pleasure and communal exchange, were temporally erected in the physical space of the gym. The elevated awareness of the symbolic dynamics of social interaction and self-presentation, as a protective means of mediating contingent or unpredictable encounters in urban life, is glimpsed in pickup ball. To some degree, the preoccupation with positive self-portrayal on the court—the strong desire to avoid awkwardness and embarrassment—mirrors the need, however problematic, to maintain a seamless and transparent display of hypermasculine competency and respect in the context of urban public life.

The production and meaning of spatial form in the context of pickup basketball is crucial to understanding the ways in which black performativity is enabled, expressed, and understood by all participants. It is the means by which cultural space is always experienced in the dialectical play between material and temporal structures on the one hand and the interpretive modes of perception through which racial subjects construct meaning on the other that gives pickup basketball its capacity to issue expression and performance differently by race. The following sections detail some empirical indicators of the three modalities of black performativity in the context of pickup basketball—aesthetic, vernacular, and body-self management.

BLACK METAPERFORMATIVITY AND THE AESTHETICS OF PLAY

In pickup basketball, actors employ what Goffman terms "expressive equipment" to communicate talent, skill, authenticity, and desirability as a player: "In the presence of others, the individual typically infuses his activity with signs which dramatically highlight and portray confirmatory facts that might otherwise remain unapparent or obscure. For if the individual's activity is to become significant to others, he must mobilize his activity so that it will express *during the interaction* what he wishes to convey."[19] The projection of confidence and competence establishes one's attractiveness as a player, one "with game." The importance of this dynamic cannot be overestimated in pickup basketball, as participation and interaction often occur without previous acquaintance or any prior basis for the evaluation of athletic competence. Prior to even stepping on the court or taking a shot, self-produced signals of ability and authority can hint at or determine one's potential status within this universe, including the distribution of playing time.

Any number of strategies are enlisted to acquire status recognition. Clothing is a semantic vehicle for suggesting, interpreting, and establishing skill. The currency and model of shoes, the cut and style of shorts, and the insider basketball references on T-shirts are important initial indicators of legitimacy. Within the expressive economy of black urban space, we must take seriously semiotician Umberto Eco's quip "I speak through my clothes," as adornment and sartorial displays present primary means of communicating to others that one is, even if lacking a particular catalog of skills or talents, attuned to the importance of positive public self-presentation.[20]

The mundane process of warming up also presents opportunities for performing competence and style. Black players often approached pregame shooting sessions with a casual detachment and physical pace far slower than game tempo. The form of the shot or dribble (embellished, fluid, on view for others) took precedence over content (adjusting flaws, preparing for game-speed pace). Black players often demonstrated elaborate personalized catalogs of finger roll layups and complex dribbling maneuvers that would appear to have little instrumental value in a game setting. However stylized, these practices communicated, on a metaperformative level, a particular approach and disposition toward the game and playing space. In contrast, white players often appeared to be more focused on literally "warming up"—loosening muscles, practicing particular shots, and correcting for perceived deficiencies in technique. In black urban spaces, aesthetics and athletic performance are collapsed. Form and content incorporate into effective performances of what Nelson George calls "intimidation through improvisation," thus signaling that looking good is paramount and a necessary concomitant to *being* good.[21]

Even before engaging in actual play, from the moment one enters this space, players are communicating with and assessing one another through the symbols of clothing, manners, comportment, and bodily expression. During the game, the meta-performance remains a fundamental structuring principle. Style, however, can bring a player only so far; he also must deliver in terms of actual performance. The most persuasive aesthetic presentation is the one that is supported and amplified by skillful and effective play. Indeed, there is a continual risk of overstating, misrepresenting, or not delivering on one's athletic capacities: "when stylistic expression is not accompanied by a successful execution, the result is humiliating, because the audience regards the performer as having laid claim to a greater expertise than he can demonstrate."[22] Players must present a self that is generally consonant with their level of skill. The player with a reputation for skill has a wider plane on which to project an image of talent and can even take risks or play carelessly, knowing that a general level of respect has been established, even if his actions are momentarily unconvincing. Highly skilled players also may feel less pressure to fully aestheticize their play or take risks and rather let their "game" speak for itself.

This presentation-skill dialectic is prominent in pickup basketball as players "announce" themselves in often highly stylized bodily performances and gestures while demonstrating a wide range of technical skill. Self-presentation corresponds in varied ways to actual talent: the capacity to score, defend, rebound, and so on. The following are excerpts from my field notes describing two core players. Their performative mediation of the skill-presentation dialectic indicates the dynamic contours of racial performativity in this context.

PLAYER 1:

His aesthetic presentation seems to mirror his playing style. His playing attire often reflects an attentiveness to detail—socks folded over to appear doubly thick and tidy, for instance.

He is a talented player, but not necessarily in terms of high skill or physical endowment; he *looks* good. His playing style is smooth and crafty; he has a lot of "moves." He rarely engages in small talk or banter, but rather smiles to register notable plays or mistakes both by him or others. His game is built on confidence, but it is expressed in a passive, self-assured manner. Judging from his general presence among other players, he appears to be very well respected as both player and participant in this culture—he is rarely forced to wait long for an opportunity to play, for instance.

PLAYER 2:

As a graduate student, he is a few years older than the majority of participants at this court. He wore a pair of well-worn, black Nike midcut sneakers with thick double-paired socks shoved down around his lower shins.

He often dominates play on his court. At approximately 6'3" he is slightly above average height for this court and is a very skilled shooter and rebounder. What strikes me most about his style is his narrow and serious attention toward the competitive element of play. It appears that playing well (without mistakes, aggressively, soundly) and winning efficiently and effectively is of crucial importance for him. His approach to the final score, remaining on the court (not losing), and defeating opponents are definitive elements of his playing style.

Player 1 is black and played almost exclusively on the black court; Player 2 is white and played primarily on the white court. Both are "good" in that they are effective and capable scorers and competent defenders, demonstrating experience through a discernable "feel" for the game and so on, but the specific style criteria for establishing their ability are determined within the racial fields that generate the structures and meaning of play on each court. The crafty, assured, but nonassertive style of Player 1 contrasts with the intensely focused and determined approach of Player 2. Here, again, is the distinction between process and outcome. Player 1 focuses on process, the series of competitive moments that unfold during the course of play. Player 2 plays instrumentally and subordinates process to outcome, the final score.

If these players were to switch contexts, the racial styles that define their approaches would contrast with the cultural structures of play. In white-dominant games, black style is often read as aloof, self-centered, and less committed to winning than making the spectacular play. In black-dominant games, a white player who focuses more on hard effort and winning is likely be perceived humorously by black players, who feel he has no grasp of the appropriate level of engagement. Playing hard, with "heart," and to win and remain playing are not secondary, deemphasized features of black play, however. Rather, within the expressive register of the game's performance, the white player might be viewed as lacking a sense of the game's levity; he lacks the metaperformative distance from which to view and monitor his own performance as it communicates to others. Moreover, the distinction between black process and white outcome signifies the cultural antinomy that distinguishes historically observable Afro-diasporic structuring principles of repetition, flow, antiphony, circularity, and temporal presence from Western teleological orientations toward material progress, growth, accumulation, resolution, and outcome in expressive practices.[23] In his fruitful essay on this cultural opposition, James Snead writes, in reference to music, that "[w]ithout an organizing principle of repetition, true improvisation would be impossible, since an improviser relies upon the ongoing recurrence of the beat."[24] In light of this, a provisional ethno-racial stress may be mapped onto Max Weber's modern distinction between *zweckrational* (means to end instrumentalization) and *wertrational* (realization of values for their own sake).[25]

Over the course of my research, the most highly skilled player in my estimation was a 6'6" white participant who played primarily on the black court. The recurring theme in my field notes regards his archetypal "black" style; he had discernable athletic prowess, often dunked, and possessed a large catalog of expressive and highly stylized moves and shots. During one particularly intense, heavily observed game, he made an offensive move toward the basket and, while guarded in dense traffic, successfully executed a difficult and athletic reverse layup. The responses of the black observers on the sideline were exaggerated displays of awe: "NOO!" "Tell me he didn't just hit that," and so on. One regular exclaimed: "He's *so* city!"

This informal, affirmative assessment—"He's *so* city!"—captures the multiple operations of race, culture, and performance in pickup basketball. That comment reveals, by conflating racial and cultural metaphors, the constructed nature of "black" style. "City" has a racialized meaning that evokes a particular repertoire of actions and behavior specific to urban black culture. This acknowledgment of city (black) style in a white player tethers perceptions of talent to culture—the life-world of the city, identifications with blackness—not biology in explaining black-white differences in playing style and ability. It is also significant that this player's high status, among both blacks and whites, was derived as much from his particular playing style as his technical skill. That this style was "urban" suggests the general orientation within basketball culture that privileges urban black expressive aesthetic forms and shapes the lens through which talent is perceived. High visibility, popular white players at the highest levels of competition indicate the pervasive elevation and appropriation of the black aesthetic.[26]

Black Vernacular Style as Strategic Play

Pickup basketball is mediated through a highly ritualized and primarily nonverbal system where, as Paul Gilroy writes, "sound is displaced by vision and words are generally second to gestures.[27] The actions fundamental to the flow and process of play—the negotiation and coordination of moving bodies in physical space, the many reflexive, intuitive, and kinetic elements of basketball—rely primarily on phenomenologically derived perceptions over explicit verbal exchanges. Even the social moments ancillary to actual play, such as choosing sides or negotiating a controversial call, contain a primary nonverbal element that generates from tacit knowledge. Black vernacular speech in the context of pickup basketball offers significant instances of the incorporation and expression of unique performative strategies—hounding, signifying, celebrating, announcing, denouncing—that accompany, comment on, and mediate processes of play.

At this gym, vocal expression and interactional style differed significantly by race and court context. Typically, the degree, frequency, and intensity of verbal participation and engagement were greater among blacks and increased in intensity as the games became more homogeneous by race (i.e., in all-black contexts). This vernacular repertoire, the forms of "talking trash,"[28] includes a variety of oral and paralinguistic expressions that serve to boost, celebrate, and affirm one's own play or to denounce, embarrass, or humiliate an opponent. Verbal tactics are often linked to particular situations during play that result in a player being "shown up" or "faced" by another. Two general types of "trash talk" may be roughly distinguished by identifying the subject for whom the utterance or gesture is intended—outward gestures and inward gestures.

Outward gestures are verbal pronouncements explicitly targeted at another player. This verbal sparring is common to the sport—"You can't hold me!" "Your game is weak!" "Oooh, you got dunked on!" The intent is to call attention to a (usually opposing) player's weaknesses and thus demean or denounce. This gesture also serves, implicitly, to elevate the status and performance of the speaker-player. Outward gestures vary widely in tone (from playful to ironic to malicious) and in effect on the receiving subject (ignored, flustered, enraged, entertained, provoked).

Outward gestures typically get expressed in moments such as the following example. During a short and intense sequence of plays, a particularly talented black player on one team scored several consecutive baskets despite close defensive pressure from a black opponent. Three of these were long jump-shots from three-point range.[29] There was a growing sense that this player was "on"—as registered by excitement of the crowd and a sense of frustration from the defensive side—and that he should continue getting the ball from teammates to maintain this offensive flow. Upon making the third three-pointer, with his back turned to his defender, he exclaimed in the general direction of other players: "Who's gonna guard me?!" To which players on both teams and those observing responded with smiles and stifled giggles. The defender appeared not to register the remark or reactions to it and simply jogged back to the offensive end of the court.

Although the comment did not explicitly engage the defender, it indirectly singled out his inadequate performance. This was an outward gesture in that it was targeted at the ability of a particular player. He was not addressed directly but rather was isolated by this remark about his weak play to everyone *but* him. Indeed, its obliqueness mirrored the sense that his defensive performance was so poor as to go unnoticed, thereby mocking him even more.

Inward gestures are self-references, such as boasts or signifying acts, that insist on recognition of one's positive status in public space. In this form of self-enhancement, verbal commentary accompanies one's physical performance in projecting the complete image of talent. By elevating the status of the speaker, they also may function to weaken, indirectly, the status or image of opposing players. Ceola Ross Baber writes that the function of the signifying act is to "talk about, put on, put down, or 'sound on' through *innuendo and implication*" (emphasis added).[30] Inward gestures promote and enhance one's "onstage" status while undermining the public presence of others.

Consider a typical example of the way inward gestures provide a constant backdrop to play at this gym. During a heavily observed game, a particularly vocal black player began making some notable plays. At one point he drove to the basket under strong pressure and made a layup over a much taller defender. He immediately jogged back down the court, arms dangling by his side and head tilted back, yelling, "RESPECT MY GAME! *RESPECT* MY GAME!"

Aware that he had accomplished a difficult move, he verbally expressed what had just occurred physically, using the inward gesture as a means of self-affirmation. Whether his performance was actually "respected" seemed less relevant than the moment of boasting that it provided. Demanding "respect" in this instance served as a self-aggrandizing comment on his performance: "I am talented, I am performing well, and I insist that you pay attention to me."

The distinctive forms of black vernacular style in basketball point to the ways that racial politics implicate the game in often subtle ways. Concerns with taunting and exhibitionism in popular sport are increasingly prominent dimensions of sport's public discourse. The tenor of this discourse is typically premised on criticisms of behavior that emanate from the distinctly racialized sites of black urban space. New racial anxieties have emerged since the late 1970s as black athletes have moved out of the role of innocuous entertainer and resisted the symbolic and structural forces that police black cultural expression such as signifying gestures.[31] For Baber, "signifying serves a socializing function in the black cultural community. . . . it helps them to develop an endurance for and resistance to insult and thereby assists in preparing them for life's more serious insults and harassments, sharpening their wits and cultivating their sense of humor as survival strategies."[32]

The range of communicative forms used at this gym as strategies to announce, denounce, celebrate, signify, or intimidate were deployed, appreciated, affirmed, and initiated by black participants. The presence and reception of these practices among black players in an informal setting largely outside the gaze of white audiences suggest the complex politics that inform white responses to black cultural difference. The furor over taunting or "showboating" may in part be less a matter of the decline in "sportsmanship" and more a matter of the perceived threat to the conventions or sensibilities of many mainstream observers.

"Face," Respect, and the Managed Self

A significant aspect of pickup basketball culture is the heightened self-awareness among participants of the public feature of their performances. This was evident in the many efforts made to avoid what Goffman terms "performance disruptions" and to maintain a positive, respected personal front.[33] Impression management, whereby individuals actively call attention to their capabilities and assets while avoiding or reducing attention to deficiencies, is especially difficult in an activity such as basketball, a dynamic physical process in which players capitalize on human error: the defensive lapse, unforced dribbling error, missed layup, fouls, turnovers, and so on. Imperfection in athletic performance is expected to a degree by observers and participants, but adequate self-impression management is a continual preoccupation.

There seems to be a general sense among players that certain unforced errors, missed shots, or mishandled passes, for instance, are common and thus unremarkable. Rather, the constant threat of being discredited by the performance of another player, to be "faced," is the underlying impulse in impression management. The face, or the retort "in your face," is a standard rhetorical figure in black culture that is premised on gestural paybacks in competitive contexts. Similar to signifying, the dozens, or various other performances of improvised and contestatory verbal exchanges, it signals and registers, often humorously, the outcome of a game's intragame mini-competitions.

The "face" is "that intangible at stake in any man-to-man playground encounter that makes even single plays memorable."[34] It is "an acceptably arrogant claim of excellence on the speaker's part."[35] The temporary undermining of status that is activated by being faced depends largely on context. It usually occurs when a player is made to look awkward, inadequate, silly, or weak as a result of an opposing player's performance. A blocked shot, a stolen dribble stolen, and an inadequate defensive effort are all potential sources for "getting served" or "being faced." The ultimate act of degradation is to be "dunked on" by an offensive player. In this masculine universe, to unsuccessfully stop the most forceful shot in the game is often portrayed as denigrating, even emasculating, because of the particular physical and symbolic violence by which face is lost and status undermined.[36]

Pickup games often ebb and flow with moments of pitched intensity juxtaposed with lulls of unremarkable competition. For players and observers, these "moments" generate excitement because they demonstrate a successful mediation of the delicate balance of chance and skill, intentionality and risk, and coordinated yet competing physical efforts—the spectacular dunk, a series of difficult shots, unexpected wins for undertalented teams, and so on.

On weekend afternoons the courts were unusually crowded, games were especially competitive, and an "eventlike" atmosphere often enveloped the black court. On one typical weekend, I observed a game along with a large and boisterous audience of waiting players and street-clothed observers. The game was close and at one point both players and bystanders were animated by a rapid series of exciting plays, including some long jump-shots made consecutively by one player and a crowd-pleasing dunk from another. Meanwhile, the level of verbal commentary between and among observers and some of the players escalated. A moment was clearly developing. Then a loose ball broke away toward midcourt and a lone player moved out ahead of everyone, retrieved the ball, and confidently began dribbling toward his basket for an uncontested layup or dunk. Unaware that he was pursued, he casually shot a stylized underhand layup and BOOM!!—a trailing defender slapped the ball so hard that it audibly careened off the backboard and violently out-of-bounds.

Like those innumerable playground "moments," the environment exploded in collective, game-stalling recognition and celebration. The mocking giggles, exaggerated "oohs," and laughter acknowledged both the skill of the block and the very public loss of face by the shocked shooter. The defender modestly returned to the other end of the court and waited for play to resume. Clearly embarrassed, the shooter almost immediately dismissed the play by saying to no one in particular: "That ain't shit!" He avoided eye contact, appeared narrowly focused on resuming play, and firmly waited for the ball to be retrieved.

Goffman defines face as "the positive social value a person effectively claims for himself by the line others assume he has taken during a particular contact. . . . an image of self in terms of approved social attributes."[37] "Face-work" is the catalog of face-saving practices deployed in moments when social image is threatened. Rather than concede to his own error or recognize another's good play, the player whose shot was blocked employed a face-work maneuver that signified that the blocked shot "ain't shit." By focusing on resuming play while ignoring a compromised face, despite the undeniable level of excitement and the comments and behavior of those around him, he further attempted to remove his emotional investment in the preceding play and communicate unspoiled status.

The dynamics of "face" vary in value and meaning, depending upon context and cultural space. That both avoidance and pursuit of the denigrating act were observed especially among black participants is significant and perhaps points to complexities of identity, respect, and status in the context of persistent black disempowerment. When the security derived from institutional representation or symbolic and material capital is denied, self-management and the effective negotiation of the social environment become a critical means of maintaining respect and security. Even the temporary and arbitrary loss of respect of the "faced" actor in a pickup basketball game can potentially attenuate black peer status, whereas these symbolic gestures of worth may be much less significant for white participants, whose investments in status are less tethered to intersubjective encounters and personal performances in public space. The boundaries of the game's ritual space and the external spaces of urban life at times blurred as threats to face are met with the status-saving strategies of a hard, uncompromising street authority. The frustrating extreme of this embattled individual management culminates in games that are continually stalled, devolve into fights and in some cases ended, because opposing players or teams cannot resolve contested calls.

· · ·

Pickup basketball is a rich universe to explore dynamic features of black expressivity. The game is a source for and enables varied productions of black cultural style and performative practices. These practices emanate from the larger constellation of expressive codes and modes of self-presentation that are significant features of Afrodiasporic subjectivities.

Three dimensions of black performance were observed in this study: the aesthetics of play, black vernacular styles, and positive public self-management. Black aesthetic playing styles that foregrounded the stylization and process of play were counterposed to a normative white style that focused on hard and aggressive play, risk-aversive tactical team function, and a singular attention to outcome. For many black players, style, talent and competence were expressed through what I have termed the metaperformative register, a secondary cultural and structurally embodied physical and expressive self-production that occurs during and articulates with general structures of play.

The second black performative element was the sometimes strategic use of vernacular styles to comment, signify, denounce, and generally negotiate the nonverbal, extralinguistic corporeal dimension of physical play. Both inward and outward gestures were widely used in structuring black play.

Finally, an exploration of image self-management in pickup basketball reveals some of the ways that threats to black public status are mediated through expressive style. The maintenance of "face" is a significant component of play and is imbricated with broader racial politics of respect and disempowerment in urban space.

NOTES

1. David Leviatin, "The Evolution and Commodification of Black Basketball Style," *Radical History Review* 55 (1993): 154–64. As of 2006, the increasing ascendancy of non-U.S.-born players in the NBA (approximately 20–25 percent of active and inactive players) has reconfigured the sites of origin of players but not necessarily affected black overrepresentation.

2. Michael Eric Dyson, *Reflecting Black* (Minneapolis: University of Minnesota Press, 1993), 73. Also see Robin D. G. Kelley, "Playing for Keeps: Pleasure and Profit on the Postindustrial Playground," in *The House That Race Built: Black Americans, U.S. Terrain,* ed. Wahneema Lubiano (New York: Pantheon Books, 1997).

3. Michel de Certeau, *The Practice of Everyday Life* (Berkeley: University of California Press, 1984), xix.

4. Erving Goffman, *The Presentation of Self in Everyday Life* (Garden City, N.Y.: Anchor Books, 1959), 22. I use the term *performativity* differently from, for instance, Judith Butler's deployment, which focuses on the material effects of speech acts in discourse. See *Bodies That Matter* (New York: Routledge, 1993). Performance here is more closely related to the traditions of symbolic interactionism and ethnomethodology. Butler's project is not unrelated, however, and is crucial for understanding dimensions of the discursive production of "blackness" in this context, for instance.

5. As with sport generally, pickup basketball is sharply delineated by sex and gender markers. In my research I was almost exclusively in contact with men, and my conscious use of only masculine pronouns reflects the somewhat calcified boundaries of this cultural universe. There is important work to be done on the complex imbrications of gender, pickup basketball, and black cultural life.

6. John Hoberman, *Darwin's Athletes* (New York: Mariner Books, 1997). Hoberman provides an impressive overview of the ways that ideological and cultural-historical forces shape scientific and informal discourses of sport, race, and biology. Yet his general claim regarding African Americans and sport—that black support for and complicity with what he calls the black athletic superiority narrative (athletic over other modes of success) devalues other modes of achievement (specifically

those of the mind)—risks reproducing a particularly insidious form of victim blaming. His intervention is especially problematic because even where it rescues black ability from the racist trap of
biological essentialism in the name of black liberation, it generally ignores the historical-material
conditions that structure black marginality. He is unable to account for the fact that talent might
be celebrated not as racial politics, but as a particular aesthetic or corporeal poetic. He ultimately
denies the pleasures of black leisure by making black sport only a political issue that is intimately
linked, indeed mutually exclusive, to black educational achievement.

7. Representative examples of the type of racial theorizing that address the vexed and shifting nature
   of racial formation include David Theo Goldberg, *Racist Culture* (Oxford: Blackwell, 1993); Etienne
   Balibar and Immanuel Wallerstein, *Race, Class, Nation: Ambiguous Identities* (London: Verso, 1991);
   Stuart Hall, "New Ethnicities," in *Stuart Hall: Critical Dialogues in Cultural Studies,* ed. David Moreley
   and Kuan-Hsing Chen (New York: Routledge, 1996); and Michael Omi and Howard Winant, *Racial
   Formation in the United States: From the 1960s to the 1990s,* 2d ed. (New York: Routledge, 1994).

8. Donal Carlston, "An Environmental Explanation for Race Differences in Basketball Performance,"
   Journal of Sport and Social Issues 7, no. 2 (1983): 47.

9. Ibid.

10. Gary Sailes, "An Examination of Basketball Performance Orientations among African American
    Males," *Journal of African American Men* 1, no. 4 (1996): 37–46.

11. Pierre Bourdieu, *Outline of a Theory of Practice* (New York: Cambridge University Press, 1977), 86.

12. See Loïc J. D. Wacquant, "The Social Logic of Boxing in Black Chicago: Toward a Sociology of Pugi-
    lism," *Sociology of Sport Journal* 9 (1992): 221–54; Loïc J. D. Wacquant, "The Pugilistic Point of View:
    How Boxers Think and Feel about Their Trade," *Theory and Society* 24 (1995): 489–535. Wacquant
    asserts that the "boxer is a living gearing of the body and the mind that explodes the opposition
    between action and representation and transcends *in actu* the dichotomy of the individual and the
    collective that underlies accepted theories of social action" (1992, 224–25).

13. The spatial production of playing styles is more complicated than a simple additive account of popula-
    tion density and player distribution yields. Nelson George perceptively points out that the privileging
    of the inner-city playground as production site of players and prominent styles is largely a matter of
    "big-city chauvinism," as many significant contributions to the game have come from black players, in
    some cases the rural Midwest, West, and South (consider the locales that spawned some of the most
    "flamboyant" of recent NBA elite—Allen Iverson [Hampton, Va.], Vince Carter [Daytona Beach, Fla.],
    Shawn Kemp [Elkhart, Ind.], Tracy McGrady [Bartow, Fla.], Lebron James [Akron, Ohio], and Jordan
    himself [Wilmington, N.C.]). Yet I would hold that there is important interpretive work to be done on
    the microdiasporic articulation of black style, particularly at the nonelite level, as it is shaped by forces
    such as regional sensibility and local culture. See Nelson George, *Elevating the Game: The History and
    Aesthetics of Black Men in Basketball* (New York: Fireside, 1992), 53.

14. Nancy Fraser, "Rethinking the Public Sphere: A Contribution to the Critique of Actual Existing
    Democracy," in *Habermas and the Public Sphere,* ed. Craig Calhoun (Cambridge: MIT Press, 1992),
    109–42.

15. See Dick Hebdige, *Subculture: The Meaning of Style* (New York: Routledge, 1979).

16. Tony Jefferson et al., introduction to *Resistance through Rituals: Youth Subcultures in Postwar Britain,*
    ed. Stuart Hall and Tony Jefferson (London: Hutchinson, in association with the Centre for Contem-
    porary Cultural Studies, University of Birmingham, 1975), 54.

17. For an extended discussion of black aesthetics, process, and goal, see James Snead, "Repetition
    as a Figure in Black Culture," in *Out There: Marginalization and Contemporary Cultures,* ed. Russell
    Ferguson (Boston: MIT Press; New York: New Museum of Contemporary Art, 1990), 213–30.

18. These racialized features of social space also were observed in a similar setting on the West Coast,
    the only difference being the addition of a predominantly Asian court.

19. Goffman, *Presentation of Self*, 30 (original emphasis).

20. Umberto Eco in Dick Hebdige, *Subculture: The Meaning of Style* (New York: Routledge, 1979), 100.

21. George, *Elevating the Game*, xix.

22. Thomas Kochman, *Black and White Styles in Conflict* (Chicago: University of Chicago Press, 1981), 139.

23. Black music is, of course, exemplary here in terms of communal practice, process, and temporal presence in its creation and reception. See Olly Wilson, "Black Music as Art," *Black Music Research Journal* 3 (1983): 1–22.

24. Snead, "Repetition as a Figure of Black Culture," in *Out There*, 221. Elsewhere Snead writes: "In European culture, the 'goal' is always clear: that which always is being worked towards. The goal is thus that which is reached only when culture 'plays out' its history. Such a culture is never 'immediate' but 'mediated' and separated from the present tense by its own future-orientation. Moreover, European culture does not allow 'a succession of accidents and surprises' but instead maintains the illusions of progression and control at all costs" (220).

25. Max Weber, "The Nature of Social Action," in *Max Weber: Selections in Translation*, ed. W. G. Runciman (Cambridge: Cambridge University Press, 1978), 28.

26. Observers have periodically alluded to the black aesthetic of white players such as the no-look and behind-the-back passes of Bob Cousy or the improvisational flourishes of "Pistol" Pete Maravich. Consider the specific performance styles of recent white NBA players such as Bob Sura, Rex Chapman, and Jon and Brent Barry (Brent won the 1996 NBA slam dunk competition with a catalog of sorties that included extending the tradition of Dr. J and Michael Jordan by taking off from the foul line and dunking). Black-inflected white play has been particularly celebrated in the West Virginia–bred Jason Williams, whose popular monikers include White Chocolate.

27. Paul Gilroy, "'After the Love Has Gone': Bio-politics and Ethno-poetics in the Black Public Sphere," *Public Culture* 7 (1994): 56.

28. A number of terms refer to this signifying act—*talking shit, smack,* or *garbage,* for instance. The very proliferation of terms suggests the prominent significance of this verbal engagement in basketball culture.

29. During my observations here and in other pickup basketball contexts, extra points were never awarded for shots from beyond the 19'9" arc that designates the three-point shot in collegiate rules. Those baskets were worth the same as all others (two points). Players were nonetheless aware of the merit of the made three-pointers and often celebrated them by using the referee's official gesture: both arms extended straight above the head.

30. Ceola Ross Baber, "The Artistry and Artifice of Black Communication," in Geneva Bay and Willie Barber, eds., *Expressively Black* (New York: Praeger, 1987), 97.

31. George, *Elevating the Game*.

32. Baber, "The Artistry and Artifice," 75–108.

33. Goffman, *Presentation of Self*, 208.

34. Chuck Wielgus and Alexander Wolff, *The Back-in-Your-Face Guide to Pick-up Basketball* (New York: Dodd, Mead and Company, 1986), 222.

35. George, *Elevating the Game*, xvi.

36. See Davis W. Houck, "Attacking the Rim: The Cultural Politics of Dunking," in *Basketball Jones: America above the Rim*, ed. Todd Boyd and Kenneth L. Shropshire (New York: NYU Press, 2000), 151–69.

37. Erving Goffman, *Interaction Ritual* (Garden City, N.Y.: Anchor Books, 1967), 5.

The Marimba Still Sounds: Building Cultural Pride and Political Resistance through Afro-Ecuadorian Music and Dance

Troy Peters

FOR PEOPLE THROUGHOUT THE WORLD, MUSIC IS AN IMPORTANT ELEMENT IN cultural identification and occupies a central and multifaceted role in social life. This study explores how it is used by people of African descent in Ecuador, in particular the folkloric movement of music and dance in the province of Esmeraldas. An introductory section provides a brief history of blacks in Ecuador, with an emphasis on the coastal colonies of *cimarrones* (the Spanish term for escaped slaves). Because these people not only freed themselves but also frequently returned to the plantation to free others, for Afro-Latinos they symbolize resistance and cultural pride. The introductory section also describes the marginalized position of Afro-Ecuadorians today and presents some of my observations as an African American undergraduate there.

THE CULTURAL CONTEXT

Afro-Ecuadorians face marginalization even on the international level, as relatively few people know anything about Ecuador, and even fewer know there is a black population. I went to Ecuador as a general exchange student in winter 1999 to do research for my senior thesis as part of a bachelor's degree in anthropology. Although I knew Afro-Ecuadorians existed, my first real introduction to the people and their culture came ironically in the primarily upper-class Catholic University of Quito, more specifically in the course entitled Afro-Ecuadorian Cultures, taught by Angel Quiñónez, a black Ecuadorian doctoral student with several academic degrees. A considerable amount of the lecture material was based on his personal experiences growing up in Esmeraldas, known in Ecuador as la Provincia Negra (the black province). From those lectures and a tape played in class one day, I developed a keen interest in studying Afro-Ecuadorian music and culture.

Experiencing the Racial Context

The day I arrived in Ecuador, the woman who hosted me during most of my six-month stay said to me, as a compliment: "Ah, you're white, Troy" (I am light skinned). As a "rich gringo," I was converted to being white, even though my features indicate African ancestry. Ideas about social and racial assimilation in Ecuador assume that no one would want to be considered "black" if given the choice, although the social construction of race is still inexorably bound to skin color. After a time in the equatorial sun, my skin darkened considerably, and I no longer fell within the acceptable color range of *blanco;* despite my obvious "gringoisms," I lost some of the social stature I had upon arrival.

A number of times during travel (both on the coast and in the highlands) whites or mestizos (mixed Indian and Spanish) asked if I had Ecuadorian parents. When I said "no," most responded that I looked like I was from the coast (*parecía costeño*). *Costeño* was used so as not to offend me by saying directly that I looked black. Discourses on race (in polite conversation) often use regional terms.

The Ecuadorian population separates roughly into 50 percent mestizo (indigenous and Spanish), 35 percent indigenous, and the remainder, which consists of a sizeable black population, a smaller number of whites, and people of Asian and Middle Eastern ethnicity. It is important to understand that how individuals and groups are defined racially is influenced not only by skin color but also by other factors, such as socioeconomic status or class, regional origins, legacies, and power relations within the society.

Afro-Ecuadorians make up between 5 and 10 percent of the population, depending on who you ask and their definition of "black." The majority live on the coastal plains, in rural or urban areas, but there is a significant population in the northern highlands. The traditional image of blacks, as seen by themselves and others, is of poor, uneducated farmers or fishermen. People of African descent who wish to be socially less *negro* often refer to themselves as *moreno* (dark skinned). This choice has deep historical roots (principally the colonial equation of "negro" with "slave") and points to an important intellectual conflict. Many progressive Afro-Ecuadorians see *moreno* as a negation of self, as an attempt to forget the past and the ancestors in order to assimilate.

In the Ecuadorian racial discourse, to be a "true Indian," one must live and dress like one. Many indigenous people choose not to maintain any traditional or political ties with the indigenous community and consider themselves mestizos. Those who do maintain their heritage generally have a strong sense of pride in "acting as an Indian." The size of the indigenous population and the degree of political organization they have managed to achieve give them a strong presence on the national scene, although they are still marginalized. Many mestizos, primarily in the upper and middle classes, refer to themselves as *blanco* (white). This does not necessarily correspond to skin color or facial features because many look like any "full-blood" indigenous person. In my experience, those with money or status use the term *mestizo* only in certain situations, as when speaking academically or to tourists about the cultural heritage of the country. Among poorer mestizos, who are generally closer to their indigenous roots, the identification is used as an attempt to separate themselves from their heritage of marginalization. Thus, racial identification has phenotypic components but includes such factors as economic status, cultural pride, and historical associations.

Income distribution in Ecuador follows the pattern in much of the Third World: a very small wealthy elite, a small struggling middle class, and about 75 percent of the population living in poverty[1] From the mid-1970s until the early 1990s the petroleum industry was booming and material wealth grew, at least for the middle and upper classes. Until the end of 1998, the national ideals of modernization and financial progress among all levels of society seemed a real possibility. For the elite in particular, the desire to become more respectable in European and North American eyes was manifested in an effort to demonstrate modernity by reinforcing an image of ethnic whiteness and decreasing the social presence of nonwhites.

The ideology of whitening (*blanqueamiento*) is described by Whitten and Torres as "an unconscious psychological process accompanying the economic state of under-development in the twentieth century.[2] *Blanqueamiento* essentially accepts the implicit hegemonic rhetoric of the United States with regard to 'white supremacy' and often blames those people classed as black and indigenous for the worsening state of the nation." It is a two-pronged process of racial mixture and cultural assimilation; the goal is to become more white and European. For all intents and purposes, this is the thrust of racial ideology and practice in Ecuador. Although *blanqueamiento* is very much a phenomenon of the twentieth century, its seeds were sown almost from the time of the Spanish conquest.

Conquest and Slavery

In 1526 the Spanish landed on the coast of what it is today Ecuador, during one of Pizarro's early voyages. In the Andes civil war was raging within the Incan Empire, and when Pizarro returned in 1534, Atalhualpa had just defeated his brother Huapac. It took little time for the Spanish to conquer the still reeling Inca and claim their land.[3]

As a Spanish colony, the area was first part of the viceroyalty of Peru, with administrative headquarters in Quito. In 1563, Spain converted the territory into the Real Audencia of Quito ("Royal Colonial Court, Tribunal"), at which point it gained a certain political and military autonomy from Peru. In 1763, the Real Audencia became part of the viceroyalty of New Granada (Colombia), but the integration was never strong. After the colonies gained independence in the 1820s, Ecuador was the first to secede from the fledgling state of Gran Colombia[4]. These associations were important factors in Ecuador's later border disputes with both Peru and Colombia, especially the latter, and across the uncertain northern boundary black *cimarrones* migrated so easily that the coastal area of northern Ecuador and southern Colombia now form a contiguous cultural zone.

The slave trade came late to Ecuador as compared to other areas in Latin America. The first Africans were brought to the Caribbean colonies in 1513, but no significant numbers reached Ecuador until the 1550s, and even then the traffic was not very large.[5] After the native population died off along the coast and in the warm valleys of the highlands, the Spanish looked to Africa for new *bestias de cargo* (beasts of burden), and the first large group was brought to Ecuador to work in the southern mines of Zaruma.[6]

The Africans brought to Ecuador came from the region that extends from modern-day Ghana to Angola, mostly from the Congo and Angola, at the southern end of that range. In Spanish colonies enslaved Africans were often named after the region or group from which they allegedly came. For example, Mina, a coastal town in Dahomey land (now part of Ghana), and Lucumi, a term for Yoruba peoples in Nigeria, are still very common names among Ecuadorian blacks.[7]

For the most part, black slaves were used in the south, on the coastal sugarcane plantations and in the gold mines of the foothills, and in the warm Chota Valley in the north, on sugar plantations and cattle ranches. Some worked as house servants and farmhands in and around the major highland cities. Documents from the late eighteenth century indicate that almost half could be found on the coast, about one-quarter in the valleys, and the rest in the southern mines or scattered among various provinces.[8] In 1802, a German traveler named Humboldt counted about eight thousand black slaves and forty-two thousand *zambos* (indigenous and African mix) and mulattos (black and Spanish mix) in what is now Ecuador.[9] These figures include the large African descent population living along the northern coastal plains, in what is now Esmeraldas Province.

Esmeraldas was the site of the first Spanish landing in Ecuador but ironically was one of the last areas in which the Spanish consolidated control.[10] Esmeraldas, which is Spanish for "emeralds," was named for mythical lakes filled with the jewels and supposedly located somewhere in the area.[11] Tropical forests cover the rolling hills, and the sprawling jungle and loosely organized indigenous groups gave Pizarro's party little incentive to remain. No permanent Spanish settlements were established for decades. Archeological excavations show that relatively advanced people populated the zone in pre-Colombian times, but when the Spanish came there were only abandoned towns, with a "surprisingly" large "cultivated area with corn, bean, cacao, cotton and appetizing fruit."[12]The only *indígenas* who still populate the area in any numbers are the Chachi (also known as the Cayapa to the Spanish), who migrated from the northern highlands, due first to Incan expansion and later to the arrival of the Spanish in the 1530s.[13]

The most formidable Chachi rival was the African *cimarrón*. The first escaped African slaves arrived in the area in 1553, when a mercantile ship en route from Spain via Panama wrecked near what is now the city of Esmeraldas. The twenty-two Africans who survived, sixteen men and six women, used what they could salvage from the ship to establish themselves in the new environment.[14] The indigenous tribes considered them no different from their European "masters," and initially there was a great deal of resistance to these and other black invaders. The Chachi called blacks *juyungos* (demons or devils), and some still use the term. The *cimarrones* fought various indigenous groups but eventually allied and intermixed with most of them. The uniting factor was the threat of an even more dangerous enemy, the Spaniard.[15]

In 1577, the Real Audencia sent Miguel Cabello Balboa to pacify the blacks and *indígenas* in the area. He made contact and ultimately developed a relationship with the leader of the *cimarrones*, Alonso de Illescas, who had defeated the Chachi and other local groups to force a peace. The two founded the first settlements recognized by the Spanish in this zone, not far from the landing site of the shipwrecked Africans. Unable to control the black and Indian allies and fearful that they would side with the British pirates who were beginning to operate in the region, Cabello named Illescas the province's first governor.[16] With this limited authority, the colonial government could not exploit the resources of the province, and for more than a century there were no significant mining operations or truly viable port towns.[17] In 1735, Pedro Vicente Maldonado, an upper-class mestizo, conducted the first real topographical studies of the province, was named governor, and founded a number of towns in the northern zone, from La Tola to San Lorenzo.[18] Not until about 1900, well after Ecuador's independence, was a road built from the city of Esmeraldas to Quito, and not until the 1948 banana boom was the province meaningfully integrated into the country economically or socially.[19]

The original blacks mixed relatively quickly with the indigenous population (except the Chachi, who forbid intermixing), but the African influence in Esmeraldas today is primarily due to successive migrations of *cimarrones* from Colombia, the Chota Valley, and the southern plantations of Ecuador. The majority came from Colombia and settled in northern Esmeraldas, usually in the backcountry. After emancipation many former slaves migrated to Esmeraldas from various parts of Ecuador.[20] Despite gaining freedom, they still faced discrimination, poor working conditions, and few opportunities to own land in other parts of the country. Esmeraldas, although underdeveloped, was appealing because blacks could own land there.[21] Its relative isolation over the centuries provided a space where blacks could maintain their Africanness and create new manifestations of cultural identity.

Modern Esmeraldas Province

Peoples of African descent live in all parts of Ecuador, but there are high concentrations in a few locations. The greatest number live in Guayaquil, the nation's largest city, to which most of them migrated from Esmeraldas Province in the 1970s and 1980s. There is also a large concentration in Quito, many of whom are descended from the Chota Valley blacks.[22] A number of blacks still live in the Chota Valley and the nearby city of Ibarra. Most of their ancestors became sharecroppers after emancipation, and they now struggle to maintain their small rural communities. Although Esmeraldas Province is second to Guayaquil in number of Afro-Ecuadorians, it is the area most readily identified with black people.

Scholars consider the Pacific Coast from the southern edge of Panama to the northern part of Ecuador to be a contiguous cultural area, but significant differences separate it into northern and southern zones. The southern half, from just north of the Colombian port of Buenaventura to just south of the city of Esmeraldas, is called the Wet Littoral. According to residents, the strongest manifestations of black culture come from the center of the range, between Buenaventura and Guapi, Colombia.

The city of Esmeraldas has the only oil refinery in Ecuador, contains a population of more than one hundred thousand (fifth largest in the country), and is the provincial capital, so nationally it is perceived as a bastion of "modern civilization" in an essentially "barbarian" territory. Many in Esmeraldas share this view and look down on the primitive "blue blacks"(because of very dark skin) to the north. However, one young woman from the city told me that people from San Lorenzo de Pailón and the north see Esmeraldas as a dirty, crime-ridden place that has lost its culture: "They think of themselves as sanlorenzeños before esmeraldeños."[23] Since the southwest area of the province is at the southern edge of the Wet Littoral, a number of scholars consider it to be less affected by the African cultural influence radiating from the central Colombian coastal zone.[24] Southerners see northerners as culturally backward because of their traditionalism, and northerners see southerners as moneygrubbing and less culturally, or even morally, aware.[25] These prejudices appeared to be more a matter of regional posturing than deeply held divisions, and the dramatic increase in migration over the past few years is likely to soften them.

Travel between San Lorenzo and the city of Esmeraldas has always been difficult because, until recently, the only means was by boat. Bus transport is now available, but for decades it was easier to get from San Lorenzo to Ibarra in the highlands, and today the bus fare to there is still cheaper than to Esmeraldas. This physical separation has led to a certain amount of social and especially economic separation between San Lorenzo and Esmeraldas, which over the past half-century have become the respective economic and social centers of the northern and southern parts of the province.

San Lorenzo de Pailón is much smaller than the southern metropole. A town of about twenty thousand and relatively isolated, it is considered to have strong ties to traditional life. It also has been an important site for the development of Afro-Ecuadorian folkloric dance. The north end of town juts out into the Bay of Pailón, which is more a river delta than a bay. Freshwater, primarily from the Cayapa and Santiago Rivers to the south, and saltwater, from the Pacific to the north and west, create the right conditions for tracts of mangrove forests. The town, about a mile from open sea and surrounded by mangrove swamps, is at the crossroads of a variety of ecological niches.

San Lorenzo was established in the 1730s or 1740s by Governor Maldonado, but according to oral history, the area was populated by *cimarrones* for an undetermined time before that. They came primarily from what is now Colombia. In the 1830s the Ecuadorian government gave the Compañía Inglesa Limitada del Ecuador (English Land Company of Ecuador) exploitation rights in northern Esmeraldas, from San Lorenzo to the base of the Andes, in order to pay off debts incurred in the struggle for independence.[26] This was the beginning of San Lorenzo's role as primary trading post and port in the area.

The English entrepreneurs conducted land surveys and purchased tagua, balsa, and other local woods. They also traded for gold, mangrove bark, pelts, and medicinal herbs, and they built the first (comparatively) permanent structures.[27] The company continued operations until the end of the nineteenth century, when local unrest supposedly forced the English to sell their holdings to a German company, Casa Tagua.[28] The Germans continued in a manner similar to the British until 1930. Both left an important mark in that the town became a center where Afro-Ecuadorians, *indígenas,* and both foreign and domestic whites and mestizos met, traded, and lived.

San Lorenzo seemed the likely choice when a highland rail company sought a port closer than Guayaquil. Construction of the line between Ibarra and San Lorenzo took nearly fifty years (1915–59), but it radically changed the pace and shape of life in the port, formerly only accessible by water. Immediately after the railroad opened, the town experienced a brief tourism boom from Ecuadorians and foreigners interested in nearby archeological sites and beaches. This leveled off to a steady trickle, but the railroad brought another important development: the first permanent Catholic priests. They came from an Italian mission, the Comboniano Order (called the Vernon Order in the United States and Britain), and ultimately played a role in the movement to rescue some of the local traditions.[29]

In the 1960s the development of a larger port to complement the railroad brought further changes. The in-migration of mestizos seeking new markets and rural blacks in search of better wages offset the out-migration of blacks and mulattos, and population growth continues today. Enlargement of the mestizo minority brought rather drastic changes in the social order and norms. In combination, mestizo control of the local economy and politics, the church's influence, and schooling (now primarily in the hands of the state) have pushed traditional Esmeraldeño cultural practices severely to the margins.[30]

Nationally, faith in industrial "advancement" did not fully dissipate until 1999, when the sucre was devaluated nearly 300 percent, but in Esmeraldas Province it evaporated sooner. In San Lorenzo the failure of the Ecuadorian modernization project is evident in the general disrepair of sidewalks and buildings in the town's center. They are visible symbols of broken dreams of wealth and "modernity."

In 1997 a new catalyst for change emerged when the highway from Ibarra to San Lorenzo to Esmeraldas was completed. At this point it is used primarily by buses, light cargo trucks, and heavy logging vehicles. Even the town streets are still mostly for pedestrian traffic, although a few Sanlorenzeños have motorcycles or mopeds. The train runs every now and then to communities deeper in the forest but does not go even halfway to Ibarra. One resident told me that in recent years there is service to Ibarra only when enough tourists pay in dollars to make the trip worthwhile. Mud slides in the rainy season often cover the tracks near the base of the Andes. Two bus companies from Ibarra run three to four times a day both ways, transporting passengers and medium-sized cargo, which seemingly takes up the slack due to the train system's decline.[31] Fairly large ships still use the port, but various residents claim they are nothing compared to the ones they used to see.

The highway may be having more profound social than economic effects. One middle-aged woman told me:

> Here, before, we would go to wash our clothes in this river. Just right here. Sometimes someone would leave the soapy clothes for the next day. Then they would come back and finish. And nobody took even one piece that was there. People here cared for these things, and there wasn't any danger, there weren't any problems, there wasn't anything.
>
> And now, what? You have to totally lock yourself in. It's dangerous, and it hasn't been this way very long. . . . The robberies began about fifteen years ago, and with force, with intensity these last two, three years.[32]

She went on to say that this corresponded to the opening of the highway, which brought another population increase to the town: "Before [the highway], everyone knew each other. Now there's so much traffic, everything has changed."

The highway continues the change that San Lorenzo has experienced over the past forty or fifty years, along with the rest of Esmeraldas. The province has been integrated into a national context from which it developed independently for nearly four centuries. This integration has affected the social order in all aspects, including traditional folk music.

Music and Dance of Esmeraldas

My first live encounter with Afro-Ecuadorian music occurred at the Encuentro Afro de Expresiones Negras (Afro-Latino Conference on Black Expressions) in the coastal town of San Lorenzo, Esmeraldas. At this festival of folkloric music, which drew Afro-Latino participants from Ecuador, Colombia, and Peru, thirty or forty groups performed a wide variety of dances. They all wore bright costumes, often performed brief skits before they danced, and frequently carried such props as handkerchiefs, torches, paddles, baskets, and machetes. Most of these dances are part of a larger group called *currulao*, the name given by Colombians and some older Ecuadorians to the traditional popular music and dance of the coastal area. My informants preferred the term *marimba*, after the instrument that gives the music its distinctive sound, and that is the term used here.

I immediately decided that the traditional music and culture would be my focus, but I quickly found that traditional music is no longer a form of daily popular expression. It is essentially reserved to specific people, in special locations, at particular times of year. I began asking questions to get a general sense of where these groups performed, how they get started, and why. I discovered that local youth tend to identify with the music. Even those who do not know how to play or dance refer to it as their own, at least when speaking to me, the foreigner.

My primary fieldwork was done in San Lorenzo, but I also spent a significant amount of time at folkloric dance schools in Quito. Over the course of three months, I attended as many practices as possible in these two locations. I also traveled to other towns in the province and in the Chota Valley, in the highlands north of Quito, where I interviewed community leaders as well as people involved with folkloric dance and music.[33] Among dance group members, who usually are between the ages of ten and twenty, I conducted informal interviews and some focus groups. More-formal interviews were conducted with the group directors, whose actual names are used when they are quoted directly.

Afro-Ecuadorians have a rich musical heritage that serves as a cultural identifier both within and outside their communities. On the national level, these traditions have been used to validate racist ideas that Afro-Ecuadorians are lazy, morally loose, "hot blooded," and culturally backward. Historically, such ideas have helped rationalize and maintain a system of social inequality rooted in class and racial divisions, which continues to marginalize Afro-Ecuadorians.

Although social protest has occurred throughout Ecuador's history, serious manifestations of social identity and self-determination became most audible in the 1990s. One social space in which these have taken place is the Afro-Ecuadorian traditional, or folkloric, dance school, and I explore the processes by which blacks are attempting to rescue their traditional music from cultural marginalization, particularly in the province of Esmeraldas. Of particular interest is how and to what extent Afro-Ecuadorian folkloric dance schools create a space where postcolonial political resistance occurs, where the social norm is challenged and is being redefined in ways that affect social reality.

The discussion begins with an overview of the music of Esmeraldas, both the traditional version and a recent import, salsa. I then examine Afro-Ecuadorian folkloric dance schools and the folkloric movement and some of the theoretical conflicts that arise from the designation. Next, examples of dances are used to explore themes of collective action, cultural identity through performance, and the relevance of traditional music and dance to the current political and economic situation. Finally, I discuss the challenges to and potential importance of the folkloric dance movement for the future of Afro-Ecuadorians and offer some concluding remarks.

Traditional Music

Traditional Afro-Esmeraldeño music can be divided into religious (sacred) and popular (secular). The most common sacred form is the *arrullo*, which literally translates to "lullaby" but perhaps more accurately means "hymn." *Arrullos* have a variety of purposes within the Esmeraldeño *cosmovisión* (world vision), but they are primarily used to thank a saint who has fulfilled one's prayers. When this occurs, a person owes an *arrullo* on the saint's holy day every year thereafter. The hymn may be sung individually or in a group ceremony that may last all night.[34] Other occasions for *arrullos* are the death of a child, to celebrate his becoming an *angelito* (little angel);[35] the death of an adult, to help her reach heaven; and communal worship in towns without the services of a local priest.

Women primarily perform *arrullos* by singing and shaking *guasas* (closed cylindrical bamboo shakers), whereas men play the *bombo* (a kind of bass drum) or *cununo* (a drum similar to a conga).[36] The songs follow a basic call-and-response pattern: one participant sings an improvised verse thanking or exalting the saint, and the others answer, usually with a traditional chorus. One woman, who shared with me a video of an *arrullo* she conducted for *el Niño* (the baby Jesus) on Christmas Day, explained that the women (and usually the men) rotate between singing verses and chorus. In the video, all moved vigorously to the music but did not consider themselves to be dancing.[37]

Blacks were converted to Catholicism before they escaped slavery and established their free communities in Esmeraldas. For most of the province's history the most common contact with Spanish Ecuadorian society was through the Franciscan priests who made yearly rounds through the area. The priest conveyed a strong sense of Spanish Catholic morality, including the separation of secular and sacred, but African practices survive.[38] Although the priests taught that dancing should not be part of religious ceremonies, Afro-Esmeraldeños managed to create space for their cultural expressions. For example, they converted some spiritual celebrations into secular ones by covering the shrine of a saint or the Virgin Mary with a cloth and then dancing.[39]

The primary popular or secularized dance in Esmeraldas is the *marimba*, but in San Lorenzo it is not the only form. *Marimba* music is essentially percussive, played on the marimbas (a type of xylophone with keys made of palm wood and bamboo sounders), *cununo* and *bombo* drums (typically played by males), and *guasas* and maracas (played by women). Call-and-response singing is also characteristic. In many traditional songs, males and females alternate between singing the lead and the chorus, and the lyrics express their respective ideas on gender relations, local gossip, and so on.[40]

In the early 1960s *marimba* houses (sites where dances occur) and saloons that played nationally popular music on jukeboxes existed side by side.[41] At that time, just after opening of the railroad, an interesting dynamic was established between the two. *Marimba* dances were free and more or less spontaneous, held whenever the house owner (usually the builder) decided, whereas saloons were for paying customers and flourished in times of plenty.[42] But by the 1960s, due to the increased presence in San Lorenzo of highland mestizos, *marimba* moved into the saloons. The influx of tourists brought by the railroad, and the money they were willing to pay to see "real" folkloric dancing, meant that local musicians wanted to be paid money for their services, not the reciprocal gifts of food or drink offered by the houses.[43] When asked if *marimba* dances are conducted for public participation anymore, many informants responded that they are not, because the musicians want to charge for them. Older people and the poorer immigrants from the backcountry who cannot pay miss them.[44]

Marimba dances include the *bambuco, caderona, anderelle, patacoré, agua larga, torbellino,* and in some cases *mapalé.*[45] The *bambuco* and *caderona* are the ones I saw performed most often. The *bambuco* is the most popular and, according to some, the easiest to learn. Couples dance the basic side-to-side *marimba* step while enacting a mock pursuit: each dancer alternates between attraction to and rejection of the other. In Spanish, *caderona* refers to the hips and waist of a woman. In the 1960s (and probably before), this dance, like the *bambuco,* expressed the social and sexual tensions between males and females. The songs were usually about the sexual allure of the woman and her ability to draw a man away from another woman.[46] Today, the *caderona* focuses more on the black woman as a sensual being rather than sexual object. Dance groups attempt to portray this the woman's movements and her mild but persistent indifference to the pursuit of the male partner.[47]

Salsa

Salsa has been the dominant popular music in Esmeraldas since its importation in the 1970s.[48] Many young people say they like and identify with it because it speaks to "love, friendship, and the things that happen in life."[49] In his study of the province,

Marcelo Naranjo states that the Esmeraldeño connection to salsa and other African-derived rhythms makes sense because these, like traditional Afro-Esmeraldeño music, are rooted in the same polyrhythmic structures.[50] Furthermore, many of the lyrics in salsa speak against racial marginality and exploitation, with which Afro-Ecuadorians readily identify.

Yet, salsa has even closer ties, according to one sixteen-year-old male member of a folkloric dance group from Limones, who considers salsa to be Colombian. His grandfather was Colombian, and he as well as the many Afro-Esmeraldeños who had a Colombian ancestor feel that salsa is theirs. He views salsa as a folkloric rhythm like *marimba*, except salsa has gained commercial success.[51] These ideas have some historical basis; some of the traditional rhythms, such as *cumbia*, that helped form salsa in the 1970s came from the northern Atlantic coast of Colombia.[52]Yet, because the physical and cultural geography of Colombia divides black cultural traditions fairly strictly between Atlantic and Pacific coasts, it is unlikely that the same cultural group created salsa and *marimba* and migrated to the coast of northern Ecuador.[53] Regardless of historical reality, the fact that many Afro-Ecuadorians believe salsa is part of their tradition is important to the overall discussion of identity. Many of the young people in folkloric dance groups listen to salsa and have begun to introduce its rhythms into their *marimba* drumming.[54]

Dance Schools and the Folkloric Movement

Bombo y Marimba was the first Afro-Ecuadorian folkloric dance group in San Lorenzo and, according to some, in Ecuador. Documents reveal that it was founded in 1969 by a local professor, Segundo Llanos, and a group of young people who wanted to have a better understanding of the music and traditions of their ancestors.[55] Initially, the group performed dances more or less as they were expressed in the *marimba* houses, adding only choreographed entrances and exits.[56]

A couple of the early members indicated that their parents were pleased to see them carry on the traditions of their grandparents. One man said his mother took him to Bombo y Marimba when he was about sixteen, because she thought he should know how to dance.[57] A woman mentioned that as a child she was interested in the dances her grandmother attended but could never go to see them. A few people said their grandparents would go off to dance *marimba* but would not allow them to come along. Yet, many middle-aged people reported that in their youth there was more interest in the Caribbean sounds of salsa, and *marimba* was considered "old people's music." By the early 1970s it appears that the older generation was reluctant to allow their children and grandchildren to visit the *marimba* houses, and most of the younger generation had no desire to do so because they preferred the new, exotic, "modern" music. These two forces, both due to increased outside influence, marginalized *marimba*, but at least some segments of the population, young and old, held onto the desire to maintain cultural traditions.

Bombo y Marimba has now been joined by Berejú and Patacoré. The Berejú was founded in the early 1980s by a former dancer from Bombo y Marimba, the late Lydia Quiñónez, and her husband. Another breakaway group formed Patacoré not long after. By the late 1980s all three operated in mild competition, but circumstances are changing. The declining economy has forced many Sanlorenzeños to leave for the cities to find work, which has created a severe drain on the population of young adults who can perform and teach. Berejú has been combating the effects of migration by training new performers in its school. This is the only group with its own private space, thanks to a grant in the early 1990s from the Instituto Nacional de Niño y Familia (National Institute for Children and Family).

Bombo y Marimba and Patacoré do not hold regular practices (other than in preparation for a performance), and there is some frustration that they have not been able to obtain sponsorship for acquiring their own space. They are essentially one group because of lack of funds and the migration of so many of their members. Inés Morales, director of Patacoré, has limited time because of her obligations as president of Fundación Cultural Afro (Afro-Ecuadorian Cultural Foundation), the organization that puts on the Afro-Latino festival. Oliver Mina, director of Bombo y Marimba, was directing a fused version of the two groups during the research period.

Membership intersects among the three groups on a number of occasions, and performance techniques have cross-pollinated as well. At one Berejú practice, children between age twelve and fourteen were learning a basic *bambuco* choreography. Those with some experience sang a call-and-response lyric about *el Berejú*, which seemed something of a theme song for the group.[58] Later, at a practice of the older Bombo y Marimba–Patacoré group, the same song was sung while working on an entirely different choreography.[59] Given the size of the town and the interaction of dance groups, it is likely that the song was carried over by performers who originally learned it in the Berejú school. Although managerial and financial differences have created some divisions among these organizations, social connections help maintain informal ties that facilitate a folkloric movement. Young people want to reclaim traditional Afro-Ecuadorian ways and knowledge, not from a desire to escape into the past but in an attempt to build a strong, positive black identity and to remove the negative connotations that have formed around being *negro*.

The problem of negative images in Ecuador is highlighted by an examination of the media. Few black people or *indígenas* are shown on television or in magazines, and images are highly stereotyped, such as the "black" mascots with which a number of products advertise. These are usually stylized drawings that represent blacks almost like monkeys, or at least like primitives, much like Sambo images in U.S. advertisements in the early twentieth century. Other stereotypes emerge in news reports on crime and violence in Guayaquil or Quito.

More positive images come in the form of athletes, beauty queens, and musicians, but all of these must be qualified. As in many countries, black athletes in Ecuador are lauded for their "natural," sometimes "primal," physical abilities, as opposed to the hard work, finesse, and intelligence of white athletes. One poster in Quito for a boxing match depicted a snarling black man who stood menacingly, his name printed below: Carlos "*el Bestia*" (the Beast) Quiñónez.

Miss Ecuador of 1998 was black, and there was at least one other before her. This represents significant change in a country where such insults as "*negro feo*" (ugly black) are common and where such sentiments as "with this wide nose, how attractive am I going to be?" are uttered often, and seriously, by whites and blacks.[60] At the same time, black and mulatto women are coveted by many because of their "primal" sexuality.

Blacks may be acceptable as musicians and entertainers but not as neighbors or workmates, except in a menial status, so young Afro-Ecuadorians are looking to their cultural heritage as a way to build self-esteem and strengthen group identity. An important space for this reclamation is the dance schools, which teach this philosophy to the young dancers and, through performances, to the country as a whole. Dance schools such as Bombo y Marimba, Berejú, and Patacoré provide a socially acceptable space in which the young learn older ways.

The idea of utilizing folklore is apparently a necessary concept for cultural retention and production in San Lorenzo. At one performance during the 10 August fiesta, the announcer always referred to "la hermosa música folklórica de nuestros abuelos/antepasados" (the lovely folkloric music of our grandparents/ancestors).[61] In my experience, Sanlorenzeños rarely speak of *marimba* music without qualifying it as ancestral. It is part of the past that they now remember fondly but may not see as part of their normal routine. Many respondents gave the impression that, whether involved in *marimba* dance or not, they had some interest in acquiring at least a passing knowledge of their ancestral traditions. Therefore, the folklore concept suggests a fond recollection and reproduction of traditional ways but without abandoning the desire to be acceptably "modern."

The term *folklore* is problematic for a number of Afro-Ecuadorian intellectuals. In Quito, one dance group director stated that it separates people from their own culture and their own identity. For her to understand who she is, she must know who her ancestors were, because "they are within us."[62] Folklore implies exoticism, which in turn implies someone else's culture: "If I put on Indian clothing, and danced to indigenous music, then I'd be performing a folklore, because it isn't mine."[63] Her attitude is, perhaps in part, a reaction to the view of Ecuadorian academics during most of this century that Afro-Ecuadorian culture is an exotic folk culture performed by "primitives." As in many parts of South America, this academic work was part of the Creole (European people and culture in the New World) reconstruction of national identity. "Quaint" or "primitive" traditions were to be cataloged and then eliminated in favor of a modern, European-type state and social order.[64]

Academics who work with Afro-Latino and indigenous cultures also are sensitive to the issue. Many of them believe cultural self-determination requires self-identification and pride in that identity. They see serious flaws in reducing the past to folklore, which can result in such images as the "poor but happy" black person of yesteryear. To them, this image ignores the important and difficult social problems—historically and today—that need to be addressed. Still, the important cultural space that folklore provides for capturing the past should not be discounted either for Afro-Ecuadorians living in the rural and ancestrally black areas of the country or for those in the cities.

When asked what role the dance schools play in his group's political agenda, Pablo de la Torre, president of the Confederation of Black Ecuadorian People, responded:

> Basically the [dance] groups have been around for about eighteen years. In the beginning they just performed traditional music and dance. They danced just in the past, and it was fine. But . . . in 1996, some of the groups began to understand that music and dance could be a weapon, a weapon in defense of the environment, in defense of territory, in defense of our identity. Music is very useful for winning *cimarrones*, for awakening consciousnesses, for motivating a people. [The groups] just can't give the message of the happy smiling black. Yes, we're happy, but we are hungry. Yes, we're happy, but we need medicine. Yes, we're happy, but we have to struggle and improve ourselves.[65]

According to de la Torre, in the past folkloric groups were too concerned with the "traditional" and not concerned enough with making statements about the here and now. It seems that many of the groups are moving beyond the first task, of looking back to find identity, and realizing the danger of ignoring the present while "lost in the past." They have found a use for the traditional forms as a way to convey ideas about the current situation, as a space for building militancy. De la Torre's statement points to the important role performance plays in this process.

MARGINALITY, PERFORMANCE SPACE, AND STRUGGLE

Victor Turner theorizes that, on a universal level, performed social drama is an activity that is set apart and that partially disorders the established norm.[66] It allows the social order to be examined, questioned, and reformed; it is a means of exploring other social possibilities for the future. Although the universality of this theory may be debatable, the notion of performance as set apart, of its in-betweeness, which Turner calls the "liminal," is useful.[67] The liminal "is often the scene and time for the emergence of a society's deepest values in the form of sacred dramas and objects."[68]

> The group acting though its delegates or representatives bends or throws itself back upon itself, to measure what its members, or some of its members, have done against its own standards of how they should or ought to have conducted themselves. Processes, mediated by procedures or established ways of doing things, are set in train, the aim of which is to defuse tension, assess irrational deeds against standards of reasonableness, and to reconcile conflicting parties—having convinced them, through showing them the damaging effects of their actions on group unity, that it is better to restore a state of peace than to continue in a state of hostility.[69]

The importance of performance as social critique is obvious. It can challenge interpretations of real events and offer potential solutions. De la Torre speaks about music as a tool for "awakening consciousnesses and motivating the people."[70] Performers may analyze critically the social structures within a group and on a broader level.

> But the performance characteristics of liminal phases and states often are more about the doffing of masks, the stripping of statuses, the renunciation of roles, the demolishing of structures, than their putting on and keeping on. Antistructures are performed, too. But, still within the liminal frame, new subjunctive, even ludic, structures are then generated, with their own grammars and lexicon of roles and relationships. These are imaginative creations, whether attributed to individuals or "traditions." These become the many performative genres we have discussed.[71]

In the liminal space, masks may be removed and traditional social roles questioned. In addition, the "imaginative creations" can draw on tradition, as in the Afro-Ecuadorian context: the folkloric dance groups look to a partially idealized ancestral identity for answers to modern social problems. They construct this ancestral past in the present, for the present, using current understandings of the past to provide a sense of authenticity for both the audience and the performers.

A closer look at dance performances illustrates cultural expression created on a personal and public level. It also shows how groups are simultaneously hampered and strengthened by larger social, economic, and political issues in their effort to gain cultural autonomy. The following analysis examines performance as a means to address both intracommunal issues, such as gender relations and collective responsibility, and intercommunal issues, such as political voicelessness and exploitation.

To a certain degree, the dramatized choreographies presented in San Lorenzo address the issue of voicelessness. They often refer to oral history and fables or mythological-religious beliefs of the people. I call them dramatized because either they begin with a short skit that establishes the theme of the dance or the entire dance tells a story. Two such dramatizations occurred at the 1999 cultural festival in San Lorenzo: "Fabriciano" and the "Dance of the Devil." Both were very well rehearsed, performed, and received by the crowd, which was three-quarters local, and most of the audience probably knew the stories.

The first comes from oral history, which tells of a fisherman, José Fabriciano, who became a soldier in the revolution of Carlos Concha, a liberal general at the turn of the twentieth century who tried to overthrow the government with the support of poor black farmers from Esmeraldas. After a four-year absence, Fabriciano returns back home to La Tola, and finds that his wife is marrying another man.[72] The festival performance, by a southern Colombia group called Cauco Grande, began at this point, with a brief skit of a wedding and the arrival of a battle-weary, disheveled man holding a cane in one hand and a machete in the other. Upon seeing the ceremony, Fabriciano cries: "I am Fabriciano, *carajo!* I'm a damned man. At the mouth of La Tola they have screwed me."[73] Then the music starts, and all the performers begin dancing; the women move toward the wings, and the men unsheathe their machetes to attack the belligerent Fabriciano. During the fighting, all the performers kept essentially on beat, but audience's attention focused on the amazingly fast and intricately choreographed duels, conducted with real machetes. Fabriciano eventually defeats his attackers (which at times include females), kills the groom, and forces his wife to dance with him at machete point. He then calls out: "I am Fabriciano, *carajo!* I'm a bad man. On my arrival in La Tola I've already killed a man."[74]. He and his wife dance until he moves her offstage.[75]

When asked what the dance was about, a distinguished Afro-Esmeraldeño writer said: "To be black is to wield the machete." This statement seems less strange if one visits the small communities of the province, where children and old women are seen carrying machetes as frequently as men who work in the lumber industry. Historically, the machete was a tool of slavery, used to cut sugarcane; it was also a weapon of resistance used to rebel and escape. The Esmeraldeño in the countryside use the machete as a work tool and a form of protection. For black people in general, it symbolizes both the slave and the *cimarrón,* and the performance made reference to this symbolism.

The "Dance of the Devil" (el Baile del Diablo) was performed by Estrella del Mar, a group from Limones in northern Esmerladas, and it began with music to which six couples danced onto the stage. They are apparently near a cemetery or in the forest (traditionally considered places where demons can harm people), away from their town at night, and soon the Devil is attracted by the music. He dances the same step as the others, in a more exaggerated fashion, and is unobserved until he moves to the first couple and begins dancing with the woman, much more aggressively and erotically than her original partner. When she dies of exhaustion, he quickly kills her partner before going on to the next couple and repeating the process. Finally, the last male realizes what is happening when his partner dies and tries to fight off the Devil. Knowing he cannot win, he pretends to die, and the Devil leaves the stage. The survivor gets up and performs a ritual to revive his fellow dancers.

Once all are alive again, they dance in celebration of their good fortune until the Devil passes by and is surprised to find his victims still alive. More determined this time, he dances even with more vigor, in the same pattern of seduction and death, but in each case he carries the dead offstage, presumably to hell. When he returns for the final pair (the same last couple in the previous attack), both recognize that he is there, and the man again confronts him. They fight a hard battle, both staying on beat with the music, until the Devil wins out and carries the man away. He returns for the woman, but she is ready for him. She pretends not to see him, but when he dances nearer she moves away repeatedly. Finally, the Devil approaches rapidly, the woman trips him, and he falls to the ground on all fours. She quickly jumps on his back and rides him offstage triumphantly.[76]

This choreography demonstrates visually some of the lyrics implied by the *bambuco* in the traditional *marimba* house setting. In those songs, men were sometimes identified with the Devil, someone who could seduce and have many women, and women wanted to ward off the Devil. The performance thus can be understood as a metaphor about gender roles that also draws on Afro-Ecuadorian folk myths. For example, to frighten their children into good behavior, parents and adults still tell them about the Devil and other demons who try to lure people into unsafe places.[77]

In both dances there is an element of what Turner calls "flow quality," an atmosphere the performers create with their dramatic, musical, and physical virtuosity to impress the total message of the production on the audience.[78] The props, costumes, and colors help bring the audience into the scene and better transmit the message. Perhaps even more important than the messages conveyed, these dances help preserve culture. The once vibrant Esmeraldeño oral tradition of stories and poetry is quickly dying off, at least in towns where electricity is common, and entertainment is becoming a more passive experience. Performances that recall these stories in fact maintain them, even if in a different form and context. Some may argue that the community is looking to the past for a culture that is no longer relevant, but close analysis reveals that the central themes in both of these performances are still very important today.

In terms of gender relationships, the Fabriciano story comments on matrimonial bonds and transgressions. The normal assumption in Esmeraldas would be that, after four years, a woman already should have taken on another husband and would be justified in doing so. Although Fabriciano is portrayed in a negative light for his actions, male interviewees seemed to understand and identify with his position. As a soldier for Carlos Concha, he is struggling to gain control over his economic and political destiny, which Concha promised the poor blacks who joined him.[79] According to one: "Carlos Concha is my patron / come from heaven; / if Carlos Concha dies / the black man is left alone."[80] Hopes of betterment were riding on his shoulders, and his failure may have increased feelings of powerlessness. Many disenfranchised men in macho societies compensate by trying to exert control over spouse, family, and friends. Fabriciano may be a flawed symbol of Esmeraldeño masculinity (spousal abuse is said to be fairly common in the province), and his story also reflects aspects of the region's political history over the last century and a half. Despite the ambiguity of Fabriciano's character and motivation, the dance conveys the idea that his actions are not acceptable. In this "liminal" moment, it is possible that people in the audience view themselves from the outside, which offers the possibility for reflection and potential solutions. Furthermore the story of Fabriciano is fairly well known, even among those who proclaim absolutely no interest in folkloric music.

The "Dance of the Devil" is, in part, a commentary on male infidelity. It is significant that the woman ultimately defeats the Devil. In the *marimba* houses, the contest between the male *glosador* (lead singer) and the female *respondedoras* (chorus) ends with the women getting the last word, or "defeating" the man. The underlying idea is that some women will eventually harness the restless energies of a man. By riding off in control of the very incarnation of that restless male energy, the victorious dancer symbolizes the empowerment of women.

The "Dance of the Devil" also incorporates the same social lessons taught to children by the stories from which the dance comes: there is peril when certain boundaries are transgressed. Traditionally, when people were lost in the jungle or swamps, a *bombo* drum was sounded to guide them back to safety. Towns and villages, the collective human spaces, are safe; the jungle and swampy areas, although work sites during the day, become very dangerous at night. The dancers ignore these taboos, and only a resourceful person is saved. The Devil is portrayed as fallible (the typical view in Esmeraldeño cosmology), which demonstrates an optimism for the future, unlike the story of Fabriciano. The extent to which these dramatizations may be classified as strictly folklore is problematic. In many ways they capture fundamental aspects of human existence that transcend time, such as gender roles and relations and the socialization of children, yet they address contemporary cultural identity and social issues directly related to the quality of life of Esmeraldeños.

MUSIC AND DANCE IN DEFENSE OF THE ENVIRONMENT, IDENTITY, AND ANCESTRAL TERRITORY

Around 1991, traditional dance groups began to incorporate overtly political themes, and by 1995 the practice had become sufficiently established to inspire a cultural festival "in defense of the environment, identity, and ancestral territory." The protection of forests around various towns has become a paramount theme in recent years. A number of informants in the highlands and on the coast indicated that the government had been planning the highway from Ibarra to San Lorenzo since the 1970s, but it was only completed a few years ago. This was done at the behest of and with financial support from the lumber companies that operate in the northern part of Esmeraldas. Since the days of the English Land Company in the eighteenth century there has been a thriving lumber industry in the area, on a large scale since the 1960s. [81] The construction of the highway provides greater access for trucks, and the amount of trees removed has increased considerably in the last couple of years. Many of the men in San Lorenzo and surrounding villages gain wage labor from the industry, but there are losses as well, such as fewer forest animals near the towns. Because these were cheap sources of food and materials, protein meals are slowly becoming special occasions, and crafts once made from these materials (primarily from skins) are declining.

The most serious environmental threat is destruction of the mangrove forests. For decades, shrimp exporting has been big business in southern Esmeraldas and the province farther south, Manabí. The mangroves provide excellent breeding conditions for shrimp and a host of other marine life, such as crab, conch, and shellfish. In northern Esmeraldas the seafood trade also has long been lucrative but smaller in scale, due to the labor-intensive methods of collection.

The forests have never been "owned" by anyone. Early squatters conducted a limited business by cutting wood, used locally for construction and heating needs. Problems began in the early 1980s, when large-scale shrimp farms farther south cut down huge tracts of forest to create pools, which produced many times more shrimp than traditional methods. By the early 1990s, more than 80 percent of Ecuador's mangrove forests had been destroyed.[82]

Unlike the lumber industry, shrimp farming provides little gain for the people of Esmeraldas or San Lorenzo, as only a few workers recruited from Manabí are seasonally employed. Not only do the farms destroy the mangrove habitat, but also the chemicals used to maintain shrimp monoculture kill off many of the organisms that could survive without the mangroves.[83] Furthermore, the mangroves were a natural protection against erosion and severe weather for the coastal towns, and their loss places additional financial burden on an already depressed area.[84] Ultimately, the people of Esmeraldas lose money, food, and protection.

The destruction of coastal mangroves and inland tropical forests has made the people of the province more dependent, economically and culturally, on the rest of the country. According to Pablo de la Torre, "The natural environment is fundamental for a culture. Without land nothing has any meaning, not the poetry, not the music, and not the dance. . . . The only way to persevere in time and space in this country is by means of territory, and more communal territory."[85] De la Torre, along with other community leaders and dance school directors in San Lorenzo, decided in the early 1990s that in order to preserve the music and culture, it was necessary to fight to preserve the land.

According to Fanon, "The Negro, never so much a Negro as since he has been dominated by the whites, when he decides to prove that he has a culture and to behave like a cultured person, comes to realize that history points out a well-defined path to him: he must demonstrate that a Negro culture exists."[86] For de la Torre, music can be a weapon. Music groups in San Lorenzo, Esmeraldas province, and Colombia are fighting territorial and cultural loss not only through their performances but also through political activism, including protest marches in Quito against the destruction of the mangrove forests. In the early 1990s, marchers were teargassed by the police when they neared the legislative palace, but protest leaders convinced the police that the demonstration was peaceful, and they were allowed to pass. In the plaza in front of the palace, traditional instruments accompanied songs of protest.[87]

The annual Afro-Latino conferences in San Lorenzo bring music groups from all over the province and from the Chota Valley in the highlands, as well as Colombia, Peru, and even Brazil. They all face similar issues at home, and during the conference they discuss these, create pan-American alliances, and give wider exposure to their respective situations.[88] At the 1999 conference, most used short skits to introduce their dance performance, and these usually featured a village of poor Afro-Esmeraldeños, living on the coast or deeper in the forest. The villain often was a drunken, poorly dressed, and generally unpleasant lumberjack or shrimper who was devastating the local livelihood. The townspeople did not know what to do until one person moved them to collective action, at which point they defeat the villain and save the land and their way of life. Then they danced a traditional *marimba* step.[89]

One performance, by a group from the southern Esmeraleño town of Muisne, was particularly striking. Their skit started with a poor fisherman walking home one night. He is approached by a shrimper wearing tattered clothes who offers him a bottle of liquor for his mangrove land. The man, tired and in need of the drink, accepts the deal, assuming the shrimper cannot use all the land. They exit, and women carrying baskets enter; at each corner of the stage is a person holding branches to represent trees. The women begin working at the tree roots to collect conch and crustaceans. They independently dance as the marimba sounds lightly in the background. They discuss the importance of the food to them and how much they might make from the day's harvest; then they exit. That night the shrimper enters with a bulldozer, a construction of bamboo poles, and newspaper with a person inside. The bulldozer knocks over one of the trees, and the shrimper sets up four poles with a rope tied around them to represent a shrimp pool.

The next day the women come out and find that part of the forest is gone. They are surprised to see a pool and go to examine it, but the shrimper tells them to get off his land. The women hurriedly collect their baskets and return home to inform the townspeople about what has happened. The men laugh about such craziness and continue drinking or telling stories. The next day the women return with a few men, who are surprised and frightened when they see the pools, so they return home to call another town meeting. The man who sold the land tells his story to a distraught and concerned gathering. The men lament their doom, and the women discuss what to do. The collection of food from the mangroves is traditionally their responsibility, and they feel they must resolve the problem.

The women decide to act collectively and go out at night to protect their mangroves from the shrimper, regardless of "ownership." As the swamps are unsafe places at night, the men consider this crazy, but the women convince the townspeople to go with torches and reclaim the land. Under orders from the shrimper, the bulldozer moves slowly toward the crowd, but before it hits, a torch is thrown at the bulldozer, which goes up in flames. The fire is quickly stamped out, and the town celebrates with a dance. All the musicians play vigorously, and the performance ends.[90]

This skit raises a variety of issues, such as the sale of land and proprietary rights. Traditionally in Esmeraldas, working the land established a claim to it; borders were loosely fixed, and agreements on communal land use and work were made on a relatively informal basis. The *cimarrón* heritage diminished the likelihood of signing deeds with colonial or national governments for the land. In the 1960s and 1970s, when mestizos began to migrate to Esmeraldas in larger numbers, they frequently laid claim to lands occupied by blacks because "officially" no one owned it.[91]

In 1998, indigenous and Afro-Ecuadorian political groups pushed the national legislature to ratify a new constitution that contained articles on land reform, including protection of the ancestral and communal lands of both groups. This helped reduce outright confiscations, but corporations are now buying land at a fraction of its worth from the farmers and fishermen, who are lured by what seems large amounts to the poor and uneducated. Some community members tell of people who exchanged their lands for radios and other technological novelties, as well as corporate representatives who provided alcohol at meetings in order to inebriate black farmers and "ease" the transactions.[92]

In the skit described earlier, both the trickery of the shrimper and the short-sightedness of the fisherman are portrayed. The performance also touches upon the traditional importance of *concha* to poor people, as a source of food and income, as well as a more recent development: the active participation and leadership of women in social protest and mobilization against mangrove destruction. A female school-teacher who also ran a fishing cooperative was involved in the early organization of the environmental movement, and she pointed out that a number of local women's groups played an essential role.[93] Moreover, although there are men who direct dance groups, a significant number of group directors and festival organizers are women. At least seven or eight of the nearly thirty groups that performed at the 1999 festival were groups of women singing *arrullos* in defense of the environment, especially the mangroves. Thus, in the skit, the representation of women as leading the mangrove defense reflects their empowerment in the recent history of this movement. Deforestation affects the entire community, but especially women, and this explains their vigorous activism.

Mangrove protection has been a more unifying cause in San Lorenzo than deforestation by the lumber industry, a sector that employs a considerable number of men in the area. In contrast, the shrimp industry accounts for very few jobs, and it threatens an important food source as well as an income source for women. Traditionally, there were no particular taboos against the removal of trees, and there was no significant conception of the conservation of some "natural order."[94] Yet, consciously or not, the land was not overused. The speed and volume of mangrove destruction has forced the people of Esmeraldas to realize the consequences of excessive land exploitation, and only recently in the San Lorenzo area is the same realization occurring regarding jungle deforestation due to highway construction. The "overnight" appearance of shrimping pools in the skit refers to the sudden shock of these rapid changes.

The skit does far more than simply refer to historical events and processes; it exemplifies the importance of the liminal as a space for disrupting the social order in order to solve real-world problems. First, the organization of protest is significant because it reinforces the importance of community responsibility and collective action. Second, the symbolism of going out at night into the dangerous swamp implies that every means possible must be used to prevent exploitation by outsiders. Even the act of torching the bulldozer, while not necessarily advocating violent insurrection, suggests that communities may have to take drastic measures to gain more control over their land and the direction of their lives.

According to Inés Morales, a local schoolteacher and organizer of the conference, the dance groups "use the ancestral forms as a historical base to say something about the reality of today which we are living in."[95] They are appropriating the space of folkloric dance and infusing messages of political resistance and change. They not only challenge the daily social norm but also engage and create the past to solve problems in the present. Morales explained: "Through the music we are influencing the child who is watching, and the adult who is listening. Already within the child there is growing a perspective, an attention to this issue of the environment."[96] Through the spectacle, colors, and skills of the dancers, organizers are using the liminal space to push their community to awareness and action. Simultaneously, the direct and obvious statements made through music, drama, and motion control the discourse, so that outsiders cannot easily misinterpret the message that these dance groups are expressing.

CONCLUSION

Afro-Ecuadorians as a whole, and the Sanlorenzeños in particular, are at a crossroads. For traditionally black areas, the rate of change has grown tremendously over the last twenty years and shows no sign of slowing. In August 1999 U.S. Marines arrived in San Lorenzo to set up operations to patrol Colombian drug trafficking. As of the end of that year, they were building a highway to Colombia. What was once an isolated backwater is becoming an international intersection.

One Afro-Ecuadorian intellectual, Dr. Angel Quiñonez, explains the dilemma. If the black people of Esmeraldas try to isolate themselves in the forests and hills of the province, they will be unprepared to protect themselves against the outside interests that come to exploit the natural resource of the area. If they continue to integrate into the broader national culture without pride in what is theirs, they will lose themselves in the margins and will be unable to defend any autonomy they may have. Therefore, they must learn from an early age to value their heritage and ancestry because that is what determines who they are. Only with self-pride can they successfully confront the changes occurring locally and in the country at large as well as determine their own path.

Afro-Ecuadorians are in a struggle for cultural survival as a distinct group, or what may be called an ethnic bloc, "a conscious reference group for those who share recurrent processes of self-identification."[97]The ethnic bloc seeks self-determination and representation for the collectivity on a political level. Unlike a colonized nation that seeks to regain power and control of state and territory, the ethnic bloc lies within a particular national border and struggles to redefine its position under a racialized nationalist hegemony.[98]

Guillermo Ayoví, an internationally known *marimba* musician who helped found some of the earliest dance schools, sums up the importance of the music and the folkloric movement: "First of all, the *marimba*, and everything we do in regard to folklore, is our identity. This is because we left the chains of slavery through [our music and culture]. Now, as we are free, what we [the folkloric groups] have had to do is respect that heritage, because it was the way that we gained this condition. Through the culture, and the *marimba*, a purely black music, which is part of that culture. It was the music that gave us the key. That's what it is."[99] Music, as a representation of culture, provided the people with a connection, an inspiration, and a motivation to free themselves, to establish communities where they could express and renew their own culture. It gave them a place where they could store remnants of their traditional ideas and forge new ones.

The traditional Afro-Esmeraldeño music is an integral part of Afro-Ecuadorian culture and identity. Because of the rapid changes sweeping their society, black Ecuadorians face much uncertainty but also great possibility. Those involved with the folk dance movement are following the path of their ancestors and using the music as a way both to maintain themselves and to explore new directions. Whether the people will challenge the social order or lose more of their autonomy is the important question. In Afro-Ecuador, music is more than entertainment; it is the historical archive, the sacred text, and the call to protest. It is their sorrow bound together with their joy; it contains who they are as a people, where they came from, and where they are going. In short, it is central to their identity. In order for Afro-Ecuadorians to persevere, so too, in some form or another, must the music.

NOTES

This chapter is based on research for an undergraduate honor's thesis in anthropology. Fieldwork was conducted in Ecuador between February and August of 1999, and the original thesis was written during winter 2000.

1. Lilyan Benítez and Alicia Garcés, *Culturas ecuatorianas ayer y hoy* (Cayambe: Abya-Yala, 1998).
2. Norman E.Whitten Jr. and Arlene Torres, *Blackness in Latin America and the Caribbean: Social Dynamics and Cultural Transformations* (Bloomington: Indiana University Press, 1998), 1:8.
3. Enrique Ayala Mora, *Resumen de historia del Ecuador,* 2d ed. (Quito: Corporación Editora Nacional, 1993), 13.
4. Benítez and Garcés, *Culturas Ecuatorianas Ayer y Hoy,* 135.
5. Argentina Chiriboga, "El endoracimo en el Ecuador," in *El negro en la historia del Ecuador: Esclavitud en las regiones Andina y Amazónica,* ed. Ráfeal Savoia (Quito: Centro Cultural Afro Ecuatoriana, 1999), 129.
6. P. Rafael Savoia, ed., *El negro en la historia de Ecuador y del sur de Colombia* (Quito: Centro Cultural Afroecutoriana, 1988), 206.
7. Henry Medina Vallejo, *Comunidad negra y cambio cultural* (Quito: Centro Cultural Afroecuatoriano, 1996), 38–39.
8. Manuel Lucena Salmoral, *Sangre sobre piel negra: La esclavitud quiteña en el contexto del reformismo borbónico* (Quito: Abya Yala, 1994).
9. Daniel Serrano Quiroz, "El problema de la gente de color en Esmeraldas," manuscript, 1975, 11, cited in Carlos Alberto Coba, *Literatura popular afroecuatoriana* (Otavalo: Instituto Otavaleño de Antropología, 1980), 29.
10. P. Claudio Zendrón, *Cultura negra y espiritualidad: El caso de Esmeraldas, Ecuador* (Quito: Centro Cultural Afro Ecuatoriana, 1998), 32.
11. Quiñónez lecture, 2 June 1999.
12. Julio Estupiñán Tello, *El negro en Esmeraldas: Apuntos para su estudio,* 2d ed. (Santo Domingo de los Colorados: El Pionero Impreso, 1972), 59.
13. Marcelo Naranjo V, *La cultura popular en el Ecuador.* Volume 4: *Esmeraldas* (Quito: CIDAP, 1984), 36.
14. Savoia, *El negro en la historia de Ecuador,* 30.
15. Estupiñán, *El negro en Esmeraldas,* 45–46.
16. Savoia, *El negro en la historia de Ecuador,* 35.
17. Over the last half of the sixteenth century, twenty-six Spanish expeditions were sent to pacify Esmeraldas and were defeated by "the courage and strategy of the negros in defense of their liberty." Luis Moscoso Vega et al., eds. *Cultural, Educational, Tourist, Industrial, Commercial, Agricultural and Livestock Information Handbook of the Republic of Ecuador,* vol. 2 (Cuenca: Cientifica Latina Editores, 1980), 596.

18. Naranjo, *Esmeraldas,* 37–40.

19. Zendrón, *Cultura negra y espiritualidad,* 37; Naranjo *Esmeraldas,* 31.

20. The first act toward Afro-Ecuadorian emancipation was in 1821 when Simón Bolívar offered liberty to all slaves who fought for independence from Spain. In 1851 José María Urvina declared manumission for the children of all black slaves. And finally Eloy Alfaro freed all those still enslaved after he took power in 1895. Quiñónez lecture, 7 June 1999; Ayala, *Resumen de historia del Ecuador,* 138–39.

21. Quiñónez lecture, 7 June 1999.

22. The Chota Valley is a separate and unique culture with its own traditional music, *la bomba.* Although it is taught in dance schools in the valley, it seems that the music is still a commonly popular form. It is important and deserves further study.

23. Field notes.

24. Quiñónez lecture, 12 April 1999.

25. Field notes.

26. Norman E. Whitten Jr., *Class, Kinship and Power in an Ecuadorian Town: The Negroes of San Lorenzo* (Stanford, Calif.: Stanford University Press, 1965), 25.

27. Ibid., 25.

28. Apparently the problem was British construction of fences and other relatively minor disruptions of the social norm. See Whitten, *Class, Kinship and Power,* for further details.

29. Ibid., 32.

30. Ibid.; Norman E. Whitten Jr., *Black Frontiersmen: Afro-Hispanic Culture of Colombia and Ecuador* (Prospect Heights, Ill.: Waveland Press, 1974).

31. During my fieldwork two bus companies ran four or five times a day between Esmeraldas and San Lorenzo. These were entirely passenger trips.

32. Aquí, antes nosotros veníamos a lavar en este rió, ¿no? Aquí no más. Y uno a veces, dejaba la ropa jabonada allí para el otro dia allí. Y se venía el día síguiente para terminar. Y nadie llevaba ni una pieza de las que estaban allí. Las Personas aquí cuidaban estos puestos, y no habían peligro, no había problema, no había nada.

Y ahora, ¿qué? Hay que encererrarse totalmente. Hay peligro, y esto no hace mucho tiempo. . . . Los robos han empezado, tal vez, unos 15 años, y con fuerza, con intensidad estos últimos dos, tres años. Interview, 26 June 1999, San Lorenzo.

33. I met with most informants through contacts made in Quito or San Lorenzo. The network of Afro-Ecuadorians involved in social, political, or cultural awareness is comparatively small, and nearly everyone has at least a passing acquaintance.

34. Interview, 27 June 1999, San Lorenzo.

35. The death is celebrated because a young child or virgin adolescent has not had the opportunity to sin and therefore will go immediately to heaven. In the case of an adult, whose destination is uncertain, hymns have a more solemn purpose. This belief apparently came by way of the Spanish from north African moors (see Whitten, *Black Frontiersmen,* 152, and Vicente Blasco Ibáñez, *La barraca* (Madrid: Ediciones Cátedra, [1898] 1998), 176–85.

36. Interview, 27 June 1999, San Lorenzo.

37. Field notes.

38. Bantu cultural beliefs from the Congo and Angola are evident among Afro-Esmeraldeños, but these are not as strong as Yoruba traditions in Cuba, or Vodou, with its Dahomean connection, in Haiti (Whitten, *Black Frontiersmen;* Zendrón, *Cultura negra y espiritualidad,* 118.

39. Zendrón, *Cultura negra y espiritualidad,* 109, 264.

40. Whitten, *Black Frontiersmen,* 115.

41. Ibid., 201–2.

42. Ibid., 124.

43. Ibid., 183–201.

44. Field notes.

45. The *anderelle* has local indigenous roots in the name and rhythm, as well as Spanish *pasadoble* influence in the steps. *Patacoré* is a song and dance with a Colombian origin that was seen as a method to remove illnesses brought on by bad spirits. *Torbellino* (translation: whirling Dervish. is named for its many spins, and the lyrics describe the problems of unruly children (Escobar Q. 1998, 70. *Agua larga* (literal translation: large water. comes from a local indigenous rhythm and is one of the older styles still played (interview with Guillermo Ayoví, 1 July 1999). *Banbyci* was the most popular dance when *marimba* was still the popular dance in the San Lorenzo in the sixties. Its steps mimic a flirtatious relationship between man and women, and the lyrics concern all matters of daily life topics (Whitten, *Black Frontiersmen*, 114–15). Today *bambuco* is the most common dance performed by folkloric dance groups.

46. Whitten, *Class, Kinship and Power*, 115.

47. Field notes.

48. Among the middle class and the more racially mixed youth in San Lorenzo, there is a growing appreciation for European dance music associated with salsa, such as techno and trance. Young people still dance to salsa, but there is growing racialization of dance halls where predominantly salsa is played. Such establishments are considered almost exclusively for poorer, less urbanized, and phenotypically African people, and therefore more "dangerous." Field notes.

49. Field notes.

50. Marcelo Naranjo, *Esmeraldas*, 222.

51. Field notes.

52. Angel G. Quintero Rivera, *¡Salsa, sabor y control!: Sociologia de la musica "tropical"* (Mexico: Siglo XXI Editores, 1998).

53. John Storm Roberts, *Black Music of Two Worlds* (New York: Praeger, 1972), 83.

54. Field notes.

55. Field notes.

56. Mireya Ramírez Castrillón, *Folklore esmeraldeño* (Quito: Banco Central Ecuatoriana, 1984), 342–49.

57. Interview, 28 June 1999, San Lorenzo.

58. In Afro-Esmeraldeño mythology, Berejú is a being akin to the devil (with roots in indigenous beliefs. who plays marimba to lure dancers away from towns. One must play a countermelody on marimba to escape him (Naranjo, *Esmeraldas*, 322).

59. Field notes.

60. Chiriboga "El endoracimo en el Ecuador," 92.

61. The tenth of August is a national holiday, marking the date in 1809 when the "first cries for independence" were heard in Ecuador. It is the main local event in San Lorenzo. Field notes.

62. Interview with Sonia Viveros, 26 July 1999.

63. Interview, 26 July 1999.

64. See Domingo Faustino Sarmiento, *Facundo: Civilización o barbarie*, in *Literatura hispanoamericana: Una antología*, ed. David William Foster (New York: Garland Publishing, [1851] 1994) for an example of these ideas in Argentina. Sarmiento called for the destruction of both indigenous and gaucho culture in order to build a cultured European state. He also thought the customs of these groups' customs should be cataloged so that they could become "icons" for the new nation. Interview with Marta Escobar, 18 June 1999, Quito.

65. Interview, 10 August 1999, San Lorenzo.

66. Victor Turner, *The Anthropology of Performance* (New York: Performing Arts Journal Publications, 1986).

67. Marvin Carlson, *Performance: A Critical Introduction* (New York: Routledge, 1996), 20–21.

68. Turner, *Anthropology of Performance*, 102.
69. Ibid., 104.
70. Interview, 10 August 1999, San Lorenzo.
71. Turner, *Anthropology of Performance*, 107.
72. La Tola is a small town on the coast between San Lorenzo and Esmeraldas (see figure 2).
73. *Carajo* is a common Esmeraldeño expletive that refers to an old Spanish prison island. It carries force and meaning somewhere between "hell" and "Goddamn" but has a much wider and more varied use. Ramírez, *Folklore esmeraldeño*, 41.
74. Ibid., 42.
75. Field notes.
76. Field notes.
77. Two other local mythological figures, la Tunda and el Duende, also seduce or pretend to be a relative in order to lure an adult or child into the forest and in some cases to hell (Naranjo, *La cultura popular*, 231).
78. Turner, *Anthropology of Performance*, 107.
79. Most historians view General Concha as a fairly stereotypical populist leader, interested in gaining power and willing to use the masses for his own purposes. Even if he had won, some argue, the Esmeraldeños probably would have lost. Nevertheless, the idea that has survived among Afro-Esmeraldeños is that the rebellion was a real chance at true autonomy. See Zendrón, *Cultura negra y espiritualidad,* or Nelson Estupiñán Bass, *Cuando los guayacanes florecíar* (Quito: Libresa, 1954) for further information.
80. Ramírez, *Folklore esmeraldeño*, 41.
81. Whitten, *Class, Kinship and Power,* 26.
82. Rob Rachowiecki, *Ecuador and the Galapagos Islands: A Lonely Planet Travel Survival Kit* (Hawthorn, Australia: Lonely Planet Publications, 1997), 361.
83. Field notes.
84. Rachowiecki, *Ecuador and the Galapagos Islands,* 361.
85. Interview, 10 August 1999, San Lorenzo.
86. Frantz Fanon, *The Wretched of the Earth* (New York: Grove Press, 1963), 212.
87. Field notes.
88. Field notes.
89. Field notes.
90. Field notes.
91. Naranjo, *Esmeraldas,* 65–68.
92. Field notes.
93. Field notes.
94. Whitten, *Class, Kinship and Power;* Whitten, *Black Frontiersmen.*
95. Interview, 29 June 1999, San Lorenzo.
96. Interview, 29 May 1999, San Lorenzo.
97. Whitten and Torres, *Blackness in Latin America and the Caribbean,* 1:8, following Geertz 1973
98. Whitten and Torres, *Blackness in Latin America and the Caribbean,* 1:8.
99. Interview, 1 July 1999, Bourbon.

Transnational Politics: A Note on Black Americans and the Paris Peace Conference of 1919

Ruth Simms Hamilton

IN NOVEMBER 1918 AN ARMISTICE WAS NEGOTIATED TO END WORLD WAR I, followed by the Paris Peace Conference at Versailles in January 1919. Leading black American organizations and cultural workers turned their attention to this important event, which along with the war heightened their transnational consciousness. Networks and relationships that transcended nation-state or colonial boundaries already existed, built around shared interests and goals. Through newspaper and radio reports and knowledge brought home by travelers, those in military, diplomatic, and missionary service, or participants in pan-African conferences, black Americans were made aware of the diaspora.[1] World War I and the Treaty of Versailles represented opportunities to learn more.

To paraphrase C. Wright Mills, everyone talks about observations and interpretations to others, but the terms by which one reports are likely to be the phrases and images of other people that are taken as one's own. For most of what is called "solid fact," "sound interpretation," or "suitable presentations," we are dependent on the cultural apparatus, or observation posts, centers of interpretation, and presentation depots. The black cultural apparatus is composed of all the organizations and milieus in which artistic, educational-intellectual, political, religious, and scientific work goes on, as well as the means by which these works are made available to "circles, publics, and masses."[2] In terms of diaspora experiences immediately following World War I, especially in the United States, this note will briefly explore three areas. The first is the major knowledge transmitted to the various publics and masses. The second is African diaspora cultural workers or key actors who participated in defining and interpreting issues and setting agendas. Cultural workers may include artists, educators, intellectuals, journalists, political activists, religious workers, scientists, or others who define reality and establish canons of taste and beauty.[3] The third is some of the institutions and organizations involved in producing and distributing information regarding world peace. Because quantitative measures of transnational consciousness are lacking, attention is directed toward the nature of activism, the agency of diaspora cultural workers, and the cultural apparatus used to reach various publics.

In January 1918, President Woodrow Wilson developed a fourteen-point plan for "reconstructing the world" to set the agenda for the anticipated Peace Conference, which began at Versailles in early January 1919 and lasted five months.[4] Two of the points were of particular concern to black Americans: (1) free, open-minded, and absolutely impartial adjustment of all colonial claims, and (2) formation of an association of nations (League of Nations) to help keep world peace, guided by specific covenants to afford mutual guarantees of political independence and territorial integrity to both great and small states. As discussed in "Reassessing Diaspora Connections and Consciousness: Global Africa and World War I,"[5] German colonies in western and southern Africa were battle sites in World War I, and one decision at the conference regarded the disposition of those territories. A related issue was the extent to which African people would be active participants at the world forum for peace. Abyssinia [Ethiopia], Liberia, and Haiti were independent nations, but would they have a voice in the discussions? Haiti was occupied by the United States, and Liberia was its unofficial colony. Furthermore, would the Africans under German colonization have representation, or who would speak on their behalf? These issues were widely discussed before and during the Peace Conference and at the Pan-African Congress held in Paris in February 1919.

RIGHT OF AFRICANS TO SELF-DETERMINATION

Although various positions were taken, depending on political-cultural orientation, three major themes emerged around which most black cultural workers and organizations coalesced.[6] First, there was strong agreement that Africa must be ruled by Africans. Second, German colonies should not be returned to Germany. Third, Belgium should not be allowed to retain its African holdings. Most black newspapers and periodicals, including the *Star of Zion,* the *Afro-American* (Baltimore), and the *Savannah Tribune* (Georgia) were strong advocates of these positions. For example,

Sol C. Johnson, editor of the *Tribune*, argued throughout the peace settlement that Africa for the Africans was consistent with the history of other world people, and the principle of self-determination should be no different for Africans.[7] Johnson's position was echoed by Elias Camp Morris, organizer and first president of the National Baptist Convention, and by the Negro Ministerial Council of Dallas, Texas.

Exactly what should happen to the German colonies was a matter of debate. Emmett Jay Scott, the Negro special assistant to the secretary of war, was clear that the colonies should not be returned to Germany or any other nation; he called for an international commission (including one black American) to govern the colonies. J. W. E. Bowen, vice president of Gammon Theological Seminary in Atlanta, suggested organizing the German West African colony of Togo into a "black international republic" under protection of the United States, Great Britain, and France: "This republic could be protected, fostered, and built up for blacks in Africa and America." W. Calvin Chase of the *Washington Bee* advised returning German colonies to Africans or transferring them "to the United States, to be held in trust for black people." Instead of Africa for the Africans, he proposed "Africa in the future for Africans."[8]

A much broader plan was advanced by the leading scholar of the period, W. E. B. DuBois. His "Memorandum on the Future of Africa" called for an internationalized portion of the continent—more than 2.5 million square miles and more than 20 million people—comprised of Portuguese Africa, the Belgian Congo, and the former German colonies. DuBois maintained that

> while the principles of self-determination cannot be applied to uncivilized peoples, yet the educated blacks should have some voice in the disposition of the German colonies. In settling what is to be done with the German colonies the Peace Conference might consider the wishes of the intelligent Negroes in the colonies themselves, the Negroes of the United States, and South Africa, and the West Indies, the Negro governments of Abyssinia [Ethiopia], Liberia, and Haiti, the educated Negroes in French West Africa and Equatorial Africa and in British Uganda, Nigeria, Basutoland, Swaziland, Sierra Leone, Gold Coast, Gambia, and Bechuanaland, and in the Union of South Africa.
>
> This Africa for the Africans could be under the guidance of international organization. The governing international commission should represent not simply governments, but modern culture, science, commerce, social reform, and religious philanthropy. It must represent not simply the white world, but the civilized Negro world.
>
> We can, if we will, inaugurate on the dark continent a last great crusade for humanity. With Africa redeemed, Asia would be safe and Europe indeed triumphant.[9]

The memorandum was sent to the U.S. secretary of state for consideration as an option at the Peace Conference; it was endorsed by the NAACP and became a framework for the 1919 Pan- African Congress in Paris and its resulting resolutions. Needless to say, the Wilson administration noted its receipt and ignored it.[10]

Another important voice was that of Marcus Garvey, the founder and head of one of the largest mass movements of the period, the Universal Negro Improvement Association (UNIA), also known as the Universal Negro Improvement and Conservation Association and African Communities (Imperial) League.[11] Speaking to five thousand persons at the Palace Casino in New York, Garvey and other participants celebrated the end of the war, called on the Allies to return German colonies to African rule, and passed a resolution that was forwarded to the United States, Great Britain, France, and Italy.[12] Its substance was very similar to the memorandum of DuBois:

> self-determination for all colonies in which African peoples predominated; equal rights with Europeans for Africans in education, work, and travel; the end of discrimination and segregation of African people where they lived side by side with other races; the restoration of lands seized from Africans in South Africa; the eviction from Africa of all those who interfered with or violated African customs; equal representation of blacks in any scheme of world government; and most important, the turning over of "captured German colonies in Africa . . . to the natives with educated Western and Eastern Negroes as their leaders."[13]

A. Philip Randolph, editor of the *Messenger* (along with Chandler Owen), wrote a manifesto that echoed positions complementary to those of DuBois and Garvey. Randolph called for more-enlightened world politics to provide independence and autonomy for Africa; an international agreement to abolish worldwide racial discrimination economically, politically, and socially; and a supernational commission composed of the world's "educated classes of Negroes" to develop and govern the former German colonies. This supernational entity would develop an educational system "to teach 'chemistry, physics, biology, horticulture, geology, mining, engineering and political science' and supervise the construction of transportation systems and communication networks."[14]

Many of those associated with the diaspora cultural apparatus had earlier taken positions that reinforced the colonial ideology to civilize, Christianize, and Westernize Africans. Even DuBois was of the opinion that there was a hierarchy of colonialists, with the French at the top of the system. Did not the French share the commonality of oppression of black people with other European nations?[15] Such a view is not unlike the ludicrous argument that the slavery of the Spanish or Portuguese was more humane than that of the British, French, or Americans. In any case, with the end of the war and more time to witness the plunder and brutality of colonial powers, black cultural workers came to reevaluate and modify their positions. There was wide agreement that Germany should be denied continued ownership of its possessions in Africa. Some type of international and multiracial body should oversee the gradual return of Africa to Africans. An important role remained for the talented, educated, "civilized," and "Westernized" continental Africans and diaspora cultural workers. Although this view was patronizing and paternalistic, it represented a shift in the diaspora relationship to Africa. Envisioned was a transnational role for black cultural workers, who should act upon and speak to the issues of human rights and self-determination for African peoples worldwide.

The Transnationalization of Experiences

Many blacks in journalism, education, government service, and political and civil rights organizations clearly saw the relationship between global and local events and the sense of common destiny of African people.[16] For them, the Peace Conference was an opportunity to put the black condition in the United States on a world agenda, along with the plight of Africans and other peoples of the diaspora. For example, Lewis Garnett Jordan, a Baptist minister from Mississippi, in an address to his colleagues in Louisville, Kentucky, argued that since the war affected Africans it meant reverberations for Africans all over the world. The editor of *New York Age*, Fred R. Moore, wrote that the Peace Conference concerned all black people, whether in Africa or worldwide, and should be a forum to express their grievances.[17]

One of the most articulate arguments came from James Weldon Johnson, an attorney, field secretary of the NAACP, U.S. consul to Venezuela (1906–1909), and author of the lyrics to the Negro national anthem, "Lift Every Voice and Sing." At a mass meeting of the NAACP in New York on 6 January 1919, Johnson's presentation was entitled "Africa at the Peace Table and the Descendants of Africans in Our American Democracy." He linked the interests of the NAACP in Africa to the "liberation of the Negroes and the elevation of the Negro in the public mind": "This question of the future of Africa had focused international attention on the just claims of blacks all over the world."[18] DuBois reinforced this position by putting forth the idea of "the centralization of the race effort and the recognition of a racial fount. To help bear the burden of Africa does not mean any lessening of effort in our own [the black American] problem at home. . . . Amelioration of the lot of Africa tends to ameliorate the condition of colored peoples throughout the world." He proclaimed: "The African movement means to us what the Zionist movement means to the Jews."[19]

African and Diaspora Representation at the Peace Conference

John Bruce, a New York journalist, wrote in 1918 that when "all the warring nations assemble around the council table, there will probably be no black or colored man there, and no white man there will be quite as interested in the questions in which the vital interests of the black and colored races are involved as would have been a black or colored man, had one been there."[20] African and diaspora peoples were clearly interested in attending the Paris Peace Conference. The African Native National Congress (ANNC) sent a deputation to England in 1919 to make known its need to be heard at Versailles. The group based its right to be present on the fact that more than six hundred men of the South African Native Labor Contingent (SANLC) died in the sinking of the SS *Mendi,* along with many others, casualties of the war. Furthermore, King George V, in a 1917 visit, commended the men of the SANLC for being part of his great armies that were fighting for the liberty of all his subjects throughout his empire, regardless of race or creed. Lord Buxton, governor general of the Union of South Africa, had promised that their loyalty would not be forgotten. South African blacks, in pursuit of their liberation from oppressive white domination, viewed the Peace Conference as a transnational forum to publicize their struggle for self-determination and citizenship. Predictably, they were informed by the British Colonial Office that the government could not interfere in the internal affairs of the Union of South Africa.[21]

Black Americans widely discussed and acted upon their interest in participating in the Peace Conference. For instance, the UNIA elected Ida Wells-Barnett, A. Philip Randolph, and Eliezer Cadat, a Haitian and UNIA commissioner, as delegates to the conference. DuBois sent a letter to President Wilson proposing the inclusion of black Americans in the U.S. delegation. He argued: "The International Peace Congress that is to decide whether or not peoples shall have the right to dispose of themselves will find in its midst delegates from a nation which champions the principle of the 'consent of the governed' and 'government by representation.' That nation is our own, and includes in itself more than twelve million souls whose consent to be governed is never asked. They have no members in the legislature of states where they are in the majority, and not a single representative in the national Congress."[22] Although Wilson ignored DuBois, other organizations selected delegates, including the National

Equal Rights League (NERL), the NAACP, the National Medical Association (NMA), and the Hamitic League. The latter, composed primarily of British West Indians and black Americans, selected Arthur Schomburg, a Puerto Rican bibliognost, and John Bruce. The NMA took the position that "our unselfish devotion at home and our heroism and supreme sacrifice on the battle fields of Europe merit representation in the make-up of the Peace Conference."[23]

Acting on a suggestion of Emmett Jay Scott (special assistant to the secretary of war), William Monroe Trotter, editor of the Boston *Guardian,* organized the National Race Congress for World Democracy. In December 1918, approximately two hundred fifty delegates representing organizations from across the United States met in Washington, D.C., at the Metropolitan African Methodist Episcopal (AME) Church. One outcome was the nomination of nine people to attend the Paris meeting. Two were women: Ida Wells-Barnett, former editor of the *Chicago Conservator* and a leading antilynching activist, and Madam C. J. Walker, a wealthy entrepreneur and philanthropist. Madam Walker, seeking to unite various groups interested in the Paris Conference, held a meeting at her New York mansion on 2 January 1919. Among those attending were the Reverend A. Clayton Powell Sr. of the Abyssinian Baptist Church of New York; the Reverend Frederick Cullen, a member of the Silent Protest Parade delegation to the White House; A. Philip Randolph; and Marcus Garvey. They formed the International League of Darker Peoples (ILDP) and adopted the previously mentioned manifesto written by Randolph.[24]

Among all these delegates, none was granted a passport. They were branded "Negro subversives" by U.S. military intelligence and the State Department. The attorney general reported to Congress that a concerted movement among a "certain class of Negro leaders" was creating radical opposition to the government and the "established rule of law." Moreover, President Wilson, a Democrat, did not even include Republicans among his official delegation, and he certainly did not want to be embarrassed by black Americans who were likely to raise controversial issues, especially about racial oppression, which would put him and the United States on the defensive: "Wilson and Lansing [secretary of state] . . . wished to keep . . . African Americans on the western shore of the Atlantic throughout the negotiations."[25] DuBois, already in possession of a passport and the editor of *Crisis: A Record of the Darker Races,* was able to secure passage on a ship carrying representatives of the U.S. press. Monroe Trotter was denied a passport but stowed away on a freighter headed to Paris. Elizier Cadat of UNIA arrived in Paris under a Haitian passport.

Efforts to put the agenda of Africa and its diaspora before the world were not abandoned. For example, when members of the Japanese peace delegation arrived in New York, in the "spirit of race internationalism" the ILDP sent a floral arrangement "as a token of friendship and brotherhood." On 7 January 1919, Madam Walker, on behalf of the ILDP, hosted a meeting at the Waldorf-Astoria Hotel for "a small League delegation and S. Kuriowa, a Japanese envoy and publisher of *Yorudo Choho,* a Tokyo newspaper." The purpose of the meeting was to persuade the Japanese, who would be seated at the Peace Conference, to put the race question on the table. Kuriowa assured them that Japan would support the principle of racial equality for the majority of the world's population.[26]

The Japanese government did instruct its delegates to push for a provision that recognized racial equality and eliminated discrimination in international affairs. In an effort to reach consensus, the Japanese presented different versions of a racial equality clause to be included in the covenant of the League of Nations. One draft even avoided using the word "race," but the change made little difference to the outcome.

As public discussion of the proposed racial equality amendment intensified, the Japanese delegates tested a revised amendment that avoided the word "race" entirely and called only for the "equality of nations and just treatment of their nationals." This, too, failed to meet with approval. . . . Despairing of ever winning a private endorsement from the Anglo-American members, the Japanese presented the amendment in the League Commission. . . . During the discussion [U.S. presidential advisor Colonel Edward] House passed Wilson a note warning that if the Japanese amendment passed, "it would raise the race issue throughout the world." The President [Wilson] made a last effort to head off a vote by assuring the members that the principle of equality was implicit in the structure of the league. . . . The measure received eleven out of seventeen votes. China sided with Japan. Nevertheless, Wilson as chairman of the commission, ruled the measure defeated on the dubious grounds that it did not have unanimous support.[27]

Eighty-two years later, the United Nations, under the leadership of Secretary General Kofi Annan, a Ghanaian, sponsored the World Conference against Racism, Xenophobia, and Related Intolerance in Durban, South Africa, 31 August–7 September 2001.[28] African delegates representing nation-states were active participants and demanded acknowledgment that colonialism had left a legacy of racism not unrelated to landlessness and other problems confronting the continent presently. This time, Africa and its diaspora had a voice. The legacies of slavery and colonialism were discussed, although they were largely overshadowed by the turmoil in the Middle East, the condemnation of Zionism as racism, and objections to Palestinian treatment by Israel. In the end, official delegates completed a document that, among other things, condemned the "abhorrent barbarism of slavery" and declared that "states have a moral obligation to halt and reverse the lasting consequences of slavery, apartheid and genocide."[29]

The agenda of the 1919 Peace Conference was quite encompassing: the settlement of war claims and, more profoundly, the future distribution of world political and economic power, the outcome of which largely prevails in 2001. Moreover, it established covenants to govern the League of Nations, the predecessor of the United Nations. Despite differences in agenda and historical circumstances, there are a few similarities in the actions taken by the United States in 1919 and at the 2001 UN conference on racism. The Bush administration decided not to send Secretary of State Colin Powell, a black American, to the conference; blocked discussion of reparations for the descendants of slaves; and sent a low-level delegation that one journalist characterized as practicing "minimalism," that is, watching and listening but not taking an active part in the proceedings.[30] This minimalist delegation walked out on the third day of the conference. In 1919 Woodrow Wilson rebuffed all proposals to include black Americans as official delegates or as observers, refused to meet with them before or after the conference, and ignored their input regarding the future of Africa and racism.

The U.S. government under Wilson, a twentieth-century Democrat, and Bush, a twenty-first-century Republican, has not differed much in its approach to addressing racism and discrimination resolutions. Wilson simply ruled lack of consensus and quashed the racial equality resolution put forward by Japan. The Treaty of Versailles made no reference to racism, and the German territories in Africa were "recolonized" under a mandate system.[31] Bush simply had the delegation walk out rather than sign an international declaration to condemn slavery and international racial discrimination. As in 1919, in 2001 the U.S. government displayed its arrogance and did not address the concerns of black Americans. Racial inequality is deeply ingrained in the American mind and behavior, but it is also a world phenomenon that spans historical and social space at local, national, and transnational levels. The diaspora communities of consciousness, nonetheless, continue their protracted contestations with growing networks of action at all levels.

THE PAN-AFRICAN CONGRESS IN FEBRUARY 1919

Before leaving the United States for Paris, DuBois communicated with a network of national and international colleagues that he would convene a pan-African congress in Paris. There were no concrete plans, but DuBois had laid out many of the issues in his "Memorandum on the Future of Africa," in particular African self-determination and the situation of black people worldwide. According to Jacobs, "the meeting had no impact on the peace conference, and its significance lies only in the fact that it helped solidify an international consciousness among black people throughout the world."[32] But that was no small accomplishment.

For the first time since the Berlin Conference on West Africa and the "scramble" unleashed by it, the principles of self-determination and the fundamental rights and liberties to which subject African peoples were entitled had been articulated by accomplished men and women who purported to speak for DuBois's darker millions. While their immediate and practical consequences would be negligible, a powerful idea to bind up the wounds of the world had been launched in Paris.[33]

Upon arrival in France, DuBois had obstacles to overcome, specifically the opposition of President Wilson and Prime Minister Lloyd George of Great Britain to the congress and the assurance of Georges Clemenceau, prime minister of France, that such a meeting would not take place. Wilson and his delegation were "fearful that the Pan-African Congress would be used as a forum to embarrass the United States" and that DuBois "would bring up the subject of the injustices and discrimination that African-Americans experienced in the United States and would point particularly to the brutality of lynching."[34] As noted above, the U.S. State Department denied passports to black Americans planning to attend, and Great Britain instructed colonial administrators not to issue travel documents for the congress. The Americans and British must have been discomforted to learn that Clemenceau had reversed position and given permission for the Congress to be held.

The intervention of Blaise Diagne of Senegal made the congress a reality. He

was one of seven black members of the Chamber of Deputies and high commissioner for the [French] Republic with special authority for French West Africa, a title so exalted that he outranked all of France's white servants in the colonies. Diagne was France's ideal African *evolue,* another of those colonials for whom the opening words in French elementary school primers—*"Nos peres, les Gaulois"* ("Our Fathers, the Gauls")—defined for a lifetime a conception of self.

In the hour of greatest need, when German gunners had been close enough to site their artillery on the Eiffel Tower, Diagne raised . . . [more than six hundred thousand] African soldiers for France in one year . . . [in addition to those] for labor duty. Like DuBois, Diagne had wagered on greater rights for his people in return for fighting and dying in war. . . . He was also George Clemenceau's trusted factotum. Through Diagne came news that the French government would permit DuBois to hold his conference.[35]

Another factor was financial underwriting by the NAACP and the extraordinary work of two remarkable women. One was Madame Calman-Levy, the widow of a prominent publisher who made her salon available and helped plan and lobby on behalf of the congress. The other was Ida Alexander Gibbs Hunt, an Oberlin graduate in literature and languages who used her language skills and political astuteness to coordinate, publicize, and serve as assistant secretary of the congress.[36]

Diagne, president of the congress, gave the opening address to approximately fifty-eight delegates.[37] Most sources agree on a total of fifty-six: sixteen delegates from the United States, thirteen from the French West Indies, seven each from Haiti and France, three from Liberia, two from the Spanish colonies, and one each from Abyssinia [Ethiopia], Algeria, the Belgian-ruled Congo, British Africa, Egypt, England, the Portuguese colonies, and San Domingo. Two men from England attended: John Richard Archer, president of London's African Progress Union (an organization that linked Afro-Americans to other African peoples), a labor leader, and the first British-born black councilor, alderman, and mayor; and Edmund Fitzgerald Fredericks. Although living in England at the time, Fredericks was "from British Guiana, and later became a member of the Georgetown legislative council and chaired the colony's Negro Progressive Convention."[38]

Most of the black Americans who attended were already in Paris and were recruited to serve as delegates. Among them were Dr. John Hope, president of Morehouse College; Mrs. Addie Waites Hunton, a black member of the YWCA in France; George Jackson, a missionary; Rayford Logan, a black soldier stationed in France; William Henry Hunt, U.S. consul general in St. Etienne, France, and husband of Ida Hunt; Dr. Robert R. Moton, president of Tuskegee Institute; Nathan Hunt, secretary to Dr. Moton; Lester Walton, managing editor of *New York Age;* and William H. Jernagin, pastor of Mt. Carmel Baptist Church in Washington, D.C.[39] Hunton, former dean of the State Normal and Agricultural College of Alabama, bursar of Clark College, and student at the Kaiser Wilhelm University of Strasbourg, was one of few women attending. She spoke to the importance of recognizing the global contributions of women and including them in the struggle for change and development.[40] The president of the French National Association for the Rights of Women was also a participant.

It seems that most speeches addressed colonial rule in Africa, but the delegates avoided being too critical and tended to laud the progress being made under colonialism. Diagne opened the congress with praise for French colonial rule, and other Francophone Africans pointed to the progress being made under the Third Republic. A Belgian delegate "could not suggest that the Africans there enjoyed equality and liberty . . . [but emphasized] the reforms underway in the colony. . . . Echoing the theme of 'lusotropicalism,' or the notion that the Portuguese in the tropics knew how to colonize without resorting to racism, M. d'Andrade, the Portuguese colonial delegate, told the congress about 'the opportunities and liberties given the natives in the

Portuguese colonies.' "[41]The delegates from the United States and England were not under colonial rule but were nevertheless racialized and lived under early-twentieth-century structured inequalities; they were more critical of their nation-states. Black Americans such as DuBois (secretary of the Congress) and George Jackson expressed profound concern about the treatment of blacks in the United States. White Americans who attended were more optimistic and conciliatory; they emphasized changes taking place, the exemplary positive steps of the Pan-African Congress, and the need for blacks and whites to work together.[42]

DuBois's memorandum provided the framework for the final resolutions passed by the delegates.[43] The major ones called for the League of Nations to administer the former German colonies, to establish a permanent bureau to oversee the political, social, and economic welfare of the "natives" of Africa. Furthermore, "The Negroes of the world demand that hereafter the natives of Africa and the peoples of African descent be governed" according to six explicated principles covering land, capital, labor, education, health, and the state. The expectation was that these resolutions would affect the Peace Conference, and DuBois hoped to present them to Wilson. They reached one of Wilson's advisors and had no effect on the final deliberations at Versailles.

The most important outcome of the Pan-African Congress was its influence on those who attended, including their personal interactions and the long-term implications for the development of a transnational diaspora consciousness and activism. Did these undertakings presage nationalist movements for self-determination and liberation from colonial rule that began with Ghana in 1958? Were they connected to the various struggles for liberation, black power, and civil rights in the last third of the twentieth century? Certainly, diaspora issues became increasingly relevant at local levels among the geo-socially dispersed communities of African descent. The global and the local mediate each other. It can be argued that the Pan-African Congress in Paris, although operating in the shadow of Versailles, put the rights of citizenship and self-determination on the world stage. It was a turning point and a seminal political strategy of the period. Although blacks in Britain and the United States continued to struggle for their civil rights at home, the congress provided an opportunity to "denationalize" citizenship issues and the struggles against racial inequality. That is, nation-states and colonial territories are not the only sociopolitical space within which group interests may be represented. Using international venues such as the Pan-African Congress, activists of the early twentieth century lobbied for their rights at a transnational level. An area that requires more research is how African diaspora identity formations are negotiated transnationally as well as nationally, and how these identities are mediated within the larger web of social relations.

REACHING THE BLACK AMERICAN MASSES, PUBLICS, AND CIRCLES

A number of postwar black American cultural workers were active transnationally. Some were more well known than others, and most were affiliated with organizations that varied in terms of size, demographic and social constituencies, ideological and cultural orientation, and geographical and economic bases and resources. They included journalists, independent and syndicated writers, entrepreneurs, intellectuals and educators, ministers and missionaries, civil servants, political activists, and scientists and other professionals. Many of these men and women knew one another and shared overlapping political and social spaces. To what extent did they reach beyond their interpersonal networks to larger publics, to DuBois's "twelve million black souls"? How did they spread information about the Paris Conference, the Pan-African Congress, and transnationalized diaspora experiences in general? The following discussion is more speculative and heuristic than factual and conclusive.

Most of the black American cultural apparatus at the time falls into three intersecting and overlapping groupings: commercial, political, and educational-religious. Long before World War I, for example, there were newspapers owned, edited, or both by black men and women, such as Ida B. Wells (*Chicago Conservator*, 1895–97), Sol C. Johnson (*Savannah Tribune*), and Fred R. Moore (*New York Age*). The first meeting of the National Afro-American Press Association was held in 1884 in Washington, D.C., and the Negro Press Association of Georgia was very active as early as 1893.[44] In 1891 there were "about fifty-five well-established Negro newspapers and journals. Thirty-seven [67 percent] are in the Southern states; seven are monthlies and two are semi-monthlies. The aggregate weekly circulation of all is about 850,000 copies. . . . The largest circulation, 15,000, is claimed for the *Indianapolis Freeman*."[45]

At the turn of the century most cities and towns with a significant black population had at least one newspaper, and some were widely read across the country, such as the *Afro-American* (Baltimore), the *Chicago Defender*, and the *Pittsburgh Courier*. Copies were sold in black neighborhoods by boys and girls on the street, at newsstands, and in drug stores. The *Defender* was particularly successful. The circulation of 50,000 in 1916 rose to 125,000 in 1918, and during this period it became a national newspaper. It had "representatives throughout the country and often employed railroad porters and waiters to distribute the papers in the South. By 1916, the *Defender* circulated in seventy-one towns. . . . The postwar *Defender* published a thirty-two page paper each week and turned out both city and national editions with a combined circulation of about 180,000."[46]

From 21–23 June 1919, the Conference of Editors of Colored Newspapers in the United States was held in Washington, D.C. Invited to the capitol by Emmett J. Scott, special assistant at the War Department for Negro affairs, the thirty-one editors who attended addressed issues affecting "American blacks and Africa." At the end of the meeting, they issued a Bill of Particulars and sent a letter to Scott opposing the return to Germany of its African colonies and calling for an international commission to govern these areas.[47] It can be assumed that through their personal networks and newspapers, these actions were widely circulated among their collective readership. These commercial enterprises were important sources of knowledge about Africa: "Unlike other businessmen and unlike the politicians, the editors were compelled by the nature of their occupation to speak out on racial affairs, but they were not of one voice on matters of racial ideology. . . . The raison d'etre of the Negro press was to protest prejudice and oppression." Newspapers, like other black businesses, "consciously tried to secure Negro customers by emphasizing the importance of their enterprises to the cause of race advancement."[48]

Organizations such as the NAACP, the National Equal Rights League (NERL), and the UNIA were largely political. Their efforts were directed toward changing state policies in the interest of black people, such as equal rights and access to resources and opportunities; security under the law, especially protection from lynching; and full enfranchisement. They shared common goals but differed in ideology and approach. The Hamitic League was considered radical and leftist in contrast to the interracial and reformist NAACP. The NERL also was more radical than the NAACP, with which it competed for members among the black educated middle class. Ida B. Wells-Barnett joined the NERL and abandoned her involvement with the NAACP: "Both she and Trotter [a major actor in the NERL] remained wary of the NAACP's predominantly white leadership, preferring 'an organization of the colored people and for the colored people and led by the colored people.' "[49]With the exception of the UNIA, most of these organizations had internal critics who were concerned that the priority should be on racial discrimination and inequality at home. Their challenge was to create transnational awareness by playing on the relationship between the local and the global. All these organizations needed financial and moral support to carry forward their agenda.

Religious and educational groups organized many political activities. Rallies, major meetings, and conferences were held at churches and colleges. Many of the college and seminary presidents were also ministers, and these institutions were important sources of well-educated cultural workers. There were ancillary groups, such as the Negro Ministerial Council of Dallas, Texas, in most cities with a number of black churches. Religion was a major force in black communities, and churches were a significant locus for generating interest in and awareness of global Africa—from the pulpit, through news bulletins, and at special meetings. Most denominations are hierarchical organizations, and at regional and annual conventions information was gathered and passed on to the local congregation. Itinerant visitors, such as missionaries and African students like John Chilembwe, were also not unusual during this period.[50]

Nearly all national organizations had regional, divisional, or local branches, and cultural workers often had memberships in various groups, both of which ensured spillover effects to larger numbers of people. Madam Walker, for example, belonged to the NAACP, the NERL, the International League of Darker Races, the National Association of Colored Women, the Court of Calanthe, and the Mite Missionary Society. In April 1916 she organized two hundred New York beauty culturists into the first chapter of the Madam C. J. Walker Benevolent Association. At the time there were approximately thirteen thousand licensed black beauty practitioners, but with the "underground" economy the figure may have totaled twenty thousand.[51] On 31 August 1917, more than two hundred delegates from nearly every state in the country attended the Madam Walker Beauty Cultural Union Convention at the Union Baptist Church in Philadelphia. Many of the sessions were open to the public, and Madame Walker was concerned that her agents not only become good entrepreneurs but "politically conscious citizens." The convention sent a telegram to President Wilson expressing outrage regarding lynchings and race riots. Given the transnational involvement of Walker, it is reasonable to assume she spoke on global topics as well.

Political organizations produced publications for their membership, such as the NAACP's *Crisis: A Record of the Darker Races.* The Boston *Guardian,* edited by William Monroe Trotter, expressed the ideas of the NERL, and the *Negro World* was the news organ of the UNIA. *The Messenger,* edited by socialists A. Philip Randolph and Chandler Owen, first appeared in 1917, initially for hotel bellmen and, in 1925, for the Brotherhood of Sleeping Car Porters, which Randolph was instrumental in organizing. It should be noted that readership far exceeded paid circulation for all black newspapers, which were shared among friends and in reading rooms at lodge halls, churches, libraries, and social or other organizations.

The *Negro World* was the most widely circulated publication and was read not just by UNIA members. As late as 1926, the UNIA had roughly 1,000 branches, of which 725 were in the United States. The ten states with the largest number of branches were Louisiana (74), Virginia (48), North Carolina (47), Pennsylvania (45), West Virginia (44), Mississippi (44), Ohio (39), Arkansas (38), Florida (32), and New Jersey (31). The District of Columbia, Iowa, and Rhode Island had 2 each. Nebraska, Oregon, Utah, and Wisconsin had 1 branch each. Only eleven states were without UNIA branches:

Idaho, Montana, Nevada, New Mexico, Wyoming, Minnesota, North Dakota, South Dakota, Maine, New Hampshire, and Vermont. C. Eric Lincoln notes: "For all the castigation of his many critics, Garvey enjoyed the admiration of hundreds of thousands of lower-class Negroes, who followed him with enthusiasm and money, and who received from him a new estimate of their worth and their future. His movement fired the imaginations of people desperate for a new hope and a new purpose, however unrealistic. 'Its spirit of race chauvinism had the sympathy of the overwhelming majority of the Negro people, including those who opposed its objectives.' " By midsummer of 1919, Garvey claimed to have 2 million members in 30 branches. His newspaper, the *Negro World*, was printed in French and Spanish as well as in English, and at its peak, it claimed a circulation of more than two hundred thousand, "reaching the mass of Negroes throughout the world."[52]

The *Negro World* was Garvey's main propaganda organ and was read aloud as a standard part of UNIA meetings wherever the organization existed. It had outstanding writers, such as T. Thomas Fortune, a leading Afro-American journalist of the time.[53]

Crisis: A Record of the Darker Races, under the editorship of DuBois, started with a circulation of one thousand in 1910, reaching twenty-two thousand in 1912 and forty-five thousand in 1916. At its peak in January 1918, 53,750 copies were sold. It appears that extra printings of the publication around the time of the Pan-African Congress reached one hundred thousand readers, who followed "the world's destines in a stream of superbly narrated, often confessional, letters [from DuBois] filling *The Crisis.*"[54]

Various means were used to mobilize support. The NAACP organized mass meetings in New York in January 1919, and keynoters spoke on Africa in the world democracy; resolutions were passed, and a cable was sent to President Wilson. Trotter's National Race Congress for World Democracy not only selected delegates for the Peace Conference but also involved the public in signing petitions, drafting resolutions, and raising funds for transnational activities, which were participatory channels used by most organizations.

Cultural workers also traveled to many different communities to give public presentations. Depending on their oratorical skills or public persona, their reception was often exceptional. Monroe Trotter, for instance, led a delegation to the White House to challenge Wilson's policies and was expelled from the meeting after a heated exchange with the president. Thereafter he drew large crowds, many out of curiosity to see and hear the man who, from their perspective, had stood his ground against the powerful.[55] Garvey has been described as the second-best propaganda device of the UNIA, after the *Negro World:* "The excellence and power of Garvey's oratory was probably the single most uncontroversial of his attributes. Indeed it is difficult to think of any other fact concerning Garvey on which such diverse persons as communist leaders, J. Edgar Hoover of the Department of Justice, NAACP anti-Garveyites, British colonial police officers and Garvey's followers all agreed."[56] In this period before the advent of television and mass communications, the public arena was "up close and personal."

On 18 December [Garvey] and Ida B. Wells-Barnett appeared before the Baltimore Branch of the UNIA at the Bethel Church in Baltimore to drum up support for the delegation [to the Peace Conference]. "During the month of January 1919, . . . Garvey and a whole team of speakers including A. Philip Randolph, Chandler Owen, and William Monroe Trotter, ranged from Boston to New York City, to Newark, to Washington, D.C., to Chicago, and to Louisville addressing the various branches of the UNIA and raising money for the delegates."[57] Black Americans were indeed exposed to much information, although its effect on transforming identity and consciousness cannot be quantified. The "masses" and "classes" were mobilized in a variety of ways to affect U.S. policy toward Africa and its diaspora at a time of major world political and economic transformation. Cultural workers formed their own networks of communications and devised ways, conventional and ad hoc, to work for a common cause, although their differences with one another should not be underestimated. Knowledge, images, viewpoints, meanings, and interpretations were derived from a multifaceted cultural apparatus. Newspapers, newsletters, journals, rallies, congresses, conferences, parades, mass meetings, podiums, pulpits, and beauty salons and other businesses were all part of the production and delivery systems of cultural workers and organizations. Conceivably, these experiences, many face-to-face over several hours, were more intense than the short sound bytes and brief explanations of television news today.

NOTES

1. For details see Milfred C. Fierce, *The Pan-African Idea in the United States, 1900–1919* (New York: Garland Publishing, 1993); Peter Fryer, *Staying Power: The History of Black People in Britain* (Atlantic Highlands, N.J.: Humanities Press, 1984), chaps. 9 and 10; Sylvia M. Jacobs, *The African Nexus: Black American Perspectives on the European Partitioning of Africa, 1880–1920* (Westport, Conn., and London: Greenwood Press, 1981); and Kenneth James King, *Pan-Africanism and Education: A Study of Race Philanthropy and Education in the Southern States of America and East Africa* (Oxford: Clarendon Press, 1971).

2. C. Wright Mills, "The Cultural Apparatus," in *Power, Politics and People: The Collected Essays of C. Wright Mills*, ed. Irving Louis Horowitz (London: Oxford University Press, 1963), 406.

3. Ibid.

4. A. J. P. Taylor, *The Struggle for Mastery in Europe, 1848–1918* (London: Oxford University Press, 1954); and Gary B. Nash et al., eds., *The American People: Creating a Nation and a Society* (New York: Harper and Row, 1990). For the fourteen points, consult any major encyclopedia under "Woodrow Wilson."

5. Ruth Simms Hamilton, "Reassessing Diaspora Connections and Consciousness: Global Africa and World War I," *Routes of Passage: Rethinking the African Diaspora*, vol. 1, pt. 1 (East Lansing: Michigan State University Press, 2007)

6. For in-depth discussion, see Jacobs, *African Nexus*, chap. 11; and Elliott Skinner, *African Americans and U.S. Policy toward Africa, 1850–1924: In Defense of Black Nationality* (Washington, D.C.: Howard University Press, 1992), chap. 10.

7. Editorial, "Self-Determination," *Savannah Tribune*, 15 February 1919, as quoted in Jacobs, *African Nexus*, 263.

   Note: My first job, as a grade school student, was selling newspapers on Thursday afternoons out of the office of the *Tribune*, watched over by an elderly Sol C. Johnson, a family friend and godfather of my brother Merilus Johnson Simms. I worked at the *Tribune* throughout my childhood, over summers during college, and for a short time after college graduation.

8. Jacobs, *African Nexus*, 249 and 253.

9. W. E. Burghardt DuBois, *The World and Africa: An Inquiry into the Part Which Africa Has Played in World History*, an enlarged edition, with new writings on Africa by W. E. B. DuBois(New York: International Publishers, 1965), 9.

10. David Levering Lewis, *W. E. B. DuBois: Biography of a Race, 1868–1919* (New York: Henry Holt and Company, 1993), 561–62; and Skinner, *African Americans*, 391–92.

11. Tony Martin, *Race First: The Ideological and Organizational Struggles of Marcus Garvey and the Universal Negro Improvement Association* (Westport, Conn.: Greenwood Press, 1976), 6.

12. Ibid., 11, and Skinner, *African Americans*, 394.

13. Skinner, *African Americans*, 394.

14. A' Lelia Bundles, *On Her Own Ground: The Life and Times of Madam C. J. Walker* (New York: Scribners, 2001), 257.

15. Jacobs, *African Nexus*, 48 and 243.

16. Jacobs, *African Nexus*, provides details about the backgrounds of the various cultural workers, along with their viewpoints, 241–57.

17. Ibid., 246 and 248.

18. Ibid., 252.

19. Lewis, *W. E. B. DuBois*, 564, quoting "Letters from Dr. DuBois."

20. Jacobs, *African Nexus*, 246.

21. See Hamilton, "Reassessing Diaspora Connections," for details on the SANLC; and Albert Grundlingh, *Fighting Their Own War: South African Blacks and the First World War* (Johannesburg, S.A.: Ravan Press, 1987), 135–38.

22. W. E. B. DuBois, *The Autobiography of W. E. B. DuBois: A Soliloquy on Viewing My Life from the Last Decade of Its First Century* (New York: International Publishers, 1968), 271.

23. Bundles, *On Her Own Ground*, 256.

24. See ibid., chap. 20, for details.

25. Ibid., 256.

26. Ibid., 258.

27. Marc Gallicchio, *The African American Encounter with Japan and China: Black Internationalism in Asia, 1895–1945* (Chapel Hill, N.C.: University of North Carolina Press, 2000), 24.

28. Two earlier conferences on racism were more narrowly focused. In 1978 the theme was decolonization, in 1983, apartheid. The U.S. government boycotted both conferences.

29. This is based on unofficial reporting that requires further verification. See Rachael L. Swarns, "A Focus on Slavery and the Palestinians," *New York Times*, 9 September 2001, A8.

30. John H. Cushman Jr., "U.S. Delegates in Durban Practiced Minimalism," *New York Times*, 4 September 2001, A8.

31. "In the final division of the former German African colonies, 42 percent were placed under the guardianship of Great Britain, 33 percent under France, and 25 percent under Belgium." Southwest Africa (Namibia) was "granted" to the Union of South Africa. Jacobs, *African Nexus*, 241 and 240.

32. Ibid., 258.

33. Lewis, *W. E. B. DuBois*, 578.

34. Fierce, *The Pan-African Idea*, 211. For more on the inside politics of the Congress and other specifics, see Lewis, *W. E. B. DuBois*, chap. 19; and Skinner, *African Americans*, chap. 10. Jacobs, *African Nexus*, provides a succinct summary of key points, 257–59, as does Fierce, 208–14.

35. Lewis, *W. E. B. DuBois*, 567.

36. Ibid., 568 and 575; and Skinner, *African Americans*, 404.

37. There are discrepancies in the various sources about the exact numbers, and there appears to be no complete listing of all the names.

38. Peter Fryer, *Staying Power: The History of Black People in Britain* (Atlantic Highlands, N.J.: Humanities Press, 1984), 290–94 and 321.

39. Lewis, *W. E. B. DuBois*, 568 and 575; Skinner, *African Americans*, 420 n. 114; and Jacobs, *African Nexus*, 257.

40. Further details about this extraordinary woman are discussed in Dorothy Schneider and Carl J. Schneider, *Into the Breach: American Women Overseas in World War I* (New York: Viking Press, 1991), 170.

41. Skinner, *African Americans*, 405; also Lewis, *W. E. B. DuBois*, 676, and Fierce, *The Pan-African Idea*, 212.

42. Skinner, *African Americans*, 405.

43. For a complete listing of the resolutions, see Fierce, *The Pan-African Idea*, 212–14; and DuBois, *The World and Africa*, 11–12.

44. T. Thomas Fortune, *The New York Negro in Journalism* (New York: New York State Commission National Negro Exposition, 1915), reprinted in Hollis R. Lynch, *The Black Urban Condition: A Documentary History, 1866–1971* (New York: Thomas Y. Crowell, 1973), 43–44; and Clarence A. Bacote, "Negro Proscription, Protests and Proposed Solutions in Georgia, 1880–1908," *Journal of Southern History* 25 (November 1959): 471–98, 477.

45. Samuel J. Barrow, "What the Southern Negro Is Doing for Himself," *Atlantic Monthly*, June 1891, 807–14, reprinted in Lynch, *Black Urban Condition*, 8–11.

46. Allam H. Spear, *Black Chicago: The Making of a Negro Ghetto, 1890–1920* (Chicago and London: University of Chicago Press, 1967), 185. Spear draws from Emmett J. Scott, *Negro Migration during the War* (New York: Oxford University Press, 1920), 30, and Roi Ottley, *The Lonely Warrior: The Life and Times of Robert S. Abbott* (Chicago: Henry Regnery and Co., 1955), 136–37 and 188.

47. Jacobs, *African Nexus*, 247.

48. Spear, *Black Chicago*, 79–80 and 115.

49. Bundles, *On Her Own Ground*, 214–15.

50. See Hamilton, "Reassessing Diaspora Connections," regarding the Chilembwe uprising in Nyasaland (Malawi). Also see George Shepperson and Thomas Price, *Independent African: John Chilembwe and the Origins, Setting and Significance of the Nyasaland Native Rising of 1915* (Edinburgh: University Press, 1958).

51. Bundles, *On Her Own Ground*, 211.

52. C. Eric Lincoln, *The Black Muslims in America* (Boston: Beacon Press, 1961), 56 and 58.

53. Martin, *Race First*, 92–93.

54. On the growth of the publication, see Lewis, *W. E. B. DuBois*, 413, 416–17, 459, 474, 490, 514, 539, 544, 564.

55. Bundles, *On Her Own Ground*, 163.

56. Martin, *Race First*, 100.

57. Skinner, *African Americans*, 412–13.

The African Diaspora in the Twenty-first Century: The Past Is Prologue

Elliott P. Skinner

THE PEOPLES OF THE AFRICAN DIASPORA FACE A CRUEL DILEMMA. AT THE VERY moment when they can establish institutional networks to destroy the racism that has relegated them to the bottom of most contemporary societies, they are increasingly attracted by the prospect of differential access to the political and economic resources of those societies. As the world moves into a new century, they must ask whether they can afford to cease mobilizing against the barriers of race and color in the hope of gaining equal access to the common resources of our planet. How the peoples of the African diaspora answer this question will condition their future and that of their descendants.[1] Whether we like it or not, the problem of the twenty-first century will be the struggle of humankind to use planetary resources in the interest of all, irrespective of race, religion, class, or gender.

When Dr. W. E. B. DuBois contemplated the twenty-first century, he prophesied that its greatest problem would be "the color line, the relation of the darker to the lighter races of men in Asia and Africa, in America and the islands of the sea."[2] It was clear to him that the issue of color, which had emerged as a symbol of the conquest and domination of the globe by European peoples, had lost little of its power and was, in fact, growing. It was also clear to him that it would be his task, and that of the wretched of the earth, to resolve that problem. In this regard, he and his generation were largely successful; DuBois not only lived to see most of Africa and Asia freed of European political domination, but even as he lay dying in an independent Ghana, on the other side of the Atlantic, African Americans were marching in thousands on

Washington, crying "Freedom." Prophetically, DuBois had written in a poem years before: "I heard the song of children crying free, Free: And I died."

That a Massachusetts-born African American should end his days in Ghana, a country he helped to make free, is another index of the centuries-long struggle of African peoples to collaborate in the drive for dignity and freedom. They had found it necessary to develop personal networks and institutional linkages in order to deal with the trauma of contact, slavery, colonization, discrimination, and segregation in the various lands in which they found themselves, groaning under different masters.[3] In the process, the sociocultural systems, languages, and even physical types of these African-derived peoples changed. But the European-controlled global system that progressively enveloped them was so pervasive that African peoples felt the need for concerted common action to defend themselves. Moreover, the types of networks and institutions they developed and the fate of these reflected and continue to reflect the major historical transformations of the global system.

African peoples will still need to create and sustain the networks and institutional linkages that have served well in the past; these are still needed and will be needed in the immediate future. The reasons are obvious: Africa-derived people are often the poorest of the poor, the most oppressed of the oppressed, the most despised of the despised, the most rejected of the rejected, the most excluded of the excluded, and to paraphrase Franz Fanon, the most wretched of the wretched of the earth. Moreover, most of the least developed societies are found on the African continent. The people of the African diaspora live primarily in poor nations, and when they are citizens of more affluent or rich countries, they are nearly always on the bottom of the social scale. The battle always has been to change this.

For purposes of analysis, it might be helpful to consider the history of these networks and institutional linkages as falling into five major periods. The period starting with the Age of Discovery extended through the height of the slave trade and the rise of capitalism, terminating with revolts among both blacks and whites against slavery and economic exploitation. The abolitionist period was characterized by the drive to end slavery, repatriation of some New World Africans, and the defense by other New World blacks of what was then called a "black nationality." The Pan-African period dawned with the twentieth century and was characterized by increasing contacts among African peoples (facilitated by migration and urbanization), major regional and world wars, the rise of socialism, the start of decolonization, and the beginning of the Cold War. The major struggle of African peoples for civil rights coincided with the proliferation of sovereign nation-states in Africa. The contemporary period is characterized by the end of the Cold War, the emerging issues of race, class, and ethnicity among African peoples, and a global call for economic, political, social, and cultural equity.

It is now conceded that Africans did not go gently into the holocaust of slavery. The revolts on the slave ships and on the plantations amply testify to the speed with which Africans from different regions could and did unite to face a common danger. Throughout the Caribbean, New Spain, New France, Brazil, and the North American continent, African captives and their descendants often took advantage of the European imperial wars to change their conditions. Some in Brazil, Jamaica, and Surinam won their liberty, retreated to the hills and forests, and attempted to re-create African communities.

Africans in English North America took advantage of the revolutionary fervor to seek to return to Africa and, when not successful, fought on both sides of the War for Independence. Crispus Attucks was among the black Americans who joined the rebelling whites, while others sided with the British; when Britain lost, many of the black loyalists were transported to Britain, Nova Scotia, and the West Indies, where they linked up with other Africans.[4] Taking advantage of the French Revolution, the Africans in Haiti struck for their liberty, creating in the process the first modern black nation-state. But deathly afraid of what many historians called "a contagion of liberty," and fearing Haitian support of such revolutionaries as Simon Bolivar and Gabriel Prosser, the United States and the European power effectively quarantined the heirs of Toussaint l'Ouverture. This did not stop Bolivar and San Martin from freeing most of South America from Spain. The exploits of the African and mulatto soldiers and sailors under these two generals were heroic but, as was true for their similars in Brazil, never were rewarded as they deserved.

During this age of revolution, Africans in the New World created and used many types of networks to improve their lot. In 1775, Prince Hall, born in Barbados but then living in Massachusetts, organized the African Masonic Lodge. He wished to help his distressed brethren then in slavery and to improve the minds of the freedmen by "searches and researches into men and things." In 1787, Richard Allen and Absolom Jones organized the Free African Society to help "people of their own complexion whom they beheld in sorrow because of [these people's] irreligious and uncivilized state." This organization led to the founding of the African (Protestant Episcopal and Methodist Episcopal) churches, which subscribed to the biblical maxim that "princes shall come out of Egypt and Ethiopia shall soon stretch forth her hands unto God" (Psalms 68: 31). The AME churches would later provide liberating institutional links between Africans on the continent and in the diaspora.

The New York African Free School was emulated throughout the country and would in time produce such graduates as Alexander Crummel and Henry Highland Garnet. These men not only fought to improve the lives of blacks in the United States but also served as missionaries and diplomats in Africa. Paul Cuffe, who founded one of these schools in Massachusetts, later established relations with the African Institution in Britain. This organization, founded with the help of such freed slaves as Olaudah Equiano of Benin, had earlier sponsored the repatriation to Sierra Leone of the unwanted black poor of England, some of the loyalist Afro-Americans, and rebellious Jamaican maroons who had been sent to Nova Scotia. Cuffe transported a number of Afro-American freedpersons to Africa and founded the Friendly Society of Sierra Leone, to open a channel of intercourse among African peoples.

The conflict between Cuffe, Allen, Forten, and other black leaders with the white sponsors of the American Colonization Society, established to repatriate freedpersons, is well known. But it is also true that many of the early colonists, such as Alexander Crummel, Lott Cary, and John B. Russwurm, viewed Liberia not only as a place of refuge but also as a site from which they could spread Christianity and civilization to the Africans. They dreamed that, through what they called "a reflex action," a strong and powerful Africa would reciprocate by protecting its far-flung children and elevating the status of black people.[5] This desire also led other African Americans, such as Martin Delany, to create the African Civilization Society and to attempt to join forces with Samuel Crowder, a black missionary of Yoruba Sierra Leonean origin, to use their skills to develop Nigeria.

African Americans sought to internationalize their struggle against slavery by going to England for what Benjamin Quarles has called a "duet with John Bull." What is significant is that some of these abolitionist black preachers left London to serve in the Caribbean. They were convinced that they had to enlighten black people everywhere. Many blacks in Africa and in the diaspora also stressed the need for this kind of cooperation. When West Indian–born Edward W. Blyden came to the United States in 1863 as part of a delegation from Liberia to seek "aid in building up a negro nationality of freedom and Christianity on the continent of their ancestors," he declared:

> For supposing that it were possible for black men to rise to the greatest eminence, in this country, in wealth and political distinction, so long as there is no Negro power of respectability in Africa, and that continent remained in her present degradation—she would reflect unfavorable upon them. . . . If no Negro state of respectability be erected in Africa—no Negro government permanently established in that land—then the prejudice in question [against blacks] will make its obstinate stand against all the wealth, and genius, and skill that may be exhibited by Negroes in North or South America. The work is to be done in Africa.[6]

Blyden was quite aware that educated African Americans had already established networks to help one another and Africa. Robert Campbell, from Jamaica, who had accompanied Delany to Nigeria, went back to Lagos to edit a newspaper. Joseph Smith, Henry Barnes, Charles Bannerman, and Thomas Hughes, from various parts of Africa and the West Indies, were advising King Aggrey of Fanti land (Ghana) about how to deal with the encroaching British. And Africanus Horton, a Sierra Leonean doctor then serving with the British army, was among those who helped launch the Fanti Federation.

While the nightmare of the U.S. Civil War eliminated chattel slavery and enabled the country to embark upon what was called its Manifest Destiny, African peoples in the United States were still not free. True, Lincoln recognized Haiti and Liberia, the first two modern black nation-states (both of which, significantly, were created by Africans from the diaspora), but the struggle of the African Americans had barely started. They would increase the pace of their fight both in Africa and America. It should be pointed out that African Americans eagerly seized the opportunity to work on behalf of black nations. And despite the problems of "returnees" with indigenous Africans, the record shows that almost every person chosen by the United States as its envoy in Africa was a firm believer in the biblical notion that "Ethiopia" (whether the real one in Africa or the "symbolic" one that existed wherever African peoples were found) "would soon stretch forth her hands unto God."

Those who served in Liberia used economic as well as sentimental arguments to urge U.S. intervention on behalf of their hosts. For example, revealing his frustration over the lack of response to his urgent cables, Henry Smyth wrote Secretary of State Seward of having "the honor once again to remind the Department of the importance to the [U.S.] government of securing some direct influence in Africa, for the commercial advantage to be obtained." He said that it would be "idle to indulge the thought that the English and French Governments are influenced by humanitarian, civilizing motives solely in the acquisition of territory on this continent." Smyth insisted that their main motive was "the prospective commercial wealth that will accrue to these governments and peoples from such effort." He argued that while the United States might believe it had enough land, it needed markets for the articles being produced in its factories. Conscious that he was being overbearing, Smyth closed a rather long cable with the "earnest hope that Africa may not be wholly neglected by us commercially, and your indulgence for the length to which your attention has been taxed by the perusal of this."[7]

During and after the scramble for Africa, African American diplomats on the continent were not unaware that the lenses through which the United States viewed Africa were distorted by racism. Their problem was how to support Africa while demonstrating their loyalty to the United States and that their vision of links with Africa was in America's truest interest. Smyth felt constrained to note that "race allegiance is compatible with patriotism, with love of the land that gave us birth. . . . The sentiment, the something stronger than sentiment which makes an English American proud of his connection with Britain, a French American proud of his connection with La Belle France and a German American fondly attached to the memories of the fatherland, and all European races of their Aryan descent, has something that partakes of the moral sublime."[8] Smyth's aggressive diplomacy often raised more than eyebrows in both Monrovia and Washington. He once suggested to Secretary of State Frelinghuysen that, as a foreign mutual friend of England and Liberia, he should "make such suggestions favorable to the Negro nation's rights as may tend to a final and speedy settlement of the matter in justice and equity to both nations, should you feel called upon to interpose. . . . This, I am advised, is the desire of the [Liberian] President."[9]

In a revealing postscript, Smyth added:

> The civilized Negro in Africa under foreign domination, as the civilized Negro out of Africa under like control, suffers in his liberty, because it has not the element of imperium. "Imperium et Libertas" must be the motto and practice of the Negro, if he is to have self respect; if he is to merit the respect of others. I hope it may be found in consonance with the foreign policy of our Government to aid Liberia in a retention of her self respect unimpaired, her control of her territory, her prestige which is the consequence of her control.[10]

African Americans resisted the attempts of Belgian King Leopold II to gain empire in the Congo. George Washington Williams (considered the first real black historian in the United States) denounced the king's administration, charging him with "deceit, fraud, robberies, arson, murder, slave-raiding, and general policy of cruelty" to the Congolese, whose "lives and fortunes" were entrusted to him by the "Conference of Berlin, 1884–1885."[11] The U.S. State Department helped to exonerate the Reverend William H. Sheppard, charged with sedition by the Belgian government for criticizing Leopold's atrocities, and Booker T. Washington by supporting the U.S. branch of the Congo Reform Association, which contributed to the end of Leopold's personal rule in that African country.[12]

The fortuitous circumstances that led to linkages between African Americans and black South Africans convinced both groups that God worked in mysterious ways his wonders to perform. One of the several imitators of the Fisk Jubilee Choir took South Africa by storm in 1888, demonstrating to the Africans and to some whites what "civilized" Africans could do. A group of Zulus founded a choir, toured Europe, and were invited to the famous Atlanta Exposition, where they were stranded. Rescued by an AME preacher, one young woman was sent to Wilberforce College, from which she wrote her relatives, extolling her treatment by the African Methodist Episcopal Church. The news led a group of black Christian separatists in South Africa, who needed apostolic legitimacy, to seek affiliation with the AME. Nothing could have better pleased such African Americans as Bishop Henry McNeal Turner, an "emigrationist" who was then having a verbal battle with Booker T. Washington about whether people of African descent should go to Africa or remain in the New World.

Once the link was established, Turner visited South Africa, and his disciples gave sermons not only on Christ crucified but also on Africa for the Africans. Bishop Levi Coppin wrote from there that when a man in America was "denied civil and political rights on account of being a descendant of Africa," this was patently "unjust" and "ungodly," but when it happened to blacks in South Africa, "besides being unrighteous and unworthy of our Christian civilization, it is ridiculous in the extreme." He concluded that there was only one right thing for the "African, Africander, Afro-world wider or colored man by whatever distinguishing title to do," and that was to unite in order to prove that "merit does not inhere in color"; rather, given the opportunity, blacks can rise to that "dignity of which mankind alone is capable."[13]

A few adventurous African Americans who visited South Africa sought to help their brethren by protesting segregation and discrimination in the Boer republics of the Transvaal and the Orange Free State. Anxious to capitalize on some anti-British sentiment in America in his struggle against British domination, Paul Kruger sought to mollify African Americans by making them "honorary whites." This, however, did not prevent them from aiding the British, the lesser of the two evils, in the Boer War.[14] The truth was that during the waning days of the nineteenth century, the position of African peoples in the global system had reached its nadir. Except for the Ethiopians, most people of African origin felt that they had to compromise with white power in order to survive.

As the twentieth century dawned, people such as DuBois, who felt that the color line had to be breached, decided to do something about it. In Britain, Henry Sylvester Williams grew concerned about the fate of Lo bengula of the Matabele nation (in what is now Zimbabwe), whose lands were coveted by Cecil John Rhodes. Williams launched an appeal to gather in a congress and launched the Pan-African movement in the process. This meeting was itself a marvel of networking among African peoples. They consciously piggybacked upon the Paris Exposition of 1900 to get their way paid to Europe. Ironically, it was that "compromiser" and "anti-emigrationist" Booker T. Washington who did much to publicize the conference in the United States. I also suspect that he was responsible for W. E. B. DuBois being able to go to Paris and then to London. Taking advantage of the emerging might of the United States, his own advanced academic standing, and the platform offered by the congress, DuBois launched the first of his "appeals" to the nations of the world on behalf of African peoples.[15]

Meanwhile, too busy "with the world's work" to go to London, Booker T. Washington used his power and prestige to send his students to Togo and the Sudan as agricultural extension agents. Then, almost single-handedly, he persuaded the administrations of Theodore Roosevelt and William Howard Taft to protect Liberia from imperial Britain and France. It was also due to Washington that Tuskegee served as a model for comparable institutions, such as the Reverend John Langalabalele Dube's Zulu Christian Industrial School at Ohlange in Natal, the South African Native College at Fort Hare, the Lovedale Industrial School in the Cape of Good Hope, the Lumbwa Industrial Mission in Kenya, and numerous other institutes in the Gold Coast and Nigeria.[16] And while the Wizard of Tuskegee advocated industrial education for the masses of persons of African descent in lands dominated by whites, he "certainly did not promote industrial education as a caste education suitable especially to Africans, as white men after his death did."[17]

DuBois, for his part, was determined to use an educated, talented tenth to confront the white world and never lost an opportunity to demonstrate the brilliance of persons of African descent. He was convinced that if the banner of racial excellence was to be lifted high for all the world to see, then it would have to be placed there by "black hands."[18] DuBois was behind the founding of the NAACP to deal with the problems of African Americans, but he devoted much attention to African peoples in the global system. At the 1911 Congress of Races in London, he met and conversed with such black South Africans as Walter Rubusana and John Tengo Javabu, who were still smarting over Britain's betrayal of their people at the Peace of Vereeniging. The hope of DuBois for the conference, which in retrospect he ranked in importance with the Bolshevik revolution of 1917, was blasted by the salvos of World War I. That conflict brought together more different types of persons of African descent than ever before; it also enabled DuBois to launch his Pan-African movement, which he viewed as an "organized protection of the Negro world led by American Negroes." DuBois later organized conferences in Paris, Brussels, London, Lisbon, and New York, and he lived long enough to see Pan-African meetings in Africa.[19]

While soldiers of African descent from all over the world were buried in Flanders Fields, there was also a gathering of blacks in the United States, a great movement from the American South and the Caribbean into northern ghettos. They were about to create a sociocultural milieu with revolutionary potential. One such migrant, Marcus Garvey, a long-time admirer of and correspondent with Booker Washington, founded the Universal Negro Improvement Association (UNIA) to preach the gospel of "Africa for Africans, at home and abroad."[20] A network of more than 1425 UNIA cells created by seamen throughout the Caribbean, Latin America, and Africa would prove to be a political time bomb for the dominant Europeans long after Garvey was exiled from the United States.[21] Into New York also streamed Langston Hughes, Zora Neale Hurston, Louis Dunbar, Claude McKay, Alain Locke, and others who would launch the Harlem Renaissance. This movement linked up with the incipient negritude movement led by Price Mars in Haiti, Leopold Seda Senghor in Senegal, Aime Cesaire of Martinique, and Leon Demas of Guiana, then students in Paris. In Paris also was Josephine Baker, bringing with her from Saint Louis both the blues and jazz. In eastern Nigeria, Nnamdi Azikiwe heard about this ferment and in time encouraged Francis Nkrumah to study in the United States. DuBois, the foremost black intellectual of the period, articulated the feelings of blacks about events in Africa and the wider world in *The Crisis.*

In 1931, DuBois mobilized African Americans against the joint American, British, and German demand that the League of Nations supervise the administration of Liberia's affairs.[22] Thanks in part to pressure from him and others, Liberia did not lose its independence. Ethiopia was not to have the same good fortune. Long smarting from the Italian defeat by Ethiopia at Adowa in 1895, an aggressive Benito Mussolini invaded that country in 1935. African Americans immediately mobilized to help, joining in Emperor Haile Selassie's plea for justice before the League of Nations and creating the International Council of Friends of Ethiopia, the United Aid to Ethiopia, and the Ethiopian World Federation. In an article for *Foreign Affairs,* "Inter-racial Implications of the Ethiopian Crisis," DuBois asserted that blacks had "lost faith" in the ability of the United States to listen to "an appeal for justice" from black people. A dejected Haile Selassie warned that Italy's conquest of Ethiopia was a prelude to World War II.[23] It seemed that the only black hope was Joe Louis, whose pugilistic exploits won the admiration of African peoples the world over.

As during the earlier imperial wars, African peoples exploited the contradictions of their masters in the second global conflict. Felix Eboue of French Guiana mobilized colonial black soldiers to help De Gaulle save the honor of France, thereby making possible the Brazzaville (Congo) conference and ultimate freedom for French Africa. African Americans fought for the right to fight, so as to reap the fruits of liberty after the war. African students such as Nnamdi Azikiwe and Kwame Nkrumah, marooned in the United States during the war, helped their hosts but also reminded them that African peoples took seriously the promises of the Atlantic Charter and the Four Freedoms.

Nevertheless, both Ralph Bunche and W. E. B. DuBois, sent by President Truman as members of the U.S. delegation to the inaugural meeting of the United Nations at San Francisco in 1945, were disappointed by what they encountered: Britain advocated a world of free democratic states while holding millions of Africans and other peoples in thralldom; Jan Smuts waxed sentimental about "humanity" yet was convinced that anyone who viewed the blacks in South Africa as being as human as whites was "mad, quite mad"; U.S. Secretary of State Byrnes chastised the Soviets for lacking democracy, but in his native South Carolina the African American majority did not have the right to vote.[24] In disgust, DuBois left the conference for Manchester, England, to participate in the Fifth Pan-African Conference, where the banner was passed to the Africans who would create new states.[25]

The Cold War that soon erupted enabled African peoples once again to use their networks to improve their lot by exploiting the contradictions among some of their rulers.[26] Unwilling to heed the call of African Americans to help with the decolonization of Africa, one white U.S. diplomat said: "We have no desire to assume the responsibility borne by other powers and, indeed, our principles, our existing commitments, and our lack of experience all militate against our assumption of such obligation."[27] More-perceptive Americans, who recognized that the United States needed to understand an emerging Africa and a liberated Asia, created Foreign Area Fellowships that enabled many brilliant young African Americans to visit and study in regions where African peoples lived. They would take the batons from such older scholars as Horace Mann Bond, St. Clair Drake, and E. Franklin Frazier, and some moved from an academic career into politics and diplomacy.[28]

The diplomacy pursued by a number of African states eventually resulted in that "reflex action" which many African Americans had dreamed about earlier, namely, that a strong Africa would warn the United States to treat its black citizens with more respect. President Dwight Eisenhower, during whose administration the Bureau of African Affairs was created in the State Department, had to invite a Ghanaian minister to breakfast in the White House to compensate for his being refused a glass of orange juice in a Maryland restaurant. African Americans were delighted when Dr. Marie Gadsend had the honor of being sent to Guinea to teach English to President Sekou Toure and his cabinet. In her footsteps hundreds of enthusiastic African Americans strove to create and strengthen links between Africa and the United States. Mel Whitfield, a Jamaican American, went to East Africa to help train a number of future Olympic medalists; Drs. Bobby and Sara Lee went to do dentistry in Ghana; Julian Mayfield went to Ghana and provided editorial copy for its president; Maya Angelou went to Accra to learn African music and dance; the Reverend James Robinson, from Harlem, sent his Crossroaders all over Africa, laying the foundation for President John Kennedy's Peace Corps.[29]

As to be expected, not all these grafts took, and some were downright dangerous. As the Africans got caught up in their local, national, and global problems, and as African Americans became engaged in a difficult civil rights movement, tensions often developed in the African world. The Cold War created problems between Africa and the United States. African Americans were confused by U.S. reluctance to take sides during the Biafran War, while being prodded by a strong Biafran lobby to support the secessionists. The death of Lumumba and the fall of Nkrumah caused consternation among African peoples.[30] These developments led a number of scholars to suggest a reevaluation of Pan-Africanism and to question the viability of the networks and institutions that Africans and African Americans had elaborated in the past.[31] It was feared that the good will between the United States and Africa, which began with the Kennedy inauguration, was rapidly dissipating, and that this would affect the relations between African peoples on both sides of the Atlantic.[32]

Noting these difficulties, one African American scholar called for a clear distinction between cultural pan-Africanism, which he likened to negritude, and political pan-Africanism, which recognized that African peoples had different and potentially antagonistic political systems. He suggested that while both Africans and African Americans might continue to use the former for their common liberation, this was not possible with the latter. It was felt that since African peoples were citizens of different independent states, their futures might involve issues that superseded race. For example, African Americans faced the problem of becoming fully integrated into a multiethnic and multicultural nation-state, whereas other African peoples faced international problems or class conflicts within racially homogeneous states.[33]

There is no denying that the changing fortunes of African peoples around the globe have led to conflict in the past and can lead to problems in the future. Nevertheless, if history is any guide, unless racism disappears quickly and completely, it is more than likely that African peoples will need networks for self-help for a long time to come. They will have to be flexible and create new institutions when disaster threatens. For example, during the Sahelian drought, when a preoccupied President Richard Nixon did not act in time, African Americans joined with Africans living in the United States to create RAINS (Relief for Africans in Need in the Sahel). Their gifts were only a "widow's mite," but they used their contacts with the Black Caucus in Congress and with the State Department to sensitize Americans to the situation. The Black Caucus so badgered the administration for relief aid that military planes were used to transport food to the Sahel. An attempt also was made to get infrastructure assistance for Africa, but this was unsuccessful in the face of Nixon's determination to end the Vietnam War and protect his Portuguese allies, who were still involved in a difficult decolonization struggle in Africa.[34]

African Americans were especially dismayed when it became quite clear that Nixon's policy of benign neglect toward them was replicated in his attitude toward

Africa, especially the southern portion. They learned with dismay that Secretary of State Kissinger's Cold War concerns had led him to formulate National Security Study Memorandum (NSSM) 39, which supported Portugal in Africa, as well as the whites in Rhodesia and South Africa.[35] Meeting in Washington, D.C., in 1976, black Americans took the president to task for not scheduling talks with President Kaunda of Zambia, who had important advice on southern Africa. They also were distressed when Congress decided to exempt chrome from the UN trade embargo against Rhodesia and when the United States used its very first veto in the UN Security Council to defeat a resolution expanding sanctions against the Smith regime.[36] Out of such concern was born TransAfrica, a black political lobby committed to changing U.S. policy toward the entire black world.

The Congressional Black Caucus, supported by TransAfrica, played a significant role in preventing the Nixon administration from committing the folly of military adventurism when the Portuguese empire fell, which would have placed the U.S. southern Africa policy in jeopardy. The caucus listened politely to Kissinger, who, for the first time, asked them for an audience, but they refused to be alarmed by the "domino theory" that all of southern Africa might fall to the Soviets. The secretary of state visited black Africa for the first time but failed to resolve the crisis in Rhodesia, which he viewed as the key to détente in the region. He also failed to involve the United States in Angola, dismayed when Cuba, vaunting its Africanity and supported by the Soviet Union, entered the fray when the South Africans invaded that country.

President Jimmy Carter's election gave Congressman Andrew Young the opportunity to engage in what I have termed an Afrocentric policy toward Africa. African Americans had long felt that the United States needed a new mind-set in order to deal effectively with Africa and that America's best hope for cooperation with the people of that continent lay in looking them fully in the face. Working closely with the frontline states, UN Ambassador Andrew Young and his deputy, Donald McHenry, persuaded the British to resume control of Rhodesia and to prepare the basis for an independent Zimbabwe.

Carter's presence in the White House also stimulated the Reverend Leon Sullivan, a member of the board of General Motors, to elaborate a set of principles by which he hoped U.S. companies doing business in South Africa could help bring about change. As first proposed in 1977 and amplified in 1978 and 1979, the code called for the desegregation of all eating, comfort, and work facilities; equal and fair employment practices, including no discrimination against the rights of Africans to form or belong to government-registered trade unions; equal pay for comparable work; the advancement of blacks to management positions; and an improved quality of life for black employees outside the workplace, such as in housing and transportation. There was some resistance by U.S. companies, but a number of them decided to adopt these principles in the hope of achieving racial peace in South Africa.[37] The Carter administration appreciated Sullivan's initiative, especially since it came out of the American experience. Although UN Ambassador Donald McHenry did a creditable job when Young departed the post, he could not bring about the decolonization of Namibia or induce racial peace in South Africa. An embattled President Carter, preoccupied with problems in the Middle East exacerbated by the rise of militant Islam, retreated from active cooperation with Africans to bring about change on their continent. Once again, African and African American cooperation fell victim to other concerns. A frustrated U.S. electorate turned the country over to Ronald Reagan.

Reagan's presidency, like that of Richard Nixon, presented African Americans with an unceasing battle to preserve their gains at home and help African states deal with severe teething problems. They mistrusted assistant secretary of state for African affairs, Chester Crocker, who had been chosen because his major premise and promise was to combat the Soviets and engage "constructively" with South Africa so as to bring about change without revolution by the black majority.[38] African Americans and Africans were convinced that Crocker was wrong in viewing Africa through the prism of the Cold War and feared that he favored cooperation with South African whites against the black majority, which was worse.

When South African military and intelligence personnel appeared at the U.S. State Department and in the U.S. mission to the United Nations as soon as the Reagan administration came to power, this was viewed as an ominous sign. More ominous was the thrust of the scope paper Crocker prepared for Secretary of State Alexander Haig before his meeting with South African foreign minister Pik Botha. Through means still unknown, the memorandum of a secret conversation between Crocker and Botha was procured by TransAfrica and leaked to the *Washington Post.* Here was clear evidence that the United States was prepared to take South Africa's views on southern Africa into greater consideration; that it was willing to discuss the nuclear energy needs of that state; and that in exchange for South Africa's willingness to accept the U.S. lead in the fight against the Soviets, there would be a new level of "friendship and cooperation between the United States and South Africa."[39]

Using TransAfrica as a base of operations, African Americans created the Free South Africa movement, picketed the South African embassy, and began to mobilize on campuses throughout the nation against disinvestment in apartheid. Sharing the view that "time was running out for South Africa" was the report of a study commission on U.S. policy there, sponsored by the Rockefeller Foundation. Headed by Franklin A. Thomas, president of the Ford Foundation, and with other African Americans among its members, the commission warned that all the ingredients of "a major crisis" were present in South Africa and concluded that "the dangers of political instability, large-scale racial conflict, and the growth of Communist influence are real." The commissioners were convinced that if the United States did nothing or adopted the wrong policies toward political freedom and civil liberties in that troubled land, the effect on the United States would be great indeed.[40] Challenged to defend his approach, Crocker said that the United States was not going to "choose between black and white" in South Africa.[41]

African Americans were not prepared to accept these reactionary views and vowed to persuade the United States to join the almost worldwide consensus that South Africa should be pressured into abolishing apartheid, deemed repugnant to all civilized people. The Reagan administration, however, stuck to its policy of "constructive engagement," despite increasing riots and civil disobedience in that country; demonstrations at home and the willingness of black Americans and their allies in the Free South Africa movement to be arrested; the mounting wave of divestiture by U.S. companies; and the growing effort in Congress to impose sanctions. When the Nobel Peace Prize was awarded to Bishop Desmond Tutu for his creative attempts to resolve the problems of his country peacefully, President Reagan himself sought to convince Tutu that apartheid was not uncivilized and un-Christian.

It was not until South Africa made callous attempts to blow up U.S. oil installations in Cabinda and attacked Botswana that Mr. Reagan changed his ambassador. It was not until almost seven hundred Africans had died, Botha had rejected any but his own plans for political change in South Africa, and the passage by Congress of relatively mild sanctions seemed almost certain that the president issued an executive order applying even milder sanctions. On 9 September 1985, he released the following statement: "I, Ronald Reagan, President of the United States of America, find that the policies and actions of the Government of South Africa constitute an unusual and extraordinary threat to the foreign policy and economy of the United States and hereby declare a national emergency to deal with that threat."[42]

Mr. Reagan's decision to name Ambassador Perkins, an African American, to the Pretoria post was probably the most cynical act of a man still not convinced that a new policy toward South Africa was in the best interest of the United States. Probably without realizing it, he attacked the core of South Africa's problem, namely, its commitment to the color line as a badge of privilege that gave unequal access to the strategic resources of that society. By naming an African American as his representative to the most racist state in the world, Mr. Reagan had obviously intended for people to believe that he had no racial feelings and that African Americans had achieved equality in the United States. Of course, no one was fooled. Ironically, this symbolic act forced the South Africans to recognize that their equation of color with resource control was losing meaning in the global system. Much to the satisfaction of all African peoples, President De Klerk of South Africa was forced to release Nelson Mandela, thereby signaling that he was prepared to deal with the issue of race and yield political power to the black majority. It will probably be a long time before the color problem dies away in South Africa, but it should progressively lose its value as a symbol of privilege.

Looking at the immediate past as a portent of the future, it is no accident that African peoples have had so important a role in the demands for two new global institutions: the New Economic Order (NEO) and the New Communications Order (NCO). Secretary of State Kissinger reacted with scorn when the NEO demand was broached at a GATT meeting in Kenya, but it is quite clear that the Bretton Wood Accords that came out of World War II are losing their efficacy and will have to be changed if African peoples on the mother continent and in the diaspora are not to starve in the face of plenty. African Americans played a significant part in obtaining the almost unanimous agreement that the United States should aid the famine-stricken millions in the Sahel, especially in the Sudan and the Horn.[43] Led by the black lobby TransAfrica, U.S. humanitarian groups forced Mr. Reagan to deny that his administration was playing politics with the lives of famine victims. African Americans and others in the diaspora willingly contributed their talents when entertainers from around the globe dramatized the African famine with the theme "We Are the World."

People of African descent everywhere are aware that they must collaborate to end their poverty and economic dependence. Africans received the support of African American economists in the United States and the Caribbean when they suggested that the African-inspired Lagos Plan of Action had more validity for their continent than the Berg Report commissioned by the World Bank. African Americans on the staff of subcommittees in the U.S. Congress or working through business associations have considered networking with African, Caribbean, and Pacific countries to help restructure unequal terms of trade, so that each can become an equal partner in the global economy instead of remaining beggars and paupers.[44]

There is little doubt that the decision of Moctar M'Bow, former director general of the UNESCO, to support the call for a New Communications Order contributed to his difficulty with Western nations and led to U.S. withdrawal from the UNESCO. The United States has always insisted that the NCO would jeopardize freedom of expression, ignoring the fact that the present system of international communication continuously projects a negative image of Africa and its far-flung peoples. Moreover, attempts to change this image encounter major obstacles. Dr. Ali Mazrui stirred up a hornet's nest when *The Africans* (a television series) was aired. Much to his surprise, and that of his collaborators, the Reagan administration took umbrage at Mazrui's criticism of the Europeans, claiming that he was very anti-West and, by implication, anti-American. All this suggests a continuing need for African peoples to establish networks and institutions that will enable them to explain themselves to one another and to the world.

As people of African descent face the twenty-first century, they doubtless will have to deal with the lingering problem of color and race, even while the true issue of the future will be the equitable distribution of the planet's resources among its manifold populations. Once viewed as the impossible dream, the ability of modern technology to provide goods in abundance is now clearly realizable. Supersonic aircraft, soon to be joined by space shuttles, will bridge continents in minutes. Electronic media already permit the world's people to communicate almost instantaneously. Genetic engineering holds the prospect of allowing humankind to erase, or curb, age-old scourges. Will these opportunities be used to benefit all people, or will new imperial systems arise to garner most of the global resources?

People of the diaspora must maintain and continue to build networks to educate themselves so that they can obtain an equal place among peoples of the world. Whether in the United States, Africa, or elsewhere, the peoples of Africa need a great deal more education. The challenge is to train teachers who can reach young people in the ghettoes and bidonvilles who have been judged uneducable. There is also the need for our institutions of higher learning to cooperate with one another so that young scholars can find the environments that will enable them to overcome prejudice and discrimination and do their best work. Diaspora peoples need to meet each other in conferences, at cultural events, and in the boardrooms of major multinational corporations. By doing so they will honor and continue the work done by their ancestors.

NOTES

1. In this text, persons of African descent in the diaspora will sometimes be referred to as African-derived peoples, African Americans, black Americans, Africans in North America, blacks, etc.
2. W. E. B. DuBois, *The Souls of Black Folk* (1903; reprint, Nashville: Hemphill Press, 1979), 13.
3. The dilemma posed for black peoples by the feeling of racial solidarity, as opposed to the recognition of their situational reality, has featured prominently in the social anthropology of St. Clair Drake. In *Black Metropolis*, this problem was phrased in the following terms: "Race consciousness breeds a demand for 'racial solidarity,' and as Negroes contemplate their existence as a minority in a white world which spurns them, they see their ultimate hope in presenting some sort of united front against the world." Drake's growing experiences in the United States, Great Britain, the Caribbean, and a number of African states as a practitioner of Pan-Africanism began to shape his theoretical views of that phenomenon. While he certainly understood the importance of the economic, social,

and political underpinnings of Pan-Africanism, he felt that its psycho-cultural dimensions were quite important. He proposed that what he called "pragmatic pluralism," and that a "creative minority" of social scientists should take the lead in evaluating African cultures, bearing in mind the concept of "cultural relativity." Drake suggested that, given the vast differences in African cultures, this was the only way to deal with the realities of the modern world. Any other approach would make "individual attitudes toward African culture unauthentic and relations between Africans and non-Africans awkwardly guilt-ridden." For Drake, then, Pan-Africanism, as praxis, from a psycho-cultural viewpoint, called for accepting the need for racial solidarity while at the same time recognizing situational reality. See St. Clair Drake and Horace R. Clayton, *Black Metropolis* (New York: Harcourt, Brace and Company, 1945), and St. Clair Drake, *An Approach to the Evaluation of African Societies in Africa Seen by American Negro Scholars* (New York: American Society of African Culture, 1958), 11–12.

4. In English North America in 1773, a group of blacks wrote the governor of Massachusetts begging to "leave the province, which we are determined to do as soon as we can, from our joint labours, procure money to transport ourselves to some part of the Coast of Africa, where we propose settlement." Herbert Aptheker, ed., *Documentary History of the Negro People in the United States* (New York: Citadel Press, 1963), 1:7–8.

5. John H. Bracey Jr., August Meier, and Elliott Rudwick, *Black Nationalism in America* (New York: Bobbs-Merrill, 1970), 77–156; and Sterling Stuckey, *The Ideological Origins of Black Nationalism* (Boston: Beacon Press, 1972), 195 ff.

6. Hollis Lynch, ed., *Black Spokesman: Selected Writings of E. W. Blyden* (London: Frank Cass, 1971), 18.

7. From John Henry Smyth to Secretary of State Seward, no. 326, 7 August 1879, *United States National Archives*, 722–23.

8. Adelaide Cromwell Hill and Martin Kilson, *Apropos of Africa* (London: Frank Cass and Co., 1969), 94–97.

9. Ibid.

10. Ibid.

11. Ibid., 106–7.

12. Ruth M. Slade, "English-Speaking Missions in the Congo Independent State, 1878–1908," *Académie Royale des Sciences Coloniales, Classe de Sciences Morales et Politiques*, Memoires in 8o, n.s, vol. 16, fasc. 2 et dernier (Brussels, 1959), 105–6; and William H. Sheppard, "Yesterday, Today, and Tomorrow in Africa," *Southern Workman* 39 (August 1910): 447.

13. Levi Jenkins Coppin, "Letters from South Africa," in *Apropos of Africa*, 247–48.

14. Williard B. Gatewood Jr., "Black Americans and the Boer War, 1899–1902," *South Atlantic Quarterly* 75 (spring 1976): 226–44.

15. O. C. Mathurin, *Henry Sylvester Williams and the Origin of the Pan-African Movement, 1869–1911* (Westport, Conn.: Greenwood Press, 1969). Bishop Walters of the AME Church was made president of the conference, and DuBois gained renown for his stirring Declaration to the Nations of the World concerning the rights of African peoples.

16. Louis R. Harlan, "Booker T. Washington and the White Man's Burden," *American Historical Review* 71 (January 1966): 441–67.

17. Thomas J. Jones, ed., *Education in Africa* (New York: Phelps-Stokes Fund, 1922); Louis R. Harlan, *The Wizard of Tuskegee, 1901–1915* (New York: Oxford University Press, 1983), 273–74. This was particularly true of the "agents of the Phelps-Stokes and the Jeanes Funds and colonial administrators." That Aggrey, the only African member of the commission, did not agree with its major thrust is seen by his work as vice principal of Achimota Prince of Wales College and School, where he produced such academic types as Dr. Danquah and Kwame Nkrumah, who used their education in the struggle to free the Gold Coast and create independent Ghana.

18. W. E. B. DuBois, *The Conservation of Races*, occasional papers no. 2 (Washington, D.C.: American

Negro Academy 1897).

19. W. E. B. DuBois, *The Autobiography of W. E. B. DuBois* (New York: International Publishers, 1968).

20. Robert A. Hill, ed., *Marcus Garvey and the Universal Negro Improvement Association*, vol. 1, 1826–August 1919 (Berkeley: University of California Press, 1983), 1.

21. See Tony Martin, *Race First: The Ideological and Organizational Struggles of Marcus Garvey and the Universal Improvement Association* (Westport, Conn.: Greenwood Press, 1976). Many Africans welcomed the sentiments of solidarity expressed by Garvey and agitated for freedom; others, such as Blaise Diagne, a deputy from Senegal to the French Parliament, and President King of Liberia, considered Garvey a presumptuous radical. Both Diagne and King opposed the notion of Garvey that their salvation could come from the black diaspora.

22. W. E. B. DuBois, "Liberia and Rubber," *New Republic* 44 (November 1925): 326–29. DuBois conceded that Liberia may have been guilty of many misdeeds: "She lacks training, experience and thrift. But her chief crime is to be black and poor in a rich, white world; and in precisely that portion of the world where color is ruthlessly exploited as a foundation for American and European wealth."

23. W. E. B. DuBois, "The Inter-racial Implications of the Ethiopian Crisis," *Foreign Affairs* 14 (October 1935): 88–92. In vain did African Americans call upon the United States to aid Ethiopia. Secretary of State Cordell Hull equivocated on applying the sanctions of the Kellogg-Briand Pact to Italy. And when the United States finally applied sanctions, it did so equally against victim and aggressor. It also permitted Italy to violate the oil embargo and excluded cotton from the list of essential war materials that could not be sold to that nation.

24. DuBois, *Autobiography*, 225.

25. George Padmore, *Pan-Africanism or Communism* (New York: Doubleday, 1971), 7.

26. Ibid. American leaders were aware that the country's policies were harmful to their cause. One declared: "Racial discrimination in the United States has produced unfortunate reactions on the part of many educated Africans. In addition, our ECA [Marshall Plan] program is an important object of suspicion, since there is some tendency to regard this program, as it applies to the overseas territories of the European powers, as a device to strengthen or perpetuate the hold of the European powers over the African territories."

27. Ibid.

28. Lincoln, Howard, and Fisk Universities were honored by the emerging African leaders, who were grateful that, for generations, they and their scholars had welcomed Africans. The delegates of these universities had a place of honor at Ghana's independence. Later, St. Clair Drake would accept an invitation from Nkrumah to teach at Legon, and that grand old man, Dr. W. E. B. DuBois, also would go to Accra to fulfill a lifelong dream, editing *Encyclopedia Africana*, and would die there.

29. Leslie A. Lacey, *The Rise and Fall of a Proper Negro* (New York: Macmillan, 1970), 167 ff.

30. The conflict in the Congo created tensions not only between the so-called Monrovia and Casablanca groupings of African states, but also between the United States and the Soviet Union, in addition to civil war in that unhappy land. But when Lumumba was murdered, the charge that the U.S. Central Intelligence Agency was involved led black Americans to riot against Adlai Stevenson in the United Nations. Coinciding as this did with the Birmingham police riot against black civil rights demonstrators, some Africans rejected out of hand the friendship offered by President Kennedy.

31. Like many scholars active in the movement, Drake felt that the temper of the times demanded a new approach to Pan-Africanism, both in theory and praxis. In " 'Hide My Face?' On Pan-Africanism and Negritude," he used as a take-off the words of a spiritual: "I ran to the rocks to hide my face; / The rocks cried out, No hiding place, / There's no hiding place down here." The article appears in *The Making of Black America*, ed. August Meier and Elliott Rudwick, (New York: Atheneum Press, 1969), 66 ff.

32. Ibid.

33. Drake's views of Pan-Africanism had become almost inseparable from that of the "race relations cycle" of Robert E. Park. In other words, ethnic solidarity had to yield to situational reality. Drake did suggest that while some Afro-Americans may go to live in Africa, and others may have business, government, and other specific interests there, "the idea that American Negroes have any mission to 'redeem' Africa in either a religious or secular sense will disappear" (Drake and Cayton, *Black Metropolis*).

34. The reappearance of Pan-African links between blacks in the United States and South Africa is a contemporary manifestation of the longevity of the ethnic solidarity movement. In many significant and increasingly related ways, the United States and South Africa share certain features. Both emanated from the expansion of Europe, one employing African slaves in order to develop, the other conquering, often enslaving, and exploiting Africans in order to exist and prosper. In both, racist ideologies have provided the rationale for prejudice and discrimination against blacks. See St. Clair Drake, "Negro Americans and the African Interest," in *The American Negro Reference Book*, ed. John Davis (Englewood Cliffs, N.J.: Prentice-Hall, 1966), 662–705.

35. Showing the kind of disdain for blacks historically felt by most white Americans, Dr. Henry Kissinger dismissed the revolutionary movements in Rhodesia and Portuguese Africa as posing danger to the vital interests of the United States. National Security Study Memorandum (NSSM) 39, an analysis of the situation in southern Africa prepared in 1969 under Kissinger's direction, questioned "the depth and permanence of black resolve" and suggested that only the South African whites could ameliorate the plight of the blacks in that country.

36. Ibid.

37. See Study Commission on U.S. Policy Toward Southern Africa, *South Africa: Time Running Out* (Berkeley: University of California Press, 1981), 462–64.

38. Richard Leonard, *South Africa at War* (Westport, Conn.: Greenwood Press, 1983), 248 ff. Almost echoing Kissinger's NSSM 39 but more cleverly crafted, Crocker's theory of constructive engagement postulated that, given the resistance of the dominant Afrikaners to change, the sufficient power of the South African Defense Force to prevent both internal and external threats against the regime, and the fact that the black communities did not possess the means for a direct assault on white power, there was little likelihood that the situation would change soon.

39. Ibid.

40. *South Africa*, 455.

41. Pauline Baker, "The Lost Continent?" *SAIS Review* 3 (winter–spring 1983): 112. Paradoxically, while Crocker acknowledged that white rule was strongly entrenched in South Africa, he warned that criticism by the United States or the implementation of economic sanctions or other pressures could trigger sudden "devastation." This led to a response that this was "the first time the United States ever articulated a policy of neutrality on racial oppression to rationalize a policy of strategic alliance. If we cannot be for or against whites or blacks as such, we can be for black claims of equality and against white policies of oppression—a critical distinction."

42. "Reagan Orders Sanctions on Pretoria," *New York Times*, 10 September 1985, A1, A12. Unfortunately, the president followed the announcements with remarks indicating that this order did not really represent his views and affirmed his support of the policy of constructive engagement by sending his ambassador back to Pretoria. An embarrassed White House staff and a saddened nation heard with disbelief the president's uninformed claim that Pretoria had abolished segregation and discrimination against blacks just as the United States had previously done. Given such blindness, one is left with the view that the United States is not yet prepared to abandon its policy of seeing Africa through a glass, darkly.

43. As in the early 1970s, there was the charge that the U.S. Agency for International Development had not asked a reluctant administration and Congress to allocate enough money for Africa. This was

compounded by the concern that the Reagan administration was not above playing politics with its aid to the starving Ethiopians and that the Marxist-Leninist government of Ethiopia wanted to use food as a weapon against the irredentist Eritreans.

44. Robert S. Browne and Robert J. Cummings, *The Lagos Plan of Action vs. the Berg Report* (Washington, D.C.: African Studies and Research Programs, Howard University, 1984), 11 ff. Berg allegedly placed "the major problem for Africa's economic deterioration on the improper policies pursued by many African nations and offered policy prescriptions which were, in many cases, politically difficult for African leadership to implement." This was judged insensitive by critics, who insisted that it was time for the United States to pay close attention to the Lagos Plan developed by the Africans with the long-term development of their continent in mind.

Contributors

Getahun Benti graduated from MSU in 2000 in History-Urban Studies, worked with Dr. Ruth Simms Hamilton as research assistant (1991–1999) and later as visiting research assistant professor (2000); currently associate professor of African history at Southern Illinois University-Carbondale, Department of History.

Josildeth Gomes Consorte is a professor of Anthropology at the Catholic University of Saõ Paulo, Brazil. Her concern with the black question in Brazil is not new and has been expressed through teaching and research on race relations and Afro-Brazilian religions, particularly on the politics of religious syncretism.

Raymond Familusi is a Ph.D. candidate in the department of sociology at Michigan State University. His dissertation examines relations of race, place and identity in late–twentieth century black political movements on the east coast of Canada (Nova Scotia). His research interests include expressions of place and identity among the descendants of nineteenth-century African "returnees" in Sierra Leone and Nigeria. He was a researcher-in-residence with the African Diaspora Research Project at Michigan State University.

Ruth Simms Hamilton was a teacher and researcher at Michigan State University for thirty-five years, and she won many awards for her work. Ruth taught courses on international inequality and development, comparative race relations, international migration and diasporas, Third World urbanization and change, and sociological theory. She was professor of Sociology and Urban Affairs, director of the African Diaspora Research Project, and a core faculty member of the African Studies Center and Center for Latin American and Caribbean Studies at Michigan State University. TIAA-CREF, a national financial services leader, created the Hamilton Research Scholarship in 2004, in honor of Hamilton's work in minority and urban issues.

Michael Hanson is a Baron Davis and Carmelo Anthony understudy and also assistant professor in the Communication Department at the University of California, San Diego. His work examines black cultural politics, particularly music, diaspora, performance and identity.

Anne Meyering, is associate professor of history at Michigan State University. She was introduced to the *Portrait d'une négresse* in the Louvre during her work on the life of the artist's son, Denis Benoist d'Azy, a French treasury department official, industrialist, and legislator.

Edward Paulino, is an assistant professor at John Jay College of Criminal Justice, City University of New York, and a Dominican New Yorker. He received his Ph.D. in Latin American history from Michigan State University. His dissertation focused on the nationalization of the Dominican-Haitian border during the dictatorship of Rafael L. Trujillo in the Dominican Republic.

Troy Peters, received a bachelor's degree in cultural anthropology from the University of Michigan. He worked as a research assistant for the African Diaspora Research Project prior to his Peace Corps assignment in Niger, West Africa (January 2002 through January 2004).

Mark Shapley is a lecturer in Africana Studies at Wayne State University and is currently producing a documentary film entitled *Tawahado: A Journey into the Judaic and Christian Legacies of Ethiopia* exploring Ethiopian Judaic and Christian religious traditions.

Elliott P. Skinner was Franz Boas Professor of Anthropology at Columbia University, New York, and U.S. ambassador to Upper Volta (Burkina Faso). In addition to field work in Guyana and among the Mossi in Burkina Faso, Dr. Skinner studied adaptive strategies among the Sahelian populations and is the author of many publications.